The Limits of Strategy is a terrific book on two counts – first as a highly insightful romp through the history of the transformative industry of our times, written by someone with a unique perspective on how events were actually shaped; and second as a thought-provoking study of how strategic insight, management ability, corporate culture, and industry dynamics interact to determine a company's success or failure, with lessons to be drawn whether your company is 170 days old or 170 years old.

Wick Moorman, CEO, Norfolk Southern Railroad

"An insightful analysis of all the key IT companies and individuals during the formative period of the industry. This book explains the competitive interrelationships between the different companies and how the IT industry evolved as a result. The lessons in the book are vital to any CEOs managing a business regularly disrupted by new entrants, new technologies, and different business models regardless of industry."

Larry Ellison, Founder and CEO, Oracle Corporation

Very few people get to witness from the inside a massive new economic sector as it is formed and evolves over a quarter century while permeating all aspects of our lives. Ernie von Simson did just that, studying the computer industry, interviewing its leaders, and shaping the thinking of those of us who implemented this technology during these explosive years. But "The Limits of Strategy" goes way beyond a faithful reconstruction of the "what happened" to discuss the many personality quirks that are often called corporate strategy and that often led to unimaginable misfortune and disaster. Ernie has insight that was not captured by the public media. This is worth reading as human nature does not change quickly.

Scott McNealy, Founder and retired CEO, Sun Microsystems

Ernie von Simson has written a tour de force in his revealing insights into the corporate strategies of the dominant American and Japanese computer manufacturers during the explosion of the industry over a quarter century. From his unique vantage point as principal investigator and master strategist behind the successful, and highly respected, Research Board, Ernie offers fascinating perspective on the limits of strategy from the real life stories of the leading participants…in essence, it's the people, stupid! A great read in general for the lessons to be had, and for the people like me who were involved, there is plenty to learn about the other guy to make this a real page turner.

George Conrades,
Chairman Akamai, Retired SVP, IBM Corporation

"Ernie von Simson's "The Limits of Strategy" is a book that can be enjoyed at multiple levels. It is an excellent, detailed history of the computer industry from the 1970s to 2000, a time when the industry grew explosively and transitioned from backroom mainframes and supercomputers that few people cared about to the post-industrial, information age of the personal computer and the World Wide Web. As co-head of the Research Board, Ernie had a ringside seat to this history, as well as personal access to the people who made the history happen.

Then again "Limits of Strategy" is a superb business book on strategy, leadership and innovation. Each of its twenty chapters stands alone as a case study of how a company and its leaders reacted to turbulent times, whether it was coping with fast growth or trying to survive major technology and market changes. These case studies stimulate the mind, and provide excellent material for quite a number of graduate and executive management courses.

Finally, "Limits of Strategy" is a good read, a series of very interesting stories, full of real characters, - some of them quite well known, - and the dramas they went through in trying to navigate the turbulent waters that their companies and the IT industry in general lived through during the 25 years Ernie writes about. It is rare to find a business book that is as well written and actually fun to read as "Limits of Strategy."

Dr. Irving Wladawski Berger,
Chairman Emeritus IBM Academy of Technology

THE LIMITS OF STRATEGY

Lessons in Leadership from the
Computer Industry

Ernest von Simson

iUniverse, Inc.
New York   Bloomington

The Limits of Strategy
Lessons in Leadership from the Computer Industry

Copyright © 2009 by Ernest von Simson

iUniverse books may be ordered through booksellers or by contacting:

iUniverse
1663 Liberty Drive
Bloomington, IN 47403
www.iuniverse.com
1-800-Authors (1-800-288-4677)

ISBN: 978-1-4401-9260-9 (sc)
ISBN: 978-1-4401-9258-6 (dj)
ISBN: 978-1-4401-9259-3 (ebk)

Printed in the United States of America

iUniverse rev. date: 03/31/2010

Contents

Preface

It took nearly three decades for computers to emerge from back-office accounting machines to take on the mantle of IT—Information Technology. Today, they're ubiquitous, affecting every aspect of our lives. There is more computing capacity in my cell phone than in the mainframe that mechanized the insurance company where I first learned to program.

The quarter-century from 1974 to 2000 was when this explosive change erupted; I had a ringside seat. With my wife and life partner, Naomi Seligman, I ran the Research Board, a quietly powerful think tank that observed and occasionally guided the computer industry. We were on stage at the entrance of today's leaders and just before the departure of yesterday's pioneers. We got to know and admire the giants of those years—including Gene Amdahl, John Chambers, Michael Dell, Larry Ellison, Paul Ely, Bill Gates, Lou Gerstner, Andy Grove, Grace Hopper, Steve Jobs, David Liddle, Bill McGowan, Scott McNealy, Sam Palmisano, Lew Platt, Eric Schmidt, and many more. We saw what factors determined the winners and losers. Above all we learned how disruptive technology can work to destroy even those who understand it well. And why great leadership is required to escape massive upheavals in markets, technologies, and business models. In essence, why there are limits of strategy. The story holds powerful lessons for those facing potentially disruptive technologies today.

My own presence in the most important industry of our time was accidental. I went to Brown University, studied International Relations, then served for three years on a Navy destroyer in charge of electronics and communications. Upon my discharge, I had a few months free in New York before starting graduate school in economics at the University of Chicago. To avoid feeling guilty about quitting in September, I looked for a short-term job that required minimal training.

A systems analyst, drawing magnetic tape layouts in the Electronic Data Processing (EDP) department at U.S. Life Insurance, seemed perfect. And that career-bending accident determined the course of my life. I jettisoned my plans for Chicago and received an MBA in economics from New York University instead.

In those early days of computers, no one knew much; we were creating a discipline as we went along. After three years at U.S. Life, I answered a classified ad from the Diebold Group under the impression that I was applying to the safe-manufacturing company. It turned out to be a computer services and consulting firm founded by John Diebold, a charismatic and often flamboyant entrepreneur who was himself creating a practice as he went along—beginning with the term "automation," which he claimed as his own. He had offices on Park Avenue scented by money; all the women were beautiful, all the men were brilliant and, for a kid from an insurance company, the atmosphere was heady.

I was anointed as a consultant and sent (without further training) to help a major paper company reorganize its IT department. Fortunately, I went in tow of a more experienced man, and my instincts were good. After a few assignments on my own, it turned out I was excellent at consulting, and I loved it. Eventually, John put me in charge of an "Assignment Review Board," assessing the work of the other consultants. I was just twenty-eight years old.

Then I drew the short straw to rescue a badly fumbled project on how computing would change marketing twenty-five years in the future. I hired legitimate market researchers and did several high-level interviews myself. Even so, it was ultimately all back-of-the-napkin stuff: Who could possibly know what would happen over two decades from then? But once the findings were massaged into a report, using my personal speculations as often as the real (but spotty) data, John loved it.

That led to my being pushed, reluctantly, into full-time research. John had hired Naomi Seligman from IBM, a feisty lady quickly dubbed "the dragon lady," to head the Diebold Research Program. He wanted me to work for her as Research Director. I wanted no part of it, but he wouldn't take no for an answer. At the company Christmas party that year, I again told him that I wanted to remain a consultant. Then I watched as, unperturbed, he announced my "promotion" a few moments later.

I had lunch with Naomi, and we drew up an organization chart of the new department. It was very Navy "chain of command." Everyone in Research reported to me; everyone in Client Services reported to Naomi. If the lines were ever blurred, I'd quit. Obviously we were headed for a major collision.

We fell in love instead—the only alternative to all-out war for two such strong personalities. We worked together and revived the program into a major business, with 140 client companies in the United States and Europe. Naomi is very smart and incredibly intuitive about people and situations. I have more imagination, usually for better—although sometimes for worse.

In 1970, we started our own company. My first three business ideas bumbled along with no hint of takeoff. So we kept bouncing other ideas off a group of our friends who'd become legendary in the information technology field: Ruth Block of Equitable Life, Jim Collins of Johnson & Johnson, Jack Jones of Southern Railway, Jack Lanahan of Inland Steel, and Edward B. Matthews III of Sanders Associates. They judged the ideas we proposed uniformly terrible. Finally in 1973, enough was enough, and they suggested that we set up what became the Research Board to do research that their companies would fund.

Their prescription was that we should build a group of clients, major companies that needed to mesh their strategies with the exploding world of computing. We would investigate what developments were coming, what adjustments they should make, and how to integrate information technology into their operations. We'd scrutinize all the major technology companies and advise our clients on what the IT leaders were doing, how good they were, and who was ahead in which new fields.

For the next twenty-five years, we followed the exact model defined by the founding five. Membership was limited to the top IT executives of the largest companies, and they had to make a serious commitment to the group and its work. The members voted on the research to be done, and only they received our reports to safeguard sensitive information confided by the suppliers. Further, they committed to read the reports before coming to the meetings, where research findings were discussed; anyone who missed more than two was out. Finally, membership was limited to companies that were users, but not suppliers, of IT, to avoid conflicts of interest,

We started out with nine clients—our five friends plus four other top IT people. In the 1980s, we began the European Board, again with the help of three extraordinary IT leaders and visionaries: John Sacher of Britain's Marks & Spencer, Jean-Serge Bertoncini of France's Peugeot, and Johan Friedrichs of Germany's Hoechst.

From there we grew steadily, but kept the core group limited to fifty leading companies in the United States and twenty-five in Europe; thirty-five smaller companies joined as associate members. We met once a year in plenary session with all the clients, twice in smaller sectional meetings. The annual meetings were always in impressive locations—among the most fun, 1994 at Disney World, where CIO Sharon Garrett orchestrated the most incredible fandango ever and, at the other extreme, the awesome stage at Carnegie Hall in 1998.

Meanwhile, our visits to the computing and communications companies began slightly awkwardly in the early years. But relations inevitably improved as they verified we didn't work for IT vendors, didn't leak sensitive information, and almost never talked to the press. Moreover, we came to our two- or three-day visits to a given company forearmed with position papers on everything written about our subjects for the past two years. We developed a cadre of excellent researchers topped by Cathy Loup, Abby Kramer, Jim Roche and our clever offspring, Ann Seligman and Charlie von Simson. Over time, the leading executives came to respect us because we were fair, serious, and objective. Obviously, talking to us was also in their interest, because our clients were their largest customers. "There is nowhere to get more sales points in the room than at Research Board meetings," a senior IBM executive once remarked.

By the time we sold the Research Board to Gartner Group in 1999, we had written nearly one hundred reports. Every year, we would assess the overall condition of the industry—which companies were doing what, and how well; what big breakthroughs seemed near. We also researched how the largest enterprises used new technologies to the best advantages as well as demographics and the labor force and the relationship of IT departments to the other activities in a company. What we learned, we recorded in thousands of written pages and in our memories. The lessons learned over that entire period are distilled and related here.

Introduction

Potentially destructive change is a constant in business. Some changes are foreseeable and avoidable. Others are total surprises. And in a third category are changes that are fully visible like a funnel cloud on the distant horizon but inevitably destroy even the most successful enterprises anyway. Despite the endless care given to business forecasting and strategy formulation, these virulent changes have recently impacted automobiles, consumer products, pharmaceuticals, telephones, and, of course, the computer industry.

The godfather of business velocity may be Joseph Schumpeter, who believed that the entrepreneur with something new and disruptive is always the engine of the economy. "In capitalist reality, as distinguished from its textbook picture, it is not [price] competition that counts, but rather competition from new commodities, new technologies, new sources of supply, new types of organization—competition that commands a decisive cost or quality advantage and that strikes not at the margins of profits and outputs of existing firms, but at their foundations and very lives."[1] The problem for the computer sector over the past fifty years is that dislocative change has too often come not from one source but from a spectrum. Innovation has created new technologies that have demanded new cost models, new distribution channels, and, by definition, new managerial skills and organizational forms.

None of this is gentle or gradual as Schumpeter implied by his seminal term "creative destruction." The consequences of "change arising from within the system so displace its equilibrium that the new equilibrium can't be reached from the old only by infinitesimal steps. Add successively as many mail coaches as you please, you will never get a railway thereby."[2]

In our analysis, 1992 was a killing year for the four computer companies most important to business buyers. All four had been dominant suppliers of minicomputers for the past fifteen or twenty years. But then came the microprocessor, portable databases, Microsoft, and the Unix operating system, which weakened the hold of computer companies on their existing customers and slashed their profit margins. On July 16, 1992, the CEOs of both Digital Equipment and Hewlett-Packard were pushed into retirement. On August 8, Wang Laboratories declared bankruptcy. In December, IBM halved its dividend for the first time ever, forcing the resignation of its CEO a month later.

How did this happen? Are the deadliest changes unavoidable because strategy is too easily thwarted by cluster bombs such as technological velocity, cultural inertia, obsolete business models, executive conflict, and investor expectations?

All four men were smart and experienced. Two were founders of their companies; the others, highly successful career executives. But all of them were simply overwhelmed by the profound changes in technology, cost structures, business models, and markets disrupting the computer industry. And while I found no single explanation for what happened, I did see definite common themes. You will find them recurring again and again in the many stories of this book, both in the chapters devoted to individual companies and in the chapters describing the changing landscape and culture of the computer industry. The common threads are:

- Vision alone isn't enough. The chief executives of DEC, HP, IBM, and Wang fully understood the implications and possibilities of the microprocessor, but still couldn't adapt to it.

- Competition can blind you. IBM's intense struggle over mainframes with Fujitsu and Hitachi distracted all three companies from identifying the new breed of competitors, including Compaq and Sun. So did DEC's continuing preoccupation with Data General and Wang, its neighbors in Massachusetts.

- Strong cultures can be a straitjacket. IBM didn't fail because of Bill Gates's negotiating skills or Microsoft's brilliant programmers, but because the PC market was driven by consumers. IBM, totally focused on its large business customers, had no expertise in the consumer market and little interest in developing it.

- Cost structures can block change. DEC and Wang didn't fail because of disruptive technology, but because they couldn't adjust their business model to cut the costs of sales and R&D by ten to fifteen percent of revenues.

- Great sales organizations are often the crown jewels of successful companies. But they can also become the most powerful barrier against changes in product innovations or distribution models, however necessary.

- First movers can fail, too. The PC leaders in 1980 were Apple, Commodore, and Radio Shack. All used the microprocessor to pursue outdated business models and lost their lead positions to latecomers with better perspective.

- Forcing the retirement of a CEO can become an especially thorny issue when the CEO is a founder who has led the company's early success. But a failure to force a timely change can ruin a company, as we'll see at DEC and Wang but notably not at IBM.

Navigating through the storms of dislocative change requires exceptional leadership.

Especially since even the most experienced CEOs can actually be handicapped by their past successes. As Richard Foster points out in his fascinating book *Innovation: The Attacker's Advantage*, leaders being challenged by disruptive competition tend to keep doing what previously made them successful. When steamships were outmoding sailing vessels, builders of clipper ships kept expanding their designs—until, in 1902, a seven-masted clipper ignominiously capsized and could be seen from passing steamers drifting upside down off the Scilly Islands near the southwestern tip of England.[3]

In other words, almost any strategy an incumbent CEO can devise will be useless in the face of truly disruptive technology, because it begins a new game that demands a completely different business model and, equally, a different management discipline. That is where strategy meets its limit and leadership dominates. And that's the message of this book.

Chapter 1

A MAD DASH THROUGH HISTORY

Before we start, let's consider a highly compressed synopsis of the computer industry's self-immolating and resurrecting history to set the book's timeline and a few overarching trends. Information Technology began modestly enough in 1822 when Charles Babbage introduced a forerunner to the computer with his beautifully handcrafted electromechanical calculator. Herman Hollerith pushed the still-fuzzy concept a key step closer to what we now know as the computer with his punch-card tabulating equipment. First used in the 1890 census, punch cards were gradually adopted for business use. Two decades later, Hollerith was able to sell his tabulating business for the then princely sum of $1 million, assuring his comfortable retirement.

Heading up the group of entrepreneurs that made Hollerith a wealthy man in 1911 was the pioneering Charles Flint, who merged a time-clock company and a scales company with the tabulating business to form the Computer-Tabulating-Recording Company, or C-T-R. It was this entity that CEO Thomas J. Watson Sr. would rechristen as International Business Machines in 1924. And when James Rand Jr. bought Porter Punch, a small tabulating company, a year later, he initiated a nose-to-nose sparring match between his Remington Rand and Watson's IBM that would survive for sixty years.

Though Hollerith punch cards became indispensable to various business operations, the decks were prone to flightiness as cards were lost, missorted, and otherwise abused. One well-traveled tale concerned cards soaked in a water-pipe break and then dried in the oven of a friendly pizza joint.

The first actual computers were built from vacuum tubes during World War II; the Brits built the Colossus, and two fellows from the

University of Pennsylvania, J. Presper Eckert and John Mauchly, came up with the ENIAC (Electronic Numerical Integrator and Computer). Meanwhile, IBM was sponsoring Howard Aiken's construction of the Mark I at Harvard. Essentially a giant electromechanical tabulating device, the Mark I's first programmer was Grace Murray Hopper, a phenomenon in her own right.

Hopper was a mathematician, physicist, serial innovator, and U.S. Navy Captain, a rank attained after she joined the Naval Reserve to support her country in wartime. During these early days, when even one of her multiple accomplishments was considered unusual for a woman, Hopper recalled a summer evening in Cambridge when the lab doors had been left open to dissipate the day's heat. When the computer choked the next morning, a moth was found caught in one of its electromechanical switches—"the first bug," she later quipped, and, indeed, she is widely credited with discovering exactly that.

The Magnetic Fifties

Commercial computing began with Eckert and Mauchly's Universal Automatic Computer (Univac), and, perhaps more important, with their substitution of magnetic tape for those pesky and problematic punch cards. The two inventors had left the University of Pennsylvania on March 31, 1946, to form a company called first the Electronic Controls Corporation and soon the Eckert-Mauchly Computer Corporation. That company was sold in 1950 to IBM's longtime rival, Remington Rand. At first, Tom Watson Sr. resisted the move to electronics, largely out of fear that magnetic tape would kill IBM's immensely lucrative business in punch cards. Tom Jr.'s longer vision persevered.

Before the decade ended, the computer was in its second "generation," with transistor technology supplanting the vacuum tube. Simultaneously, computers made their first real penetration into the business office, as punch-card records were slowly transferred to magnetic tape. Soon, mainframes were pervasive, often visible in "glass houses" located near the headquarters lobby so that visitors could marvel at a company's modernity as captured in the herky-jerky movement of the tape drives.

The Do-It-Yourself Sixties

The 1960s marked my entry into the industry, eventually affording me a front-row seat from which to view the computer revolution. Naomi entered the industry in 1965 as a freelance market researcher working mostly for IBM. Around 1963, I designed and programmed a business application on a pair of transistor-based IBM computers that supported an entire insurance company with less memory and fewer cycles than today's wristwatch.

By mid-decade, the industry consisted of IBM and the so-called seven dwarfs: the Burroughs Corporation, the Control Data Corporation (CDC), the General Electric Company (GE), Honeywell, NCR (officially the National Cash Register Company until 1974), the Radio Corporation of America (RCA), and the Univac division of Remington Rand—by then part of the Sperry-Rand Corporation. Every dwarf took shelter under IBM's pricing umbrella to mark up the cost of its hardware fivefold for 80 percent gross margins. Big Blue could hold to its 15 percent annual profit growth and surround its major customers with armies of "free" sales representatives and systems engineers, who invaded executive offices with one idea after another, many half-baked.

Efficiency was no better among the seven dwarfs. All were shielded from competition by the handcrafting of software; a customer couldn't switch to a different computer without laboriously rewriting and then retesting every applications program. "Switching cost" was the iron advantage undergirding the entire computer industry's flabby business model.

Given that restrictive oligopoly, computer vendors could benignly double price/performance ratio every five years more or less. And computer power presumably increased exponentially with cost, as stipulated by Grosch's "law" (named for Herb Grosch, the gifted computer scientist and grumpy industry gadfly who was serially hired and fired from IBM by both Watsons). Though this "big is beautiful" price/performance relationship was widely accepted, its validity was questionable. Most computing-power metrics are horribly unreliable and too easily manipulated by computer marketers. Besides, the pricing wizards at IBM and elsewhere set prices with an eye toward encouraging customers to buy bigger computers than they really needed. Grosch's law owed less to electronics than to complacent business models and oligopolistic pricing.

In the late 1960s, IBM won what was arguably the largest bet ever made in the computer industry. Tom Watson Jr. had invested heavily in the development of System/360, a line of small to large computers that were software-compatible and that used the same peripherals—that is, tapes, disks, printers, and so on. Previously, customers couldn't switch to a larger or newer computer without reprogramming all of their applications—a deal breaker if there ever was one. Watson's gamble changed all that and gave IBM products an edge its competitors lacked.

The appeal of IBM compatibility was enormous, and System/360 completely upended the existing computer industry. RCA and GE quickly exited the field, with Honeywell eventually following, and CDC became a computer-services company. Against IBM, the only real survivors from the "mainframe" era were, ironically, Tom Sr.'s two fiercest opponents: Unisys, the stepchild of Jim Rand after Univac and Burroughs merged in 1986; and NCR, the brainchild of John H. Patterson, the man who had brought the elder Watson into the office-equipment business and then fired him.

The Chips Fall in the Seventies

In 1973, Naomi and I formed the Research Board and began almost three decades studying the computer industry during its most innovative and formative period. From our vantage point, we saw that success brings its own challenges, which for IBM meant both an antitrust suit and, more important, scores of new market entrants.

First came the leasing companies, clippers in hand, to undercut IBM's prices with discounts on secondhand gear. Plug-compatible peripherals and mainframes followed, and they used IBM's own 360 operating system to cut the equipment newcomers' research-and-development and field sales expenses. Worse yet, compatibility wore down a customer's apprehension about linking its own applications to a vendor of uncertain business viability. Should the fledging die, the customer could quickly and painlessly go running back to Big Blue.

At the same moment, the minicomputer industry was birthed. Starting around 1968, dozens of small companies formed in response to early-mover DEC's successful introduction of the Programmed Data

Processor (PDP) line. Most of these start-ups built business models with lower product costs and gross margins than those burdening mainframers. For one thing, the minis used high-volume circuit technology, which was both cheaper to buy and simpler to deploy than the exotic ware the mainframes demanded. The minis were also cheaper to operate, since they didn't require a special priesthood or glass houses; regular office workers could fire up the machines without much training.

Grosch's law was quickly repealed. Now small was better, in a sense. The computing power provided by minicomputers, and then microprocessor-based servers, was far less expensive than what came from mainframes, a result of the minis' lower-cost technology and leaner gross margins. Most of the new wave was still burdened with the disadvantage of "proprietary operating systems," however, meaning that every manufacturer's software was incompatible with its peers.

But lurking just over the near horizon was the microprocessor, which carried the essentials of a computer processor on a single silicon chip. Developed first by Intel in 1971, and very shortly thereafter by Texas Instruments, the chips revolutionized computer development and radicalized the entire industry in the process. Many chief executives failed to appreciate the threat in time to save their companies. But so did the heads of Intel, the National Semiconductor Corporation, Motorola, and AT&T's legendary Bell Labs. First movers into PCs like Commodore, Radio Shack, and a kite string of lesser pennants fared no better.

Meanwhile, Grace Hopper had left Univac to lend her talents to the U.S. Navy, becoming the computing world's transcendent figure and bridging the gap between Howard Aiken's mechanical marvel and the microprocessor. Captain Hopper had begun mentoring Naomi whom she sponsored in 1968 for the American Management Association's Leadership Council. With their matching Vassar pageboy haircuts, one white and the other chestnut, they noodled, with Grace providing two pieces of stellar advice: "learn knitting" to avoid talking too often, and "leave your prestigious Diebold Group vice presidency to start the new firm with Ernie."

Captain Hopper was wonderful with young people and new ideas. Our interviews with her at the Pentagon were always attended by the twenty-something Navy ensigns and electrician mates whom she had somehow identified as computing wizards. She was godmother to the newest forms of computing that are only today becoming fully realized. She was certainly among the earliest proponents of replacing the exotically powered and priced mainframes with cheaper, more approachable minicomputers. She also imagined that hundreds, even thousands, of microprocessors might one day perform computationally intensive tasks that would overwhelm even the largest supercomputer. "When our pioneer forebears were trekking westward and their wagons were too heavy for the oxen, they didn't grow larger oxen, they harnessed more of them," she liked to say. "They didn't harness a herd of rabbits, either," we'd mutter under our breaths.

But Captain Hopper was much closer to the truth than most of us. To illustrate her argument when speaking at Research Board meetings and other venues, she would hand out roughly keyboard-long pieces of wire: "That's a nanosecond," she'd tell her admirers, who numbered in the thousands. "It's the maximum distance that light—or an electrical signal—can travel in a billionth of a second." And, by implication, that was the maximum dimension of a computer targeted at optimal throughputs. Today, microprocessors operating together are a given. Google alone harnesses hundreds of thousands of these rabbits.

A clear counterpoint to Hopper's concept came from the legendary supercomputer builder Seymour Cray. Dr. Cray was reputed to have begun designing each new model by building a box sized to provide the proximity required for his ultimate computing targets, if all the components could be crammed inside. But the required amount of ultra-high-performance circuitry creates enormous heat, comparable to the surface of an electric iron. So Cray mined his considerable genius to develop the "packaging" (e.g., the circuit boards) and especially the cooling mechanism. One of his most famous deca-million-dollar masterpieces was shaped like a banquette (complete with seat cushions) with liquid Freon running through the "backrest" to draw off the heat.

Dr. Cray had a curious personal ritual that could characterize the computer industry as a whole. Every spring he'd begin building a sailboat on the cliffs overlooking his Wisconsin lake that he'd finish in time for summer sailing. Then in the autumn, he'd burn the boat to ashes to clear his mental pathways for starting again the next year.

"Burn the place down," replied Steve Jobs to my question on how Apple could have escaped the Mac's success (after Steve had founded NeXT). The remark was simultaneously typical Steve and a terse, if inadvertent, reflection of the heavy baggage inherent in outdated business models. The only way to escape prior success is to burn it down?

Minis Fade in the Eighties

The beginning of the end for the minicomputer companies was preordained by three separate events. First, microprocessors replaced minis embedded in the machinery produced by assorted companies. Second, IBM finally entered the market with a half-dozen of its own minicomputer models. And finally, software compatibility eroded the customer's cost of switching to another vendor. After that, the old proprietary model was dead.

Minicomputer companies, led by Digital Equipment, followed the IBM System/360 approach and created hardware lines with a single operating system. Then the circle of compatibility widened beyond the product line of a single supplier when Larry Ellison began writing his Oracle database in a "higher-level" language that could be readily "ported" to different operating systems. It was a three-bagger for the industry's most envied iconoclast. Larry drew customers by lowering their switching costs across computer suppliers. As his customer count grew, so did Oracle's appeal to the developers of applications packages— first in accounting and payroll, later in supply-chain management and other fancy stuff. And more third-party software lured even more customers to Oracle.

Switching costs were hammered down again by the spread of UNIX (popularly Unix), an operating system first written around 1969 by Bell Labs' scientists. The initial version of Unix attracted scientists and hobbyists but was ill-suited for business use, lacking reliability and productivity tools for average programmers. By the early 1980s, though, Unix was being commercialized by Sun Microsystems and NCR. Some old-line hardware vendors tried to stem the assault by creating their own Unix flavors, such as IBM's AIX and Hewlett-Packard's HP-UX. But the different Unix brands were still enough alike to draw the independent developers of applications software—initially, scientific and engineering tools and, eventually, business applications.

The Disappearing Act of the Nineties

The draw of large numbers was flattening industry profit margins. Larger volumes permitted sharply lower prices; success bred more success. Bill Gates was separating Microsoft and its Windows operating system from IBM's over-engineered, underperforming OS/2. He began to appear at industry meetings with a chart like Table 1.1 that illustrated economies of scale on operating systems costing roughly $500 million each to develop.

Table 1.1   Software Economies of Scale

	Units Sold	Unit Cost
Mainframes	2,000	$250,000
Minicomputers	20,000	25,000
Unix	100,000	$5,000
Windows	10,000,000	$50

Having a single Microsoft operating system would assure compatibility all around, both for PC makers like Compaq and Dell and for the all-important independent software vendors. Of the fifty midrange computing players active in the 1970s, only IBM and Hewlett-Packard survived, joined by latecomer Sun. Digital Equipment (acquired by Compaq), Wang, and all the rest had either disappeared completely or were severely reconstituted.

The apparently victorious PC sector gave no quarter, devouring siblings and offspring alike. The era had dawned with giddy hopes of a cottage industry of fruitful and inexpensive innovation. The kiddy corps would strike down the wicked establishment, or so many had hoped. But consolidation came quickly. The lack of switching costs between computers had encouraged this fertile excess; now it drove consolidation around one or two survivors. Today, 75 percent of all profit in the software sector is earned by just four companies: Microsoft, IBM, Oracle, and SAP.

Industry consolidation and the commoditization of PC hardware ran on the same track. As PC switching costs were driven to near zero, innovation in manufacturing and distribution became more important than innovation in product design, as Dell irrefutably demonstrated. Of the myriad personal computer brands of the 1980s, only Apple, Dell, HP, and Acer survive today as significant players in the United States. Even one-time leader Compaq is gone. Most of the others vanished without a trace.

If the magnitude of the implosion wasn't clear, it came into sharp focus on June 16, 1992, when DEC's legendary founder and CEO, Ken Olsen, was abruptly forced into retirement after a string of losses and uncharacteristically wrongheaded decisions. On that same day, Hewlett-Packard CEO John Young was allowed to announce his retirement, pushed out by founders Bill Hewlett and Dave Packard. Young's organizational restructuring had left the company mired in bureaucracy just when industry turbulence was mandating fast action. In August, Wang Labs declared bankruptcy, an entirely preordained interment following a trail of repeated failures by the once-visionary An Wang. And in October, IBM announced its first-ever quarterly loss, causing CEO John Akers to lose first his bonus, and soon his job.

How could Akers, Olsen, Young, and Wang have failed so publicly and suffered such discomfiting personal consequences all within the span of four months? As we've already said, all four were thirty-year veterans of their companies; Olsen and Wang were founders. All were certainly aware of the transitions that periodically rock the technology industry. Failure wasn't caused solely by the advent of the microprocessor or its impressive debut as the power inside the personal computer. After all, Dr. Wang was the brilliant electrical engineer credited with inventing "core" memory in the early days of computing. John Akers was the IBM lifer who had passionately supported the personal computer from its birth, much to his own eventual disadvantage. Ken Olsen was a star engineer who built the second most important computer company in the world. John Young had been CEO of the pundits' most admired instrumentation company for six years when he wrested personal control of its growing computer side. None of these leaders could be faulted for sheer stupidity or ignorance of the business.

Star Walkers

In the end, the minicomputer establishment was immolated by five young men:

- Larry Ellison, at Oracle, extended compatibility across many of the most popular minicomputer brands, and later the Unix variants, through the Oracle database. As a result, customers were relieved of the switching costs by which the minicomputer companies had previously maintained account control and 60 percent gross margins.

- Scott McNealy, at Sun Microsystems, pushed compatibility across an even wider arc by making an early commitment to Unix while DEC, IBM, and even HP tarried, conflicted by their long-standing dependency on proprietary operating systems.

- Bill Gates, at Microsoft, made the flow a torrent, realizing the power of volume compatibility more clearly and actionably than any of his illustrious contemporaries did.

- Steve Jobs, at Apple, used Mac's user interface to propel a radical change in customer-support requirements, blasting away the foundations of the minicomputer companies' business models.

- Michael Dell, at his eponymous company, radicalized the manufacture and distribution of computer hardware.

The personal similarities and coincidences among these men are not without interest. For instance, Gates, Jobs, McNealy, and Dell were all in their twenties when they founded the companies they would lead to the top tier of their industry. Gates, Jobs, Dell, and Ellison leapt into their careers after spending little more than a year in college, though all were brilliant and exhibited a remarkable range of interests. (McNealy was the only college graduate in the group, with degrees from both Harvard and the Stanford University business school.) Ellison and Gates started their companies the same year, 1973, made their initial public stock offerings one day apart—on March 12 and 13, 1986— and went on to dominate the American software industry.

In terms of primary skills, I would judge Ellison as the most deeply immersed in his company's technology, Gates the best and most relentless tactician in both technical and business terms, Jobs the most creative inventor, and McNealy the clearest-thinking strategist. McNealy believed in attaining higher margins by differentiating his company's product line, while Dell believed just as strongly that IT products were, inevitably, low-margin commodities that did not lend themselves to differentiation. Neither extreme was entirely accurate as it turned out.

While one-time industry movers and shakers were falling by the wayside, one original member of the computer industry survived—not without upheaval and distress, but with name and company still intact. The next chapter relates the saga of Big Blue, the house the Watsons—father and son—built and renovated with such craftsmanship that it still stands strong nearly eighty-five years and multiple iterations of the computer industry later.

Chapter 2

THE STRATEGIC GOLD STANDARD:

The Watsons

A successful strategy hinges on a leader's vision and steadfast determination to challenge and, if necessary, disrupt the company's own business model, despite subordinates' fears and customers' grumblings. Both Watsons did just that at IBM. Tom Sr. jettisoned major pieces of a sleepy conglomerate to usher in sixty years of supremacy in the newfangled business of data processing. Tom Jr. navigated IBM through three critical and hazardous transformations: the move into electronic computers with the attendant replacement of his father's highly profitable punch-card business; the settlement of the 1956 antitrust suit in a capitulation that actually enhanced IBM's competitiveness; and the creation of the System/360, the product line that would effectively terminate his father's competitors.

In the 1930s, IBM's tabulating equipment held 90 percent of the punch-card market. And no small measure of its continuing success can be attributed to the smooth succession of command from father to son in 1956, when the eighty-two-year-old Tom Watson Sr. relinquished the presidency to Tom Watson Jr. The younger Watson was just forty-two, but he had already accumulated a lifetime of experience with the company. Rather than a dying man's nepotism, this was actually an astonishingly successful transition, especially for an industry where founders generally stayed too long and were replaced only in extremis by executives too weak to maintain or regain competitiveness.

In the 1960s, Big Blue used its IBM System/360 computer line to pound its seven traditional competitors. Unwittingly, however,

System/360 also spawned a whole new computer industry of "plug compatibles"—both mainframes and peripheral equipment that could displace IBM's own mainframes, tapes, disks, and printers. What is more, the competition came not from doddering survivors of the electromechanical age but from robust newcomers, notably a bevy of entrepreneurs and the Japanese giants—Fujitsu, Hitachi, and Nippon Electric. Once again, the company rose to the challenge.

Throughout those years, the Thomas J. Watsons—first the father and then the son—remained firmly in control, making farsighted decisions that would keep their company planted atop an industry undergoing unimagined change.

The Founding Father

The old man was tough as a tree trunk, having started his career selling everything from sewing machines to investments from the back of his horse-drawn carriage. His management expertise came later from John Henry Patterson, the legendary czar of "the Cash," otherwise known as the National Cash Register Company (NCR), whose relentless business practices would eventually spark a government investigation and the antitrust conviction of his young protégé. Tom Watson had helped set up unmarked storefronts to covertly crush resellers of NCR cash registers by undercutting their prices until they collapsed. Though Watson took the heat as NCR's front man, an ungrateful Patterson fired Tom in 1913, in part, many suspected, as a potential competitor.

Two years earlier, a band of entrepreneurs led by Charles Flint had lashed together a time-clock company, a scales company, and the Hollerith tabulating-equipment business to form the Computing-Tabulating-Recording Company (CTR). Flint was every bit the stuff of business legends in the mold of J. P. Morgan or Cornelius Vanderbilt. Before CTR, he had put together the United States Rubber Company and the American Chickle Company (the maker of Chicklets, Dentyne, and other chewing gums). He bought the ships that formed the Brazilian Navy, sold the Russians $35 million worth of submarines, and (unsuccessfully) peddled the patents for both the Wright brothers' airplane and Simon Lake's submarine to various foreign governments.

Watson was hired as CTR's general manager in 1914, a year after departing from NCR, though still under the cloud of a pending one-year jail sentence—which he would never serve—for his antitrust conviction. Brinkley Smithers, the son of one of Flint's co-investors, who himself headed up IBM's Washington, DC, office for a time in the 1930s, told Naomi and me that his father, Christopher Smithers, initially "hired Watson for sales. My father didn't let him near the money." But Tom soon controlled the money and the company after being awarded CTR's presidency and, in 1924, renamed it International Business Machines.

Watson showed considerable interest in his engineers' development of the newest tabulating equipment. But he focused on sales right down to the carefully constructed image, described with artistic flourish by a fawning reporter in the January 1940 issue of *Fortune* magazine: "He dresses with relentless conservatism—a dark suit of expensive worsted relieved by a timid stripe, a decorous tie of moiré so heavy it seems made of wax, knotted perfectly in a dazzling collar.... When he begins to talk, he is the kind of slightly bashful, dignified gentleman who would be the last person on earth to try to sell you anything. Therefore you lose consciousness of your sales resistance. The lines of his face have accented the tenuousness of his lips, giving him a somewhat Presbyterian cast. As he continues to speak, however, his whole face lights up with the vaguely wistful sincerity, the slightly imploring earnestness that can be noted even in his sternest photographs."

The "bashful, dignified ... slightly imploring" Watson navigated the Great Depression with a strong hand, especially against electromechanical rivals like Burroughs Adding Machine, National Cash Register, and Remington Rand (which retained a 10 percent market share in tabulating equipment for decades). "From a corporate perspective," said the writer of a November 1931 piece in *Fortune,* "it is far more noteworthy that in 1930, IBM did record business, made record profits, paid record dividends, increased its personnel, enlarged its plant capacity and ended the year with a net of $7,357,817 (equivalent to 21 percent of its net worth)." Better still would be 1931, despite the lingering Depression, the writer promised.

At the time, IBM manufactured four product lines—time clocks, scales, meat and coffee grinders, and tabulating machines—encompassing 600 models. The most important line, of course, was tabulation; it provided about 50 percent of the company's revenues and

65 percent of its profits—from what the *Fortune* reporter called "those two prettiest types of modern profit, 'machine rental' and 'refill.'" Burbling on, the writer explained that IBM got its revenues by leasing out, servicing, and repairing its tabulating machines and by selling the cards used in the machines. The latter, it pointed out, made up "a very substantial portion of the division's business for, with its machines using upwards of three billion cards a year, the sales revenue at $1.30 per 1,000 amounts to over $4,000,000." At this point, IBM's forefront customers were "paper flow" concerns, especially government agencies, insurance companies, and banks.

Watson made a savvy move in choosing rental over outright sale. Rentals offered many advantages, especially for a monopolist in a Depression-era sales climate. "The consumer need make no capital expenditures to install their products," according to the *Fortune* piece. "A salesman can go to a prospective customer with a simple proposition: 'Your present costs are so much; with our machinery installed, your costs (including rentals) will be so much less—resulting in a net cash savings not only next year and the year after, but at once.'" In later years, computer sales reps would have sold their wingtip shoes for such a powerful pitch.

IBM's card-refill business invited comparisons with the film used in Eastman Kodak cameras, the spark plugs that went into General Motors' automobiles, the tubes for RCA's radios, and the blades in Gillette razors. But unlike blades and tubes, there was no competition for cardboard, insisted *Fortune,* implausibly: "I.B.M., however, has so far found itself secure in the market for tabulator cards for its machines, because the cards must be made with great accuracy on a special paper stock which, so far, at least, has not been successfully imitated." Pure gibberish, of course, and the 1956 antitrust settlement would verify that cardboard is just cardboard. Still and all, IBM's punch-card monopoly was a reflection of unshakable account control over its customers.

In 1933, Watson bought the Electromatic Typewriter Company, which would eventually give IBM its most powerful entry into the office market. But at the time, the foundling's annual sales were only $11 million, and the business would lose money for the next fifteen years—until Tom Watson Jr. hired Ivy Leaguer Wiz Miller in 1948. (Watson Jr. later called Miller his first important personnel decision.

Wiz "taught his salesmen to use this blarney on the secretaries and started making the [Selectric] typewriters in different colors like red and tan," recalled Watson Jr. "He even made a white typewriter that my father presented to Pope Pius XII...."[1]) From then on, the Office Products division grew at 30 percent annually until it effectively owned the office typewriter market. Only the personal computer would slow this awesome pace and displace the Selectric in the office—and that was thirty years later.

World War II midwifed the electronic computer with the simultaneous development of several machines, including the Colossus, the ENIAC, and the Mark I, the latter created under IBM's patronage. The Mark I, though, was electromechanical, not a genuine computer like the ENIAC, admitted Watson the younger. "When ENIAC was first unveiled," he said, "it created a huge stir because it was fundamentally different. It had no moving parts, except for electrons flying close to the speed of light inside its vacuum tubes."[2]

After the war, J. Presper Eckert and John Mauchly, the ENIAC's inventors, left the University of Pennsylvania to build commercial computers at their newly formed Eckert-Mauchly Computer Corporation (EMCC). Needing capital to finance their dream, in 1949 they sold 40 percent of EMCC to American Totalisator Company, the maker of racetrack display devices that toted up the odds in pari-mutuel betting. When American Totalisator's CEO was killed in a plane crash the following year, the company's new owners decided that the computer venture was alien to their main business. Their withdrawal threatened EMCC with a funding cutoff just as its inventors were building their first Universal Automatic Computer (Univac I). Mauchly and Eckert turned to Tom Watson Sr. for funding, but the old man said no.

Junior later contended that IBM failed to buy EMCC because it was preoccupied with the antitrust suit: "When they came in, Mauchly slumped down on the couch and put his feet on the table—damned if he was going to show any respect for my father. Eckert started describing what they'd accomplished. But Dad had already guessed the reason for their visit, and our lawyers had told him that buying their company was out of the question. Univac was one of the few competitors we had, and antitrust law said we couldn't take them over. So Dad told Eckert, 'I shouldn't allow you to go on too far. We cannot make any kind of arrangement with you, and it would be unfair to let you think we could. Legally, we've been told we can't do it.' Eckert understood perfectly. He leaped to his feet and said, 'All the same, thanks very much for your time.' Mauchly never said a word; he slouched out of the door after an erect Eckert."[3]

No slouch, Mauchly recalled the meeting quite differently. The elder Watson "gave us a sermon for 15 or 20 minutes," he said, "the gist of which was that there was no such thing as invention, just discovery. He was playing down the value of patents. Then he shook hands and turned us over to someone else who offered us each a lab and a small salary and a chance for the greater glory of IBM. So we turned them down."[4] Given the Watsons' unblinking competitiveness, Mauchly's recollection was likely closer to the truth.

A few months later, EMCC was acquired by Remington Rand. Soon thereafter, in 1951, Remington Rand delivered the first Univac, with three more to follow in both 1952 and 1953, seven each in 1954 and 1955, fifteen in 1956, and a few more after that as electron tubes gave way to transistors. Total shipments were tiny by today's standards, but the outlook was promising; there were early commitments from the U.S. Census Bureau and the Prudential Insurance Company, both among IBM's ten largest accounts.

The Son Who Succeeded the Founding Father

"Many people had the impression that my father and I never agreed on the subject of electronics," remembered Tom Watson Jr. "But, oddly, electronics was the only major issue on which we didn't fight. I like to think that if I hadn't been around to push, Dad would have eventually put IBM into electronics anyway, because he loved calculating speed."[5]

Well, maybe. But computers threatened a much larger upheaval than merely displacing mechanicals. The still-lucrative punch-card business would be backwatered by the Univac's magnetic tapes despite old Watson's tenacious rearguard defense. "My father initially thought the electronic computer would have no impact on the way IBM did business, because to him, punch-card machines and giant computers belonged in totally separate realms. A computer revolution might sweep across the scientific world, but in the accounting room the punch card was going to stay on top.... IBM was in the classic position of the company that gets tunnel vision because of its success."[6]

Whether the father and son agreed or not, there was no avoiding the fact that IBM lagged badly in new technology. Its "monkey wrench" labs engaged exclusively in electromechanical gears rather than vacuum tubes until Tom Watson Jr. built a new research facility and filled it with experts in electronics. Remington Rand's progress with Univac helped persuade his father of a profound technological shift, leading IBM to announce, in 1953, its first so-called scientific computer, the 701, nineteen of which would be produced over the next two years. In 1955 came the commercial 702, but only fourteen were delivered over its two-year life cycle. Upgrades followed, including the 704 scientific machine, which featured faster tapes and an advanced core memory with a 36-bit word account. Additional models followed until the 700 series was obsoleted by the advent of the transistor, but their impact on industry was minimal.

The ferocious contention over cards versus tape roiled not only father and son but also various factions in the sales force as well as IBM's most important customers. The battle proved a rite of passage for young Tom, then in his early thirties, proving his ability to make critical decisions based on his own analysis that went against the prevailing wisdom.

Harvard business philosopher Clayton Christensen notes that companies that fail to embrace new and ultimately disruptive technologies typically draw false comfort by listening closely to their best salespeople and customers.[7] That would have been an easy choice for Watson Jr., because the best sales reps were solidly opposed, while customers were ambivalent at best, schizophrenic at worst.

But, naysayers aside, tape's advantages—storage space, speed, and fewer manual operations—were obvious and compelling. A senior methods analyst at Prudential Insurance reckoned that a million binary digits could be stored on just one cubic inch of tape as opposed to the five hundred cubic inches and three thousand punch cards required otherwise.[8] In 1948, the vice president in charge of electronic data processing at Met Life warned young Watson: "Tom, you're going to lose your business with us because we already have three floors of this building filled with punch cards and it's getting worse. We just can't afford to pay for that kind of storage space. I'm told we can put our records on magnetic tape."[9] Given that Met Life was a significant customer of both IBM and rival Univac, the message was unmistakable. Similar warnings came from the president of Time Inc., bemoaning the bulky equipment needed to process three cards per subscriber into mailing labels. "We have a whole building full of your gear. We're swamped. If you can't promise us something new," he threatened, "we're going to have to start moving some other way."[10]

But no matter how convincing the arguments in favor of the changeover, it still wasn't clear that magnetic tape was ready for industrial use. At a 1953 computer conference, another Met Life vice president cautioned that the safety and efficacy of the new technology was yet unproven. Where were the guarantees against "accidental erasure, loss of information through breakage, kinks, dimensional instability, flaking and other such occurrences," he asked. "Nor have we been satisfied that the devices currently being employed to read and write on magnetic tape can be relied on to do so with accuracy."[11]

Though the technical fears proved unfounded, the switch to tape did run into organizational and procedural roadblocks (as have subsequent radicalizing technologies). According to a 1952 study by the Society of Actuaries, "most customer executives were amazed at the amount of work required to train personnel, revise procedures, and program applications."[12]

The biggest complaint was lack of access. Whereas punch cards and their relevant data were typically close at hand for problem-solving clerks to view, the tapes were closely guarded by tape librarians and their information distributed back to the various business departments as smeary listings in a time-consuming and cumbersome print process. Certainly, the old man was aware of the access limitation as early as 1947. "Having built his career on punch cards," young Tom remarked, "Dad distrusted magnetic tape instinctively. On a punch card, you had a piece of information that was permanent. You could see it and hold it in your hand. Even the enormous files the insurance companies kept could always be sampled and hand-checked by clerks. But with magnetic tape, your data were stored invisibly on a medium that was designed to be erased and reused."[13]

Indeed, Watson Sr. had strongly backed the development of cards with three rows of 180 columns each—a nearly sevenfold capacity improvement on cardboard the size of a file folder. As recorded in an early history, at a meeting held at the Endicott, New York, laboratory in June 1946, "T. J. Watson Sr. had practically demanded a card 'large' enough to use as an original document rather than one into which only selected information from an original document could be squeezed.... By January 1947, the increased capacity program was second only to the SSEC [IBM's first digital calculator] project in size and apparently second to none in importance. Thus, in plans at least, the Endicott laboratory already had its own new record-storage medium that possessed all the advantages of the unit record then in use and presented none of the system problems associated with tape."[14] In reality, the prognosis for an impossibly awkward, file-folder-sized cardboard sheet was ridiculously limited.

The roiling uncertainty continued at least through 1949, when Watson Jr. organized a team of eighteen systems experts for a three-month study, in part to mollify his father. Unfortunately, the task force came back with the conclusion that punch cards were the best thing in the world for accounting jobs and that magnetic tape had no place at IBM. The top salesmen agreed. It was a defining moment for young Watson, foreshadowing Clayton Christensen's conclusions fifty years later. "I was beginning to learn that the majority, even the majority of top performers, are never the ones to ask when you need to make a move," said the then thirty-five-year-old Watson. "You've got to feel what's going on in the world and then make the move yourself. It's purely visceral."[15]

Ironically, the most successful first-generation computer was the underpowered, tape-card hybrid IBM 650. First delivered to the John Hancock Insurance Company in 1954, the 650 with upgrades continued to be produced until 1962. About 1,800 of the machines were manufactured, a figure that dwarfed the few dozen installations of the more powerful 700 series. For thousands of people, the 650 was their first hands-on experience with a computer, and, not coincidentally, its success helped extend IBM's punch-card revenues for a time—though no longer as a primary business.

At about the same time, IBM encountered a new threat, as both its punch-card exclusivity and rental-only policies were challenged by a Justice Department buoyed by antitrust victories over the Aluminum

Company of America and United Shoe Machinery. The old man was prepared to defend his past practice to the precipice. His son was not surprised by the attack, given the dominance of IBM equipment in business settings.

"We charged premium rents for a premium service, and our growth and profits were astounding—year after year, we were making about 27 cents, pre-tax, on every dollar of revenue," Watson Jr. recalled. "Yet, as lucrative as the business was, we'd attracted very little competition, and we still held about 90 percent of the market for punch-card machines. To the Justice Department, all this was proof that IBM was a monopoly. Sometimes the investigation seemed to die down, but then we'd report another record year, or the Antitrust Division would win some other big case, and they'd be after us again."[16]

In 1950, the Watsons visited U.S. Attorney General Tom Clark with an imaginative market definition drawn as a pyramid. Punch-card equipment was in its tiny apex, with adding machines, posting machines, and bank-teller machines in lower levels, and, lower still, ledger books and pencils. "Our own estimate—straight out of Dad's head," Watson Jr. remembered, "was that IBM only did about 2 percent of all numerical calculations in American business.... The attorney general wasn't persuaded by our pyramid, and I couldn't blame him because I wasn't convinced myself."[17] A compromise was feasible at that stage, with a penalty far short of forcing IBM to divest itself of any of its businesses. Just granting manufacturing rights and putting machines up for sale as well as rental might have been enough. But the old man was adamantly and viscerally opposed to any compromise, still smarting, perhaps, from his collision with the feds while at NCR. As a result, the next five years were marked by ongoing disputes, both legal and familial.

In January 1956, Watson Jr. finally persuaded his dying father to let the IBM lawyers sign the antitrust consent decree, effectively ending the company's lock on the punch-card business and the rental-only equipment policy. The accelerating pace of technological advancement had effectively mooted the entire issue anyway, making long-term rentals increasingly risky and hastening the decline of revenues from IBM's magically formulated punch cards.

Whereas Hollerith electromechanical tabulators had retained their currency for sixty years, the triple-step leap from vacuum tubes to transistors to integrated circuits had occurred in the space of just fifteen years, and product life cycles would shrink to only five years in the 1960s and 1970s, and fewer still after that. Moreover, outright sales were the wave of the future. "Settling the case was one of the best moves we ever made," Watson Jr. said later, "because it cleared the way for IBM to keep expanding at top speed. With Dad, the consent decree was always a sore spot, and we never discussed it again. But there was no longer any doubt for either of us that I was running the show."[17] The following May, Watson Sr. finally ceded the chairmanship to his son. Six weeks later, IBM's founder was dead.

The Antidote to Founder's Blight

Too often, once-entrepreneurial companies have been fatally damaged by their aging founders' refusal to release power. How did IBM escape this founder's blight? By his late seventies, Watson was at least ten years older than An Wang of Wang Labs or Ken Olsen of Digital Equipment when they failed to save their companies from new competition. The elder Watson was hardly complacent, but he was not ready to accept a new technology and new business model. Unlike Wang or Olsen, however, Watson Sr. had a sharply outspoken subordinate in whom he had considerable if unspoken confidence.

According to Watson Jr., the rancor with his father was fierce and ongoing, at least on business issues. Their ferocious exchanges pepper chapter after chapter in the son's autobiography. In one instance, Watson Jr. relates: "I completely lost my temper. 'God damn you, old man! Can't you ever leave me alone?' I said. I didn't strike him, but I ripped my arm away with great vigor.... We were right on the brink of estrangement—both of us felt it—and neither of us wanted to jump over the edge. Dad came very close to firing me"

On another occasion, "But usually I'd come back at him hard, and we'd have one hellacious fight. He'd get livid. His jowls would shake. All the old family tensions would come boiling out, and I'd let him have it with everything I had...."

And souring a celebration, "Dad and I were so addicted to fighting that we even managed to make a struggle out of my promotion to president of IBM."[18]

It's impossible to imagine Fred Wang, in the setting of a traditional, patriarchal Chinese family, raising his voice to his father and company founder An Wang. And at Digital, most of the strongest executives—those who might have influenced Olsen—had already jumped ship for new opportunities in Silicon Valley by the time the company was sinking. "Ken's been right so many times, no one dares disagree," Naomi and I told his closest colleague in explaining our suggestion—fruitless, as it turned out—that it was time for the Grand Dragon (as Ken was fondly known) to retire. Neither Wang Labs nor DEC survived its founder.

By contrast, IBM's transition was perhaps the most fortuitous in the history of the computer business. Besides being no stranger to the business, Watson Jr. was notably farsighted about the technical and regulatory changes affecting the company. And he clearly had a taste for risk, as evidenced by his often lonely push to convert from cards to tape.

By all accounts, Watson Jr. also had a tolerance for turbulence in his choice of direct reports—or was at least willing to brook the kind of challenges that characterized his relationship with his father. "I managed IBM with a team of 15 or 20 senior executives," he wrote. "Some of these men were my friends, but I never hesitated to promote people I didn't like. The comfortable assistant, the nice guy you like to go on fishing trips with, is a great pitfall in management. Instead, I was always looking for sharp, scratchy, harsh, almost unpleasant guys who could see and tell me about things as they really were. If you can get enough of those around you and have patience enough to hear them out, there is almost no limit to where you can grow."[19]

Watson Jr.'s management style leaned far more toward decentralization than had his father's. He handed off authority to his direct reports rather than managing everything through a very few highly trusted, long-time subordinates. On the top rungs at IBM were men like Al Williams in the chief financial officer's slot, Vin Learson who headed the 360 effort and eventually took over as the chief executive officer, and Bob Evans who oversaw development. These genuinely smart, tough, and often disagreeable guys set the contentious tone at IBM. And just as the boss speculated, growth soon flooded the flagship data-processing division, which included everything from components to software to manufacturing to field sales for both electronic computers and tabulating machines. (Typewriters and a few other items were separate.)

In May 1959, Watson divided the company in half at the $10,000 monthly rental line, leaving about thirty thousand people on each side of the divide. Explained the company news magazine: "As Tom Watson said, 'The management concept is decentralization, wherein more of the responsibility for key decision-making and for profit is set at operating levels below corporate headquarters.... GPD [General Products] is responsible for all product planning, development and manufacture of equipment presently represented by the punched card, RAMAC and 650 class. DSD [Data Systems] does the same for equipment in the 700 series and above."[20]

The realignment looked good on paper, but the dividing lines were often breached amid the rapidly changing technology. For example, the new 1410 model, which should have been included with the larger computers, was actually moved to the General Products division to force compatibility with the smaller 1401. Evans and a colleague took engineers from both teams to Rocky Point, a resort in upstate New York, where they "nailed the door shut" until agreement could be reached between the camps. The resultant stridency seems improbable today, when perhaps a half-dozen operating systems dominate the industry and anything new would be stillborn for lack of third-party software. But in 1959, operating a computer was still a craft, and computer engineers were the artisans who tweaked and polished each new entry to the point where everything from operating system to customer applications required unique software. "There were people that threatened to quit the company if we made the decision [for a compatible machine]," Evans remembered.[21] Fortunately, he didn't let such threats deter him.

By 1960, with the transition from vacuum tubes to transistors concluded, IBM offered eight solid-state computers, ranging from the 7070 to the 1401 and 1410. Two years later, IBM unveiled the 1440 with the first disk storage and, in 1963, the follow-on 1460, which featured a faster printer and faster memory. A string of new capabilities to be sure, but largely inefficient for customer use, as Watson clearly recognized: "Different software and different peripheral equipment, such as printers and disk drives, had to be used with each machine. If a customer's business grew and he wanted to shift from a small computer to a large one, he had to get new everything and rewrite everything, often at great expense."[22]

Betting the Company

Watson initiated arguably the largest gamble in computer history, the System/360. By design, the 360 would make obsolete all of IBM's existing computers—mostly rentals—by offering a family of compatible computers that would rent from $2,500 to $115,000 a month. The obsolete machines would be returned, applications would require major adjustments, and the customer's selection of vendors would be reopened. The risks to the company were enormous, but so were the potential benefits.

For the first time, all of IBM's new mainframes could run the same printers, tapes, disks, and other peripherals. And customers could move their applications without having to reprogram larger and larger boxes as their workloads expanded. What sounds obvious today presented enormous costs and risks in terms of management, money, and company reputation. As the scale of the project unfolded, deadlines were missed, costs rose, and competitors began to pick off IBM's now-restive customer base.

The September 1966 issue of *Fortune* headlined "IBM's $5,000,000,000 Gamble," calling it "the most crucial and portentous—as well as perhaps the riskiest—business judgment of recent times." Building these new lines would subject IBM to tremendous upheaval, making and breaking careers. While Vin Learson prospered, Tom Watson's brother Arthur, who was known to friends and colleagues as "Dick," didn't. Dick had been in line for a top job at IBM, but had the misfortune to fail in trying to lead System/360 development. "The expense of the project was indeed staggering. We spent three-quarters of a billion dollars just on engineering. Then we invested another four and a half billion on factories, equipment, and the rental machines themselves. We hired more than sixty thousand new employees and opened five major new plants. It was the biggest privately financed commercial project ever undertaken. The writer at *Fortune* pointed out that it was substantially larger than the World War II effort that produced the atomic bomb," Watson wrote in his autobiography.[23]

The massive project began on a remarkably shaky platform. Learson brought together engineers from both large and small computer divisions into a committee dubbed "SPREAD," for systems, programming, research, engineering, and development. The committee met for a couple of months in late 1961 until "Vin got impatient," Watson said. "Two weeks before Christmas he sent [the engineers] to a motel in Connecticut with orders not to come back until they'd agreed. That was how the plan for System/360 was born—in the form of an 80-page report delivered on December 28."[24]

Two months? Eighty pages? Learson's Christmas-season binge was the product of an extraordinary mix of hubris, ignorance, and strength of will. The monumental project was launched with less planning than a typical company-payroll system would get. Not surprisingly, the results were delivered many years after the date pre-announced to the restive customer base—falsely, as Watson later admitted under oath at the trial of the lawsuit brought by competitor Control Data. "By the spring of 1964, our hand was forced and we had to, with eyes wide open, announce a complete line—some of our machines were [announced] 24 months early, and the total line an average of 12 months early," he said.

The new operating system proved to be the greatest challenge. The $500 million spent in 1960 would, in today's dollars, be five times what Microsoft spent on new operating systems in the 1980s. And software wasn't the only gamble; System/360 also marked the first time that IBM ditched transistors in favor of integrated circuits that it opted to fabricate itself rather than relying on the merchant market as it had previously. Furthermore, all the peripherals had to be redesigned to mesh with the new 360 architecture. Later, Bob Evans confessed to a reporter that he called the project "you bet your company," adding that it was still "a damn good risk, and a lot less risk than it would have been to do anything else, or do nothing at all...."[25]

The noted IBM historian William Rogers summarized the Watson gamble succinctly and with his customary lucidity: "To guarantee continued command of the market, it became necessary for IBM to take a massive step forward—at a risk which some old company hands feared, notwithstanding its great resources, could break the company. Over a period of four years in the 1960s, IBM spent nearly as much money to develop, redesign, program, and systematize its full line of computers as its gross sales of $5,345,000,000 in 1967. By dumping in staggering amounts of capital, far more than any combination of competing companies could or would commit, and by striding into the market with systems and equipment distinguished by all of the advance design and compatibility technology the company could develop, imitate or buy, IBM could keep most of the market to itself. Otherwise, the market might become fragmented, even thoroughly competitive, with quite a few separate companies carving out segments of the burgeoning field, leaving IBM one among many. The vision of rampant free enterprise developing in a market overwhelmingly dominated by IBM was a recurring nightmare to management.... In the end, the cost of processing 100,000 computations on the old first generation models was reduced, according to IBM, from $1.38 to three and a half cents."[26]

The risks were huge, but so was the payoff from widening the distance between IBM and its traditional competitors. On the eve of the first System/360 installations, its rivals, ranked by the 1967 dollar value of their computer installations, were Sperry Rand (i.e., Univac), Control Data, Honeywell, RCA, NCR, GE, and Burroughs. Though collectively known as "the seven dwarfs," each competed skillfully against IBM in specific markets ranging from Univac's foothold in real-time computing to Burroughs's expertise in memory management. And bad blood between the dwarfs and the industry megalith often made the competition all the more brutal.

Despite their individual strengths, the System/360 lowered the boom on the dwarfs. By 1967, IBM was winning the battle on the basis of compatibility, technology, and business viability. As a young consultant at the Diebold Group, I encouraged a tiny if symptomatic fracture in the widening divide between IBM and its competitors in my evaluation of computers and computer manufacturers for a midscale pharmaceutical company in upstate New York. Even after extensive vendor interviews and spreadsheet comparisons, I couldn't find anywhere that IBM's System/360 line was substantially ahead of either Burroughs or RCA except printers, perhaps. But it also wasn't behind by enough in any area that mattered to my client to warrant the additional risk of joining up with a dwarf that might be gone five or ten years later, thereby forcing a rewrite of all of the company's applications software to mesh with another manufacturer.

General Electric was the first to exit the computer field in 1970, selling its business to Honeywell for $234 million—not a brilliant acquisition since Honeywell's product line was completely incompatible with GE's systems. RCA followed suit in 1971, selling its computer assets to Sperry Univac and reducing the dwarfs to a BUNCH (Burroughs, Univac, NCR, Control Data, and Honeywell).

In 1972, pundit Herb Grosch predicted at a heavily attended conference of the Association for Computing Machinery (ACM) that none of the BUNCH would exist by 1980 and that "the weaklings will drop out in the next two or three years." By 1973, IBM probably hoped Grosch would be wrong, given the pressure of the antitrust suits and ongoing scrutiny from the courts. As Naomi and I wrote then: "Of course, the problem facing IBM is that the competition often seems to be getting weaker than it was before—without IBM's prodding. Honeywell appears to be resting on GE's laurels, Burroughs on the B5000 series with its clever operating system, CDC on civil suits mostly against IBM, and all on the good will of the Federal Bureaucracy whose nonsensical RFPs [Requests for Proposals to supply a service or commodity] and bidding processes inevitably award the dance to the weakest sisters."

Grosch's prognostication was not entirely correct. NCR remains a real contender today, maintaining its stronghold in retail computing through an early move to Unix point-of-sale equipment and a later acquisition of data warehouse Teradata. Honeywell, after several mergers, is strong but long since out of the computer business. CDC is diminished to only a consulting capability. Burroughs merged with Univac to become Unisys, largely dependent on government largess and the personal computer business.

Thus, most of the dwarfs exited stage left as the System/360's near-total triumph simultaneously opened the market to new competitors angling for product-compatibility from stage right. In other words, the cast of newcomers wrote themselves into a script Big Blue thought it was writing just for itself.

Leasing Companies

The first assault came from computer-leasing companies that had scuffed IBM's shoeshine since 1956, when the consent decree ended old Tom's rental-only policy and gave customers the purchase option. Young Tom's doctrine of long-term software compatibility made the purchase option even more attractive by boosting resale values with the implicit guarantee that secondhand buyers' programs would work.

Compatibility brought the leasing companies to boisterous adolescence while creating considerable distress within IBM. Everything depended on "residual value," the price the leasing company could expect to get from resale to another user once the equipment came off lease. Their profit projections depended on the blind faith that IBM would continue its predictable five-year product life cycles with a straight doubling in price/performance. With that assurance they could price (and depreciate) their gear on an eight-year life span, with the expectation of a 40 percent residual even after IBM had delivered its next-generation equipment.

The stress on IBM was evident from internal memorandums discovered in preparation of the 1973 Telex suit against IBM; more will follow. Third-party leasing had become so attractive that a worried IBM district sales manager wrote in a 1967 memo to the Armonk, New York, headquarters: "Frankly, our salesmen are aggressively marketing for leasing companies. They are using the leasing companies as a sales tool. If this activity is within corporate sales objectives, fine! If not, action should be taken to change the sales plan."

It wasn't fine at all, snapped a memo from the financial analysis department. Admittedly, the field might have been misled because "IBM's policy toward the leasing company industry has vacillated considerably during the past several years. The posture we are to present to this industry, however, was finally crystallized by F. G. Rogers' DP Branch Managers Letter #450: 'Third parties that are vendors of data processing equipment are *competitors* of IBM.' The facts leading to this conclusion are crystal clear."

Crystal, indeed. The memo next projected that the leasing companies' "uncontrolled" inventories would grow from $720 million in October 1967 to $1.3 billion, or 12.5 percent of IBM's installed base over the next year. And who knew what after that?

The Debut of the Plug Compatibles

The makers of plug-compatible peripherals (e.g., tapes, disks, and printers) bet their futures on computer users' ability to plug into IBM's 360 with little if any software modification. Some of these peripherals were technically better than IBM's offerings; all were noticeably cheaper because their suppliers had the use of IBM software without its super-sized expenses for software development and support, never mind puffy sales and administrative overhead burdens.

The first PC disk maker was probably Athena, which came on the scene in 1968. Its most memorable impact was on the share price of its parent, Comstock-Keystone Computer Company, which vaulted from fifteen cents per share in June to eight dollars in July, at which point the SEC halted trading. A brief gold rush commenced as the plug-compatible manufacturer (PCM) ranks were joined by a large cast of heretofore unknown actors with names like Marshal, Potter, Bryant, and Talcott, and later, Calcomp, Memorex, and Storage Technology.

"Cheap capital was a key part of the business case," mused Les Kilpatrick, the founder of Calcomp, an entrant in the sweepstakes, whom I met a decade later. "When you sold one dollar's worth of product," he told us, "you could raise a hundred dollars of investment."

By the end of Watson Jr.'s tenure in 1971, the PC peripheral companies had claimed 30 percent of the IBM market. We at the Research Board contrasted Armonk's benign dismissal of the dwarfs with its combative stance toward the new arrivals: "IBM seems to view the competition in two slices," we said. "The other mainframe manufacturers seem to have been given the protected status usually accorded to vanishing species, and there is good reason to suppose that IBM would view their future demise with as much alarm as their future success, given the pressure of various antitrust suits and the ongoing scrutiny of the courts. On the other hand, there are the peripheral manufacturers who have become the people to turn to when the customer wants to save money or, often more important, wave a bloody flag at IBM. Part of this attitude may be based on the very real potential of the peripheral market as a growth sector. Part results from IBM's rant that these vendors are often technological thieves and parasites."

The threat of plug-compatible mainframes began in the last days of Tom Jr.'s tenure (and, ironically, with the new antitrust suit) when top-ranked computer designer and IBM Research Fellow Dr. Gene Amdahl defected with two colleagues in a dispute over mainframe design. Amdahl was the near-mythic designer of everything from the 702 vacuum-tube computer to the 360. Now unemployed and laid low by a back injury, Amdahl spent the next eight months thinking about cost performance in large-scale computing until he developed what he later called "a startling piece of information about how that relationship affected a high-performance machine."[27] What he had apparently discovered was a way to achieve high yields in the fabrication of silicon chips with twenty times the number of logic circuits IBM could produce.

As Lloyd Thorndyke, a vice president at Control Data, observed to us: "Gene Amdahl will always occupy a special place in the industry in large scale integration. The rest of us wondered if anyone could ever achieve an acceptable level of reliability, given the heat problems we expected." The leapfrog in circuits per chip gave Amdahl a competitive technical advantage in lowering the costs to make these boxes and then reducing the points of failure.

Gross margins and profits wholly incomprehensible by today's standards provided a much more compelling reason to enter the plug-compatible mainframe market. IBM's 1974 annual report listed gross margins of 67 percent on a pretax profit of 27 percent (versus approximately 25 percent and 10 percent, respectively, for the best computer companies today). Our own between-the-lines analysis speculated that product costs were actually around 11.5 percent, a conclusion supported by industry estimates of 10 percent to 13.5 percent. A senior executive at National Semiconductor recalled that company's decision to get into the business after its product analysts concluded that IBM spent only $95,000 on parts to build a mainframe costing $2 million. The opportunity was doubtless irrefutable, as evidenced by the host of hopefuls—Itel/National, Fujitsu, Hitachi, and Magnuson among others—entering the market alongside Amdahl.

Of course, the rise of the plug-compatible mainframes could only come at the expense of IBM's most strategic product line, providing not only the best profit margins but the basis for its legendary account control as well. Using IBM's operating system let the fledglings cut R&D expense. Equally important for the customer, it nearly eliminated the switching cost of moving back to IBM.

Amdahl's contentious yet dependent relationship with IBM led us to coin the term "alience" to differentiate it from the friendly if generally impotent "alliances" so beloved by the computer industry (at least for photo opportunities). At the time, Amdahl's reliance on System/360 was largely regarded by IBMers as something between an unpleasant nuisance and criminal exploitation. In fact, it turned out to be a model for the future, as Unix, Linux, and Microsoft all attracted their own "aliences" and thereby ruled the day.

Unbundling Services and Software?

IBM and the old-line mainframe suppliers had offered a pricing package that "bundled" hardware, software, and maintenance. Their mindset was clear from a June 1968 note (Telex) from strategist Hillary Faw that opened: "Any IBM executive who suggests that our data processing service contract price should be partially unbundled is likely to be regarded by his associates as a man in need of a vacation.... [Service bundling] has proved to be eminently acceptable to data processing customers as well as to other systems manufacturers."

But bundling came under legal attack from the leasing companies as letting IBM discriminate against customers who acquired their equipment from third parties. Faw continued that some unbundling may be necessary "because of recent environmental changes" such as the Justice Department's inquiry into whether bundled field maintenance represented "a single charge for a combination of services [that] could be regarded as a tie-in sale under the Clayton Act." Legal action from Justice or private lawsuits by leasing companies could well "be far more damaging to IBM than self-imposed unbundling," he warned. Maintenance was soon unbundled.

Another Faw memorandum dealt with software bundling, which left the independent software vendors in competition against an IBM product included in the price of the hardware and thus superficially "free." Applied Data Research (ADR) was a highly successful vendor cofounded by Martin Goetz that offered mainframe-related software tools. Its lawsuit occasioned a memorable fight-or-flight legal strategy memo from Faw: "What are the options available to IBM?" Here's how he laid them out:

- Option 1: "Fight the ADR action in the hope of winning the argument that control programs are in fact so interrelated with the hardware as to be indistinguishable from it."

- Option 2: "Stay as we are and buy out ADR and all other software houses with whom we will be in conflict." That could be expensive since "as word spreads that IBM is in the practice of buying itself out of conflicts, we will be exposed to being victimized by charlatans who go into a business to be bought out."

- Option 3 was preferred (albeit, very cautiously): "Fully price on a cost basis all programming systems not yet in the public domain including separate prices for all segments of each system."

Then Faw quickly retreated from the abyss of his own cleverness: "This is mentioned as an option merely to remind us that were we to elect Option 1 and lose our case, this could be forced upon us."

Ironically, software unbundling and full pricing was eventually deployed by Lou Gerstner as a major opportunity with 2008 software revenues exceeding $22 billion and providing for almost half of IBM profits. On the basis of revenues alone, unbundling should have come much sooner. More importantly, software "compatibility" across hardware vendors was embraced by the industry. Within just ten years, suppliers of mass operating systems from Sun Microsystems to Microsoft would do everything and almost anything to attract the maximum number of independent software packages. IBM would eventually adopt the same approach.

Transitions in Leadership

The struggle to develop System/360 put a great strain on IBM management, starting with the Watson brothers. Dick was forced out of CEO contention when Learson seized control of the struggling 360 effort and was, subsequently, named president in 1966. Tom later voiced regret over his brother's treatment: "As it was, we remade the computer industry with the System/360, and, objectively, it was the greatest triumph of my business career. But whenever I look back on it, I think about the brother I injured...."[28]

The years 1969 to 1970 were disastrous for Tom Watson personally. On January 17, 1969, the Justice Department filed a second antitrust suit that would distract IBM management for the next thirteen years. Then the Nixon-era recession started, and IBM stock soon lost half its value. Brother Dick left the company to become ambassador to France, and sister Jane was dying of cancer. Tom's marriage was hanging by a thread, though it was later repaired. And in November 1970, at age fifty-seven, Tom suffered a serious heart attack.

The following June he retired, though he temporarily remained as chairman of the executive committee. Vin Learson was elected CEO for an eighteen-month stub tenure, an anomaly reflecting his "long and dramatic career" and Watson's early retirement. Then, in January 1973, Tom stepped down as chairman, and Learson and Frank Cary stepped up as chairman and CEO, respectively.

By any measure, Thomas J. Watson Jr. was an extraordinary CEO. He assumed the top role just as the company was facing massive changes in technology and competition, and he handled the switch to tape, the first antitrust suit, and System/360 magnificently. Fortuitously, he ceded the chairmanship just as IBM was encountering powerful new antagonists in the form of minicomputers and plug compatibles.

In a macabre sense, his father's terminal illness and his own brush with death were beneficial to the company in that they forced timely transitions of the top executive. Almost every other major computer firm would be less fortunate.

Chapter 3

REORGANIZING TO REARM:

Frank Cary at IBM

The organizational structure of an enterprise can be a battering ram of corporate strategy in one period and an enervating dead weight in the next. In the 1960s, Tom Watson Jr. centralized the development staffs to unify development of System/360 as a line of mainframe models arrayed from small to large along a carefully graduated price ladder. Each division was charged with working a slice of the entire system product line that would mesh compatibly with every other slice. In other words, the Systems Products Division engineered everything from processors to tapes to communications devices, while Systems Development programmed software for operating systems, storage, and telecommunications, and Advanced Systems tried to juggle all the parts and pieces for the next-generation announcement. IBM's crown jewel was the Data Products Division, whose "blue-suiters" sold the products and provided every CEO from 1911 until 1993, when outsider Lou Gerstner broke the tradition.

Typically announced on the same day as the processors were new tapes, disks, printers, and telecommunications controllers— each enhancing the others' market potential even at risk to its own. And further neatening the customer's decision was the bundling of software and service costs into the system's purchase or rental price. One price covered everything. To coordinate this parade of computers, peripherals, software, training, and pricing, IBM established a process of forced reviews that subjected almost everything and anything to "concurrence" or "non-concurrence" by various executives across the vast organization. Every product plan drew endless meetings and memos signaling agreement or disagreement in sometimes ferociously combative prose.

The concentration of effort was fine so long as the competition mirrored IBM's end-to-end systems offerings, but it became a noose once the industry fragmented. Then dozens of specialized competitors fed on the IBM market, taking advantage of their insurmountable cost advantages and ability to target especially vulnerable points in the product line. They also knew that IBM's cumbersome management process would impede its response. IBM needed powerful leadership to chart a new course. And the question that rippled through the industry was whether or not the new CEO, Frank Cary, was up to the challenge.

Many outsiders thought not. In their judgment, Cary would be a mediocre leader at best. Our friends at *Fortune* chuckled over his request for an invitation to one of the luncheon meetings the magazine regularly scheduled with top-rung business leaders. The journalists couldn't conceive of the power-conscious Tom Watson Jr. or Vin Learson ever asking to be included. Our own view of Cary's management skills, cobbled together from random sources outside IBM, was aligned with the doubters. But all of us were wrong. Frank Cary was the first professional manager to head a traditionally entrepreneurial company that had outgrown its traces. His style may have been more modest than his predecessors, but, as Watson himself later acknowledged, "Trying to make himself famous was what any Watson would have done. But it wasn't Frank Cary's style, and the fact was that for eight years he ran the company as well as it had ever been run."[1]

Relocating Leasing Company Inventories

The earliest competitive threat encountered by the new Learson/ Cary team was likely the leasing companies, whose resale of secondhand gear at depreciated prices depressed the prices IBM could charge for new mainframes. The extent of this drag on product introductions was aptly described in the Watson days by a note (another Telex memo) from Bob Evans evaluating a new high-end mainframe against its predecessor. "The machine failed in the marketplace because it was considerably overpriced," Evans said. "The present System Manager's estimate is that it was at least $20,000 too high on approximately a $100,000 CPU/memory. The business analysis failed to take into account the effects of leasing companies lowering the effective price of Model 65s and the high purchase multiplier."

The leasing companies also doused expectations for IBM's own leasing program, still cherished over outright sales for the closer working rapport created with customers, in part by letting them try out unproven products without making a long-term commitment. More important were IBM's dearly held expectations for orderly—that was 15 percent annual—financial growth. Specifically, leasing revenues gave IBM the financial predictability "to correct mistakes [in revenue projections] and adjust for unforeseen changes" that "might make it difficult to maintain uninterrupted employment" and, eventually, even increase "the exposure to unionism." (Telex again.)

The executives at IBM headquarters in Armonk, New York, couldn't retaliate through pricing alone, however, because of its high overhead, the government's continuous antitrust scrutiny, and the fragility of the leasing companies. Any prodding from IBM might cause these flimsy firms to collapse under pressure from their worried bankers, fretted IBM strategist Hillary Faw in an August 1968 memo on "the potential secondhand systems inventory already outside IBM control … Financial analyses have indicated many leasing companies will begin to suffer debt retirement difficulties at approximately the same time they are experiencing significant user placement problems," Faw said. And their failure could instigate a possible riot of losses and failures that might well subject Big Blue to "treble damage exposure of unbelievable magnitude" in a trust-busting judge's courtroom.

Considering all that, "one of the few legitimate ways to manage leasing company activity is to introduce new technologies," IBM counsel Bartow Farr advised in 1966 (Telex). Sounds obvious, but computing is a complex business. Every strategic question tends to get tangled up in a host of competing interests and contradictory considerations. A technology shift that abandoned or at least disadvantaged the programs written for the older mainframe would infuriate IBM's best and biggest customers. In that nightmare scenario, customers might opt instead to reprogram to one of the more cost-effective new minicomputers just starting to appear on the market. Never "reopening the customer's purchase decision" was an article of faith everywhere in the computer industry. Product incompatibility should never put a customer in such a bind as to drive him to another supplier. By analogy, consider the consumer electronics supplier who introduced a CD technology that obsoletes the customer's music collection.

Even so, continued activity by the leasing companies convinced IBM management to introduce a new mainframe technology that opened a gap just large enough to devalue third-party inventories. The difficulty and danger of that navigation between impacting inventories without discomforting customers was evident in a stutter-step product decision, the unintended consequences of which would plague IBM for the next decade.

At issue was whether the just-announced 370/155 and 370/165 models should be replaced after only eighteen months by the 370/158 and 370/168. The "5s" were linear replacements for the top of the 360 line. The "8s" would introduce a brand-new (for IBM) feature of memory "relocate," which let the customer process more programs at the same time to realize a higher price/performance ratio. Unfortunately, the only way that enhancement would be available to 370/155 and 370/165 owners, including the pesky lessors, was through the purchase of a Rube Goldberg-like add-on called a DAT box (for Direct Address Translation).

Extraordinary levels of internal review, debate, concurrences, and non-concurrences are visible in a series of Telex memos reflecting the horrendous complexities of the decision:

December 1970: The memory "relocate" feature represented at best a "modest improvement in the price/performance of S/370," wrote Jack Bertram, then heading Advanced Planning. "We have not seen a persuasive case ... [that] relocate obsoletes and devalues the purchased inventory." Perhaps the capability was later strengthened.

April 1971: In fact, the impact might be too great, worried Planning Vice President Dean Phyphers, noting a tangle of problems: "significant 1971-1972 revenue impacts, troubles in handling purchase customers, FET [memory] demand mismatch, 370 model churning and rental life problems, and major funding exposures ... My net is that we are in trouble on product strategy."

September 22, 1971: Perhaps Phyphers was right, warned Bertram, repeating his non-concur. "[T]he announcement of Olympus [158] and Pisces [168] will have a significant retardation effect on the revenue from previous 370 equipment."

November 5, 1971: Organization indecision was intolerable, wrote a restive COO Cary to CEO Learson. "As far as I'm concerned, the decision to do relocate was made two years ago. We have spent millions of dollars, but we have not—for some good and some not-so-good reasons—completed the business analysis justification for it. My own intuitive judgment is that relocate will be a successful program and [should] finally be announced and implemented in the IBM line." It was past time for "the strongest kind of management action ... with the laboratory management to assure that they understand the Group Plan is (*a*) to relocate and (*b*) to solve the memory problem. If this is done, I think that it will settle most of the churning that is going on in the laboratories."

December 22, 1971: Amazingly, the debate meandered on. "Selected fine-tuning analysis" was requested by the Management Committee according to the minutes of its meeting. "Beitzel was asked to evaluate the worldwide effect of an Olympus without Pisces." Just eight months before scheduled product announcement, there was still a chance one of the two high-end machines would be stillborn.

But by now, two other important competitive factors favored the move: First was the need to match the up-to-date memory-handling capabilities successfully offered by Burroughs in several strategic markets, notably banking. Equally problematic were reports that defector Gene Amdahl was readying a high-end, plug-compatible mainframe for introduction around 1972. Delaying the 370/165 until the relocate feature was ready would leave only the aging 360 to defend the market against a newcomer with much higher-density circuitry, thus accentuating any Amdahl press splash. Something newer and better was needed—and fast.

Both relocatable machines were introduced in 1972, and customers who had purchased the older gear were predictably furious over the artificial add-on. The DAT box quickly became "dat joke," and customers who bought one were ridiculed by peers as someone not quite in the know and, by implication, less favored by their key supplier. From IBM's perspective, the near-term revenue impact was uncomfortable as rental customers prematurely jettisoned their 370/155s and 370/165s.

And some purchase customers chose to insulate themselves from future unpleasant shocks by tilting to rental, thereby delaying IBM's revenues.

The Leasing Companies Get Whacked

But the revenue shortfall and customer discontent was justified in Armonk because operating-lease companies with large inventories of the secondhand, technically handicapped 370/155s and 165s were busted. Resale prices of the two-year-old 370/155 and 370/165 immediately dropped by 20 percent, while the price of secondhand 360/65s plummeted from 40 percent of original list to 20 percent or less, when they could be sold at all.

The stark situation engendered by IBM's pugnacious business decision was recalled for us by Mike Morrell, a staccato-talking executive at Leasco in 1977. Leasing companies on less-than-full payout contracts were stranded with acres of returned equipment. More than one hundred fifty mainframes were downgraded to performing simple tasks like printing, and large shipments of technically rusting inventory were sent to Europe, "though no one knew what to do [with them] when they arrived," he said. Calm didn't return for another two years along with full payout leases on the 370/158 and 370/168 machines. But by 1975, the amateurs were back "like Ali Baba and the 40 thieves," all offering the same inadequate financing formula. "Another shakeout is coming like the leasing sector's misjudgment with the last generation. Hiroshima again." He was right.

In 1977, we also visited Peter Redfield at Itel, the classic highflier in a perch high up in San Francisco's TransAmerica building. Every plush office seemingly sported a brass telescope for scanning the harbor, along with a stunning, bare-legged assistant to help with focus and settings. Presiding was Redfield—urbane, charming, and always ready with an overly complicated answer. The economics were based on "realistic interest rates, various tax considerations, and an assumed 40 percent residual after eight years," he assured us with bland confidence. That 40 percent had worked five years earlier, but it sounded improbable in the new mix of residuals and product lives and the impact the newer minicomputer companies were making. Saying that we didn't understand discounting, Redfield showed a bit of temper but remained adamant in his analysis.

Regaining our composure, we quickly returned to the high road of strategy. The ever-savvy Redfield had already begun buttressing a weakened market position with a few "free" services. To lease a new machine, for example, Itel would work to resell a customer's existing IBM gear, though without ever taking ownership. Still, we parried, mainframe prices had to decline, partially as a consequence of the invasion of the minis. "We're positioned for cautious growth," retorted Redfield. "This isn't going to be a whirlwind industry again. Transportation-equipment leasing is our anchor to windward. As for our own mainframes, we're riding the crest. We'll enjoy good times for at least the next eighteen months." And he did, although Leasco's Morrell called Itel's financial statement "all hot air" pumped out of "overly optimistic residuals."

Bartow Farr had nailed it back in 1966: Technology was the best way to counter the leasing companies. Ultimately, the leasing companies fled the scene, just another blip on the computer-industry screen that faded in the vapor of their inflated residual assumptions. Itel sold its computer-marketing and field-support unit to National Semiconductor, which then operated as National Advanced Systems.

Crippled in Concurrence

Given the indecision over the 158/168, Frank Cary certainly wasn't blind to the crippling effects of IBM's cumbersome product-rollout process. A 1971 Data Processing Group statement (Telex again) worriedly surveyed the drop in mainframe sales, citing the general lack of "dramatic new design concepts" to whet the appetite of the market, and, perhaps most important, a loss of "account control" that it attributed to vested interests within the company; the forced unbundling of hardware, software, and maintenance under threat of lawsuits and regulatory actions; greater account complexity and larger quotas; competition from the PCMs; and so forth. Many years later, the memo's closing observations still resonate: "The game of the sixties was overall systems price/performance. We won that game ... [the] system is now in place and the market is satisfied with it. The current market philosophy is 'who has the cheapest boxes [computers] for my systems?'" Already, boxes—not systems—were the focus. Watson's System/360 triumph left organizational baggage that Cary would now have to jettison.

Cary rushed to change the game, even while Vin Learson, the architect of the previous regime, was still CEO. Almost immediately, the new COO chartered an internal task force to study the issues behind the managerial disarray. On October 5, 1971, a four-page memo, blandly entitled "Characteristics of the Present Structure and Management," was issued by SVP Richard Bullen and Assistant Treasurer Hillary Faw. The memo covered eleven points. Some concerned the ubiquitous conflicts between operating divisions and the corporate staff. Others made (often unpleasant) judgments about specific personalities. Most substantive were four points directed at failures that had dogged new-product development—especially that of the misbegotten "Future System."

1. Product planning didn't work, especially as a division separate from the actual product-design engineers. "By merely changing leaderships, we are not likely to get to the fundamentals of the problem ... [In fact], the problem set erupted." There were too many variables for an end-to-end product plan.

2. The problem wasn't scale: "We are convinced that the fundamentals have nothing to do with the business volume, size, or the numbers of people involved. Sheer size of itself could not create the kinds of problems we now see."

3. The root problem was sheer complexity—both in product line and in the growing clout and complexity of the competition, which the memo described as "loss of control over our environment." The centralized "Group Management System [was] unable to manage departures ... outside the mold of preserving the old system." The stress from "large vested interests" resistant to change was hobbling IBM's ability to react.

4. The software development division (SDD) was itself a profit center, divorced in management and motivation from the other product divisions. In producing System/360 a decade earlier, this organizational structure forced end-to-end consistency in the

software offering. But at this point, it was creating conflicts of interest and a bureaucracy at odds with the hardware divisions.

The task-force memo also complained openly about the quality of the current staff and interference from on high, specifically CEO T. Vincent Learson: "Adding to the inadequacies of the management system ... TVL has had his fingers directly in this pie for some time." It was long past time for a wholly different, less dynastic, more professional approach to corporate organization and management. All the changes of the past five years were merely tinkering to no positive effect: "We have made a review of all the structural changes made since 1965. This told us we had made a long series of unfortunate moves directed at size. These involved profit decentralization attempts which were never in fact fully delegated by the Corporation. Throughout all of this time, the system and the people were frequently subjected to irrational, unrealistic dictates from top management. The result was a compounding of confusion."

Cutting the Straps

Taking Bullen and Faw's analysis to heart, Cary wasted no time in beginning a decentralization that would defend the company against an array of feisty and fast-moving new entrants. The first action came on January 13, 1972 (before he'd even been named CEO), when he announced that the Data Processing group—previously overseen by a Watson favorite, George "Spike" Beitzel—was being split in two. Sales, maintenance, and advance planning were combined into the Marketing and Services group, while components (e.g., chips), product development, and software development were shifted into the Data Processing Product group under John Opel, who would follow Cary as CEO. Meanwhile, Beitzel trundled off to head the General Business Group (GBS), where two divisions fielded separate sales and maintenance organizations. GBS would later invent what was then IBM's most modular, unbundled, competitive, and generally coolest minicomputer, the Series/1. (Coincidentally, the group's vice president for sales, Jack Reilly, a.k.a. "the Grey Fox," became a good friend and sounding board for our ruminations on the company. We'd meet him many more times.) The already-independent Office Products group made a foray into office automation from IBM's beachhead in Selectric and magnetic-card typewriters.

Though the decentralization seemed just the thing for accelerating product innovation and shortening development cycles, the immediate outlook for field operations was messier. Enterprise customers (i.e., the largest corporations) would now suffer visits from three different pairs of wingtips: the Data Processing rep for mainframes, the GBS version for minicomputers, and the Office Product guy for typewriters and other secretarial gear. There was probably no alternative, since traditional salesmen wouldn't touch any minicomputer or office system not connected to a mainframe. But the cost of this field fragmentation soon became unsustainable, especially after IBM and its competitors began selling their low-end offerings through computer stores and other channels of indirect distribution. Clearly, the organizational structure still needed fine-tuning.

Simply bisecting IBM's traditional computer business was hardly enough to fix the inadequacies cited by Bullen and Faw. The mainframe, peripherals, and communications businesses were still too entangled to allow for hot pursuit of competitors. So in September, 1972, Cary decisively upended Watson's organizational orientation, jettisoning functional consolidation for three vertically integrated, largely autonomous product groupings that each combined hardware engineering and manufacturing. The three field operations were unaffected. The Systems Products Division now oversaw all the traditional mainframe lines from top to bottom; Systems Development encompassed all software plus telecommunications products; and General Products, the only division based in California, was responsible for tapes, disks, and database software.

Just one week later, the sixty-year-old Learson retired as chairman, citing the importance of youth in a business "as technical and competitive as this" and leaving the Chairman's title to Cary. The *Wall Street Journal*'s take (September 27, 1972) on the reshuffling quoted unnamed observers to the effect "that Mr. Learson's departure didn't indicate any hidden problems or major changes in IBM's course. The line of succession was amply prepared, and Mr. Cary is highly regarded inside and outside the company." Naomi and I were surprised that Learson did not stick around for a year or two of transition. Of course, it was hard to overlook that

Cary had just axed the artifact of Learson's proudest accomplishment, the organization he had built to create the System/360.

The Obsolescence of Future System

Effectively axed, too, was the idea of a revolutionary "Future System," once envisioned as a product that would encompass radically new hardware, packaging, storage media, operating system, and object-oriented programming language. Besides the fact that the computer and peripheral divisions were too disconnected to permit system-wide product coordination and introduction, the Future System (F/S or FS) no longer made sense from a market perspective. Already by December 1970, the threat to the traditional "systems" approach posed by Gene Amdahl's resignation a year earlier was evident in a non-concurrence from John Bertram opining that "the assumed date for FS (December 1977) is too late in that it leaves a basically box-oriented architecture exposed to additional PCM incursions and, in particular PCM-CPUs [the mainframes]." Viewed in that light, FS was a dying duck, although development would linger for another three years.

Critics like Charles Ferguson, the coauthor of *Computer Wars: The Fall of IBM and the Future of Global Technology*, made much of the Future System's disintegration. "F/S was IBM's own quiet Vietnam," he said. "The confidence of top management was badly shaken ... The old IBM never shrank from cannibalizing its own; it went after them with the same aggressiveness, enthusiasm, even exuberance, that it aimed at the competition ... [T]he aftermath of F/S brought subtle, but profound, changes in management attitude at IBM. Armonk never lost its appetite for big, expensive projects. But F/S was the last time a centrally driven technology initiative ever challenged an existing profitable product line."[2]

There may be some truth to Ferguson's assessment, but the fact is the system-wide approach that successfully introduced System/360 was simply outdated by the fragmentation of the competition and its own complexity. IBM had to move to a box, or single-product-based, approach. I don't believe management lost confidence, but, rather, gained forward-looking judgment. Moreover, many F/S components found their way into subsequent products. Circuitry and packaging appeared in future mainframes, new disk technology became standard for both IBM and its Japanese competitors, and elements of the operating system resurfaced in IBM's successful System 38 minicomputer and follow-on AS/400.

In any case, IBM could not afford to lose backward compatibility with its System/360-370 and risk having customers revisit their purchase decisions or, at best, retard demand while they reprogrammed old systems rather than developing or buying new ones. In fact, no company—not Intel, Microsoft, Sun, or Oracle—could afford a new product so distanced from past architectures that it made customers' applications obsolete.

But Cary's restructuring couldn't ignore the consequences of the split between hardware and software in the Systems Development Division. Once the hub of activity for the all-encompassing System/360 operating system, now the division was the source of persistent problems and product gaffes—as exemplified in the rapidly expanding telecommunications arena. A late and underfeatured network system scheduled for release in 1974 was blasted as "completely unacceptable" in a withering March 1972 memo that continued: [The product] "will not be used in any system or advanced function forecasts ... Why do we need to wait almost three years and spend large programming resources to get back to where we are?" More complaints followed.

Enough was enough. On May 30, 1975, Cary jettisoned the functionally specialized business units in favor of new self-sufficient product divisions. Software responsibility was switched back to the product divisions, and the Systems Development Division was renamed the Systems Communications Division to denote its new (and overdue) focus. Bob Evans, the patron saint of compatibility, was replaced by Allen Krowe, a dynamic financial executive whom we'd soon meet as he attempted to salvage the wreckage of an earlier era. Advanced Systems Development was disbanded, which allowed each division to plan new product offerings with an eye toward besting its direct competitor. Three years later, the mainframe division was split in two. The high end under Jack Bertram was free to develop exotic bipolar technology to compete with Dr. Amdahl and the Japanese. Meanwhile, the low-end half under Jack Kuehler was gearing up to compete against the minicomputers using merchant-chip technology.

Our friend Jack Reilly aptly summarized IBM's new outlook: "Whether we like it or not, IBM is now in the box business, not total systems. We can't afford the delays, confusion, lack of software accountability, and endless coordination it takes to deliver total systems."

The newly decentralized product divisions were now free to unleash a flurry of competitive counterattacks against the four rival camps: plug-compatible mainframes, plug-compatible peripherals, leasing companies, and the emerging minicomputer sector. Both the leasing companies and plug-compatible mainframers like Amdahl had been slowed by the 158/168 announcement. The new structure would also beat back the plug-compatible peripheral companies tailgating too closely behind IBM.

Tailgaters Get Their Comeuppance

Markets dominated by a single player invite newcomers and even also-rans to try a tailgating strategy. For the tailgater, the idea is simple: manufacture products that are very similar—especially in their functions and/or software components—to those of the dominant player. That way you can ride along on the larger competitor's own customer base and product development to gain pricing and R&D cost advantages that will offset the incumbent's economies of scale in manufacturing and distribution. The outlook for the strategy improves against a competitor encumbered by a change-resistant cost structure and customer base. Initially, IBM's products were too tightly strapped together into systems to provide a fast and adequate response against the mono-product competition—until, that is, Frank Cary cut the straps.

Prior to 1972, IBM's tapes, disks, and printers were seriously disadvantaged against the plug-compatible manufacturers (PCMs), which targeted IBM's existing customer base with IBM's own software while avoiding its bloated gross margins. More importantly, the PCMs could respond quickly and without coordinating their product plans across other devices.

At first, Armonk responded frantically, unveiling a flurry of tactical weapons that often backfired. Substantial price cuts hurt IBM more than the opposition, while silly software tinkering pointlessly complicated the life of the IBM field engineer.

The futility of these jabs at innovation was made clear in a memo (Telex discovery again) outlining the conclusions of a 1971 study team organized under VP Bob Evans, who oversaw development: "In the storage products areas, competitive skill in reverse-engineering—copying [our products]—is improving to the point that new technology gives IBM little more than six months lead over the competition." All the team could suggest was to slow the maintenance response times for breakdowns in mixed IBM/PCM configurations. This self-defeating (and possibly illegal) idea was quickly dropped. But a sensible and competitive response was badly needed.

Decentralization freed the product divisions from the five-year intervals orchestrated for System/360. Shortening the product life span of IBM's peripherals (and, hence, the competition's) was a two-pronged strategy. One part was technical and consisted of midlife "kickers," or minor enhancements, that boosted IBM's relative advantage over plug-compatible peripherals. The second was financial and aimed at the many customers who had opted to rent rather than buy in order to take best advantage of the shorter product cycles. Now IBM offered a two-year, fixed-term plan that featured prices lower than those available on a pure rental while simultaneously reducing a customer's flexibility to install competitive gear. Taken together, this pincer narrowed the PCM's "window of opportunity," noted Peter Redfield, the chairman of Itel, the leasing company, in a memo (likely solicited for the Telex suit): "For the peripheral equipment industry, the product life cycle seems to be shortening. The [earliest disk-generation] cycle was 60 months long. The [next disk] production cycle could easily be as short as 15 months. The [current disk] cycle, which began with IBM deliveries in early 1971, could end as soon as December 31, 1973."

His memo continued, "If IBM has delivered, say, 80 percent of the total expected industry shipments and markets them under a two-year [fixed-term plan], any independent would be foolish to attempt to participate only in the last 20 percent. This explains why independents entered the 2314 [earliest disk] market (with its longer product cycle at around the 90 percent point), whereas it is inconceivable that an independent would enter the 3330 [disk] market if the same were repeated today."

Peripheral makers that offered little innovation but depended on IBM plug compatibility were decimated by Cary's strategy. Some tried antitrust lawsuits to recoup their losses and market positions. Telex's initial and unexpected victory in its 1973 antitrust case against IBM temporarily buoyed the crowd of competitors. But by late 1977, the Telex judgment had been overturned on appeal, and the other rivals had lost their battles, too. Memorex, for instance, seemed strategically befuddled despite having a very strong CEO and the patience of its key debt holders. Elsewhere, California Computer Products, after being routed in the courtroom, replaced its founder and CEO, Les Kilpatrick. "If Les Kilpatrick was a cowboy, [his successor] is a cook," I quipped about their different management styles. Now CalComp was exiting the disk business and hoped to rediscover its profitable niche in plotters. Instead, it soon disappeared inside Lockheed Martin.

I dimly remember Kilpatrick as a long-boned gent with his feet sprawled under the restaurant table, who looked as if he'd squint under his hat brim—if he'd worn a hat—while drawling his continuing resentment of both IBM and the courts. "I'm a red-blooded Texan who believes that not even IBM is above the law," he averred. Certain the judge had ruled incorrectly, Kilpatrick told us that his company's legal team "proved that IBM had 70 percent of the market. IBM said 32 percent ... the case should have gone to the jury." Today, the Department of Justice's 70 percent market-share threshold for defining monopoly isn't applied to Intel, Microsoft, Cisco, and others. But these days, people have much less confidence in government intervention than they might have had then.

"What were the business prospects for CalComp and other PCMs?" we asked Les. "Terrible, for several reasons," he answered, "starting with capital shortages. Why invest in flaky computer technologies when General Motors is selling at five times earnings? And developing a sales organization is very difficult. Hardware prices are dropping so rapidly that software may be the only profitable product. Software has economies of scale. If enough copies can be sold, programming inefficiencies are irrelevant." The Texan exhibited bull's-eye prescience!

Going forward, only peripheral companies with their own software or specialized hardware would survive. Storage Technology benefited by being last to market, thus avoiding the larded hubris of the first movers. Its salvation came from offering a mainframe-connected tape robot that IBM didn't have. The EMC Corporation subsequently opened up a new software-intensive market with storage systems that could traverse processors running different operating systems. EMC's strategy reflected the reality that IBM's mainframe operating system was being squeezed into a smaller and smaller corner of the market.

Management Transitions

Frank Cary led IBM until January 1981, when he turned sixty and was replaced as CEO by John Opel, though he stayed as chairman for two more years and remained as a director for ten. Cary's decentralization had accelerated product development at IBM, battered the plug-compatible peripherals and leasing companies, and midwifed the PC. But there was also innovative excess, especially in the minicomputer market where seemingly every product division managed to gin up an entry. "The current laissez-faire attitude toward interdivisional competition seems to be changing the organizational model from General Motors to the Court of the Medici," we snickered.

Opel soon initiated an organizational review aimed at predicting the competitive landscape over the next ten years, designating, to the surprise of some, his predecessor and designer of the status quo to head the reassessment. In yet another tribute to Cary's open-mindedness and organizational savvy, the reassessment marked a substantial reversal of the decentralization he'd initiated in 1971. The competition had changed markedly as armies of upstarts gave way to a few big guns, most notably Digital, HP, Wang, and, potentially, the personal computer.

This was the moment for consolidation, both to cut excessive programming expenses and to attract a higher number of independent software vendors. So Big Blue was reconfigured into three major organizations—large computers, midrange computers (including PCs), and field operations. Axed were both independent business units: Office Products (Selectrics) and General Systems (Series/1), established by Cary to quick-start the minicomputer business outside the crushing influence of the glass-house bigots. The three organizations were set up as follows:

- John Akers was chosen to head the peppiest group, signaling that yet another sales executive was being groomed to replace Opel. (Krowe became VP Finance.) Information Systems and Communications contained all the competing minicomputers, the nascent personal computer, and a catchall of communications products, typewriters, and copiers.

- Jack Kuehler would head the mainframe-oriented Information Systems and Technology group.
- C. B. "Jack" Rogers led the newly consolidated sales and support group. The all-important National Accounts Division under George Conrades would cover the top 2,200 accounts.

Banking on the power of the company's mainframes, the competitive edge of the 4300 model, and the IBM personal computer—and reveling in the recent weakening of the antitrust threat—the company set its annual growth targets at 18 percent, a heady goal even factoring in the effects of inflation. Euphoria ruled at IBM.

Cary's legacy would be much like young Watson's. Both had ably led IBM through periods when the company made bets against tough competition. Both had forcefully used organizational models to promote their vision of the future. And while the organizational model each created was successful during his tenure, neither of these models would survive the challenges encountered by their successors. The good news was that Cary's decentralization had revitalized IBM's mainframes and peripheral product lines. The bad news, as we'll see, was that the different divisions spawned different and often uncompetitive minicomputers, each with its own hardware and software developers, spare-part inventories, training materials, and sales support. It was creativity run amok that would bedevil John Akers a decade later.

Chapter 4

THE COMPETITIVE LIMITS OF TECHNOLOGY:

Amdahl versus IBM

Tailgaters seldom gain permanent advantage from technological superiority alone. The incumbent simply has too many other strengths. Dr. Gene's Amdahl Corporation initially hoped to leapfrog IBM with advanced semiconductor components. But IBM countered, first with an unforeseen product upgrade, then with denser logic chips, and finally with a radical shift in chip technology. Like a self-righting punching bag, Amdahl repeatedly bounced back into the lead but was ultimately crushed under the enormous power of IBM's superior research, business scale, and market positioning.

Dr. Gene's first plug-compatible mainframe was targeted at IBM's 370/165 (on which he'd done some early work) but was whacked by the unexpected announcement of the 370/168 and, therefore, dead on arrival.

Many years later, Amdahl recalled how he'd been blindsided: Lacking "the virtual memory [of the 370/168] ... we dropped the first model and put aside any expectations of being able to ship a product for nearly a year and a half."[1] When the product delays proved ongoing, Amdahl's investors—including Fujitsu, the German minicomputer maker Nixdorf, and Edgar Heiser, a Chicago-based venture capitalist—got testy. And who could blame them with nothing to show for the $27 million they'd invested to date? "Tension in the boardroom reached a peak in early 1974, when Amdahl's enterprise almost went under," revealed *Fortune* magazine in September 1977. "Chief among the problems was a collapse in management."

The board forced Amdahl out as CEO and pushed his two founding colleagues out the door altogether. Five vice presidents subsequently departed after the board enlisted the scrappy, white-haired Eugene R. White to run the company. White, a former GE and Fairchild Semiconductor executive, brought the executive presence Gene Amdahl lacked. And both Genes deserved equal credit for the early company's success.

On arrival, White found the company without management, product, customers, money, or morale. The most immediate tasks were to reorient the design team toward the 370/168 and to resolve the funding shortage. For that, the two Genes approached Fujitsu executive Toshio Ikeda, a.k.a. "Mr. Computer of Japan," and came away with $35 million on top of the $11 million Fujitsu had previously invested, in return for a 41 percent equity stake and access to Amdahl's intellectual property. The agreement also called for the Japanese giant to manufacture ten mainframes based on an Amdahl-built prototype in exchange for exclusive rights in some markets.

When the brilliant and somewhat eccentric Ikeda (he reputedly kept a computer team awake during one grueling night by belting out Schubert's *Winterreise* song cycle in German) suffered a fatal fall at Narita Airport a short while later, Fujitsu's relationship with Amdahl took on a much harsher tone. Amdahl CFO Cliff Madden, who remembered Ikeda as "very much the rising star," said that "his successor was well regarded, but didn't have nearly the same stature. The circumstances gave other powerful factions within the company, such as international marketing, a bigger voice," he told us.

In the early years of the partnership, any animosity was likely cloaked by high hopes for Amdahl's success. Fujitsu manufactured the first boxes to help Amdahl conserve capital, and its engineers worked "shoulder to shoulder in Sunnyvale [California] throughout the development of the Model 470/V6," Amdahl's first successful product, related Gene Amdahl in a December 1975 *Infosystems* interview. The first six processors were installed at the National Aeronautics and Space Administration (NASA), Computer Usage Corporation, and four universities. The seventh spelled commercial credibility when Dave Blackwell, the doughty chief information officer of the Massachusetts Mutual Life Insurance Company, took the career bet of persuading top management to buy from the upstart Amdahl, even as a near-hysterical IBM dispatched fleets of blue helicopters to land on Mass Mutual's lawn, dispensing a mix of dire threats and halcyon promises. Amdahl had secured a beachhead in commercial data processing.

At our first research visit to Amdahl in March 1976, the tough talking Gene White boasted of twelve letters of intent to purchase, twenty excellent prospects, and 121 that he categorized as "Class A." Since half the letters of intent came from government agencies, which were required to accept the lowest bid from a group of competitors, we viewed White's enthusiasm with a jaundiced eye. But we were wrong. Business boomed, and the future looked rosy, with twenty-seven customer installations and a fifty-million-dollar public offering in the wings. "Amdahl in '76: from oblivion to a comer," gushed a *Datamation* headline in February 1977.

IBM Strikes Back

But this popular wisdom took a hit barely one month later (March 25) when IBM introduced its new 303X series mainframe, dubbed "the Big One" by *Think* magazine and "the big bombshell" by *Datamation*. At the same time, IBM announced a 30 percent price reduction on the existing 370/168. "Impact of IBM moves seen as serious," headlined *Electronic News in September,* foreseeing disaster for the plug compatibles. Unsaid but still momentous was the removal of the word "System" in front of 3033, a signal that, from now on, IBM would announce mainframes as stand-alone products. The System/370 would have the distinction of being IBM's last end-to-end system.

Also significant was the surprisingly low number of circuits integrated on a single chip. Naomi and I had toured IBM's massive foundry in Fishkill, New York, a month before the 3033 debuted. Our host was its head and VP Erich Bloch, a German refugee who received the National Technical Medal from President Reagan (with Bob Evans and Fred Brooks) for work on System/360 and later became the first Director of the National Science Foundation to come from industry. Erich allowed that by standardizing on its 2-kilobyte Duchess memory chip for almost a decade, IBM had fallen behind industry frontrunners like Texas Instruments. But holding that low level of integration was by design, Bloch emphasized with accented intensity. "We're in the business of computers, not watches or toys." Because for computers, the packaging to which the chips were bonded contributed as much to cost and speed as did the chips themselves. Bloch was probably right in the near term, but IBM's tardiness on circuit integration ceded advanced-technology bragging rights to Amdahl.

In any case, the 3033's price/performance ratio was good enough to create a flurry of customer orders. As we wrote at the time: "IBM was amazed and astounded by the surge of 303X orders.... Order certification (which forbids customers from selling delivery positions) is apparently not very successful. Brokers, lessors, and customers alike are offering early positions on 3033s for hefty premiums. This explains why one IBM senior sales type asked us if customers would be receptive to or incensed by the idea of an earnest money binder to flush out the tourists. (Oh, happy days!) Two particularly edgy customers were advised by senior IBMers to try Amdahl." A joke, no doubt.

The backlog backfired. IBM inadvertently gave Amdahl a huge boost when results of its "delivery lottery" pushed some customer shipments all the way into 1980. Much to the giant's consternation, its own squeeze in production capacity was driving some of its closest and most important customers into the arms of the upstarts. "Always build excess production capacity and never make the shortage worse by cutting prices on announcement day" were the overriding lessons IBM executives would have cause to remember in later years.

When Naomi and I visited Amdahl later that year, the company's most visible problems were a ubiquitous office-construction program and an overcrowded parking lot. White opined that the much-ballyhooed 3033 represented neither a fire-sale nor a shot at Amdahl. Rather, he saw it as a longer-range excursion to more robust hardware that would support IBM's emerging networking strategy.

He wasn't much worried about other plug compatibles, either. Most, like CDC and Magnuson, White pointed out, were stuck at the low end of IBM's product line. And although Itel drew some tax advantages from its leasing business, its equipment was largely engineered in Tokyo, meaning it was over-engineered and, therefore, not cost-effective. The Japanese "throw in everything but the kitchen sink," he remarked dismissively. As for the semiconductor companies, they didn't understand end customers and were too secretive to provide future direction. The bottom line, in White's view, was no new competition in large mainframes: "The technology is too demanding. This isn't like the plug-compatible peripheral business. They struggled to stay even with IBM's newest product announcements. We're ahead."

The only issue for Gene White was software, specifically IBM's multiple virtual storage, or MVS, operating system, on which Amdahl and the other mainframe-compatible companies depended. "The public domain status of the operating system is the key issue, and we don't think IBM can tamper with that," he said with no visible fear of contradiction—and he was exactly right. Nevertheless, the legal battles and technical skirmishes over the public status of the MVS would preoccupy Amdahl and Fujitsu for years to come.

The Poke from Tokyo

Amdahl's glowing successes didn't soothe a growling Fujitsu. Since 1975, Amdahl's dependency on Fujitsu's technology had sharply declined, going from 90 percent in mid-decade to 79 percent in 1977, when Amdahl first engaged Motorola as an alternate supplier, to just 43 percent in 1979. Fujitsu feared it might be pushed aside, especially in the all-important North American market where hopes of selling its own machines were cherished by strong factions, most notably again, International Marketing.

In 1977, during the initial planning for Amdahl's follow-on machine, Fujitsu had proposed that Amdahl become strictly a sales and service organization, leaving the design and manufacture of the product up to the Japanese. But, as Cliff Madden recalled for us three years later, "We said no. Amdahl was an engineering company with an experienced team. Although Fujitsu had learned from us on the V6, we thought the Japanese had the wrong product perspective for the United States. They wanted to pursue the absolute level of throughput, with a strong emphasis on scientific computing. We thought cost would be equally important. But we also thought Fujitsu was the best component supplier in the market, especially for 400-gate [i.e., circuit] chips which would be the basis for the next generation systems."

The Japanese were impatient. After all, didn't everyone recognize the inevitability of the country's eventual global dominance in technology? So, on September 7, 1978, the partners signed an agreement giving Fujitsu unquestioned control over Amdahl's high-technology components, while reserving the North American market for Amdahl and Japan for Fujitsu. Amdahl also committed to buying 50 percent of most commodity components and 80 percent of logic chips fabricated with proprietary technology from Fujitsu. More important, nondisclosure restrictions on its own and Fujitsu technology effectively precluded Amdahl from using a second source for chips. Thus, Motorola, which by then was working on a 5,000-gate chip with Control Data, was now off-limits. A tight bind for Amdahl, and we called the contract "the most pivotal document that customers or prospects could read."

Blinding euphoria seemed to be the only explanation for Amdahl's acceptance of such a one-sided contract. Its revenues rose by 70 percent that year, while gross margins widened to 50.8 percent from 47.5 percent; in addition, the stock had been split but still doubled in price again before the third quarter was out. Dr. Gene's technology looked invincible. And as so often seems the case, the Fujitsu accord was forged at almost the precise apogee of Amdahl's fortunes and the beginning of its gradual decline. Later, Gene White would argue that we'd misunderstood the contract or missed the subtext behind the language.

In 1979, Amdahl and IBM both witnessed an unexpected switch from sales to leases. One reason was IBM's brand-new 4300 minicomputer, which boasted a four-to-one price/performance improvement. Many assumed that mainframes would follow suit, prompting the DAT-box customers to rush to insulate themselves from the embarrassment of buying another mainframe that would quickly be devalued. "Unexpected Conversion to Leasing Hits IBM as Users Await New Series," headlined *Electronic News* on June 18. The accompanying article surmised that "Amdahl's recognition came suddenly, in as much as it was telling analysts early in June that it expected little direct leasing beyond its normal 10 percent of shipments." Now the second-quarter lease rate looked to be more like 40 percent. Too bad, given record interest rates and Amdahl's soon-to-be evident liquidity problems.

The company's 1979 financial report showed a 7 percent decline in revenues to $21.3 million, a deterioration of gross margins to 39.3 percent in the fourth quarter from 53.3 percent in the first, and a whopping increase in short-term debt to $468.8 million from $29.8 million a year earlier. Computer shipments, as the report noted, had increased approximately 21 percent, setting a record. So the revenue shortfall was "largely attributable to a significant shift in customer preferences towards leasing, which began in the second quarter … and to price reductions," the report disclosed. Amdahl attributed the shift toward leasing to uncertainty stirred by rumors of a new IBM product coming to market and to rising interest rates.

The bad news was too much for Wall Street; Amdahl's share price plunged from the low 70s to 16 1/2 by year-end 1980. The nearly six million shares held by Fujitsu lost upwards of $300 million of their value, more than double the company's entire pretax income of $134 million that year. The slide, coming only a year after Fujitsu had signed away market access to North America, doubtless strengthened the determination and internal clout of the International Marketing faction.

One early casualty of the downturn was Amdahl's bid against NCR for Comten, a supplier of telecommunications controllers that would have broadened Amdahl's product portfolio in an area where IBM was weak. Explained an Amdahl spokesman to *Computerworld (January 1977)*: "We felt that to be competitive with the NCR offer, which was really one-half cash, we would have had to increase our offer in stock another $3 or $4." A proposed merger with struggling Memorex, the maker of plug-compatible storage devices, also fell through. Once again, questions about the relative valuations of the two suitors soured the deal. The proposed swap of ten for twelve shares "was not enough," complained some shareholders and analysts, especially those who recommended Memorex last summer at almost twice that valuation," wrote the *Economist* magazine in September 1979. The fact that Fujitsu also offered both telecommunications controllers and disk storage did not strengthen the spurned suitor's hand.

IBM's Apparent Swoon

November 1980 brought some good news and cheers of relief from beleaguered Amdahl when IBM's announcement of its "next generation" 3081 drew jeers from the computer industry. It appeared that IBM's two "dyadic" processors coupled into a single box still delivered only

11 MIPS (millions of instructions per second), or slightly less than Amdahl delivered with just one processor.

The press had a field day. *Datamation* opened its January 1981 "News in Perspective" column with an electric jolt: "IBM's newly announced 3081, dubbed the first H Series machine by many analysts, is the legacy of a strategic error made four years ago," (presumably referring to the demise of Future System).

Jubilant strategy planners at Amdahl advised us that "IBM senior executives reached their job plateaus ten years ago, and IBM technicians learned their craft ten years before that; today, they're ossified." A cagey Fujitsu source ("Call me only a senior Japanese executive") chimed in with this observation: "Our company is thirty-two years old; IBM is forty-five. A man of forty-five years has money, a car, a house. A man of thirty-two years may be poor but has energy and ambition. He wins in a struggle."

Yes, IBM was over-the-hill, crowed the always-combative Gene White during our interview. "Even with our worst-case scenario, we kicked them in the ass. In fact, IBM's offering is so pitiful, their relative throughput gap against our announcement damages our credibility. We almost wish they'd made a better showing."

Amdahl's revenues, margins, and share prices soon stabilized. There was plenty of cash left from the fifty-million-dollar stock offering of the previous September. Fujitsu had reassured big domestic and foreign institutions by buying 650,000 of the 2.2 million shares at market value. *Forbes* cooed in December 1980: "The fact that Fujitsu was paying $17 million for the shares, or market value, even though it held warrants to buy up to 203 million shares at only $5 per share, greatly impressed the big domestic and foreign institutions which quickly snapped up the remainder of the offering." To Naomi and me, it seemed that $17 million to protect a $162 million investment and maintain ownership of a potential competitor was the leverage investment of the year.

Amdahl bought time, but the contest with IBM had definitely tightened. From a technical perspective, we thought Gene White had seriously underestimated both the achievement represented by the 3081 and the competitive boost it could give IBM over the next decade. It was a truly massive effort that represented substantial progress in semiconductors, packaging, cooling, engineering automation, and chip testing.

That year, we'd tramped through the Fishkill facility again. After three days of interviews on semiconductors, packaging, and design, we understood enough to get ninety minutes with John "Black Jack" Bertram (so named for his relentless management style). Now SVP of the mainframe division, the canny scientist began the interview by benignly reminiscing about his early career at DuPont while poking holes into a fat cigar with a kitchen match. After a few starting puffs, he spoke clearly and starkly about IBM's progress.

In semiconductors, IBM had advanced to seven hundred circuits (or gates) per chip from just thirty-seven in the previous 3033 generation. This higher level of integration meant that fewer chips were necessary to build the computer, and fewer chips meant faster cycles and lower manufacturing costs. Amdahl had achieved a chip density of only four hundred circuits, but two offsetting factors seemingly gave it an edge. First, IBM used just three hundred fifty of its seven hundred available circuits, and, second, Amdahl's circuits were six times more powerful, hence faster.

Over at Control Data, though, master computer architect and VP Lloyd Thorndyke struck a note of caution when he said: "I'm very glad not to be in the plug-compatible business." In contrast to the twentyfold advantage Gene Amdahl had achieved over IBM a decade earlier, Thorndyke noted that, "this time, the Amdahl advantage is extremely thin—chips with four hundred high-speed gates compared to IBM with, effectively, three hundred fifty."

IBM's investment in innovation was clearly on display on packaging. Here Bertram's cadre had created a revolutionary cube of multiple ceramic layers that held 118 chips, 400 feet of wire, and 1,800 connection pins, all contained within a five-by-five-inch space. Packing chips so closely together boosted performance, but it also created a heat-dissipation problem. IBM solved it by running chilled water through the ceramic cubes. Amdahl, who scoffed at water cooling as technologically regressive, fan-cooled its conventional eleven-by-eleven-inch printed circuit board containing 120 chips. CDC's Thorndyke, however, came down on the side of IBM, because its approach produced less vibration than fans, used less energy, and subjected computer operators to less discomfort.

Though its cold-water ploy worked, IBM was still pressured, both technologically and organizationally, by the new packaging. "I won't say packaging gaited the 3081 announcement, but it sure was good this came out when it did," Paul Low, the Fishkill general manager, told us over lunch during that year's tour. Added the PhD guiding our tour, "It's still very hectic in that area." Ceramic technology is used by IBM to this day.

IBM's design automation won kudos from the respected professional journal *Computer* (May 1979): "Many in the industry agree that IBM appears to have the most sophisticated design automation system," it wrote. Bertram had told us that day in Armonk that the system caught 90 percent of all design errors before the layout was committed to lithography and the eventual chip fabrication. And although Amdahl defended its largely manual design approach as yielding a much higher performance, it was clear that anything manual was reaching its limits. As the editors at *Computer* later explained (February 1981): "Ten years ago, one 250 millimeter chip could be designed on a seven foot wall hanging. Now it would require a layout sheet the size of two tennis courts. With very large scale integration, a logic drawing of the same chip would cover two football fields." Today, chips have over one billion circuits, but by the standards of the time, the IBM circuit design system, with its eight million lines of code strung over twenty-six of the old 370/168 mainframes, was gargantuan.

IBM had engineered more pyrotechnics into chip testing. At issue was the time interval required to test, repair, and retest a prototype chip before beginning production in volume. A year or two earlier, a Texas Instruments executive had discussed with us the "possibility" of shortening logic chip test cycles from twelve weeks "down to three weeks with a high degree of automation." Now, IBM's Quick Turnaround Testing (QTAT) process had shrunk the turnaround to twelve days, Bertram told us. No, "five days," quibbled the Fishkill engineers. Either way, months had been sliced off the product-development cycle for complex chips. "Between these design-automation and quick-turnaround test systems, we can handle two thousand to three thousand circuits per chip," said Bertram, glancing modestly at his cigar. Amdahl was far back at only four hundred.

Once again we came away with the impression of a breathless race won not a second too soon for the 3081. Why, we asked, hadn't the Big Blue-baiting press been told of IBM's achievements? "Because we don't have to; they'll find out soon enough," said Bertram beneath a halo of cigar smoke.

Puzzled by the 3081's meager throughput gain, we pressed the enigmatic Bertram for an explanation. Couldn't the engineers have harnessed throughput boosters used on earlier IBM models? "I was worried about the potential problem of trying to work through more complex circuit designs with a new level of circuit integration," he responded. "If the automated design system had proved less successful, unable to identify more than 80 percent [rather than over 90 percent] of all design flaws before fabricating prototype chips, then the total lapsed time with a more complicated design would have been unacceptable. But now we could conceivably sprinkle a handful of chips—ninety or so—and increase performance by around 40 percent." Fairy dust? We couldn't judge. But we were subsequently baffled by IBM's failure to follow up its technology lead with much more aggressive pricing—like the four-to-one gain demonstrated by the 4300.

We were nearing the end of our allotted time, and Bertram pressed ahead. "Beyond the immediate bottlenecks, we begin to confront the physical limitations of silicon as a semiconductor. In this machine, we've cut cycle time in half from the previous generation, and we could [cut it in half again] in two more rounds. But silicon isn't likely to be driven any further; that is probably the limit until gallium arsenide and even [the cryogenic] Josephson junction [electronic circuit] become commercially feasible. Meanwhile, I don't think uniprocessors can be pushed much beyond 35 or 40 MIPS."

Today's $1,000 personal computer is powered by a standard Pentium microprocessor operating at speeds that numb the brain. So the brilliant Bertram may have been right about bipolar technology, but not about the "CMOS" merchant technology that today powers everything from PCs to mainframes. Even the patient Japanese long ago abandoned the notion of ever using ultra-high-powered circuit technologies like the Josephson effect in computer applications.

As for the 3081's projected revenue growth, Bertram would only say "better than the 5 percent the market speculates but not the 20 percent I'd like." Of course, that 5 or 20 percent would have been on top of the 20 percent annual improvement IBM traditionally baked into price performance. A temporarily saturated market explained revenue growth—slim by IBM standards—of 14.3 percent in 1975, 16.4 percent in 1976, and 18.7 percent in 1977. After that came price erosion as low-end mainframes encountered vigorous competition from minicomputers, creating pressure on the big iron as well. Even a blizzard of new online applications that raised capacity consumption by nearly 39 percent in 1978 and 46 percent in 1979 couldn't turn up revenue growth to IBM's expected volumes.

Les Kilpatrick, the deposed founder of CalComp, had been especially gloomy about the outcome of the plug-compatible wars over our previous lunch: "Eventually, IBM will overwhelm everyone including Amdahl," he predicted. "I tell Gene to sell software so his customers won't have lifelines back to IBM. Or sell his stock, make some money, and then worry about business survival. I should have sold my shares at 50." "And what about the Japanese?" we asked him. "IBM made them up," he said without missing a beat, "as a way to bolster its argument in the antitrust trials that it faced adequate competition." In a sense, Les was right. From today's vantage point, both the awe and paranoia accorded the Japanese seems ridiculous.

The Possessive Partner

Much more damaging to Amdahl than either IBM or market-price erosion, though, was "partner" Fujitsu's tightening grasp. In early 1980, yet another merger deal collapsed, this one with Storage Technology. Amdahl insiders blamed Storage Tech CEO Jesse Aweida, the flamboyant super-skier who himself was subsequently ousted. But Aweida was quoted by *BusinessWeek* in July 1980 as saying, "Fujitsu quashed the deal by threatening to sell its Amdahl shares. I was willing to proceed with or without them, but the Amdahl board felt it could not proceed without Fujitsu.... So we aborted the whole thing."

Amdahl insiders brushed off the *BusinessWeek* account, calling Fujitsu's objections lighthearted or, at worst, face-saving. But the ever-reliable Cliff Madden told us some years later that "Jesse [was] telling the truth. Fujitsu sent in its international troubleshooter and resident SOB to kill the deal. When he arrived the weekend before the signing, he put the gun to everyone's head. Jesse was astute enough to walk away. The *BusinessWeek* piece was accurate."

A continent away, we trundled over to Fujitsu America headquarters in the New York City suburbs for a meeting with Dr. Norihiko Nakayama, its president and Amdahl board member. Industry sources have called him brilliant and "thoroughly amiable," illustrating his "cooperativeness" with this quote: "We are here to help Amdahl in every way possible."

That's not the case at our visit. After an uncomfortably chilly introduction, complete with Styrofoam coffee service, Dr. Nakayama offered a ninety-second survey of the global economy. Then came the message he really wanted to send: "U.S. companies want to make money marketing computers but don't want to get their hands dirty farming for new technology. Amdahl does not like to say its 580 machine has been completely designed and manufactured by Fujitsu. But if Fujitsu stops shipping, Amdahl is destroyed.... Fujitsu could not enter the market directly because of the political climate in the United States.... The generation of the sixties, when Toyota and Datsun entered directly, is not the eighties. We need joint ventures now.... Lots of U.S. businessmen already earn their meals by marketing our products." Twenty-five years later, the silliness of such hubris is clear, and today's fearful Americans would be wise to take note.

Meanwhile, Amdahl acquired a new competitor when Dr. Gene and Madden retired shortly after the aborted Storage Technology merger. "The weekend after Gene signed the papers retiring as chairman emeritus, we were having a dinner celebration with our wives," Madden told us. "I said, 'Let's start another one,'" remembered Cliff, who met us in a San Jose hotel to discuss the new venture, Acsys (later renamed Trilogy). Dr. Gene, who had endured another period of forced contemplation when his old back problems reappeared, told us that he "concentrated on the unsolved problems in computing" to take his mind off the pain. "By April, my idea looked so good, we couldn't afford not to start," he said, without divulging specifics. "A dance of the seven veils," he wagged enticingly.

As luck would have it, Naomi and I were pondering his response that evening over drinks at Rickey's, the Palo Alto motel whose bar seemingly gathered all the pilgrims of the era. Unbeckoned, a stranger at a neighboring table leaned over to say, "Wafer-scale integration; Amdahl's going to try wafer-scale integration" (meaning that Dr. Gene would try etching an entire subsystem into a single silicon wafer rather than the usual, costlier approach of chopping wafers into chips and then bonding the chips into a subsystem). With that lead, we could triangulate well enough to print at least "a rumor" in our next RB Report about Acsys. At the next Research Board meeting, Dr. Gene arrived furiously demanding to know how we'd gotten hold of this top-secret scoop. The only answer was to blame it on the incestuous and gossipy climate in Silicon Valley. So much for scoops, though; wafer-scale integration has yet to arrive.

In March 1980, the Research Board met again, this time at the Stanford Court Hotel in San Francisco to discuss high-end computing. Bertram was there, speaking calmly as though riding in a juggernaut with only dwarfs in his path. So was John Rollwagon, the president of Cray, who envisioned supercomputers one day creating animated visualizations of ballet choreographies. Attending from Acsys were Gene Amdahl, Cliff Madden, and Amdahl's son Carlton, previously at Magnuson, a maker of low-end mainframes. Someone other than Gene White took Amdahl Corporation's seat at the table. White, who was scheduled for open-heart surgery the following week, had become so incensed after reading our recommendation that the members read the 1978 contract with Fujitsu that he crashed the previous evening's dinner. Only he and perhaps one person in Japan could explain the real meaning of the agreement, he told our group, and even life-threatening surgery couldn't keep him from setting the record straight so that his largest customers wouldn't feel threatened by Amdahl's apparent dependency. We never understood exactly what he meant.

Amdahl had escaped two assaults from IBM and continued to sell mainframes for another decade under the able leadership of Gene White and, subsequently, Jack Lewis. But the leading PCM could never recapture its magical presence and technological effervescence of the seventies, as we'll see. And IBM's real competition would shift from Amdahl using MVS to a new breed of competitors armed with Unix.

Chapter 5

TRANSIENT TECHNOLOGY:

Travails of the Mini Makers

To create sustainable strategic advantage, a new-product wave should represent a radical shift in both technological assumptions and business model. The PC would fill the bill; the minicomputer did not. The mini makers' processor technology and business models were simply lower-cost versions of the mainframe scheme. The mini and the mainframe were alike in most other respects, too. They were vertically integrated products with customized circuit designs, proprietary operating systems, and wholly owned distribution channels and field-service operations. The PC would challenge each of those layers and would win on every count. The minicomputer wave would soon run its course, despite the best efforts of its executive cadre.

The fifteen-year minicomputer cycle began around 1968, and nearly a hundred companies joined the half dozen established firms over the next four years—but only half actually developed a salable product and just ten succeeded. Prime Computer and Data General led the newcomers, followed at diminished growth rates by MAI Basic Four, Four-Phase Systems, Computer Automation Systems, General Automation, Macrodata, Microdata, and Modular Computer Systems (Modcomp). Creative naming could hardly account for their early successes.

Ho-hum naming aside, the biggest winners were older, more experienced companies, notably DEC, along with Datapoint, Wang, HP, and eventually IBM, all of which entered the minicomputer space through a side door. Datapoint had been languishing as a maker of mainframe monitors when it invented the programmable terminal in 1972. That same year, Wang Labs made the death-defying leap from calculators to office computing and word processing, while HP, almost simultaneously, brought in new leadership to transform its withering minicomputer business into an industry leader.

Mainframes still offered more total power, but minicomputers were less expensive to build, didn't need special air-conditioning or costly glass houses, and had more flexible operating systems. The mainframes incorporated the clumsy and time-consuming "batch processing" methodology, which required specially trained machine operators to periodically load punch cards or tapes into the machine, which would then spew out the encoded information as updated records and printed reports. In contrast, the interactive minicomputers allowed regular office personnel to access the systems' internally stored information as needed. Gone were the ugly, space-consuming stacks of printed outputs. Better yet, the minicomputers' leaner cost model translated into cheaper products. Whereas IBM needed an 85 percent gross margin on its mainframes to cover everything from operating-system development to field operations to profits, Digital Equipment prospered on margins of just 60 percent. By 1983, IBM's price per MIPS (millions of instructions per second) on its high-end 3084 mainframe was about $285,000, compared to $190,000 on its 4300 minicomputer, $170,000 on HP's 3000, and $150,000 on DEC's VAX 780. That implied a 50 percent premium on big-iron MIPS—a clear repudiation of Grosch's law implying that MIPS costs should instead decline with scale. A combination of base technology and a new business model upended Grosch's neat symmetry.

Minicomputers flowered at corporations large and small, propelled by their price and software advantages over mainframes and their ability to function reliably at typical office electrical power and temperature levels. Telecommunications costs and unreliability were the third factor in their popularity. Work sites served by local minicomputers didn't need continuous access to telephone lines, unlike mainframes connected to "dumb" monitors. In the 1970s, telecommunications tariffs set by monopolist AT&T were projected to drop by only 30 percent over the next decade. Minicomputer price/performance would gain at least 500 percent in that same period. So local computing offered a better alternative than central mainframes accessed over expensive and spottily performing telephone lines.

Hewlett-Packard reflected the trend when it installed its own minis in seventy-two locations at an investment of just $2.5 million (admittedly, the machines were priced at cost). Twice that much was saved annually by doing most computing locally and transmitting selected data to corporate headquarters just once a day. And though the number of transmitted characters rose sevenfold between 1971 to 1973, network charges were held to $1.4 million versus a projected $7.7 million using a continuously connected central computer.

For the next several years, the minicomputer companies would thrive in at least three separate markets:

- *The original equipment manufacturer, or OEM, business.* Minicomputer companies supplied equipment to OEMs for embedding in another company's product. Factory equipment, for example, might be embedded with a computer that would make complex calculations related to chemical analysis or production-line sequencing. Unglamorous though this business sounds, at one point or another, half the boxes shipped from Digital Equipment, Data General, Computer Automation, and others went to fill orders from this source.

- *High-performance engineering and scientific workstations.* Success with these single-user minicomputers depended on attracting highly specialized application packages from third parties. Digital's initial advantage stemmed from its ongoing presence in the best engineering schools, beginning with founder and CEO Ken Olsen's alma mater, the Massachusetts Institute of Technology.

- *Local business functions.* Minicomputers were ideal for order entry, shipping, and other areas in which automation with mainframes was not economical. In this segment, the minicomputer's momentum was also accelerated by a creative ideology in which the technology sector exerted outsize influence over management practices, reflecting perhaps the sense that computing is cutting-edge and cutting-edge practices must therefore be better than whatever went before. Wrong, of course. In the 1960s, the creative ideology or "management by exception" helped turn customers away from punch cards and toward magnetic tape—a trend soon dropped with the advent of randomly accessible disk storage. This time, the technical concept was "distributed processing," pushed along by a tailwind from the decentralized management movement. According to a cadre of consultants and academics, local business units would necessarily be more responsive to local issues if they controlled their own computers. As is often the case, the fundamental idea makes sense: Certainly, business policy should be dictated by local markets and regulations rather than by centralized mainframes, clumsy software, and a specialized IT priesthood. But the core logic soon dissipated beyond any vestige of good sense as local managers were assigned programmers to build minicomputer applications solely to neighborhood requirements. The resultant fragmentation of applications and data standards and frivolous diversity in business processes retarded the corporate extension of information technology throughout the 1990s.

Early Customer Successes

In the early 1970s, corporate pioneers in distributed processing developed a fascinating array of thoroughly practical systems using minicomputers. Grace Hopper cheered the movement from the outset; her talented Navy petty officers demonstrated endless clever applications during our visits to the Pentagon. But curiously, the major computer suppliers would miss the phenomenon for almost a decade.

Seen today, snapshots of these early systems provide a clearer economic justification for the mini's popularity and underline its significance as a way station to the future Internet.

- Dow Chemical, guided by computing chief George Mommony, deployed DEC's PDP 8s to capture customer orders online in its many sales offices; by not mailing the orders to headquarters, the inventory/delivery cycle was reduced by several days.

- Missouri Pacific Railroad installed DEC's larger PDP 11s to track incoming and outgoing railcars in its switching yards.

- Continental Can used PDP 11s to devise a successful plant-accounting system in 1970.

All three of the above systems were built by central programming staffs, thereby avoiding the inefficient fragmentation described earlier.

Southern Railroad added a new wrinkle in a system that became famous as a forerunner of future "modular" programming techniques, spearheaded by CIO Jack Jones. Southern built its Sheffield Yard switching system by lacing together five of Data General's Nova minicomputers. One computer maintained files on every railcar already in or entering the yard, including the car's number, physical characteristics, contents, and destination. A second computer controlling the yard switches made sure that once a locomotive pushed an incoming car over the "hump," it glided toward the train headed for its assigned destination. The third machine activated the "retarders," which slowed a car's roll after calculating speed, weight, and wind resistance. The two other minicomputers were backups.

Jack was a founding member of the Research Board, and he'd asked us to research the common factors underlying the most reliable systems. We concluded that reliability was often associated with simplicity, or, conversely, that a correlation existed between a system's complexity and its frequency of failure. Perhaps coincidentally, the Sheffield system's specialization represented a method of containing complexity that would resurface in future modular or encapsulated programming techniques.

Beyond the cost advantages, electronic data processing (EDP) executives at Dow and Missouri Pacific reported that programmers developing minicomputer applications were far more energized—hence, productive—than their mainframe counterparts. Less positive were the reports of frequent and prolonged minicomputer outages. But even though mainframes were more reliable, a single failure could idle thousands of clerks, whereas any one minicomputer crash typically affected fewer than a dozen. And, in any event, mainframe users put themselves in double jeopardy, because computing failures occurred just as often in the fragile network of telephone circuits as in the glass houses.

Office automation represented another major opportunity for the minicomputer. Until the early 1970s, the IBM Selectric typewriter was the gold standard for secretarial desks. Then came a wave of highly specialized word-processing machines from a bevy of newcomers—companies with names like Lanier, Lexitron, Redactron, and Vydec—that offered per-station prices in the $10,000 to $20,000 range. Shaken by this attack on its Selectric preserve, IBM's response reeked of desperation.

First, it promoted a magnetic-card, text-storing device, even though its competitors were offering much more convenient tape- and disk-storage solutions. Later, it came out with a minicomputer system that cost an almost unbelievable $550 a month per seat and, worse yet, required substantial secretarial retraining. Expensive equipment combined with extensive training made these systems almost unsalable, especially to companies whose secretaries spent just a fraction of their time typing.

Finally, it hit on another piece of creative ideology, this one imported from IBM's German affiliate, originally dubbed *Textverarbeitung*, which translated loosely into "word processing." This purported to represent a new management concept of reorganizing secretaries away from their "principals" and into what old-timers might have recognized as typing pools, but with a difference: Typing pools conjured up entry-level drones, the IBM pitch went, while the new word-processing centers were made up of happier workers who enjoyed broader training, greater professionalism, and access to new career paths, which, of course, led to higher productivity. IBM further touted pooling by releasing noxious studies claiming that most secretaries spent major portions of their time drinking coffee and gossiping. So why not apply Teutonic discipline (especially if it meant higher office-equipment budgets)? The entire concept was nonsense.

Citibank tried a pool variation in a pilot program that utilized Digital Equipment desktop minicomputers for word processing, calendaring, and an early version of e-mail. A 1977 *Datamation* article, written by an executive vice president at the bank, ballyhooed his connection to eleven lucky subordinates through a network of twelve management workstations operated by the secretaries in central work areas. Proliferation throughout the bank was imminent, promised the article.

But when we interviewed the same EVP two years later, only ten managers were still onboard while the minicomputer count had almost doubled to twenty, presumably because the secretaries had gotten their own machines and moved back to desks near their bosses. "A retreat?" we asked. Lessons had been learned, admitted our host. "The one relationship you don't want to disturb is that between the manager and the secretary," he explained. Moreover, a substantial share of the correspondence traveling around the bank was too long for a system that could support little more than a cover memo. The more shocking explanation was this: "Management in the services sector is inherently so unproductive that we cannot afford any additional expenses that could retard productivity still further."

As general-purpose PCs began to gain popularity, specialized electronic word processors and secretarial systems disappeared. At one-fourth the price of the older gear, the cost of a PC could be justified if used as little as an hour a day. No longer did equipment cost make it necessary to dump word-processing professionals into glorified typing pools. Secretaries could go back to their old desks near their bosses. In the 1980s, e-mail replaced multi-carbon-copy office memos. It wouldn't be long before executives typed well enough to write their own memos. The question of secretarial productivity gave way to benchmark studies of whether PC-equipped principals still needed secretaries at all. And the creative ideology of IBM's *Textverarbeitung* vanished with little comment.

IBM Stumbles into the Market

The new minicomputing entrants blossomed under IBM's ambivalence toward the sector. Its weak initial entrants included the System 3, a small but expensive computer sold largely as the replacement for tabulating systems or as a small-business solution—even though a few very large customers like Coca-Cola, Pfizer, and International Chemical also bought the machines. Another of IBM's offerings was the System 7, used mainly for industrial-production control activities traditionally done with punch cards. And then there was the low end of the IBM 360 line, judged as hopelessly "deficient" in IBM's contentious evaluations process, flunking even the test against the now-tottering BUNCH. A 1972 critique (Telex) from IBM's sales division shrieked: "The [360] Model 20 is highly exposed. Both Burroughs and Memorex have [aimed] their new systems at the remaining installed

Model 20s." Burroughs? Memorex? Was anyone paying attention to the new competitors? Plans for the 370 line were inadequate to stem the loss. The upcoming 115s and 125s would still be too expensive or otherwise unsuitable as "migrators." Nor, they complained, could the sales representatives retain unhappy 360/20 accounts by offering transitions to System 3s, given "the limited scope and high price of those boxes. A combination of product announcements and pricing actions are required if this business is to be saved."

No action was taken, perhaps because tough pricing moves might have disturbed the evenly graduated price ladder, inadvertently affecting high-end mainframe prices. Predictably, the company's March 1973 "Quarterly Product Line Assessment" clubbed the low-end models in the 370 line: "The Model 115 is assessed as DEFICIENT ... due to architectural functions compared to the Burroughs 1726," which was also $1,000-a-month cheaper. Furthermore, its memory was "too small for" IBM's low-end [DOS/VS] operating system. IBM's other mini, the System 3/15, also drew a fat "deficient" for its lack of a "growth path" to larger models.

More indecision followed. In November of that year, another inter-executive memo recommended a "crash program to reverse the disastrous trend on the 115/125/135 part of the product line." Maybe, it suggested, "a cookbook approach (i.e., Sesame Street DOS, packaged applications programs, etc.)" was the answer, or "perhaps dedicated salesmen ... special incentives ... specialized district support." Meanwhile, DEC boomed, boasting a 1974 installed base of twenty thousand PDP 8s and fifteen thousand PDP 11s, many sold through engineering applications supplied by universities and third-party vendors. IBM clearly needed a new business model.

By mid-1974, IBM's indeterminate presence in minicomputers was covered in only two out of one hundred fifty pages of our Research Board report on office automation. Fortunately, the first happy harbinger of Cary's decentralization became apparent a few months later, when the newly formed General Systems Division released the Series/1. "It finally represents the unbundling expected since 1968," crowed Jack Reilly, the division's vice president for sales. Customers would assemble their own final configurations from a menu of hardware and software components, and they could expect far less handholding than customers of the small-business System 3 or the mainframes received. Blunting the field organization's devotion to full service would not be easy, and any sales representative who overpromised would be "separated," Jack said.

Even after the public announcement, the ever-powerful central sales organization continued to argue that the low-end 370 constituted a better answer to distributed processing than did the Series/1. More important were the high-level misgivings about the General Systems Division's unbundling philosophy, which, in fact, didn't work at first. Nor could the Division's sales force match the productivity of the minicomputer companies. High gross margins left the Series/1 wholly uncompetitive in the OEM market. Still, the product scored a few major sales, including the thousands of machines bought by the State Farm insurance company to automate its agency offices. Whatever the technical pluses and minuses, State Farm CIO Norm Vincent almost certainly achieved a customized result, the scale of which would have stretched both Wang and Digital.

The next two years were characterized by more indecision. The reconstituted Systems Communications Division initiated a second clumsy foray into the office minicomputer market. Unfortunately, its efforts were still inhibited by the product engineers' mainframe-based preconceptions. To start, they assumed that secretaries could be taught to use the same inhuman, basically unintelligible commands as those foisted on mainframe operators.

Illustrative of the gap was a pilot study of an IBM 3730 office system conducted by oil giant Atlantic Richfield on seven secretaries, all of whom were wholly capable on the Selectric, though six unsurprisingly spent only a quarter of their day typing. The results were dismal. Returning to their desks after fifteen hours in training, spread over five sessions, none of the seven could create even a simple memo. Noted the evaluation: "Their proficiency only improved after 'substantial post-training support which occupied 50 percent to 75 percent of the time of four people for three weeks, 30 percent of their time over the next three weeks and leveled off at 10 percent of their time for the remainder of the test.'"

More descriptive of the scale of the debacle were accounts of secretaries bursting into tears when confronted by computer-generated messages more appropriate to mainframes than typewriters. Deadpanned the evaluation: "It is difficult to learn more about some commands such as SYSXARCH." SYSXARCH? No wonder Lexitron, Lanier, Vydec, and especially Wang systems spread like brushfires across IBM's former preserves.

After mentioning these results without identifying the source at an otherwise wholly forgettable visit to IBM's Systems Communications Division, we received an unexpected invitation to breakfast from division president Allen Krowe. We found this large beefy man highly intelligent, ambitious, and a glutton for detail. He'd already been briefed on our remarks and possibly the Arco memo as well. So he was fully prepared with a sharply insightful and hardly defensive analysis of his product's competitive shortfalls. To start, he readily acknowledged the 3730's horrible human interfaces as being "a classic victim of the programmer culture around here. For example, that entire technician's lingo in the screen messages, like SYSTORE TEXT. Idiotic. How about 'Store this Record.' It's being cleaned up fast."

Krowe also criticized IBM's frustrating training program as "originally more complicated and unrewarding than it had to be. We were teaching spaghetti style, and the new approach is a caterpillar-to-butterfly technique. By the first coffee break, we want everyone to stand up and cheer because they can already prepare a simple memo without assistance. In one and a half days, the participants should know all the major functions they are likely to use regularly. Next, we'll teach those features …" Unfortunately, the jazzed-up training curriculum was soon devalued when Xerox and then Apple introduced easily comprehensible screen icons and embedded help cues.

Krowe's take on providing word processors with competitive levels of features and functions was this: "We've got to be on a par with Vydec, Lanier, Wang, or whoever. In fact, we have to be better." A strong statement given that we'd just been told by one of Krowe's most influential direct reports that the division would concentrate on networks and not bother "to stay up with every little feature." "Commonplace IBM bravado?" we wondered. No, Krowe strongly insisted: "Word-processing operators don't give a tinker's damn about network communications. Some day they'll use these things, but IBM can't tell them to struggle along in the interim," he observed.

But not even this powerful chief could make his prescriptions stick. The programmer culture lingered far longer than management hoped.

"Competitive function with minimal networking" was fine to say but impossible to force on the IBM lifers, especially in a division newly refocused on communications. Krowe was clearly on the right track, but the track neither reached nor rattled IBM's most calcified technical cadres. Of course, one might have questioned why the already-challenged communications division was building a word processor in the first place.

In late 1979, the Office Products Division rolled out the OS6, a functionally competitive word-processing system inexplicably fitted with a tiny screen capable of scrolling just six lines of text. Division President John Young admitted to us that the small screen had been a mistake (another sign of the developers' unfortunate mind-set). But he gamely insisted that six lines provided more visibility than secretaries had gotten from their Selectric typewriter. Huh? A typist could see the whole page. Already, prospective customers were disparaging the pint-sized screens as puny also-rans compared to the competition's half-page or better displays. The programmer mind-set so apparent in both the OS6 and 3730 was a powerful predictor of IBM's eventual failure in the consumer-oriented PC market.

Not much better impact was made by the 8100, a new minicomputer from Allen Krowe's Systems Communications Division but tightly coupled to the mainframe. That connection avoided the need for an operator, enhanced remote hardware support, and spread joy to the centrist mainframe bigots in the sales division. But the tight coupling never made sense to the distributed-processing market. Once again, the mainframe mind-set put a clamp on the innovation required by the new markets.

After a trip to division headquarters in Raleigh, North Carolina, Naomi and I met with again with Allen to probe the 8100's disappointing performance, gaps in support, and even the lingering doubts about its survival. He was again fully engaged, fastidiously picking lint from his handsome, new, and subtly off-blue wool suit even while enumerating IBM's product plans with an auditor's precision. Righting the ship wouldn't be easy, he said. Already, the blue-suiter sales reps were softening their customer appeals, and many had even stopped mentioning the box altogether.

Krowe was elbow deep in a problem that began well before he arrived as division president. He acknowledged both the delays and the capacity shortfalls, but insisted product development was back on track. "While we met our timetable on twenty-eight of thirty deliverables, we missed two of the most important. COBOL was only three months late after I worked a Raleigh team around the clock. But the marketing people reacted as though the delay were Armageddon." Capacity constraints were fixed by adding more memory. Too bad "we gave prospective customers more performance specifics than we'd ever provided before," Krowe remarked. But as with the secretarial system, even he couldn't turn around his recalcitrant programmers or block the positioning of a mainframe-centric product that was obsolete at the outset.

Luckily, a few weeks later, IBM was finally able to announce a blockbuster, a low-end mainframe shepherded through production by Jack Kuehler. The 4300 was a marvel from both a technological and a cost/performance perspective. This first E Series processor had 64-bit memory chips, new multilayer ceramic packaging, and new hardware design draped in microcode. It was manufactured and tested in highly automated facilities and boasted a four-to-one price/ performance improvement (twice the gain engineered by IBM in every other instance). "E is for Exciting," burbled the often anti-IBM *Computerworld* (February 1979). "IBM New Models Jolt the Industry," glowed *BusinessWeek* on February 12. "IBM's Latest Blitz," trumpeted *Newsweek* a day later.

Hurrying to interview the Systems Products Division president responsible for this wonder, we were led by our liaison, Sam Albert, to a large office. There we found only a slightly built young man in the mandatory white button-down shirt, but with tails hanging out and no jacket, carrying a slide projector and looking for an electrical outlet. The administrative assistant, we surmised. Naomi was becoming annoyed that the great man was late until Sam whispered that "the guy with the slide projector" was actually Jack Kuehler.

Kuehler, along with John Akers and Allen Krowe, was then rumored to be in the running for CEO. He made no secret of his ambitions for the mini-mainframe, even if his peers in the other divisions had to pay the price: "If I weren't out to take over the world, IBM would have the wrong man for the job," he pleasantly interrupted our probe about internal competition. After all, this division had been broken away from the larger mainframe division under Bertram because "we weren't doing as well as we should in that market"—certainly an understatement, given the 370/115 and other offerings.

Equally important was the 4300's new circuitry and the way in which the designers had addressed installation and maintenance costs. With its self-diagnostic circuits to isolate problems, a repairman could bring the right replacement parts on his first visit, or be coached via telecommunications links from the new Remote Service Facility. These were the first stirrings of a broadened customer emphasis away from acquisition price to "total cost of ownership," including operation and maintenance. Fortuitously, IBM was able to cut the ratio of original purchase price to monthly maintenance cost just when the weaker minicomputer companies offset falling sales revenues by moving in the other—and ultimately self-destructive—direction of raising their monthly maintenance fees.

Perhaps the only downside from an overhead-cost perspective was IBM's insistence on continuing expensive support for three different 4300 operating systems, including the old-line DOS/VSE. "I have too many operating systems and a limited number of programmers," observed Kuehler. Was that a signal that a system would be discontinued? "I couldn't weaken DOS/VSE without an international war," he said in a nod to the Böblingen, Germany, lab that was the center of its development.

Was the 4300's surprisingly low price really in IBM's interest? Yes, snapped Kuehler without hesitation. Because by then, plenty of new competitors possessed the resources and business models to push price/performance trends at the same pace, and more importantly, because the new price slope reflected a combination of factors—technical improvements in chips, packaging, and architecture, as well as unbundled software prices that served both to recover expenses and to discipline the programming groups. "Now they'll have to ask whether anyone will pay for that extra feature."

In fact, the 4300's impact on the market was tremendous. It felled leasing companies and plug-compatible mainframes while nudging the weaker tier of minicomputer companies over the cliff. At the time, National Semiconductor was manufacturing midscale IBM compatibles, and its partner Hitachi was supplying the high-end boxes. The 4300's performance leap destroyed National's nascent competitive threat. Coincidentally, another National compatible aimed at Digital Equipment was hastily withdrawn after DEC successfully petitioned to have its patent-infringement suit moved from California to its home turf in Massachusetts. At that point, National stopped manufacturing computers altogether and turned its efforts to the healthy microprocessor business and to reselling Hitachi mainframes.

Close to the end of Frank Cary's term as CEO, his decentralization effort had spawned more new minicomputer entrants than the market needed. Quipped Reilly: "One product division in Atlanta is dressing our terminals as processors, another in New York is dressing our processors as terminals, and a third in Florida is dressing naked [unbundled] minis as everything. It's incredible." Adding the System 3X for small businesses and the new personal computers originally initiated by Cary himself, we could identify eight different IBM small computers and eleven different operating systems.

"We want active internal competition, but not unbridled or wasteful competition," Krowe tried to reassure us. Product proliferation and overlap would be effectively contained by the three sales forces that existed at the time. So Office Products salespeople would leverage Selectric relationships that sometimes reached back to the 1940s, selling word-processing minicomputers to millions of office accounts. General Business would sell, mostly to small businesses, minicomputers (including Series/1 and System 36 and 38) that were relatively simpler to implement than mainframes. The big mainframes, 4300s, and 8100s would be sold to large enterprises by the crown-jewel Data Processing Division. Of course, "in the top three hundred accounts, all three sales groups are present," allowed Krowe, begging the proliferation question we'd raised in the first place. IBM would waffle for another ten years on which boxes to kill.

A Transient Sector Sags

The minicomputer's glory days were fading. The commercial distributed-processing market was choked by overcapacity, especially once most second-tier companies found themselves in direct competition with one of IBM's overwrought product divisions. At the same time, the volume microprocessors fabricated by Intel, National, and others began devouring the minicomputer's share of the OEM market. The consolidation of the minicomputer sector was relentless and brutal.

Just hearing an IBM salesman mouth the word "mini" was enough to freeze the purchasing decisions of many enterprise accounts. No one doubted Armonk's underlying strengths, and the minicomputer makers were convinced that IBM would inevitably introduce a technology more potent than anything they could offer. Most named IBM as their only real competitor, even though Armonk's puffy margins offered at least temporary salvation. The preoccupation with Armonk was often ridiculous and almost always a distraction.

Simultaneously, the decentralized-management fad was waning. Gradually, an even stronger argument for centralized development had grown up around business concepts like central purchasing, cross-regional supply chains, and the provision of a "single face" to customers across divisions and locations. Meanwhile, small, decentralized programming staffs had devolved into what a later internal study at Mobil Oil dubbed costly "pockets of incompetence"—units too small to attract competent people or achieve reasonable economies of scale (most were disbanded). Minicomputers were still in use but under the guidance of the central IT staff, to the detriment of the weaker vendors.

By the time we made our 1979 visits to around twenty minicomputer companies, many in the second tier had already begun their swoon after significant operational shortfalls and management gaffes. "Woes for the Second Tier in Minis," heralded *Business Week* on September 24, 1979. Computer Automation, General Automation, and Modcomp had "run into serious problems and [were] quickly falling behind." Among their challenges, declared the magazine, were "growth itself … [t]heir inability to come up with enough money to expand the industry growth rate," and the lack of "management skills beyond those of the entrepreneurs who launched them."

To our mind, the *Business Week* analysis focused far too much on individual companies and far too little on broader factors affecting the entire industry, beginning with overcapacity. As we noted at the time, "It may be difficult to remember that most of today's minicomputer company stars are less than a decade old. And that many tripped through their first five years in a sequence of exploration, misstep, and hairbreadth rescue with all the twists of a Keystone Cop pursuit to nowhere. But the competitive landscape is changing. Gone are the early days of minimum competition. Those wide-open spaces are vanishing with the buffalo." Excess capacity kicked off the earliest round of collapses in the minicomputer sector:

Computer Automation

The company was formed in 1967 with just $15,000 by a computer development manager from Varian. For five years, Computer Automation built automated circuit-test equipment. Then it stumbled into minicomputers with the Naked Mini and, in 1976, caught the brass ring when it won a huge order from the California-based Fireman's Fund Insurance Company. Computer Automation's revenue from commercial systems more than doubled to $17 million annually from $7 million, enough—at least in management's mind—to justify formation of a Commercial Systems division with no less than forty-nine sales offices. By 1977, total revenues had soared to $50 million, the company had zero debt, and Wall Street cheered.

But, as so often happens in technology, that was also the company's apogee. The slide started after Computer Automation stumbled badly in deciding to build a second-generation computer that couldn't run the software written just three years earlier for its predecessor. That incompatibility gaffe, not excess growth, set off a chain reaction of trouble as important customers crowded the exits. Only a year later, the company fell on its face again when exploding inventories pointed to gaps in management processes and controls. Accounts receivable mushroomed (perhaps because customers refused to accept the daffy new machine), and without cash, debt followed suit. A swarm of customers defected to IBM; bankers became angry; and the SEC began investigating whether "the officers and directors of the Company, while engaging in transactions in the Company's stock, made misleading statements."

The CEO's moist eyes signaled depression and exhaustion when we visited him during the fall of 1979. Nevertheless, he gamely looked ahead to more focused product offerings and a processor-on-a-board designed to deflect incursions by the microprocessor. Also in the offing, he told us, were several new software systems, including one then being built in San

Antonio, Texas, and appropriately code-named "Alamo." Our visit ended when a phone caller interrupted to announce that one of Alamo's twelve programmers had just punched a colleague in the eye and raced out of the plant on an intoxicated toot—or so we were told.

We never visited Computer Automation again. Its original test-equipment business helped keep the company afloat for some time. By 1992, the company was making facsimile software for local area networks. It had only eighty-three employees, and its stock was valued at just $2 million. The following year, employees bought the rights to make and repair Computer Automation's test equipment.

General Automation

This early pioneer in OEM systems was founded in 1967, floundered in 1975 on a poor technology decision, and finally collapsed in 1979 amid serious questions about the business judgment of its founder and CEO. Efforts to oust him were thwarted by his sizable equity holdings, friendly board members, and threats of legal action. The squabbling reached a climax in May 1979, when management simultaneously announced yet another drop in earnings and a grand plan to acquire singer Bing Crosby's estate (complete with helipad) for corporate or personal use. "That was the last straw," recalled his long-time friend and cofounder, who now joined the dissidents.

The new, temporary CEO had no easy answers either. After initial staff cuts, this former consultant quickly hired the Boston Consulting Group for a strategic makeover. "GA hired a consultant to hire a consultant," chortled an industry watcher with understandable incredulity. When we visited in late 1979, the CEO-for-rent was still wrestling bloated inventories and valiantly trying to hold staff defections below 40 percent. Larger product "repositioning" awaited the consultant's report. But, realistically, the only viable strategy for the CEO was to pray for an acquisition while pondering whether to renew his one-year turnaround contract. In 1980, the company reported a loss of $16 million on $126 million in revenues.

We didn't revisit this company either, though something by that name lingers as a small software integrator. Annual revenues dropped from $34.6 million in 1994 to $6.8 million in 2001, when the company had just thirty-five employees and a stock value of $1.8 million.

Modcomp

Modcomp began in 1970 making systems for NASA. It then became an early entrant into real-time factory-control systems, which were proprietary and poorly documented. Hence, switching costs were high and longevity relatively firm. Trouble surfaced early. By 1974, a respectable 35 percent growth rate somehow morphed into bloated inventories and accounts receivable. Growth wasn't the culprit, as the previously cited *BusinessWeek* article suggested. The following year, the company was accused of boosting revenue figures by booking letters of intent as actual sales. The restatement of 1975's financial results turned a $2 million profit into a $2.2 million loss. Other losses followed. Finally, in 1978, the founder and chairman was replaced by the retired chairman of Northern Telecom, with the Modcomp CFO assuming a role as president.

When we visited a year later, an SEC investigation described as "grueling" by the management team was still draining their attentions. Though the company had lost pace and position, it somehow opened a London office and delivered a high-performance system to the London Stock Exchange. Later that year, Modcomp opened an office in Cologne and sold a 25 percent equity share to an IT subsidiary of Daimler-Benz AG, the German car company, which acquired the rest of Modcomp five years later. According to company literature, Modcomp still "was firmly committed to the research and development of innovative technologies that provide real-time computing solutions for the 1990s and beyond."

But by 1996, the company had revenues of just $36.7 million, and it was sold again, this time going to CSP Inc., a maker of cluster computers for the defense industry.

Four-Phase Systems

Formed in 1964, Four-Phase Systems' minicomputer's ultra-high-speed connection to dumb terminals had made it the perfect system for interactive data entry. The company muddled along for five years before adding a professional management team. Shortly thereafter, a former McDonnell Douglas engineer used its unique capability to develop a highly successful hospital information system that let nurses quickly record patient-care events (e.g., medications ordered and given). In 1978, when Four-Phase successfully launched an initial public stock offering, hospitals accounted for 22 percent of the company's revenues and 37 percent of its order backlog. Another 50 percent came from OEMs that embedded Four-Phase equipment into their final systems. Revenues hit $160 million in 1979, the year we visited. Jubilance reined. The only real competitor was "IBM, IBM, and IBM ... especially the 8100," burbled the vice president for marketing. "We'd be out of business if IBM had announced the 8100 five years ago," he said. "But they gave us a window to develop a first-rate sales force, a solid service organization, and 1100 customers dependent on Four-Phase."

Leasing was the key to the company's strategy. Especially remarkable was its use of the phlegmatic five-year, straight-line depreciation method, a departure from the accelerated four-year schedule preferred by most of the company's competitors. That meant that 40 percent of the company's lease base was still not depreciated after three years, a risky proposition in an industry headed for three-year product cycles.

But our questions on the point brought knee-slapping chuckles from the jovial marketer. No worries about equipment life cycles, he told us. Every bit of equipment Four-Phase owned was under lease; none was languishing—without a payment stream—in some warehouse. In fact, he said, "There's even an eight- to ten-system order backlog for the first model we ever produced." Of course, that backlog was probably a sign that the later models weren't compatible with the first, so that an early customer needing more capacity would have to wait for essentially obsolescent gear.

After some badgering, our host allowed that the break-even point on leased equipment didn't occur until the eighth year. "Eighth year!" we audibly gasped. "But after the ninth year, the profits are staggering," he boasted. "What ninth year?" we wondered. This, after all, was the technology sector. One had to be suspicious of a computer-hardware company that could only lease its products at prices so low as to require eight-year payoffs, and whose R&D budget was only $11 million, or 7 percent of revenues, versus the 8 percent to 11 percent share set aside for R&D by the best of the competition. Underpriced products, underfinanced R&D, undemanding customers, overlong estimates on revenue streams—this was a formula for failure, we determined.

Back at the office, we wrote: "Is the lease base really an asset or a liability?" The answer was obvious, especially after the marketing guy blurted, "When the 8100 was announced, our prospects collapsed because it hit the heart of our product line. We had to immediately announce an upgrade even though it hurt our lease program."

Just one week later, on October 5, 1979, the *Wall Street Journal* published a requiem for Inforex, a near competitor of Four-Phase in terms of both product definition and revenue expectations. "Losses mount and optimism fades ... ," said the *Journal*. "[T]he company's earnings are washing away ... a loss of more than $3 million for the fourth quarter."

The explanation invoked a strong sense of *déjà vu*. Too many leasing customers wanted the newly announced line of equipment. The upgrade added just $200 to Inforex's monthly lease. "But the cost to Inforex to upgrade these systems or provide new ones was about $14,000 ... ," the *Journal* noted. Moreover, the old customers took quick delivery of upgraded equipment and then sent their old gear back to Inforex, where it lay idle awaiting resale. "Idle equipment costs us money," the chairman was quoted as saying. "Atop all this, Inforex's third-party leasing business [also important to Four-Phase] began drying up," the *Journal* reporter remarked, signaling the collapse of the rest of the company's business model. Leasing firms, it turned out, could no longer count on eight- or even five-year revenue streams.

Hurrying the collapse of an eight-year revenue stream, no doubt, was not IBM's much-feared 8100 but its little jewel, the 4300 with its four-to-one price/performance improvement. The ensuing business whirlwind eventually flattened not only minicomputer life expectancies but also the life spans of mainframe machines like those turned out by Amdahl. To our surprise, the 4300 was never mentioned during our visit to Four-Phase, which we chalked up to management's especially deadly blend of hubris and myopia.

The old strategy would survive into the future, insisted our host: Hold product prices at least 20 percent below IBM; hold equipment returns to one percent a month; hold replacement delivery to a crawl ("Only a squeaky wheel gets delivery in less than five months," he bragged); hold the pace of new-product introduction till forever if need be. "We held our last product generation for a year or until the 8100 was on the market," he told us. "The next generation will be held until 1981 'if necessary,' though it would be better to wait for two years or even three. We'll milk the lease base for every nickel we can."

Within three years, Four-Phase ran short of milk and nickels. It was sold to Motorola for just $253 million, a slight premium over its $234 million of annual revenues. A "troubled company with an impressive sales force," noted the press. Another three years later, in 1985, the organization was merged into Motorola's telecommunications business and essentially disappeared. The strategy of holding back innovation in the IT business is a lot like holding your breath until you faint.

Eventual Epitaph

Despite the demise of these wounded birds, minicomputer companies persisted for more than another decade. Ultimately, mass-fabricated microprocessors rendered irrelevant their idiosyncratic hardware designs. The switching costs raised by their proprietary operating systems simultaneously slowed their demise against Unix and made that demise inevitable. In the end, only IBM and HP survived, not coincidentally because they eagerly grasped the opportunity presented by the PC. None of the fifty others exists today as a computer company.

Chapter 6

FIRST MOVERS:

The Dawning of the Personal Computer

The first entrants into a new market created by a disruptive technology will establish an unassailable position and reap the lion's share of benefits in terms of customers, markets, and profits. At least, that's the theory. And, certainly, numerous first movers have achieved a sustainable long-term advantage. Take Citibank, for instance. Its early embrace of the upgraded automatic teller machine (ATM) earned it a measurable market share among precisely the most profitable customer set while its competitors were still churning out studies showing that ATMs could never be cost-effective. Citi held its position even after its competitors introduced the machines, confirming what NationsBank's CEO Hugh McColl told us years later: "IT innovation can help you gain market share, and customer inertia helps you keep it."

Today's Internet paragons like Amazon, eBay, and Yahoo may again prove McColl right, but not without a few caveats. It's true they started with first-mover advantage, but it was the succeeding layer upon layer of sound decisions and active leadership that buttressed their competitive positions and helped them fend off rivals. Latecomers could muscle aside the first movers, but only with difficulty and even better decision making and leadership. So, first-mover advantage is merely a starting point, and it's still too early to tell whether Amazon and eBay can hold their lead indefinitely. Certainly, AltaVista, the early Internet-search leader, tumbled like a dried leaf before latecomer Google.

Even that's only half the story. First movers often enter the market before it's been definitely reshaped by the disruptive technology. Too often they try to mold new technology around old business models, with disastrous results. All three of the 1980s' PC market leaders—Apple, Commodore, and Tandy—made that mistake by trying to shoehorn microprocessors into older and inappropriate models. Apple eventually succeeded, but only marginally. The other two disappeared, making first-mover *disadvantage* a *leitmotif* of the PC revolution.

Technology Upends Business Models

The history of semiconductors and microprocessors is remarkably compact, considering its force and sweep. Vacuum tubes were replaced by the transistor developed at Bell Labs in 1947, and a decade later transistor equivalents were being etched onto silicon chips as "integrated circuits." Accelerating progress prompted Gordon Moore, then the director of research at Fairchild Semiconductor, to postulate his industry-defining "law" in 1965. With some later revision to Moore's initial pronouncement, the law projects that the number of circuits that can be placed on a chip will double every eighteen months.

Amazingly, for these cynical times of revisionist everything, that projection has held up. In the forty-three years since Moore's first pronouncement, the number of circuits on a chip has exploded from thirty-two to more than two billion in 2008.

In 1968, Moore joined Robert Noyce and Andrew Grove to found Intel, which began development of the DRAM (dynamic random access memory) technology used for short-term storage of computer data and programs during processing. Two years later, while working to build a seven-chip logic engine for Busicom, a Japanese manufacturer of desktop calculators, Intel engineer Ted Hoff hit on the idea of displacing the seven chips with a single-chip microprocessor. Besides considerably reducing manufacturing costs and hardware-development time, Hoff's invention, when combined with inherently malleable software, would expand the microprocessor market to multiple uses beyond calculators.

At about the same time, Texas Instruments' engineers began work for Computer Terminal Corp. (CTC, later renamed Datapoint), which manufactured a minicomputer housed in a programmable terminal. Unlike the "dumb terminals" or mainframe monitors offered by IBM and others, this machine could perform simple tasks like validating arithmetic totals locally, thus erasing the need to transmit such data to the central data center over expensive and unreliable telecommunications links. When word of Intel's work spread, Texas Instruments reworked the original design of its underlying processor to one chip from three.

The microprocessor came to market in March 1971, ironically even while the gold rush of investments in minicomputer start-ups continued. Intel delivered its 4004 device to Busicom, beating the public announcement of TI's more powerful eight-bit device (which CTC rejected) by two months. Though still primitive, the 4004 was almost as powerful as the 18,000-vacuum-tube ENIAC supercomputer of twenty-five years earlier. According to legend, it was powerful enough to provide the guidance mechanism for the *Pioneer 10* rocket exploration of Jupiter and beyond. But it certainly launched Intel on its path to dominance in microprocessors.

The new electronic technology ravaged these incumbent business models, particularly in sectors wholly dependent on electromechanical workings. In the desktop calculator business, for example, previous leaders like Monroe and Victor Comptometer were left stranded with warehouses of obsolescing gear-and-rotor marvels that only yesterday sold for thousands of dollars, along with their appropriately priced training and field-repair services.

The end came quickly. Sam Bernstein, the vice president of marketing at Commodore Computing when we spoke, recalled his experience at Victor: "We had a $12 million R&D budget, and we spent the whole budget developing a new electromechanical unit that was a little smaller, a little faster, a little quieter, and so jammed with gears that they almost popped out when you opened the sound shielding. At about the same time, an inventor came by with the idea of an electronic calculator, which we agreed to evaluate—but not for another two years, because we were already in the product cycle with our new box. Point is, we spent $12 million on a technology that was obsolete before we started. And who survived the calculator wars? None of the traditional calculator companies." Bernstein would apply this lesson to Commodore's PCs with even less satisfactory results.

Already handicapped by their new rivals' lower product costs and expanded capabilities, the incumbents were further burdened by their vertically integrated, labor-intensive sales and service organizations. Previously the crown jewels of customer retention and general competitive advantage, now these people were the millstones around the neck of a sector auditioning as a textbook case of radical change in the essential business model. As Bernstein remembered it: "In 1970, when everyone else was selling calculators for $1,000, [Victor] had one for $195. We thought that the entire industry would sell 100,000; actually, as prices declined, fifty million were shipped [a classic case of price elasticity].... Everyone asked us, 'What about service?' I said, 'Nonsense. For $195, let them send it to the factory.' They said, 'What about salesmen? How will customers learn to use their equipment properly?' I said, 'For $195, let them teach themselves.'"

Intense competition from HP and Texas Instruments slashed calculator prices along with customer demand for salesmen, training, and field repair. Eventually, the gadgets were sold in stationery stores to people who could learn everything they needed to know from a manual and who tossed the gizmos in the garbage when they broke. Market-changers HP, National Semiconductor, and Texas Instruments would themselves be driven from the business after Asian producers turned calculators into novelty gifts.

The minicomputer industry was next in line for obliteration, as an early analysis by Edson de Castro, the CEO of Data General, suggested when we met in 1974. His table below is instructive both for its correct assumptions and for those that were off the mark. To give de Castro's insights full credit, 1974 was the year that (then) Intel engineer Larry Kildare programmed the first widely used PC operating system.

Prognosis for Microprocessors at Data General

	MAJOR	**MINI**	**MICRO**
ORIENTATION	Industries	Systems	Products
PRODUCTS	Solutions	Tools	Devices
USE	Data	Operations	Tasks
PRICE	Millions	Thousands	Hundreds
UNIT VOLUME	1,000s	10,000s	50,000s
SALES & MARKETING	25–30%	10–15%	6–8%
ORIGINS	Universities	Components	Semiconductors
MATURITY	10–15 years	8–10 years	4–7 years

De Castro's table is amazingly prescient about the maximum percentage of price that would be allocated to sales and marketing, especially since a new business model is usually the last thing recognized by an incumbent management. Where he goes off the rails—and by a mile—is in his estimate of unit volume; his projection in the "50,000s" for microprocessors is less than one percent of Intel's actual shipments today. The great significance, though, lies in what the microprocessor's enormous volume has wrought. Computers have become commodity products, with three or four "standard" hardware architectures dominating the entire IT sector (e.g., Intel's X86, IBM's Power, Sun's SPARC).

De Castro hoped to establish Data General's own microprocessor plant in Silicon Valley, but his was a lost cause. The volume semiconductor houses—Intel, Motorola, and National Semiconductor —set the standard, and as it turned out, the microprocessor represented not an extension of the mini, but a complete and radical break with preexisting technical thrusts and business models. The first fault line between the minicomputer and the PC was the former's dependence on each manufacturer's proprietary hardware designs, just as the divide between mainframes and minis a decade earlier had been exotic circuitry.

What may be an apocryphal story about Henry Ford helps to explain what was about to happen in the computer industry. As the story goes, Ford asked a market research team to project the market share of a new automobile costing six hundred dollars, or about one-tenth the price offered by the rarefied competition of his time. The team misconstrued the actual market and counted the number of chauffeurs, allegedly causing Ford to scream, "Idiots, you should have counted horses." Ford understood that a vehicle costing one-tenth the going price for an automobile would expand the market far beyond anything others might achieve with incremental product improvements. Ford's Model T eventually swamped much of the automobile industry, but more important, it opened the market to the masses. The PC was on its way to becoming the Tin Lizzie of the computer world.

Credit for the first personal computer probably goes to the long-defunct Imsai, which introduced a hobby kit in 1973. The following year, Larry Kildare wrote one of the first industry-wide operating systems, the rudimentary CP/M, in just four weeks. How we all admired his speed of execution and the product's simplicity! A year later, Kildare and his wife formed Digital Research, which would be remembered as the PC's first first-mover disappointment.

Larry's lead lasted less than a decade. Instead, it was the young William Henry Gates III who became famous by making a deal with IBM to set the industry standard. According to industry lore (which Larry denies), Bill stuck his nose under the IBM tent when Larry brushed off the blue-suiters to go flying in the sunny skies off Monterey.

Practical uses for the early marvels were sparse, despite burbling in the computer industry press about homemakers using their PCs to store recipes while their husbands ingeniously programmed the lawn sprinklers. Yet, over the next decade, the microprocessor would spur the development of a radically different business model for the computer sector. Whereas the old, vertically integrated model dictated that IBM and DEC produce their own chips, build their own boxes, add their own operating systems, networks, and databases, and then sell their systems through their own in-house sales forces, the new PC model was layered. The first layer consisted of a few semiconductor companies designing and fabricating the mass-volume microprocessors used by everyone else, while a few second-layer software houses, most notably Microsoft, built the operating systems, and so on. The new model would kill the minicomputer vendors along with the first-mover PC stars.

An Insufficient Understanding

The otherwise astute managements of companies making calculators and minicomputers didn't see the approaching PC storm. Such tempests are often difficult to forecast until the green water is already crashing over the ship's bridge. And curiously enough, it's not just the incumbents who can become confounded by their myopia, but also those who have the most to gain from the disruption. In 1976, I interviewed the heads of four major semiconductor research and production centers. Well-positioned as these executives were at Intel, National Semiconductor, Motorola, and Bell Labs, not one was particularly accurate in his forecast of how his company's latest, greatest hope would impact the market and the leader's own fortunes.

At the time of my visits, the semiconductor business was swinging from bust to boom in its typically ragged business cycle. Chip makers were competing vigorously, often pricing "down the learning curve" at cost levels that wouldn't be justified by fabrication experience and volume for another year or two. Margins were razor thin, demand erratic, and then—boom—the manufacturers would enjoy a bonanza for a year or two. It was no surprise that the heads of these companies searched frantically for something, anything, that might deliver longer product cycles, greater retention of final product value, and higher gross margins (i.e., markups on manufacturing costs)—the three grails of their perennial quest.

As spring arrived in 1976, it seemed that two years of awful sales had finally ended. Crowed *BusinessWeek* in its April 26 issue: "As quickly as it arrived two years ago, the worst recession of the short, but eventful, history of semiconductors seems to have ended. Prices are firming, delivery times are stretching out, and some customers are beginning to fear a repetition of the capacity crunch that touched off a buying panic in 1973. [But now] it's Katy bar the door."

About that time, the semiconductor companies jettisoned a raft of consumer end-products—electronic calculators, watches, and the like—that had raised great hopes for value retention just a year or two earlier. Intel disbanded its watch division, and National Semiconductor's chairman, Charles Sporck, told securities analysts that "1977 will be looked on as the year consumer products left silicon gulch." A healthy upturn in quarterly earnings was attributed, in part, to a "reduced emphasis on consumer products" along with moves that had brought the company's "business to manageable levels."

Perhaps the relief they felt after eliminating small-bore consumer products explains the semiconductor chiefs' disdain for the PC. Having tried, and failed, to attract consumers with a variety of products, they were finished. Now their gaze was turned back to the always preferable original equipment manufacturing (OEM) business, where semiconductor companies could supply chips to the manufacturers of a huge range of industrial products.

The View from Silicon Gulch

In 1977, I started a study of the microprocessor's expanding territory by interviewing the heads of major foundries with competitive products: Bell Labs, Intel, Motorola, National Semiconductor, and Texas Instruments. We didn't get beyond a gaggle of especially irritating PR flacks at TI. But all the rest had a compelling story to tell, and I was privileged to listen.

National's sparkling upturn was evident from the overcrowded parking lot at its Santa Clara headquarters. A young girl with long blond hair topped by a police hat veritably sparkled as she directed traffic with enormous energy. "Charlie's right in that building there," she pointed, big grin intact, in response to our request for directions to Mr. Sporck's office.

Charlie himself was more bristly than sparkly. A big man glaring over a large handlebar mustache, flanked by two subordinates in a nearly empty, visitor's office, with the day's agenda propped on an attaché case at his right, he motioned me to an empty chair opposite the three.

Asked about the markets for microprocessors, Sporck answered cautiously that there were three. First, process controllers in automated manufacturing was one, a promising high-margin market absent either standards or dominant players. Second was the OEMs, though the existing minicomputer manufacturers were so dominant, he told us, that any real change would be slow and evolutionary. Third was the traditional mainframe market, where National would clone IBM's "big iron" to steal a tasty piece of what they figured to be, as we learned some years later, a twentyfold markup between the cost of components and the final price. Of course, a big part of that markup would go to its leasing-company partner, Itel, in return for fielding the labor-intensive and typically awkward sales and service functions. Sporck's projections proved accurate eventually, though the company completely missed out on the PC parade.

When we arrived at Intel in Santa Clara, CEO Bob Noyce greeted us in his airy office, dressed in a very colorful, perhaps Hawaiian, short-sleeved shirt. After putting this stuffily blue-suited visitor at ease with a benign smile, he spun out his elegant and imaginative constructions of Intel's future with very few course corrections or requests for clarifications from me.

Noyce addressed three themes: desktop PCs, embedded devices, and gangs of microprocessors. The PC would radicalize the traditional computer industry, he said, and defrock the in-house Management Information Systems (MIS) analysts and programmers, whom he scorned for blocking access by "real" users and, hence, retarding their productivity. IBM, with its overpriced hardware and overcomplicated operating system, would be the first to get burned, Noyce opined. "IBM has a lock on the market because of operating systems only they understand." Customers were terrified to change systems, he told us, because they hadn't forgotten the pain of the last IBM systems upgrade only a few years earlier.

But all that would change immediately, Noyce confidently predicted, as PCs offloaded tasks then being performed through mainframe-based time-sharing. And, eventually, the development of gangs of microprocessors (just as Captain Grace Hopper had envisioned) would displace the mainframe altogether and open the way to far leaner pricing models. "The IBM or Univac markup over manufacturing costs is five to one," Noyce reported, "but, in our industry, distributors get by with just two to one." Lower prices combined with simplicity would gradually swing the market to the microprocessor-based computing platforms, leaving the corporate MIS types exposed in all their pathetic bureaucracy. "Those guys will have to be dragged kicking and screaming to anything new," Noyce predicted. "And in the end, how can anyone justify a central [MIS] department to manage typewriters [i.e., desktop computers with typewriter prices and simplicity]?"

Noyce's predictions about the microprocessor's impact on overall computer prices and pervasiveness were exactly right—and spectacularly so in his all-important profit metric. He had complained about Intel's inability to retain a larger share of the profits from its intellectual property; twenty years later, its profits exceeded those of all the PC makers combined.

But the great man was wrong about both the price drivers and the fates of IBM and the MIS professionals. In fact, PC pricing models were driven far below Noyce's two-to-one ratio over manufacturing costs; the ratio eventually shrank to almost five to four. Operating systems didn't become simpler, but the Microsoft and Unix versions did displace the proprietary systems once developed and maintained by IBM, DEC, and every other computer maker. The customer's cost of switching to another OS had protected the supplier's gross margins, but once that cost dropped, so did hardware markups.

Today's personal computers are far more complicated than the microprocessor-embedded "typewriters" Noyce imagined in 1977. To start, they're not stand-alone Selectrics but intricately networked communicators that need databases, browsers, security, and support. As a further complication, Windows OS has much more code than did IBM's mainframe equivalent, expanding the scope of work to be performed by both IT departments and armies of outside IT contractors.

Bell Labs, in Murray Hill, New Jersey, was our chosen destination in the AT&T empire. I called on Lee Thomas, superintendent of microprocessor development, and he intrigued me with an analog of the microprocessor to the fractional horsepower engine. Thomas asked me to imagine, at the engine's invention, a farmer contemplating the opportunity to employ such a machine. He might think of developing a motorized hoist for his hay bales, or he could speculate about how such engines would lower the manufacturing cost of a common household tool such as the washboard. But absent any experience with a mechanical clothes washer, the farmer couldn't begin to imagine an electric-powered one or, even less, an electric toothbrush.

So the impact of the fractional horsepower engine can be gauged, in part, by the number of homely devices appended with the word "electric," he told us. Similarly, the way to project the impact of microprocessors was to append the word "intelligent"—such as *intelligent* telephone, *intelligent* clothes washer, *intelligent* camera, *intelligent* toothbrush. Much of this happened just as Thomas predicted.

My last stop was at Motorola, outside Chicago. Motorola had built the second-most-successful microprocessor, which long powered Apple's Macintosh and backed up IBM's production of micros for its servers. The morning of my visit was consumed by a carefully orchestrated, but largely irrelevant, set of interviews with the marketing staff. "We could just put computers next to the people who understand the business and let them build their own applications," they trumpeted gleefully. As for field maintenance, the largest enterprises would happily bring their wounded PCs to local computer stores. Neither occurred. Twenty-five years later, very few business people actually develop PC software, and the chains of helpful computer stores have disappeared.

Fortunately for me, Dr. Robert Heikes, the general manager of Motorola's Semiconductor Group, provided more than lipshoots at this critical moment in the new industry. Probing questions were his forte: Should Motorola really produce and sell final systems when that approach might conflict with Apple and other important customers? Could customers really rely on the stores for product support? If not, should Motorola try to develop its own field force or try to buy a dying ember like Univac? The question of looming overcapacity, always a bleak side to the semiconductor sector, drew animated musings: Moore's Law seemed almost self-consuming, he observed. "So let's say the automobile market for micros is ten million chips a year; we alone could produce ten thousand in a few hours."

In many ways, Dr. Heikes was on target. Motorola, Intel, National, and the other semiconductor houses still don't sell final systems into the end-user market. Heikes then ended our interview by advising us not to ask him where Motorola was going in microprocessors, because he didn't know. We snickered a little as we gathered ourselves and our papers to leave his office. But many years later, his caution seems positively sage.

First In, First Out

By 1977, the PC landscape was dominated by Apple, Commodore, and Tandy Radio Shack. Commodore's awkwardly named Personal Electronic Transactor, or PET, was targeted at the home enthusiast. Sales were sparse by today's standards, and support was almost nonexistent. Radio Shack's TRS 80, meanwhile, was disparaged as the

"Trash 80" by bemused and unconvinced corporate IT executives, but its real market was as a minicomputer replacement for small businesses. Neither model was successful.

Commodore had begun life as the Ontario-based Commodore Portable Typewriter Company. In 1962, it changed its name and moved into low-priced electronic calculators, watches, and teaching machines. By 1976, the year it acquired a small semiconductor house, calculators were contributing 89 percent of Commodore's flattening top line, and of its $55 million in annual revenue, just 1.5 percent was earmarked for R&D.

Commodore drew on its once successful calculator history for its entry into personal computers. But, unfortunately, that backward-looking business model wasn't keyed to the new market. A PET with 4,000 bytes of memory was priced at $595, and 8,000 bytes cost $795. Essentially a display terminal with an embedded microprocessor and a balky keyboard baked in, the PET used a tape cassette for storage. Sold exclusively by mail, orders were accepted only when accompanied by a check. Questions from potential customers were handled over the telephone by "software coordinators," but none too gently as we watched. A minute or two into a call, our software coordinator was admonished by VP Sam Bernstein: "You're too softhearted. We can't afford to talk to these people." Ongoing support was patterned after Bernstein's calculator-minimalist model: "If they send us a circuit board, we'll replace it. If they want instruction, they can buy from [minicomputer maker] Basic Four."

The company had just shipped its first one hundred PETs, hoped to ship fifteen hundred more the following month, and was eyeing two million a year by 1979. The PC was priced high enough to be seen as a luxury appliance but low enough to discourage competition. Bernstein beamed while ticking off the PET's supposed applications: It could keep track of prospect lists, word processing, and menu planning. "Pet rock" would have been a better metaphor for a PC so limited in function and R&D resources, we decided. No wonder the company disappeared.

When we visited Tandy Radio Shack at its Fort Worth, Texas, glass-and-gold headquarters in 1981, we learned that the TRS 80's business model was keyed less to the layered PC sector than to the integrated minicomputer with its own operating system, applications software, training, distribution, and field maintenance. Our host was the gangly Jon Shirley, then vice president of merchandising but rumored to be the next CEO at some point in the future. Shirley knew the business, having started twenty-three years earlier in a Boston-area Radio Shack as a newly minted high-school graduate.

The TRS 80 was priced at just under $600 for a home computer and around $4,000 for a small business model. Tandy had developed its own operating system to correct perceived flaws in Digital Research's CP/M (Apple's Steve Jobs shared Tandy's negative view). Shirley also disdained the cottage software industry, which pundits were showering with expressions of joy and hope as a wellspring of free-spirited innovation. Hundreds of these small entrepreneurs dreamed of selling millions of program copies either through retail stores or software publishers. But only fifteen or so were turning out commercially viable software, Shirley judged, fairly it turned out.

Viability hinged on more than disciplined quality code, he sniffed; the computer-illiterate small-business owner, the software's ostensible target, also needed comprehensible documentation. "And once we went to the effort of writing high-quality documentation," he said of Tandy's approach, "we found we might as well write the code as well." Indeed, Tandy had already developed 159 business applications and fifty games for its operating system, and a floor full of programmers were grinding out five new systems a month. Not even the minicomputer companies wrote so many of their own applications.

Tandy's competitive edge was retail distribution, not hardware differentiation, averred its plush, flush, and supremely confident CEO John Roach. "Product detail must be the key concern among PC producers battling for shelf space at Byte Shop or ComputerLand, but not for us," he boasted. "We own the shelves with two hundred of our own computer specialty stores in the United States, plus another fifty overseas. We've also got the only reliable software-program documentation for every level of user sophistication, and consistent customer support in training and store service. No PC maker dependent on independent software and third-party sales and maintenance can match our control over store performance in all these areas."

In 1981, the company seemed the ultimately successful first mover. The TRS 80 was then one of the industry's top sellers, with an apparently unshakable market presence. Computer-related revenues topped $1.7 billion, or 22 percent of the company's total. Most of the canny homegrown management team, burnished by shining star Jon Shirley, had been there at least ten years and was expert in retail consumer electronics (which the company still does today). But, in truth, the company was not so much a first mover into a new technology as it was the last mover into an outdated business model. Its computer aspirations would eventually collapse.

In 1983, just two years after our visit, Jon Shirley decamped for Microsoft, where he became the chief operating officer and, later, a company director, retiring in 2008.

Galloping Hordes

In *Soul of the New Machine*, Tracy Kidder chronicles a technical team's heroic efforts to design Data General's next minicomputer under a very tight deadline. Winner of the 1981 Pulitzer Prize, the book is still widely read. But from a business perspective, it was obsolete before it ever hit the bookstores. By telling coincidence, 1980 was the year IBM famously joined Apple, Commodore, Radio Shack, et al in the PC race when a team of thirteen engineers, led by Phillip ("Don") Estridge, brought its first entry to market in just thirteen months. They did it by using already available parts.

The impact was electrifying, both for the industry and, perhaps especially, for IBM itself. "Snapping pictures" became the watchwords in Armonk. Survival depended on copying concepts and buying components from outside the company to shorten product-development cycles. A snapshot! The economic reasons for relying on mass-produced processors would soon be embraced by much of the computer business. Self-sufficient teams like that described by Kidder would be permanently disbanded.

By the 1980s, half the total PC market was in the hands of a large number of newcomers, including Altos, Compaq, Dynabyte, Exidy, Micropro, North Star, Osborne, Vector Graphics, and about fifty other fingerlings. All built their businesses around the layered model. In the first layer dwelled the microprocessor makers, Intel or Motorola; the second housed operating systems made by either Microsoft or Digital Research; in the third layer were the PC companies themselves, assembling their own boxes; a fourth layer contained Borland, Lotus, WordPerfect, etc., the builders of applications; a fifth layer, like ComputerLand, retailed the final systems; and a sixth layer installed them. One problem was that, at lower layers, the model quickly led to near monopoly, or at least market dominance, by one or two players.

The tidal wave of new competitors shared three characteristics. First, despite endless talk about the scientific geniuses behind each venture, it was almost impossible to differentiate one product from the next. "What's the difference between all these companies we've visited?" we asked Paul Ely, HP's head of computer products, in 1983. "There isn't any," he said. Or, as we discovered, none worth mentioning. The flamboyant Adam Osborne and his eponymous computer company tried to attract buyers with an embedded suite of office automation and a portable "form factor" with all the appeal of an army mess kit. Only Apple offered any real innovation.

For his part, Ely thought the future would belong to PCs that offered ubiquitous networking to IBM mainframes as well as to HP's minis. He was right—though at the time, the early movers were largely interested in stand-alones. In hindsight, anyone who thought PCs could reach their current level of ubiquity without access to the Internet was almost delusional.

A second characteristic of many of the early firms—which turned out to be a mistake—was their embrace of the minicomputer's already-obsolete processing model in which up to four dumb terminals were attached to a single microprocessor through Digital Research's CP/M. Sharing a *personal* computer hardly seemed hygienic, we quipped. But a more serious flaw was the lash-up's sluggishness and tendency to fail.

Finally, the cadre of new PC company executives spent more time selecting and seducing indirect distribution channels such as the computer stores than they spent worrying about end users. In the early years, their unwise preoccupation with retailers left the enterprise market to the establishment vendors–largely IBM and Hewlett-Packard–which had strong direct-sales presences in those accounts. In later years, their misplaced attention accelerated the disappearance of the smaller PC companies as store chains–such as one-time leader ComputerLand–collapsed, leaving the manufacturers without viable sales channels. One problem was that customers would tie up clerks with endless questions about the different computers and then buy from a discounter. Clearly, a bad business model. The newer retailers reserved their shelf space for brands with customer recognition—IBM, of course, but also Compaq, Toshiba, Apple, and a few others with well-known names. The multitude of machines outside the customer's immediate awareness were quickly swept from retailers' shelves. Looking back, any hope that the stores would help drive the sales of no-name PCs was simply ridiculous.

The Unfit Fail the Darwinian Test

Profiles of the early leaders bear out our conclusion. With so much attention given to the indirect channels, CEOs often ignored the enterprise market. And the chore of meeting us was usually left to marketing people, who, unfortunately, couldn't answer routine questions about business models, technical product differentiation, and the like.

Just so at Osborne Computer, the company Adam Osborne had founded in 1980 with the idea of bundling standard office software on a low-cost luggable computer. Thousands of his PCs were shipped in each of the company's first few years, and we were eager to learn more about the company. But when we arrived in Hayward, California, for a chat in 1983, the brilliant, photogenic, and press-pleasing Osborne was nowhere to be seen. Instead, we were greeted by a sour young woman who announced herself as the marketing vice president.

After treating us to a whirlwind tour of the showroom to admire the mess kits, our less-than-friendly guide set about spinning our questions. The Osborne's low, low $1,700 price, she informed us, was the product of a magic mix of corporate philosophy, tight product design, no frills, no advertising, no R&D staff, and a management team betting most of their salaries on stock options. Hmm. We had read rumors of real problems, and nothing we'd learned from our hostess put our minds at ease.

"That company's done," declared the always intuitive Naomi a few moments later as we made our way back to the car. I tossed my careful notes on the back seat and drove to the next PC appointment. A week or so later, the company declared bankruptcy under a mountain of debt. After a brief resurfacing, the company disappeared. Adam returned to India, where he'd spent much of his childhood, and died in March 2003.

At Altos Computer in San Jose, California, the staccato-talking CEO, David Jackson, had positioned the company against the minicomputer makers "with their five-to-one markups." Unfortunately, Altos's multi-user operating system didn't work that well. Moreover, Altos didn't have the minicomputer companies' brand recognition or field force to sell and maintain the hardware, not to mention that its total system was priced just 30 percent below its minicomputer equivalent when 75 percent might have been more realistic. Nevertheless, Jackson managed to keep Altos afloat for several more years.

At Vector Graphics in Thousand Oaks, California, the beginning was different, but the company's ending was depressingly similar to what we'd observed elsewhere. Founded in 1976 by two homemakers, Lore Harp and Carol Ely, to sell the circuit boards designed by Harp's clever computer-scientist husband, Vector produced its first PCs two years later. CEO Harp and her partner Ely successfully won significant retail shelf space through a determined combination of nifty packaging, advertising, user manuals, and personal attention to store owners. Their approach worked well at first. Sales stood at $25 million in 1981, and the company's initial public offering had garnered $12 million just before our visit.

But the bloom was already beginning to fade. As the market grew more crowded, retailers were demanding sales pull from a standout brand rather than hand-holding from its vendor. And after the Harps divorced, both the management team and Vector's product-development operation fragmented. Priced between $9,000 and $30,000, Vector PCs competed against minicomputers, and adding no-name word processing and spreadsheet applications didn't help much. The development of Vector's own idiosyncratic local area network (LAN) seemed to be a negative as well. "We can't wait for the Ethernet standard to gel," confessed the sad-eyed vice president of marketing as he slouched into the meeting room to explain that the bosses were otherwise engaged. We weren't surprised to learn that dealers and retailers were no longer a reliable source of growth. So an eleventh-hour effort was under way to connect with office-equipment suppliers and low-end consulting firms who might be more loyal, our host explained. The company was even considering sending its own field reps to visit prospective customers, a bid to override the retailer's "come see me" mentality.

After leaving Vector, we met with ComputerLand CEO Edward Faber, who told us how much he personally admired Harp and Ely. Unfortunately, the retail chain was already being sucked into a downdraft. Most of its stores would be closed by 1990.

A Survivor in Name Only

Datapoint was perhaps the minicomputer company best positioned to survive the transition to PCs. Occasionally, it's even described as the first PC company. After all, the earliest microprocessors had been designed for its PC-predecessor workstations. Moreover, it had taken an early lead in both peer networking and "client-server" computing. Certainly, its founder and chief technologist, Vic Poore, was an unusually astute assessor and implementer of future technologies. But none of that was enough to keep Datapoint from suffering an early demise.

Formed in 1968 as Computer Terminal Products (CTC), its engineer-founders stumbled on a eureka in 1970 with their invention of the Datapoint programmable terminal that could simultaneously serve as a remote dumb terminal attached to a mainframe and a support system for certain local applications. The Datapoint terminal won rapid acceptance in small offices within large enterprises, where it processed order-entry, local payroll, inventory, expense-reporting, and the like. Its lucky stumble was transformed into a *jeté de danse* by IBM's reluctance to recognize that anything could be processed anywhere without big, expensive mainframes. On that note, "dispersed processing," CTC's market-blitzing concept for the Datapoint, was "partially an accident, in all candor," recalled Poore.

By 1972, the company was working on the first microprocessors at Texas Instruments. Subsequently, it developed the industry's first local area network, the Attached Resource Computer (ARC), which could link up to 255 workstations using either coaxial cable or—more tantalizing—wireless infrared links. Datapoint gave exciting demonstrations of "light" links between its twenty-three San Antonio-area office buildings, but the buzz waned when the links proved totally impractical in other business settings.

Microprocessors, LANs, wireless connections—Datapoint had all the technological underpinnings of a successful PC entrant. What it didn't have in those early years was good management from its engineer-founders. After their stumbling produced losses totaling $6 million in 1971 and 1972, the investors rebelled and recruited a new CEO from Harris Intertype. Harold O'Kelley was a flamboyant guy who quickly changed the company's name to Datapoint, and then spent three years building a sales and service organization (under the lean, aggressive leadership of Edward Gistaro), introducing new products, and rebuilding credibility among investors.

In 1977, with revenues moving smartly higher, O'Kelley made two eventually questionable acquisitions: a disk manufacturer and the supplier of an add-on feature to office telephone switches (i.e., PBXs), which chose "least-cost routing" for still expensive long-distance telephone calls. The boom roared on at Datapoint. Revenues rose 53 percent in 1978 and another 43 percent in 1979, the year we visited. Even more dazzling were the earnings increases in those years, 82 percent and 65 percent, respectively. Datapoint's accounting treatment of its leased equipment was quite muscular, as well; it used the double-declining-balance method over four years, as opposed to the five-year, straight-line method employed by early casualties like Four Phase. Wall Street cheered. So did the MIS executives, who saw Datapoint as a lead exponent of the new distributed-computing paradigm.

But the company began to feel outside pressures nonetheless. First was the entry of three different IBM divisions into the minicomputer market. Soon the PC would nibble, then gobble, market share in the distributed workstation sector. Perhaps as a defensive reaction, executive eyes became fixated on the "integrated electronic office," which was aimed at uniting data, text, and voice in the next growth wave. The 1979 annual report was festooned with quasi-comic renderings by three artists commissioned to "let our concept of the integrated office spark the imagination." O'Kelley opened a civilized lunch with us at his club by declaring that the integrated office was the key to American productivity growth, adding that his executive team's resolve was unwavering. Less clear were his responses on why he had also decided to acquire an underscaled semiconductor facility "for quality" purposes, or why he wanted to develop a word-processing system. Neither seemed likely to achieve the volumes necessary to survive.

During Vic Poore's tenure, two favorite themes had emerged. First, like An Wang, he believed the integrated office would be the primary, perhaps only, market for computers over the next five years. In hindsight, he was nearly right but also fatally wrong. The office did indeed become a huge market—but for commodity PCs, not proprietary minis—and voice and data wouldn't be profitably integrated for another twenty-five years, initially in the smart phone. Poore's second-favorite vision was a paean to "small is beautiful." He envisioned many large problems being solved by linking small computers—hence, "attached resource computer" or ARC—rather than big, ugly mainframes or even large minicomputers.

It turned out that Poore would eventually be proven correct, at least for certain applications; witness Google and the million-odd processors in its "grid computing." But Datapoint would have been better served had Poore developed a Unix-based server strategy. And, clearly, he didn't see the microprocessor as affecting much more than manufacturing costs.

Only field boss Ed Gistaro offered a more nuanced perspective. Gistaro was a most insightful marketer and effective sales executive whose perspective mixed hardheaded realism with reactive opportunism. "No one can be sure our next idea will be as good as our last," he once said to me, "even though integrated office is our attack strategy and a market we will be able to serve with a uniquely coherent product line." But if it didn't work, the company could always fall back on the old reliable dispersed-computing concept. "We'll take the approach we've taken in the past: Extend what we're doing anyway, building on existing products and capabilities."

In the end, that approach wouldn't be enough.

Over the next three years, total revenues doubled, but mostly on maintenance charges, an unhealthy sign. Growth in new-product sales lagged, suggesting that Datapoint was losing its technology edge. In that light, the office focus, the product-development plan, and especially O'Kelley's acquisitions could be seen as serious errors. Microsoft's operating system would squash any low-volume, low-capacity proprietary alternative. The industry-standard Ethernet (and, to a lesser extent, IBM's token ring) would drive ARC from the market. (Indeed, a plaintive note in one web site chronology marks 1984 as the year "the first networked computer failed to reach critical mass.") In-house disk manufacturing would be uneconomical against the high-volume suppliers entering the PC market. The telephone add-on never added anything to the product strategy and was actually a distraction. The semiconductor facility was almost quixotic in its lack of utility. Another word-processing package would be quickly swept away by WordPerfect and, eventually, Microsoft Word. We concluded that O'Kelley, Poore, and Gistaro were either blind to the PC threat or simply incapable of executing a radical enough plan to jettison the baggage of prior success and move forward.

In 1984, Gistaro asked to meet us in New York for dinner and a strategy discussion. After we had exhausted still-feasible resurrection strategies, Ed asked, with a mixture of belligerence and pathos, "Well, what would you do with Datapoint?" "Sell it to the Japanese," we responded coolly and none too helpfully, especially considering that the Japanese were already in retreat as well.

The next year, corporate raider Asher Edelman seized control of the company, reconstituted the board with a majority of his own people, and ousted Harold O'Kelley, naming Gistaro as CEO. The press release, dated March 15, 1985, noted that several activities were being readied for a quick sale or a spin-off, including both manufacturing plants and the field-maintenance organization, which, as a New York Stock Exchange-listed company with the symbol IT, reported 1986 revenues of over $150 million.

But other than chewing the bones, the banquet was over. In 1999, the remnants, including the Datapoint name, were sold to a British firm for just $50 million and the assumption of $10 million in debt. Today's Datapoint is a U.K.-headquartered software integrator with four hundred people specializing in call-center operations; a help-desk operator can call up the customer's file on her PC screen as she answers questions over the telephone. In that sense, voice and data have been integrated after all.

Bleak Vistas

The PC pioneers too often drowned in the onrushing wave. The cottage software industry promised by the pundits never materialized, and of the ninety lucky start-ups that were showered with $180 million by venture capitalists in 1985, few provided a satisfactory return. Microsoft is the only mega-PC software company left; enterprise-applications suppliers Oracle and SAP occupy the next two spots. These three plus IBM account for well over half of total software revenues.

Whether a PC first mover or a well-positioned minicomputer maker like Datapoint, their stories ended badly. Not one of the top three PC hardware companies in 2000 were first movers in the 1980s. HP is a survivor from an earlier era, and Dell rose to its premier position by ignoring the babble about staking out preferences in the retail chains and, instead, selling direct to customers. Compaq, a true early mover, befuddled itself by acquiring DEC and Tandem; it was later acquired by HP. Gateway, though a relatively new entry, doddered into an acquisition by Taiwan's Acer. IBM sold its PC business to China's Lenovo. The market will ultimately belong to Asia.

Chapter 7

DEFEATED IN SUCCESSION:

An Wang at Wang Labs

The always thorny question of timing the retirement of a successful CEO and choosing a successor can get even pricklier when the CEO is also the founder. Too often the board of directors has retreated into complacency and dependency after years of strong leadership. Too often the CEO is left to choose his own end date—which invariably gets extended when growing turbulence threatens the greying legend's legacy.

An Wang was arguably the most brilliant CEO we ever encountered. The visionary inventor and grit-practical engineer had navigated his company through perilous straits for more than twenty years, moving from one technology wave to another with no discernible heavy breathing. Wang tended toward the ascetic, as his autobiography makes clear: "In general, I do not have much interest in the ostentation that is commonly associated with being the CEO of a large corporation. At any one time, I only own two suits, which I replace when they wear out. I prefer to have lunch by myself, and I generally use the time to read and think."[1] Today, Wang is revered by bloggers as a near cult figure, complete with posters and a book of sayings, though his former shareholders might hold a different view.

In the business world, An Wang's imprint was writ large, but especially in the daring leaps, minimalist product design, and rabid rush to market that were the hallmarks of Wang Laboratories. All of the important decisions were his—initially, to good effect. The other members of the management team were active in their own endeavors. John Cunningham, a brash, young ex-IBM sales representative nurtured by Dr. Wang and reportedly dubbed the "American son" by Mrs. Wang, oversaw sales and field maintenance. Manufacturing and finance were run by Harry Chou, a long-time friend of Wang who was smart, sensible, and seldom visible outside the company. Finally, there was the real son, Frederick Wang, a Brown University computer-science graduate who was in perpetual training to succeed his father as head of engineering, if not the entire company.

It was our practice to spend two days with significant vendors, leaving the CEO interview until the end to pull all the pieces together, clear up any misconceptions, and provide feedback on our impressions of the company's direction and management. All of these sessions were interesting and some were contentious, but none was more memorable than those with An Wang.

I remember sitting at a long, paper-cluttered table with Dr. Wang at the head, Naomi and I on either side, interweaving our sharp, or so we judged, questions from left and right. Wang, seemingly engrossed in office memoranda, would serenely cup our firecrackers and toss back the proper responses without pause. No other CEO exhibited such benign indifference to our efforts. At the end, he would look up, bright eyes beaming above a perfectly tied bowknot, and ask, "How's Fred doing?" We liked Fred and generally reported positively on some aspect of his efforts, to which the father would shake his head and respond, "Fred has a lot to learn." In a sense, that remark presages the end story of Wang Laboratories.

The "Indispensable Leader," from the Beginning

"The Doctor," as An Wang was called by everyone at headquarters, had been educated in China, where he formed an overarching respect for the Chinese culture and its sense of family obligation. In his autobiography, he disclosed that, "Like many Chinese families, we had a written history that would be updated every couple of generations by an affluent member of the family. These books gave our families a sense of continuity and permanence that I don't see in the more mobile West."[2] The book covered twenty-five generations with great certitude, and the twenty-five before with a bit less.

At age twenty-five, Wang immigrated to Boston. He had survived the Japanese invasion, an experience he recalled fifty years later when dismissing any chance of a sale or alliance with one of the Japanese technology giants: "In the 1930s, I fought them in Shanghai; today, they're doing the same thing economically [that] they once did militarily," he told us.

After receiving a Harvard doctorate in electrical engineering and one of the first patents on "core" memory, Wang began the small technology company that, in its first thirteen years, would inch ahead to revenues of just $1.3 million on "special systems." Then came a pioneering and successful foray into electronic calculators, which provided enough lift for an IPO in 1964. When that wave crested in 1969 with the arrival of competitors from far larger semiconductor companies, the careful pilot had already plotted a new course toward the intersection of office automation and distributed processing. Product announcements came just three years later in 1972. Bull's-eye! Wang Labs' revenues sizzled, going from $178 million in 1977 to $500 million in 1979, settling the company comfortably among the *Fortune* 500 before our first visit.

An Wang's autobiographical recollections are interesting not only as a portrait of the man but as an indication of what would and would not follow fifteen years later. "As we struggled to develop computers," he wrote, "our calculator sales continued to grow, but disturbing signs made me wonder how long the calculator business would remain profitable. By 1970, our sales had grown to about twenty-seven million dollars and we employed fourteen hundred people. Our earnings remained strong at three million dollars, but the price of calculators was plummeting as competition increased from other companies....

"Most of this pressure fell on the simplest of the calculators. By 1971, the base price of our 300 series had dropped to six hundred dollars.... I could see the price of the basic calculator dropping to a hundred dollars in the not-too-distant future."

Equally ominous was the imminent appearance of semiconductor chips containing all the circuits of a calculator. Both situations argued for abandoning the calculator business, though it represented 70 percent of total revenue. For Wang Labs, dropping the calculator business would be like IBM dropping its mainframe business.

"Still, after a few weeks consideration," Wang recalled, "I decided that we had to do it. And once I decided to get out, I spent another week considering how to do it. I decided we should disengage in stages.

That meant that we would stop pushing the 300 series, as well as the 200 and even the 100 series, which we had just introduced. We would continue to push the 700, the 600, and the 400 calculators, which because of their sophistication were somewhat insulated from the pressure to lower prices. We also redoubled our efforts to find new markets we might explore."[3]

John Cunningham argued against the exit, as the Doctor made a point of mentioning. But prices plunged so dramatically that calculators were soon given away as sales promotions. The inescapable conclusion was that An Wang truly was, as he himself believed, the indispensable leader in any grave situation. He was the one who could make sense out of a confusing situation and pilot his company to a safe landing. That safe landing would be in the field of minicomputers.

We first visited Wang Laboratories at its old Tewksbury, Massachusetts, headquarters in 1980, a full year after our tour of the other minicomputer makers and only after a loud complaint from Dave Blackwell, the chief information officer at Mass Mutual. He was clearly right on this one, notwithstanding our initial judgment that Wang Labs' haphazard manufacturing and indifferent field service rendered the product line too flimsy to be taken seriously. What we had missed was its role in filling a basic need for office systems among the huge "paper-flow" insurance companies and banks that others, notably IBM and Xerox, had badly fumbled.

Not surprisingly, given our late—by half an hour or several years— arrival, no one was especially glad to see us, despite a boldly visible "welcome visitor" sign with our names plugged into the appropriate slots. For about twenty minutes, we sat waiting in a corner of an oversize reception area teeming with customers.

"We aren't jumping up and down for more prospects," announced a belligerently grumpy Cunningham when he finally appeared. Wang Labs couldn't handle any more orders as large as that from RB board member Equitable Life, he announced, and, besides, we might write something negative. Somehow, we negotiated a temporary truce, and, in years to come, we would actually become friends.

Over the next two days, we interviewed many members of the Wang management group. All were totally convinced of the Doctor's genius for discerning exactly which functions the market would pay for, while avoiding senseless frills that could only confuse customers and slow product rollouts. In separate interviews with four Wang executives, each using almost the same words, we were told: "The Velvet Hammer [a fond nickname for Dr. Wang] asks an R&D team to develop a particular product. If they estimate two years until completion, he'll say one year. They'll settle on fifteen months and are grateful to finish in twenty. That's still a four-month advantage over the competition."

One of the company's characteristically snappy ad campaigns featured a baby dangling a lightning bolt. "If the baby were replaced by an elderly scientist keeping the lightning bolt on a short leash, the image could be an appropriate company logo," we wrote after that visit.

In such an environment, manufacturing and field service were merely a sideshow, managed without much interest or attention by Chou and Cunningham, respectively. Neither was much effort devoted to designing products that could be manufactured efficiently and with high quality. To the contrary, one could almost imagine engineers tossing the factory their just-developed boxes with wires left flopping out the sides. Customer assessments of sales and service were generally mediocre as well. Cunningham blamed the situation on the frothy 65 percent annual growth rate in the installed base, adding, "But we are pleased it wasn't worse in the midst of such expansion. Our wage scales are below the industry average; we'll remedy that." In terms of compensation, Wang seemed stuck in the calculator era.

Fred Wang was nominally responsible for product development, with intermittent coaching from his father. "Rudimentary" was the word Fred most often used to encapsulate the company's minimalist design philosophy: "We offer enough technology for most of our customers already. In fact, some products in development probably go too far.... Our calendaring may be rudimentary, but the real barrier to use is that people don't enter their appointments into the system.... Our message system is rudimentary, but few customers need more because they're still experimenting. I don't even have a terminal because my 'boss' [father] doesn't have one. Overall, we offer all the right technological capabilities our customers want right now."

In our report, we imagined Dr. Wang "watching new ideas emerge from his shop like flies hatching on a windowsill. Most he swats as frivolous before they can take wing, even though some may actually be honeybees...." Would his eyesight remain sharp enough to differentiate the honeybees from the houseflies?

For now, the company gained mightily from its leader's brilliance in product development, from John Cunningham's energetic flair for powering the sales force, and from the weakness of the competition in Wang's secretarial market. IBM's swarm of minicomputers gave off lots of buzz but failed to erode Wang's market in any significant way, partly because its new office systems were overwhelmingly user-hostile. The other large minicomputer companies generally steered clear of both the financial-services and clerical-office sectors. Wang raced to maintain what it thought would be an eighteen-month advantage, but, as Fred remembered some years later, it actually lasted for five years. Wang Labs reported revenues of $850 million for 1980, with future growth projected at "only" 40 percent, assuming Europe could be turned around, Cunningham said.

Startling to us was Wang's dominance of the financial-services field, which once was staunchly "true blue." Twenty-four top accounts, many in banking and insurance, now generated $86 million in revenues, despite Wang's stingy seven percent volume discount. Cunningham hoped that accounts like these would eventually provide half of total revenues, with the other half coming from indirect channels.

The largest question mark for us in 1981 was the 6,000-strong, system-maintenance organization, or "Customer Engineering" as it was known at Wang. A big plus was vice president Ray Cullen, a tough chief petty officer type, complete with a taste for unfiltered Lucky Strikes, who applied a new boot to the field force. The average time it took a Wangster to reach a downed customer had been tightened from a horrendous ten hours to a nearly respectable three. Two years earlier, Customer Engineering had lost forty-three cents on every dollar; now it turned a marginal profit, largely because of price increases. And looking ahead to 1982, a 10 percent profit on service revenues was expected, mostly as a result of tougher management and an insistence on productivity metrics.

Worrisome was the continued absence of remote diagnostics embedded into the equipment like Digital and IBM repairmen used to connect to a downed computer from their offices. They could determine if the customer was doing something wrong or what parts to bring if something was broken, thus saving a second call.

All Wang had was a new dispatching system and better training, which allowed a slight reduction in its average three-and-a-half-hour repair time. "To do much better, we would need embedded hooks and handles in the equipment," Fred Wang told us before reminding us that those things "took years to develop" in other companies. Hoping to soothe our concerns, he explained that "since most hardware failures are mechanical, we still have to dispatch someone" and, hence, there would be little cost advantage.

Remote software diagnostics, we concluded, remained far beyond the horizon, given Dr. Wang's minimalist focus. "We're not really into [remote diagnostics] yet," Fred confessed. "We generally assume the problem can be found on-site by studying the core dump [a listing of what is happening inside the computer memory]. And our software has so many layers that diagnostics would be difficult to develop.... I guess we're not very sophisticated in that area."

"Dangerously uncompetitive" was a better description, we thought.

A Cullen lieutenant confirmed that engineering didn't see remote diagnostics as critical, "given their resource priorities," and Cullen himself told us that "the company doesn't like conflict." A very apt— and, in our view, worrying—assessment.

Within a few years, field maintenance would be Wang's most important source of revenue growth, reflecting not superior performance but increased maintenance charges to a (temporarily) captive customer base. Disproportionate revenue growth from maintenance too often signals a hardware or software company in early decline.

Whither (or Whether) "Wang Without Wang"?

In 1981, An Wang passed what would have been his mandatory retirement age if he were running IBM. Amid successes in sales and product development, it was the right moment to make the first moves toward "Wang without Wang." And, indeed, the Doctor made a preemptive effort to devolve power to a five-person management committee consisting of father, son, Harry Chou, Cunningham, and the company's new manufacturing vice president, Jon Kropper. There was even a rotating chairmanship, announced Cunningham buoyantly, "so when Dr. Wang steps down, there will be an established group at the top to run the company."

But a year later, the new committee still lacked purpose and clout, leaving the issue of succession unresolved as well. The *Wall Street Journal* (April 21, 1982) chortled: "Will the son also rise? And if he does, how will the company satisfy a hard-charging 38-year-old executive who isn't a son?

"An Wang, founder, chairman and president of fast-growing Wang Laboratories Inc., is only 62 years old. But the word processing and computer industry is already wondering what role is in store for Mr. Wang's 31-year-old son Frederick. Last July, Frederick became a senior vice president of the company and last October, he was named a director, too.

"Frederick clearly is doing nicely for his age. But if he succeeds his father, the company could lose John F. Cunningham, the young executive vice president. His marketing skills were important in the company's 12-year rise to a position challenging IBM and Xerox for leadership in office automation. Questions about his future role at Wang Laboratories have already placed the executive's name high on headhunter shopping lists, industry sources say.

"Whatever the senior Mr. Wang decides will probably prevail. As of last September, he and Mrs. Wang, along with a Wang family trust, owned 55 percent of the company's Class C Common shares, whose holders elect three-quarters of the company's directors."

Early Signs of Decay

For the November 1982 visit, the Wang-arranged service dispatched an enormous white stretch limousine to meet Naomi and me at Boston's Logan Airport—to the absolute delight of the young researcher who accompanied us. But at the end of our visit, no limo appeared. Its driver, as we learned from the replacement who appeared an hour later, had stolen the car and was even then speeding toward destinations unknown. Was it an omen?

Wang was also ending an enormous building expansion, moving from one 300,000-square-foot building to three dead-white towers totaling 2.3 million square feet and costing $60 million. Another omen? We couldn't help but reflect on how often such building bonanzas erupt at what is actually the apogee of a company's fortune and just before the beginning of a terminal slide. Already squashed by 1982 were one-time minicomputer stalwarts like Computer Automation, General Automation, and Modcomp.

Any transition to "Wang without Wang" was off to a terrible start. In engineering, control had either passed to Fred, as Cunningham insisted, or it hadn't, as he also implied ambiguously. Too much distance was opening between product developers and those field people closest to the market. But, otherwise, he told us, "Fred has given the effort some direction. There were hundreds of projects without a budget or proper controls. We've reached the point where we need structure more than genius." It was hard to discern much discipline, however. R&D expense had increased from 6.5 percent of revenues to 7.8 percent, reflecting precisely a weakness in budget and structure, we thought. Wang's recent string of product gaffes was sufficient proof of an endemic problem.

The most visible failure was its stand-alone word processor, the Wangwriter—boisterously pre-announced two years earlier as the answer to IBM's successful Displaywriter, but quickly given up for dead, according to Cunningham. No matter the 1980 photograph in *Electronic News* of John with his arm draped avuncularly around the new electronic hope, or Fred, in similar pose for *Business Week*. "Wang expects to produce 10,000 units over the next twelve months," duly repeated an attentive press. Too bad the company shipped only 1,600, while an unfazed IBM moved 200,000 Displaywriters over the same twelve months.

The day of the Wangwriter had already passed. So where was a PC project befitting the founder's minimalist design strategy? It had been handed off to Fred as little more than a defensive, even desultory project bootstrapped over the objections (or at least disinterest) of the Doctor. Fred's view was at once brave and defensive: "These things bucked the tide of conventional product development procedures in every large company, from IBM onward. And perhaps the skeptics are right. The personal computer could still turn out to be a fad. But more likely, ours will assume a strategic role as an intelligent workstation and emerging replacement for the 2200" (the aging Wang word processor that had once cut a swath through the doddering competition). But Fred's hopeful scenario never came to pass. It wasn't even clear that Fred had the organizational stature to do more than substitute a microprocessor for Wang's own circuits, never mind pressuring his father to implement the harsh cuts necessary to execute the rest of the PC business model.

There were other miscues as well. A new voice-mail system failed because it was initially overpriced for the departmental market, where many of Wang's sales were made, and because the Wang sales force had a difficult time selling at the corporate VP level. On-and-off efforts to consolidate Wang's diverse product families were repeatedly ensnared in internal politics and rendered irrelevant as microprocessors chewed up Wang's low-end entries. The company bought a majority stake in Telenova, a small PBX (private branch exchange) telephone-switch company, presumably in concert with the industry's lemming-like march toward the "integrated office."

It also built its own broadband Wang Net to support the so-called convergence of voice, data, and image that management deemed inevitable, though the idea would take another twenty years to develop. There was also a rather goofy effort to create a personal-image computer, with the single function of handling graphs and pictures—though it did help Wang achieve long-term success in business image processing.

Some of these ideas were probably hatched by the Doctor. But it was Fred's leadership that sparked a growing chorus of skepticism in the middle-management ranks. Despite having earned a computer-science degree, Fred was viewed as "not an engineer like his father." At age thirty-two, he was simply much too young, his critics claimed, before observing that, "when Dr. Wang was thirty-two, he only had two employees; he didn't have Fred's management burdens." Fred was overly enamored of future technology at the expense of bread-and-butter products, we were told: "He's never even used one of our word processors." Nor could he lead as well as his father, whom "everyone really loves," we heard over and over again. "Fred will push a product schedule, but he can't make people feel they've really ever succeeded." There was a seemingly endless chorus of criticism directed at Fred. Meanwhile, product life cycles were shortening throughout the industry, placing an even-greater premium on strong and focused leadership.

Only Harry Chou remained cautiously optimistic about Wang without Wang: "The press overemphasizes the importance of Dr. Wang. He's important, but he doesn't run everything. The company can turn the corner without him." The Doctor himself gave a more nuanced response to our question concerning the company's greatest challenge: "Of course, how the company will manage without me. It should be possible if we maintain coherence and all work together."

After the formal interview ended with the usual "How's Fred doing?" the father proceeded: "I must impress on Fred not to dwell only on day-to-day concerns but observe the wider horizons, new communications methods, satellites, multi-write videodiscs, PBXs. My goal is to make the organization recognize these trends, not to design specific hardware. And by 'organization,' I mean not just Fred and his immediate subordinates, but the entire 1,700-person engineering operation."

Was Wang delusional or willfully blind to the realities? Satellites? Multi-write videodiscs? PBXs? None would have a mainstream impact on office computing. The only things that really mattered day to day were execution in product development and the PC. Wang had neither. What it had was the sorry Wangwriter. Perhaps, we speculated, the splendid minimalist was merely deflecting our attention from a planned giant product leap beyond the PC.

In any case, Wang's retirement wasn't really a problem—because it wasn't remotely a reality. One sure signal was the hole chopped between the top-floor executive penthouse and the engineering floor just below to accommodate a staircase near the elevator bank. "That penthouse wasn't very Wang-like," smiled a veteran executive. "The Doctor decided the floor separations were a visible sign that some of our executives were losing touch with their managers and with daily operations."

More important, perhaps, the staircase let "the roamer" (another of Wang's in-house nicknames) drop in freely and frequently on the development managers, effectively undercutting his son. Very Wang-like, but not the way to move toward Wang-after-Wang, we agreed. No matter—given the continuing revenue gains (whatever the source), it was easy to ignore those pesky Wall Street analysts who were beginning to carp about margin pressures and product delays.

The "American Son" Makes a Move

Throughout our 1982 visit, John Cunningham seemed visibly distracted, while Fred calmly surveyed product plans, wreckage and all. Was an organizational overhaul imminent?

A few weeks later, our suspicions were confirmed when Cunningham was named president and chief operating officer responsible for sales, service, and manufacturing, while An Wang remained chairman and CEO. Harry Chou, Fred, the developers, and various family retainers were among the Doctor's direct reports.

A year later, we saw Cunningham at his best—a quick and savvy conversationalist who peppered his talk with sharp insights about the competition and the computer industry in general. Too bad John's vision didn't stretch beyond the East Coast: His greatest fear was that IBM would turn predatory. During that 1983 visit, the American son never mentioned personal computers but still seemed hopeful that he might yet prevail, or, at least, that he might gain equal footing at the governance table.

At one point, Cunningham earnestly recounted an elk hunt while sitting out in the rain in a blind with David Packard, the cofounder of Hewlett-Packard, when the discussion turned to family trusts. "As soon as I got back, we got the lawyers to establish a Wang trust so that even after both the Doctor and Mrs. Wang are dead, they won't lose a thing." Wouldn't lose a thing after death! Naomi and I marveled at the disconnect on the flight home. But, of course, trust planning was something that a "good son" would do.

Dr. Wang bounded down the hall to find us as we were saying our good-byes to Cunningham. Perhaps he was late for a meeting, or maybe he was hoping to dispel whispered rumors of his inactivity or illness. In any event, our subsequent conversation was disconcerting.

For the 1983 report, we were canvassing industry leaders for their opinions about which technologies would dominate the 1990s. Absent from the Doctor's response were his year-earlier plans for videodiscs, satellites, and PBXs. Now he contended that looking more than three years into the future was a waste of time. But not to worry, Wang assured us, the computing price/performance ratio would continue to improve by 20 percent annually, though three-quarters of the gain would be chewed up by improved user interfaces. "Was he referring to the Mac?" we wondered. Nevertheless, prices would remain roughly flat. Demand, however, was a different story. "There will be no slowdown in demand," Wang proclaimed, "until the ratio between office computers and employees is the same as between office telephones and employees today." Wang was totally prescient about the race, but he had saddled the wrong horse. Less and less expensive PCs, not Wangwriters, would soon appear on every desk.

At least publicly, the careful pilot still refused to grasp—or perhaps accept—that the PC was the only new item on his horizon that would actually ignite an important new market. It would also elbow aside his equipment in its traditional markets, destroy his placid price/performance projection, and even undermine his company's field-service revenue. "Seventy percent of PCs in corporations are still gathering dust," he mused a moment later.

It was a critical juncture; the time had come to choose one of two directions: either join the PC crowd by moving Wang's already popular word-processing and office software to a Microsoft or Apple platform with the hope of selling millions of copies around the world, while gradually edging out of the hardware business. Or, less plausibly, Wang could recommit to the minimalist approach of emphasizing simplicity and lower cost over the gewgaws that characterized the company's later years and added cost but generated little market interest. Either path would have required clear thinking, massive downsizing, and the assumption of considerable risk, given the coming shakeout.

It's too easy to fault the Doctor for his blind spot about technology. It's likely that he fully understood the PC's implications for Wang's business model but simply couldn't bring himself to fire two-thirds of his workers. That wouldn't have been "Wang-like." No one is less able to navigate a dramatic shift in business model than the *pater familias.*

By 1984, much of the minicomputer sector was in terminal collapse. Steve Jobs had introduced the Mac; the Microsoft/IBM relationship was starting to unravel; and Datapoint's field boss, Ed Gistaro, would soon badger us for survival ideas over dinner. But Dr. Wang couldn't—or wouldn't—accept the potential power of the PC revolution barreling toward him, even when championed by his son Fred.

Neither would the Doctor step down, though battling throat cancer. Worse still, neither he nor the family retainers would allow Fred or John or anyone else to make the hard decisions necessary for the company's survival. Wang's autobiography recounts the fateful end of a last-ditch attempt at succession: "A few years earlier, in 1982, I had stepped back somewhat from the day-to-day operations of the company in order to give my executive team room to maneuver. In 1983, I designated John Cunningham as president. John, a Wang employee since 1967, came to the job by virtue of the work he had done building the sales organization of the company. He had shown that he could really motivate a sales force, and he also served as a superb spokesman in dealing with the financial community. In late 1984, however, as the computer business began to soften and our problems began to deepen, I felt it was necessary for me to move back into a more active role in running the company."[4]

The most destructive problems, though, weren't sales-related; product development was the issue, and that was Fred's bailiwick. No matter, John Cunningham soon departed for Computer Consoles, where he became the CEO. Headlines in the trade press screamed: "Top Spot Eludes Cunningham" (*Computer World,* July 29, 1985) and "Why Wang's American Son Left Home" (*Business Week,* August 5, 1985). Jon Kropper, the VP Manufacturing, soon followed Cunningham out the door.

To anyone paying attention, the obvious reason for Cunningham's departure was his realization that he could never supplant the natural heir. A few years later, he told us he'd lost so many battles to Fred as to make his COO title meaningless and his job a dead end. In retrospect, he would have been the logical successor as CEO and perhaps the only person capable of navigating the family collisions and collusions to make the drastic cost cuts necessary for long-term survival.

But a reading of An Wang's autobiography suggests that the outcome was foreordained: "This philosophy [of entrepreneurial control]," he wrote, "also influences the way I view the larger question of family control. As the founder, I would like to maintain sufficient control so that my children might have the chance to demonstrate whether they can run the company without fearing to take a risk or two. But the question of how far one should go to maintain family control of a publicly held company is a delicate one. All other things being equal, my children should be more highly motivated than a professional manager because of their substantial stake in the ownership of the company."[5] In other words, any professional manager brought to Wang was at a disadvantage from day one.

By our November 1984 visit, the company was in free fall, and the top management structure seemed almost Byzantine and certainly in disarray. Carl Masi and Robert Doretti headed up sales, but when we asked who reported to whom, they responded that "the reporting relationship is so sensitive that only Dr. Wang can explain it." It was vintage Wang—competition without conflict. Both seemed cheerful and totally satisfied with the soon-to-be-released quarterly financial results—and a good thing, too, given the previous quarter's $196 million flood of red ink. But when the profit proved to be a paper-thin $9 million, we could only wonder at their unwarranted self-satisfaction. Without Cunningham, sales productivity would not recover.

Wang Enters a Late Turn

The future of Wang Labs had always depended on its products, and the company would now attempt a strategic turn almost as dramatic as An Wang's shift from calculators to computers fifteen years earlier. And once again, the old and the feeble would be sacrificed to make way for the new, though not without considerable risk. The aging 2200 word processor still had 65,000 installations, and the obsolescent Office Information System (OIS) computer had 90,000, two-thirds of which were in major accounts. The risk of abandoning these customers was far greater than in 1972. At that time, Wang's engineering customers disappointed over the discontinued calculators were generally not in a position to slow sales of word-processing gear. That was not the case when customers for the discontinued office gear were expected to buy the new offerings as well. If customers felt slighted, competitors would welcome their business. Furthermore, abandoning the low-end word-processing market would open the gates to the PC. To reassure the increasingly edgy Wang user group, the company promised to "fully support OIS and 2200 customers. We understand how these products fit into your future," it told them, "and our development plans ensure that you have ample growth paths."

Well, not quite. Just as the smaller calculators had been the first to be discontinued in 1972, no further engineering resources would be expended on Wang's earliest and now least-powerful systems, Dr. Wang confidently told us. And we were convinced after spending a full day discussing product development with senior VP Horace Tsiang and his top staff. Of Tsiang's three hundred hardware engineers, nine hundred programmers, and an assortment of product managers and testers, no one was assigned to revamping either the 2200 word processor or the OIS system. Also abandoned was Wang Net, the quirky and overly ambitious broadband data network. Instead, Wang Labs was on a forced march toward Ethernet and the IBM "systems network architecture." It was a major retreat for the Doctor, and a late one at that.

Only the company's relatively new VS minicomputer series, a line previously led by Tsiang, would be defended against the new breed of Unix servers. One-third of the hardware engineers and 115 systems programmers were charged with doubling the capacity of the high-end processor. But whether it would gain any functional advantages or maintain enough differentiation to stay competitive in the commodity box market was unclear. The continued competitiveness of the low-end minicomputer would depend on a 25 percent price cut.

Wang's next leap forward was apparently a single office box combining telephone, personal computer, fax, scanner, optical character-recognition device, calculator, and file cabinet—"7 to 1 desktop compaction!" the Wangsters boasted. In today's terms, it was "convergence" on steroids. Perhaps a more youthful and vigorous Wang might have carried the day. Although, almost twenty years later, the concept still hasn't been realized, for numerous reasons involving both technology and human factors. To start, the fax, scanner, and optical character-recognition device did indeed converge—but into a PC accessory dominated by Hewlett-Packard. And the convergence of telephones and personal computers began first in wireless phones (to conserve pocket real estate), not desktop computers.

Then there were the technical issues. The telephone piece of Wang's "compaction" rested in part on its 51 percent ownership of Telenova. But when we asked the Telenova chairman over lunch about the $20 million to $30 million of revenues predicted by the press, he said that, actually, his company had yet to make its first sale. So we batted around some small but practical ideas with the Chairman, including a law-office system that would store client telephone numbers and track client call time for subsequent billing. But the Telenova boss decamped for warmer climes soon afterward, and yet another prospect met a dead end.

Likewise, paperless storage—something critical to the office box. At the time, the cost of storing one page image on a magnetic disk ranged between $2.28 and $9.00, depending on density. The company had high hopes for the optical disk, which its developers figured would eventually cut the costs per page to between nine cents and thirty-six cents. In the interim, they proposed using electromechanical microfilm rolls (yes, rolls) to lower the per-page cost to five cents, using mechanical arms to push access times to fifteen seconds (from the minutes or hours that might have been needed to retrieve the rolls manually). The product was improbable and, not surprisingly, never implemented. Dr. Wang's razor-sharp mind was too far ahead of reality.

Meanwhile, the operational parts of the business were atrophying. Manufacturing now reported to Fred, who had neither the interest nor the experience to make it work. And he downplayed manufacturing as, at best, a "second cousin," between "where development sent its products and sales got them." Now it had been demoted still further to a purchasing subordinate that would simply oversee close vendor relationships and conduct careful negotiation. "After all, by the time the parts kit reaches the assembly worker, it's simply a matter of snapping pieces together and passing circuit boards through a wave solder," Fred breezily remarked. Well, not exactly, but who was going to challenge Fred?

Field service remained another slighted cousin, short on product quality and lacking the remote diagnostic tools long available to most competitors. The big news for 1984 was the opening of three regional phone centers that supposedly could talk Wang customers through 80 percent of their problems. We were incredulous. Given Dr. Wang's legendary attention to ease of use and functional simplicity, how could simple operator error be the apparent cause of so many problems? Apart from the phone-rep wrinkle, the organization was stagnant: The mean time to repair was stuck at the three-and-a-half hours reached three years earlier, and the number of calls per field engineer was still 2.2 per day. Response time was the only metric that showed improvement, edging down to a mean time of two-and-a-half hours instead of three, but still no better than the industry average.

Little wonder that Wang's business metrics were sickly. Except for service-fee hikes, revenue trends were almost flat, and though gross margins had shrunk by a full 10 percentage points, to 60 percent, they were still too fat to compete against the newcomers or even against old rivals like DEC and HP. Profit margins had shriveled, too, from 15 percent to the point of dead loss in 1985, prompting the termination of 1,600 employees—another ominous first for Wang.

The future looked bleak, confided Controller Ed Bullis. "Margin improvement won't easily come from hardware, but from increasing the revenue contribution of non-hardware products and services," he said. "Unbundled software could provide significant revenue streams in two or three years." Unbundling Wang's software might have been a great start to carrying the company's widely used office systems to the personal-computer sector. But it never happened, in part because selling software (at a hundred dollars a seat) without Wang hardware would have forced a huge shrinkage in revenue, margins, and, most dramatically, head count. Wang's long-time loyalist and general counsel, Edward Grayson, closed the door on unbundling by wistfully observing, "No single business aspect of the business by itself could return Wang to 15 percent margins."

In that context, Ray Cullen, the field support vice president, tried to convince us that Wang's maintenance was cost-competitive with that provided on IBM and HP minis. It wasn't an easy sell: Wang's maintenance charges as a percentage of purchase price were now 40 percent higher than the best of the competition, an ugly cost differential that rivals were quick to point out when trying to sell their own products to Wang customers.

Meanwhile, the growing importance of service revenues (see Table 7.1) was an incontrovertible sign of an essentially uncompetitive company deep in its final flop.

Table 7.1 Service Revenues Dominate at Wang

$Millions	1986	1988	1990	1991	1992
Product Sales	1,874	2,008	1,558	1,207	899
Service Fees	769	1,060	939	884	998
Total	2,643	3,068	2,497	2,091	1,896
Service %	29.6	35.0	37.6	42.3	52.6

Source: Wang Labs Financial Reports

By 1985, talk of CEO succession had been smothered by the burden of weak demand and hard competition, especially from IBM—or so our Wang sources told us. Rather than thinking about succession "at times like this," said Dr. Wang in his autobiography, "the CEO must be prepared to take extraordinary action.... Beginning in the fall of 1985, however, I committed myself to a great deal of flying in order to reach field offices and customers. I changed my habits in response to what had happened to the computer industry and to my company the previous year." Some of the issues Wang ascribed to the industry, some to "missed delivery dates on a couple of strategic products. Outside, the problem surfaced in customer complaints about support."[6] The head count was cut for the first time in ten years, but the downsizing was far from enough.

At our visit, An Wang, the sixty-five-year-old treasure, was visibly and uncharacteristically exhausted, having just ended a grueling travel schedule to reassure customers after Cunningham's departure. But the travel had led to important discoveries, he told us eagerly. The computer business was no longer about data processing or even about office automation, but about information management. Certainly, information management, plus transfer, integration, mining, and visualization, would drive the successes of many IT vendors, old and new. But for Dr. Wang, the drive was effectively over.

Fuel-dispensing pumps at the gas station somehow became Dr. Wang's metaphor for explaining a future services business. Wang Information Services Corporation (WISC) would offer voice mail, electronic mail, and data processing to small businesses, while low-cost sales representatives working from home would displace high-cost reps working from glitzy offices. The ailing Dr. Wang had actually come up with the germ of a daring idea. But in 1985, absent the Internet, WISC seemed merely an old man's hope for reviving his namesake's dismal voice-mail product and its aging supply of minicomputers tumbling off long-term leases as customers defected to the competition.

We closed our interview by asking his assessment of the company. "Our products are superior to those of competitors," he told us, "and we have a pervasive presence in the office market. Our manufacturing capability is lousy, but we don't need more. The sales programs aren't good. Administration is lousy." He didn't mention the industry's unmistakable turn to the standard microprocessors and the operating systems needed to run increasingly complex computers and their software applications, which dashed any hope of Wang resuming its former growth and profitability. Instead, "services will help get our margins back," he predicted wistfully. "Consider industry precedent. Although the semiconductor companies developed marvelous chips, when prices fell to commodity levels, who benefited? Not them, but us, the computer companies. Now that computer prices are declining, who will benefit? Not the computer companies, but the service companies."

Wang's autobiography ended in early 1986, its tone defiantly upbeat. "The shocks of 1985 had the effect of eliminating any vestiges of complacency within the company, and we entered 1986 with a renewal of the spirit that has characterized the company for almost all of its history. In January, 1986, this revived hunger paid off when Wang Laboratories won [against IBM] ... a $480 million contract to install MIS systems at United States Air Force bases around the world."[7]

For Wang, the enemy still resided in the Hudson Valley, not Silicon Valley: "Today, thirty-five years after I founded the company, I continue to hear people question whether Wang Laboratories can survive the competition with mighty IBM. My response is that the odds against Wang Laboratories surviving in 1951, and then growing to the size it has, were a lot worse than the odds of the company's successfully competing against IBM today."[8] Clearly, despite Dr. Wang's fixation on IBM, that long-time rival was no longer the major issue. We never saw the Doctor again.

Wang Without Wang—Both Senior and Junior

Fred meticulously projected mature confidence during our 1987 visit, but his demeanor hardly reflected the company's fortunes. Recurrent losses had dragged down Wang's share price to a pitiful four dollars, 90 percent below the forty-two dollars reached five years earlier—just before Fred's R&D function fell into terminal disarray. We wondered if the real son's easy manner wasn't a reflection of his new freedom from the shadows of both his absent American brother and his seriously ill father. Fred could once again redirect development plans—away from last year's WISC service or the prior year's satellites, focusing instead on industry-specific business applications that he hoped to build or buy. Unfortunately, many computer companies, then and now, have chosen the same path, but very seldom to positive effect.

Worse was Fred's firm embrace of An Wang's wrongheaded perspective with respect to the competition. Fellow Easterners IBM and DEC were still at the top of his threat pyramid (though both would soon fall into extreme crisis), followed by a mid-layer that included Wang, HP, Unisys, and NCR, and at the bottom were minnows like Apollo and Apple.

"Wang and HP were badly burned by our own idiosyncratic experimentations," Fred asserted. That was true, but in HP's case, the "experimentations" moved preemptively toward Unix, industry standards, and long-term viability, while Wang took exactly the opposite tack. As for Apollo, it was acquired by HP while DEC was bought by Compaq. NCR would make a strong entry into the Unix market under the audacious Charles Exley, only to be acquired, sucked dry, and eventually disgorged by AT&T.

Prescience hardly described Fred's prognostications. Disastrous was more like it, given his stubborn omission of the PC threat even as Wang's traditional office position was being hollowed out by Lotus, WordPerfect, Novell, and, especially, Microsoft. Not surprisingly, the four continued to gain ground on Wang over the next two years.

In 1989, the top four PC software houses registered combined revenues of $1.8 billion, while Wang racked up a devastating $429 million loss. After telling the trade press that he had a plan to turn the company around, Fred resigned a few days later on August 7. The board meeting must have been extraordinary. Did Fred's father reject the son's technology plan as too extreme? Did his mother nix the downsizing as too brutal?

Dr. Wang, then sixty-nine, would die from cancer of the esophagus within eight months. But he returned to work part-time, naming Harry Chou, his long-time comrade in arms, as president and COO. For a company in very serious difficulty, the management structure was totally unsustainable, but there were no other internal succession candidates. Besides Chou, the only remaining executives were Ray Cullen and Horace Chiang, the vice presidents of field service and development, respectively—and Chiang's poor English worked against his taking a more public role.

During seven years of pointless internal dithering, the Doctor had remained determined to leave the company to his son, notwithstanding the availability of a more capable choice. But could the old man listen to his born successor as Tom Watson Sr. had listened to his? It's impossible to imagine Fred saying, as Watson Jr. had told a journalist after his father died: "My father and I had terrible fights. He seemed like a blanket that covered everything. I wanted to best him but also to make him proud of me. I really enjoyed the 10 years with him …"[9] Instead, it appeared, Fred received a vote of no confidence from his parents, though he was allowed to remain on the board.

Press speculation turned immediately to John Cunningham, who staunchly denied he'd even been asked to rejoin Wang Labs. But, privately, he admitted to us that he had refused an offer to return, and for three very good reasons. First, any difficult changes, especially the necessary staff reductions, would be blocked by the paternalistic Wang family retainers. Second, Cunningham was seriously concerned about the top twenty accounts that had been his greatest pride and hope for the future; since 1986, purchases by these accounts had plummeted from $330 million to $110 million. Finally, John thought that even though the old man was dying, he would clutch at control, limiting a new president to public relations and executive customer calls.

As a last resort, the Doctor reached outside the Wang circle to recruit Richard Miller, a finance executive from the consumer electronics sector who appeared especially ill suited to leading a business computer company. Nonetheless, the understandably desperate An Wang made concessions unlike anything he probably would have conceded to his American son. The Doctor's death soon thereafter explained his eagerness for a deal.

But it was too late to do more than apply a tourniquet to the losses, cut staff, and pray for a buyer to appear. In the first few months, Miller halved the company's debt by selling off the equipment-leasing business and Wang's prideful one-third interest in a Taiwan assembly plant. Then came devastating staff reductions that slashed the rolls from 29,000 to 23,500, and then to 19,000 before the year was out. It was enough to eke out a half-percent profit in the fiscal first quarter before Wang fell back into the red in the second.

Even the Doctor's beloved engineering group was decimated, and most of the hardware engineers were gone: "Boxes are not our future" was the long-overdue realization. Gone also were the operating-system engineers, with Wang finally adopting the Unix operating system and moving to support midrange IBM computers. Only the applications-development sector increased its staff, going to three hundred from two hundred.

There was also a ludicrous scheme afoot to assign engineers to ninety-day stints in customer locations, where, presumably, they would identify and develop new and salable applications. "Hundreds" of such applications had already been inventoried, we were told, not very convincingly. To avoid swamping the sales force, or so the story went, the company was purposely going slow in its packaging and shipping of these new applications to customers. More promising (and believable) was Wang's image-processing system, which actually attracted real customers among leading-edge banks and credit card companies like Citicorp. But it was too little and too late to save the company.

In 1991, Miller made a presentation to an RB meeting of CIOs, many from the huge banks and insurance companies that were Wang's accounts. Later, I learned that key Wang executives had cautioned Miller against the appearance, certain that the tech-savvy crowd would quickly drill through the façade to the hard truth of Wang's dwindling future.

And, indeed, Miller's gamble was misguided. He had little convincing to say beyond half-strategies to support IBM hardware, the search for applications, and a pending alliance with Computer Associates, whose aggressive pricing tactics had infuriated this crowd for years. The result was deadly. As the audience filed out to lunch, the CIO of one major bank muttered that he would not only accelerate the exodus from Wang but would recommend that his bank review its credit line. The insurance companies jumped ship as well. The erosion of its traditional markets undoubtedly gained momentum that day. The large accounts that had filled John Cunningham with such pride were almost the first to toss the Wang company and its products over the side.

Wang turned turtle on August 19, 1992 (though subsequently brought out of bankruptcy on a diminished basis by its next CEO, Joe Tucci). The company's history is a curious testament to the double-sided nature of leadership. The charismatic and steadfast leader can pull the organization through a difficult and contentious transition, as An Wang did with the turn from calculators to computers. But when that same leader is wrong or weakened, the results can be symmetrically calamitous. In just ten years, Wang Labs plummeted from the peak of its industry to near ruin.

Chapter 8

RETROSPECTIVE STRATEGY:

John DeButts at AT&T

The storied American Telephone & Telegraph Company (AT&T) was arguably the competitor with the best opening cards, the most hesitant gambles, and the worst relative losses. In 1979, the year before the antitrust judgment that broke up Ma Bell's extended family, AT&T was still a giant. Its telecommunications revenues (excluding Western Electric) totaled $45.4 billion, making it 50 percent larger than fellow monolith IBM. Its profits of $5.7 billion were equal to the raw revenues of the sixty-seventh largest company in the *Forbes* annual review. Its more than one million employees outnumbered those of IBM, DEC, and HP combined—enough to represent one percent of the entire U.S. labor force.

Structurally, the key elements of the so-called Bell System were Bell Labs for research and engineering, Western Electric for manufacturing, Long Lines for the network infrastructure, and twenty-three Bell operating companies (BOCs), which provided local services such as last-mile connection, installation and repair, and the yellow-pages phone book. AT&T executives liked to remind the regulators that the local market was also shared with 1,600 independents, but only General Telephone, United Telephone, and Continental had any significant scale. As one measure of dominance, the 138 million telephones in Ma Bell's system represented 79 percent of the U.S. handset market.

AT&T had plenty of punch in computing as well. The world-renowned Bell Labs had perfected the vacuum tube, invented the transistor, and operated a capable semiconductor facility that produced

AT&T's own 3B microprocessor. Its engineers had also developed Unix software in the late 1960s, salvaging it from the wreckage of the Honeywell Multix project and using Digital Equipment's early minicomputers as the platform. In 1973 (coincidentally, the year Imsai brought out the first PC), the new operating system was rewritten in the higher-level C programming language, making it portable across different hardware in a matter of months, not years. Unfortunately, the successes of those early years were wasted, because corporate AT&T was futilely preoccupied with preserving a monopoly in voice telephony. When what was left of Ma Bell was swallowed up by one of its former operating companies in 2005, the one-time giant's sorry end aptly demonstrated the enormous difficulty of turning a successful monopoly into a lively competitor.

The First Hundred Years

AT&T was blessed from its earliest days, recounts John Brooks in his book *Telephone: The First Hundred Years.*[1] On February 14, 1876, hearing specialist Alexander Graham Bell rushed to the patent office with his new invention just hours before Elisha Grey, the cofounder of Western Electric, sought to file his patent, and three weeks before Bell could actually demonstrate that his contraption worked by uttering, "Mr. Watson, come here—I want to see you."

The following year, Bell, Watson, and two financial angels, Thomas Sanders and Gardner Hubbard—both fathers of deaf children who had studied with Bell—formed National Bell Telephone, an unincorporated association. One of those children, Mabel Hubbard, married her teacher just two days after the association was formalized. The new company distributed 5,000 shares to the company's first seven shareholders. Hubbard received 1,387 and his daughter, the new Mrs. Bell, got 1,497, while her husband received only 10.

Within two years, a group of Boston financiers had forced out Hubbard, followed by Bell and Watson. By 1880, with just 47,000 phones in the United States, all the AT&T founders had left the company for comfortable lives, but with nothing like the dynastic fortunes amassed by the families of other technology pioneers.

The Boston financiers were themselves ousted by a J. P. Morgan syndicate in 1907, and Theodore Vail was installed as president. The sixty-two-year-old Vail, a former U.S. Post Office superintendent, had resigned from AT&T twenty years earlier after being passed over for president. Now he set about restructuring the company around organizational concepts that would survive for almost eighty years. A year after assuming the presidency, he minted the slogan, "One Policy, One System, Universal Service," to underscore his deep belief in a natural monopoly. And in the 1907 annual report, he argued that "two exchange systems in the same community, each serving the same members, cannot be conceived of as a permanency.... The strength of the Bell System lies in its universality."

Vail's "universality" was just another name for "monopoly," a fact that did not go unnoticed by President Theodore Roosevelt's trustbusters. In 1913, AT&T was forced to divest its 30 percent stake in Western Union, and vice president Nathan Kingsbury had to write a formal promise (the "Kingsbury Commitment") not to buy any more independent telephone companies or deny them interconnection to AT&T Long Lines. Unperturbed, Vail simply adjusted to the new reality of regulation as a natural consequence of monopoly. Before he retired in 1918, at age seventy-four, Vail had made the peaceful transition from a world of voracious competition to one of benign regulation that would in time become government protection. By then, company revenues reached $183 million, and AT&T had issued 10 million telephones to a U.S. population just over 100 million.

The next thirty years were marked by AT&T's steadily growing revenues and prodigious invention amid a benign environment of passive regulation and stable consumer rates. AT&T revenue grew to $2.6 billion, and the number of phones stood at roughly 30 million.

Simultaneously, Bell Labs set a sprinter's pace in innovation. On a short list of its achievements from 1912 through the 1940s was its success in perfecting Lee De Forest's vacuum tube (a technology that would power the first generation of computers), buttressed by its development of ship-to-shore radio, a method for transmitting pictures over telephone lines, early television, radar, and, famously, the transistor, which powered the second generation of computers and myriad other devices.

Years of aggressive rate increases in the 1940s and 1950s raised regulatory hackles; and in 1956, AT&T found itself signing a consent decree that commanded the company to stay out of any business not related to telephones in return for being allowed to retain Western Electric. Another skirmish followed when sharp cost cutting by AT&T began to undermine the reliability of its Long Lines phone system. Then, in 1964, the regulatory agency began an inquiry into the long-distance rate structure. It was this probe that would blossom into a full-scale assault on AT&T's cozy relationship with the FCC.

"Specialized" Long-Distance Competition

In 1971, the FCC announced the Specialized Common Carrier Decision allowing "specialized" competitors to enter the market with new services in long distance. The entry and subsequent expansion of new players such as MCI, Southern Pacific (later Sprint), and others was ferociously disputed by AT&T and a group of allies, including the National Association of Regulatory Utility Commissioners (NARUC) and the United States Independent Telephone Association (USITA).

Big money was at stake. For state regulators, the issues were simple: Subsidies from high-density corridors allowed "rate averaging" for low-density rural routes. So if AT&T was forced to lower rates on the high traffic routes attractive to the specialized common carriers, rural long-distance rates would rise as a consequence. Moreover, toll revenues directly subsidized local residential service. Raising basic service charges would disadvantage the deserving rural poor, NARUC grumbled on behalf of the state regulators, painting the risk of depriving phone service to the elderly in graphic terms: "Mrs. Dunn was one of the old people in the Hull pilot project … 'I fell and lay there from eight o'clock Thursday night until Saturday morning when the milkman found me and they sent for the police and they broke in. I was frozen through.'"

The FCC countered that competition would provide only "specialized" services such as data and private line, leaving AT&T the conventional, public switched voice services that constituted the bulk of its revenues. So at risk for AT&T was only 3 percent of traditional telephone service, plus 1 percent or 2 percent of new data services, which shouldn't be corralled in the "natural monopoly" anyway, reasoned the Feds.

But its neat delineations wouldn't hold.

MCI had been formed in 1968 by William McGowan, a leprechaun gambler who was canny to the core. Within its first three years, MCI acquired seventeen small regional carriers and a 92.7 percent interest in a subsidiary called "Microwave," which operated mainly in a critical corridor of the Midwest. In 1972, McGowan used the credibility bestowed by the FCC decision to float a $30 million initial public offering, and used the proceeds to start a major network construction program. Just one year later, construction halted as the company ran out of funds, leaving a network that covered fifteen major cities, including Washington, New York, Chicago, St. Louis, and Dallas. By then, MCI had spent a total of $83 million from stock sales and bank loans, including $54 million on construction, but realized just $1 million in cumulative revenues. McGowan blamed this sorry record squarely on AT&T's intransigence.

On McGowan's first visit to us in 1974, MCI still seemed an unlikely David; it had just 750 employees and 850 customers, 93 percent of whom used the circuits for voice, not data or anything else thought of as "specialized." Its biggest customers were General Motors, which accounted for 16 percent of MCI's total circuit miles while Westinghouse had 11 percent; its top seven accounts represented 46 percent of its business. Customers whom we contacted credited their decision to switch to MCI to its 25 percent price break and their belief in "a need to encourage competition." All kept one eye carefully on the exit, in case MCI's financial outlook faltered.

Though Bill McGowan was perspiring that cool autumn day, he normally exhibited the nerves of a cat burglar. A few months earlier, he had left the legal confines of the private-line business to let subscribers call anyone (including non-subscribers) in cities covered by MCI. "So wasn't that an illegal encroachment on the services still reserved to AT&T?" we pressed Bill in massive naiveté. "In this business, you need as many lawyers as engineers," he quipped to our delight.

MCI's legal skirmishing irretrievably cracked AT&T's "natural monopoly." McGowan would later concede the obvious: He had invented the term "specialized common carrier" merely to mollify the FCC. The far larger and more profitable switched voice market was his target all along.

Bill was the first CEO to meet with the still-tiny RB membership, joining us in the back room of a Chinese restaurant in New York.

He began the conversation by bragging that MCI generated $40,000 of revenue per employee versus just $27,000 in the Bell operating companies. That was about the only good financial news. As we wrote in November 1975, "MCI may be in a position to turn the corner, if it does not fall off its bicycle first. It provides customers with a cost-effective service, and it has real allies in the FCC—who are extremely concerned about the impact of an MCI demise." They needn't have worried.

Another of today's majors, Sprint, originated in 1973 as a spin-off from the Southern Pacific Railroad and was the brainchild of its powerful CEO Benjamin Biaggini. Start-up assets included the parent's own microwave network, extensive landholdings, and a railroad's core competence in working with regulators. Heading the new carrier was Gus Grant, a mature and able executive recruited from Teledyne. Early service was spotty, often taking fifteen months to set up a circuit and too long to fix a break. Early customers included heavy traffickers American Airlines, Ford, and General Electric. Grant gained acceptance from nervous customers by encouraging them to leave half their traffic with AT&T; most left 90 percent. But with MCI, SPC, and others, a new industry was born, making competition an irreversible reality for Long Lines, though AT&T would waste years defending the past.

Choked by Interconnection

Three years before the opening of the common carrier market to competition, the FCC's 1968 Carterphone decision had opened the Bell telephone network to "customer premises" equipment, including telephones and the private-branch exchanges (PBXs) used by business customers to route calls to the recipient's extension. The Bell operating companies were barred from blocking the interconnection of "foreign" (i.e., non-Bell) gear that didn't damage the network. Arguments over what constituted "damage" raged for several years.

The timing couldn't have been worse. Years of stagnation on fundamental product development had left Western Electric tottering with forty-year-old, step-by-step customer switches (i.e., PBXs) and forty-week order-to-delivery cycles. A new generation of mostly Japanese competitors were offering business customers semiconductor-based switches with more functions at lower prices and a four-week delivery, leading the operating companies to defect from Western Electric, especially in densely populated states such as New York, California, Connecticut, and New Jersey.

But elsewhere, state utility commissioners did everything possible to protect AT&T against the newcomers under the banner of assuring "universal telephone service" to needy customers in rural areas.

At immediate issue was a 1973 case involving three Lilliputians: the Home Telephone Company that served Mebane, North Carolina; Crescent Industries, an interconnection company with annual revenues under $100,000; and Apparel Inc., a company that had made a 29 percent down payment to Crescent for a seven-line telephone system. When Home Telephone refused to allow the interconnection, Crescent raced to the FCC.

As the case unfolded, Home Telephone's precarious financial situation grabbed national attention. (To start, its annual debt service totaled $120,000 on $6 million in loans from the Rural Electrification Administration.) Of the $500,000 in local-service revenues from Home's 3,600 customers, $82,000 came from three businesses with PBXs. Losing those three could perhaps end telephone service to tiny Mebane.

After the North Carolina Utilities Commission moved in 1973 to severely restrict "foreign" systems, the FCC retaliated with a four-month inquiry. Its 1974 Telerent Leasing Corporation decision determined that "where interstate and foreign communications services depend on plant facilities used in common, no state may take action on interconnection that is in conflict with action taken by the FCC." The state regulators rushed to appeal, but after several years, a court decision was rendered in favor of competition.

The results of deregulation were nearly catastrophic for the torpid AT&T. In the data-terminal market alone, the share held by AT&T's Teletype Corporation plummeted from over 90 percent to under 5 percent. The trend was temporarily reversed between 1975 and 1979, when the AT&T subsidiary belatedly introduced electronic terminals, but Teletype never regained market dominance.

AT&T's PC modems were so thoroughly uncompetitive that the Bell operating companies resorted to a broadside of anticompetitive, even illegal, tactics, as detailed in a Justice Department brief:

"The BOCs instituted and administered tariffs embodying the requirement ... [of] a Bell supplied [access device]. They lowered the rates for BOC-supplied modems while raising the rates for monopoly data services [and] refused to make available technical information ... provide conditioned circuits [ones of guaranteed quality] on a tariffed basis, instead providing high-quality circuits to users of BOC-supplied modems on an informal discriminatory basis." And so on.

As for PBXs, the once-dominant Western Electric languished in technological irrelevance. Its offering for medium-scale PBX installations was the 701 device, an electromechanical, "step-by-step" clunker developed in the 1920s, the era of the punch-card tabulator. (At the time, IBM was already installing its third generation of electronic circuitry in the System/360.) Frenzied efforts to upgrade the Western Electric product line ensued, each more inept than the last.

One of the sorriest offerings was the 770A PBX, which was rushed into combat against a Nippon Electric product. To start, the 770A's reliability and maintenance record was atrocious, a stark departure from Western Electric's usual focus, even overfocus, on quality. Worse yet, the only way the company could meet competitors' prices—and not just those of its Japanese rivals—was to cut product features that had long been available on its own older gear.

Better marketing would resolve the issue, advised a headquarters' memo to the field: "Customer dissatisfaction has been expressed when a 770A PBX system has replaced a 756A, 757A or 800A PBX. The primary reason for the operating characteristics differing from previously designed Bell System PBXs is to gain economies that are resulting in lower cost PBX systems. [If sales reps would simply review] these characteristics with the customer during the implementation of the sale, many customer irritations will be avoided."

Despite the skewed view from headquarters, salesmanship alone couldn't stem the bloody tide. A Bell Labs presentation allowed that 70 percent of the Bell System's PBX losses in the first quarter of 1973 would be in the 100-line capacity range, a market trolled by 81 percent of the company's sales reps.

In full retreat was AT&T's once lucrative business in multiline office telephones, where new companies could offer superior equipment at lower prices to highly cost-conscious small businesses. An October 27, 1972, memo to Chairman and CEO John deButts from S. E. Bonsack, in the market and service plans department, begins with soothing talk of an installed base where AT&T couldn't help but remain dominant—at least temporarily. But it then describes the alarming rate at which that base was eroding:

"Mr. deButts:

"In line with our discussion on key system losses at the October 23 Cabinet meeting, the most recent information available is outlined below.

"Key customer losses now total approximately 2,800. Based on an estimated in-service figure of 650,000 key customers with 3 or more lines, the losses equate to .43%.

"The total universe of key customers, including 1 and 2 line systems, numbers approximately 1.7 million. Against this base, our current losses equate to .16% of the market.

"A sampling of our key system competitive cases for the first 7 months of this year reveals that we lose to the competition 48% of the time ..."

Losing *half* of the deals when encountering competition? Could there be any clearer indications of technological obsolescence? DeButts should have begun a radical restructuring and decentralization of Bell Labs and Western Electric, much as Frank Cary was doing under similar circumstances at IBM. Instead, he continued to adulate a bygone era. Proclaimed the chairman in a 1972 speech: "I will admit to you that my own instinctive response to emerging competition in our business matches that of Theodore Vail, who—back in the days of the brass-knuckled competition our business experienced in the early 1900s—declared, in a statement we would now call Churchillian, 'We have established and organized this business and do not propose to see it taken from us.'" Churchillian? DeButts would not—or could not—acknowledge that Vail had been equally adept at accepting, even co-opting, the inevitable regulation—much to AT&T's sixty-year advantage.

Saved by Consultants

Despite the backward thrust of John deButts's words and actions, he drew support from several outside consultants. The company's 1969 annual shareholder meeting had heralded a consultant's positive report on Western Electric: "One of the most thorough studies made, rates Western Electric high in performance and very efficiently managed." Unfortunately, such misplaced praise simply reinforced the already regressive executive mind-set. One can almost hear the cheering from former Western Electricians who were now among AT&T's senior executives.

In 1973, McKinsey & Company consultants conducted a study of AT&T's overall competitive position. The results were baffling, considering the desperate losses in PBXs, multiline office telephones, terminals, and modems. McKinsey assessed Bell Labs as "an outstanding product development organization which has provided technological leadership in all areas of the telecommunications businesses—switching, transmission, terminal equipment, etc." The only glimmer of a problem, in McKinsey's estimation, was the Labs' possible fixation on "providing high quality service and reducing System operating costs," rather than "meeting the competition." (Someone else might well have judged those goals to be admirable, not problematic.) Career insiders were less complacent than the McKinsey team, witness an engineering VP's 1974 comment, "I could hope that in the future, Bell Labs managers would get out more and find out what the real world is like."

As for Western Electric, the McKinsey recommendations echoed the 1969 conclusions that the subsidiary "provided the Bell System with clear-cut cost advantages over other manufacturers." Thus, only nefarious trickery could explain why its products were losing out to the competition: "New competitive distributors, often using newly recruited Bell System salesmen, have moved quickly to carve out viable market niches for themselves. Using aggressive marketing and sales tactics, they have focused on areas where they believe that the Bell System is vulnerable. For example, hawking a more compact PBX with new features for hotels/motels ... these distributors have rapidly made inroads in their target segments. Competition also capitalizes on the rigidities of the operating companies' rate structures caused by regulation ... [and] competition has also offered flexible new pricing arrangements." A savvy reader might conclude that AT&T salesmen only learned to sell by leaving the Bell System. As for product problems, there weren't any, if McKinsey were to be believed.

The good news was that Western was already conducting market research projects to analyze competitive losses "and the need for new product features and pricing options." Even better, pumped the consultants, "several new products have been introduced—e.g., the 770A PBX—to halt the inroads being made by the competition." Was this an upgraded 770A? Or were they simply unaware of the 770A's functional deficiencies as described in the headquarters' marketing memo to the field?

One was left to wonder if this entire report weren't written for the lawyers and regulators to use in buttressing AT&T arguments against deregulation. Coincidentally, that same year, Bell System employees were invited to view an in-house film entitled *What Is in Our Files?* The theme was one of caution, not illegality, but it seemed designed to head off potential litigation over document discovery. The Seminar Administrator's Guide contained the following dialogue about an innocent Mr. Simpson who had embarrassed his corporation with an ill-considered memo: "What is your reaction to Mr. Simpson's memo? If you are like most people, you will say, 'I'm going back to my office and never write another memorandum.' None of us wants to be a Mr. Simpson."

In any case, McKinsey's recommendations were far more realistic than its findings:

- First, consolidate the sales and marketing effort "to provide stronger centralized leadership," but not too intrusively. "We do not believe that 195 [Broadway, then AT&T headquarters] can or should become directly involved in daily BOC sales and marketing decisions."

- Second, find a world-class marketing leader, but not an outsider. "We gave serious consideration to recommending someone outside," the consultants wrote, "but dismissed this possibility on several grounds—the most important being that it would probably be difficult to interface effectively with Bell System management on the often 'tender' issues involved in his assignment."

- Finally, the BOCs must "shift the sales force from its traditionally strong implementation orientation and relatively passive approach to selling towards a more aggressive selling posture— in effect, to develop a cadre of sales people and managers that have the capability and motivation to seek out and capitalize on important opportunities to improve service, upgrade existing equipment, and increase usage."

Because the generally sensible recommendations offended almost no one, they became politically more acceptable. It was a brilliant move. Western Electric's products and Bell Labs' development were exonerated, while marketing could be safely critiqued since it hadn't previously mattered to anyone of importance anyway. Finally, there was a bunch of Cinderella talk about how a benign AT&T could change its stodgy image.

"AT&T Goes Back to School to Learn How to Sell," blared *BusinessWeek* (August 11, 1975). The headline ran above a picture of the new marketing VP, Kenneth Whalen, holding a telephone patterned with patriotic stars and stripes. "Selling Is No Longer Mickey Mouse at AT&T," applauded *Fortune* nearly three years later; this time, the accompanying photo showed Edward Goldstein, the director of product management, holding a Mickey Mouse phone. All glitz and no regrets, we thought. How wonderful.

Following the McKinsey study, 195 Broadway took much greater control over marketing and sales. A new department, corporate sales development, was added, creating system-wide programs for sales recruiting, training, compensation, and control. After all, said the inconsistent consultants, "the basic sales and service job is the same throughout the System; the major differences between companies are in rates, which vary from state to state and in local administrative procedures." Also added were two powerful corporate-marketing functions, product management and market services. The former defined pricing and product requirements, provided product management to Bell Labs, and even recommended the purchase of products for resale on an OEM basis from sources outside Western Electric. The latter conducted system-wide market research and oversaw advertising plans.

What came next was arguably the greatest organizational shift among the operating companies since the days of Theodore Vail. Previously, the BOCs had been organized around functions or skills: "Plant" for craft union workers, "Commercial" for white-collar business offices, "Traffic" for telephone operators. The structure made considerable sense by aligning tasks with comparable unions, crafts, and clerical content, thereby providing sensible career paths for competent supervisors and executives. But now everyone would be reoriented to "tasks." Thus, "customer services" included both white-collar and craft workers engaged in the administration, engineering, installation, and repair of AT&T equipment on customer premises. "Engineering and network services" similarly involved switches and circuits outside customer premises. And "assistance services" grouped operators with the production and sale of directories.

But forcing this reorientation on the operating companies required massive changes in management philosophy. Until then, the BOCs were largely autonomous; they could respond to local regulatory environments and market pressures as they deemed most appropriate. *Fortune* magazine had noted back in May 1970 that the previous CEO, H. I. Romnes, viewed his role as "largely advisory. He does not try to second-guess the top officers of the operating companies. Indeed, he may not even talk to a company president for months at a time. They don't have to check their decisions. He says, 'performance is what counts.'"

The reshuffling was wrongheaded in its failure to distinguish between residential and business services. It was also profoundly ineffectual, fomenting resistance at the operating-company level. Indeed, as the 1977 Bell Labs Handbook warned archly: "The reader should be aware of both the traditional and the recommended organizational structures. Vestiges of the traditional structure will remain for some time and the recommended structure indicates the most probable direction of evolution." Worst of all, the changes failed to deal with a fundamental lethargy at Bell Labs and Western Electric, though they facilitated the acquisition of products for resale from outside manufacturers.

By the following year, the problems were visible enough to attract press attention. There were reports that some BOCs simply rewrote the plans handed down from AT&T, thus delaying implementation of the new organization for months. Noted the *Wall Street Journal* reported (September 28, 1978), "Plans conceived at AT&T headquarters aren't binding on the 23 operating companies and not everyone is enthusiastic. 'They create the mold and then fit everybody into it,' says a marketing manager at one operating company. 'What works in Manhattan won't necessarily work in Dubuque.'"

Meanwhile, headquarters remained adrift from reality. A 1975 "Planning Paper," issued by the public relations department, had laid out the field of play, and it all boiled down to a losing argument favoring a benign monopoly: "It is rare, for example, that anyone attacks the idea of a public waterworks. A planned industry avoids the waste, overproduction, and inefficiencies caused by abrupt and costly shifts in direction dictated by the vagaries of the market for its services and of the market to which it must go to buy its supplies … Vail's insight into the economics of technology is almost incredible: universal service is an economic system for a reliable market. He sought—and gained—the opportunity to plan." What nonsense!

A year later, John deButts made a last-ditch attempt to reassert the primacy of natural monopoly and universal service through a legislative initiative, the Consumer Communications Reform Act. A horde of AT&T lobbyists led by the chairman himself cornered Congressmen in their offices and in the corridors, initially winning 151 sponsors. But by 1977, the fever had passed, and the "Bell Bill," with just twenty-four sponsors, died in committee.

DeButts Departs

DeButts, having personally antagonized enough lawmakers to become a political liability, announced his early retirement in October 1978. His long-time Illinois Bell associate, Charles Brown, was tapped to succeed. In his last weeks, the second massive reorganization in less than four years was announced. This time, the Bell System's customer-facing aspects (marketing, sales, and field support) were redivided into business, residence, and network. "It's a profound change," the chairman declared, "not just a reshuffling of boxes on our organizational chart." (*Wall Street Journal*, December 26, 1978) Bell Labs would join corporate and the BOCs in this structure, while Western Electric would launch a serious study into its future.

Senior operating company executives publicly favored the restructuring because it called for more focus on business customers. "Segmentation was necessary to focus on distinct markets. In Connecticut, only 7 percent of our customers are business, yet they generate 53 percent of the revenue," related Haydn Owens, the impressive vice president for business at Southern New England Telephone. "The tail has been wagging the dog too long. Business is our most important customer—not the little old lady in tennis shoes with a Mercedes."

Far less upbeat were the mid-level supervisors, the backbone of the system. Their career aspirations had already been throttled by the 1974 reorganization, the 1973 Equal Employment Opportunity Commission (EEOC) decision forcing AT&T to put women on an equal footing with men when it came to promotion, and staff reductions taken in the face of technological improvements. Then came a string of defeats at the hands of the FCC, state regulators, and competitors.

As one senior BOC executive explained to us: "First we told our employees that the Federal government would never permit competition. Then the newspapers told them the FCC was moving faster and further to encourage it. Next we assured them that the Congress would reverse the trend. Then our whole congressional effort got flattened instead. Most recently, we said not to worry about the antitrust litigants, and then MCI got a $1.8 billion award. Our people don't believe us anymore."

A young friend of ours who worked as a New York Telephone manager told us, "Segmentation was accomplished very crudely ... like a sports draft. I was randomly assigned to business, and the next guy in the lineup went to network. We had nothing to replace our traditional benchmarks for performance and promotion. No one from AT&T corporate had bothered to figure out how segmentation was supposed to function. They just expected operating managers to reinvent whatever they needed as they went along."

By all accounts, deButts's final missive was a mess—nothing like the organizational chart that would be needed once the regulators were finished. The next chairman and CEO, Charlie Brown, closed his part of the presentation by stipulating that such far-reaching changes were necessary "in response to equally far-reaching changes in the society we service. Yet, we can be confident that for some years to come, we will not witness another restructuring of this magnitude."

Just eighteen months later, Brown would be proven wrong. Even as he spoke, California Congressman Lionel Van Deering was rewriting existing legislation that would totally deregulate the industry while also emasculating the FCC. In addition, the Bell System would have to give up Western Electric. For one brief moment, Brown tread the destructive path taken by his predecessors: "Let there be no misunderstanding. I have no intention of agreeing to spin off Western Electric," he was quoted in the November 1978 issue of *Fortune*. Coming to his senses, Brown would save the day with an entirely different strategy.

A send-off from *BusinessWeek* on November 8 burbled that deButts was "a corporate strategist with few peers ... As he steps down, it is becoming apparent that in his six years at the top of the world's largest corporation, he has carefully crafted a total change in strategy that few other men could have dared to undertake ... DeButts' plan is to meet the challenge of totally revamping the company's structure, broadening its concept of the products and services that are within its realm and changing its goal from that of mastering the regulatory process to meeting the needs of the marketplace." Unfortunately, *BW* was describing what should have occurred, but didn't. In our opinion, deButts's protection of the rotting hulks—whether Bell Labs, Western Electric, or the natural monopoly—totally overlooked the newly emerging threats and opportunities.

Deregulation Rules

The climate had changed. Legislators were now in full-voiced pursuit of deregulation, with no patience for further ramblings about natural monopolies. Well aware that "deregulation" was a dead-end business for regulators, a rash of resignations broke out at the FCC. The same attitude prevailed at the state level. Marvin Lieberman, the former chairman of the Illinois Commission, told us: "The question of whether or not there is going to be serious competition in the communications industry is no longer in the air.... State commissioners are no longer in the position to artificially support a particular class of rate player—not even Aunt Minnie. And the situation has already attracted a new class of commissioners; very few of the old stalwarts are left to carry Bell's message."

Even Ben Wiggens, the vocal firebrand who once headed the communications committee for the National Association of Regulatory Commissioners (NARUC), surrendered: "The state commissioners have given up. They have been fighting these issues for years, and it has only been an exercise in futility," he told our researchers. "You can't keep swimming when the ocean waves overtake you. Besides, now that regulation is so unpopular, nobody wants the job."

By 1979, the outlook was mixed at best. Deficient PBX equipment sliced seven percentage points off AT&T's market share; inexplicably, Western Electric's brand-new Dimension product was analog, not digital, and could handle only a limited number of lines. "Limping" was how several loyal AT&T executives characterized the product. Even the new marketing wizards ran for cover, telling us: "My group inherited Dimension.... [W]e were stuck with it." Competitive rates at Long Lines drew new voice traffic, and data networking grew as well. But some of the growth was cannibalistic; revenues from "wide area telephone service" (WATS) grew 94 percent at the expense of simple toll service.

Charlie Brown clearly meant to steer the leaking hulk on a new course. A senior headquarters executive, speaking anonymously, painted a future far different from deButts's vision: "First, we've got to completely forget the deButts objective of maintaining a single universal telephone system at any cost—including more regulation. In fact, there won't ever be more regulation; now what we have to do is learn to operate reasonably well on two levels, one regulated and the other deregulated.

"Next, we have to shift the preoccupation of the entire Bell System from 90 percent network and 10 percent gadgetry to the new unbounded information business. The great challenge will be how to accomplish so massive a transition with a minimal amount of uncontrolled or wasteful activity.

"Finally, we have to hold the company together so that, eventually, when the entire communications market is deregulated, the pieces can be brought back again into one integrated operating organization." Good thinking, though the "one integrated operating organization" would never be revived.

Our view remained dour: "For the Bell System, the special curse is an organizational structure that retains all of the functional characteristics of IBM at its darkest moment after Watson and before Cary. All advanced planning remains frozen in corporate, all R&D and software locked in Bell Labs, manufacturing controlled by Western Electric, service exclusively in the operating companies, and sales uneasily divided among Long Lines, the marketing program in AT&T corporate, and the account executives in the BOCs."

Congressional deliberations continued, but in 1982, the FCC returned to center stage with the results of Computer Inquiry II. This time, the blueprint envisioned an industry with three segments: AT&T and GTE (the other monopolist) would be limited to basic, largely voice services, but fenced off from customer-premises equipment or enhanced services like data; the newly deregulated portions of AT&T and GTE could offer customer-premises equipment, including computers and Unix plus enhanced services like data, provided they were totally separated from their regulated segment in management, personnel, facilities, computers, and accounting—and provided, too, they did not own any network or local distribution facilities; finally, everyone else could offer both basic and enhanced services on their own or someone else's network or local distribution facilities.

The FCC decision met loud opposition from many of the traditional parties, however diminished, but, surprisingly, not from the AT&T chairman.

Instead, on August 2, Brown announced what would be the third major restructuring of the decade after almost seventy years of placid sameness: "The shape of the future is becoming clear," Brown said. "To meet the requirements of that future, and to fulfill its opportunities, it is apparent that the Bell System will be operating in two modes. Under regulation, we will continue to provide basic telecommunications services, local and long distance. At the same time, we anticipate that we will be afforded increasing opportunities to compete in unregulated markets." Another shuffle of management chairs at headquarters left several unanswered questions, but from a historical perspective, Brown's reconciliation with the inevitable was brilliant, and finally turned the company in the right direction. Possibly there was still time to enter the Unix/microprocessor market.

Chapter 9

FOREIGN CULTURES:

AT&T's Recruit from IBM

However questionable the McKinsey consultants' assessment of AT&T's product strengths, their three primary recommendations seemed eminently sensible. Unfortunately, the suggested appointment of a "world-class" insider to work with Bell System management on "tender" marketing issues was ignored. Recruited instead was outsider Archibald McGill, reputedly IBM's youngest Group VP and a man whose undeniable marketing expertise was often undercut by an abrasive personal style. A bullying popinjay, McGill seemed emotionally incapable of addressing the "tender" issues without rubbing them raw. In fairness, he faced a constantly flip-flopping regulatory framework. But, in any event, what may have been a workable style at IBM was wholly unsuitable for an outsider at AT&T.

The two AT&T insiders who might have contended for the job of director of market management were flummoxed by the new imperative. Ken Whalen, the corporate marketing VP and former president of Michigan Bell, conceded that he "didn't understand market management." And Ed Goldstein, the Bell System's sensible director of product management, explained, "Engineers at Bell Labs are notoriously bad at assessing user needs and need a more disciplined approach," which he apparently felt incapable of enforcing. The only choice, then, was to go outside for talent. And as Archie later chortled to the Wall Street Journal on December 26, 1978, "I'm the change agent. I came here swinging the bat."

But the bat wasn't always wisely targeted, leading mainstream AT&T executives to growl at the effete shrillness of the new batsman. As the hugely capable Long Lines boss, Al Stark, breathed with unmistakable disdain, "Archie didn't grow up playing stickball behind the industrial yards in Kearney, New Jersey" like the tough old dogs who really ran the company. Enterprise-scale customers were annoyed, too. At a dinner with the Research Board, McGill responded angrily to member questions about AT&T support levels, making empty promises and even emptier threats, eventually bawling that the CIOs were "impolite." Gerald Montgomery, a clever and feisty member from J. C. Penney, memorably replied, "We've all met lots of four-flushers in our careers, but we are always polite." Archie rushed to his limo. If his goals included improved relations with large corporate customers, the evening had not been successful.

Left adrift in the uncertain churn were three different sales organizations elbowing for account control. The National Account Managers (NAM), targeted at large-enterprise accounts, had been rattling around the Bell System since 1962, mostly handing out crying towels, coordinating with the Bell Operating Companies (BOCs), and conducting an occasional traffic study for the fifty largest accounts (mainly oil companies, automotive, and airlines).

In 1977, NAM account executives trained by McGill's group were assigned to 125 large accounts, initially earning quite favorable reviews. But the strong start petered out within two years, done in, first, by reorganization, and then by demands for unnatural and unsustainable growth. "We're growing too fast," Robert Huber, the Long Lines marketing vice president, told us in 1980. "The NAM program could comfortably handle 20 percent growth per year, but AT&T [meaning McGill] is currently pressuring us for 30 percent." The NAM accounts were expected to double to five hundred in just eighteen months. "Realistically, we can absorb only half that many," Huber said. "The heart is beating faster than the legs can run."

The churn in staff turnover was the inevitable result, along with a lack of visible progress in selling data networks, workstations, and PCs to IT organizations. "Our traditional telephone people can't dance with large accounts as well as Archie's new computer breed," said Huber. A competitive product would have provided a booster shot for the NAM reps' business, but probably not enough to satisfy McGill.

The grumpiness of AT&T's Marketing VP was palpable when we visited a few days later. To start with, McGill informed us, the NAMs should and eventually would report to him rather than to Bob Huber at Long Lines. At that point, though, the cost assessments for their keep would push operating-company license fees (to AT&T) above a targeted limit of 2.5 percent of BOC revenues. "We've got to get control over the NAMs," a McGill lieutenant had told us previously in the corridor. But the boss scorned that notion, deriding the NAM teams as useless for selling anything but black telephones and railing about their 30 to 50 percent turnover rates. "Would you rather start over?" we asked. "No," chimed in another assistant. "There are too many people involved for that."

As befuddled as the NAMs was a second group, the National Account Coordinators (NAC), which dealt with intermediate-scale accounts. The demarcation line was soon breached as a result of infighting, leading *Sales & Marketing Management* magazine to exclaim tartly over "What might modestly be termed the most massive case of account conflict in the history of American marketing."

As if two jostling AT&T sales forces weren't quite enough, there was a third, belonging to the BOCs. It was supposed to be absorbed into the NAM or NAC structure at some point. But after visiting a pointedly resistant Southwestern Bell EVP in Texas, we had our doubts. "A customer deserves a single point of contact, to the extent he finds it worthwhile," Joe Hunt told us. "But the whole system would bog down if we routed absolutely everything through one NAM point.... You must keep in mind that the NAMs don't have all the expertise they need, especially in customer-premises gear. Our people grew up with that stuff. The NAMs are only learning it by osmosis from us." Translation: The NAMs couldn't even sell telephone service and equipment, never mind data networks, and certainly not computer gear.

Soon, mutinous mutterings rose to a rumble. "We are supposedly guaranteed a certain amount of additional annual revenue to compensate us for these NAM assessments," said Hunt's counterpoint at Diamond State (Delaware). "If the revenue isn't there, where do I go to collect the bill? I'll continue until the money runs out, but the NAMs may be pricing themselves out of the market."

By 1982, not everyone was delighted with CEO Charlie Brown's negotiation of the split between regulated voice services and unregulated products and data services. McGill was in full fury over the FCC's rule that an unregulated company could not own a network. In our discussion that year, Archie appeared alternately earnest, thoughtful, morose, and angry, finally accusing us of knowing too little. His rationale for demanding a network for an entity selling unregulated products revolved around the inevitable convergence of communications and computing; voice and data would merge in both technologies and markets. Besides, the forty-year asset-depreciation cycle imposed by the Feds had left AT&T's regulated network technologically uncompetitive. Any well-heeled competitor—Xerox, say, or even Exxon—could leapfrog AT&T using more cost-effective technology. "Do you expect us to stand by and watch them draw off our most basic revenues?" McGill asked rhetorically.

When we tried to ask why customers should want a new subsidiary to develop transmission facilities in parallel with the Bell core company, the discussion began to deteriorate. To us, the proposition seemed particularly startling since prevention of network redundancy was once the most convincing argument for "One System," the backbone of natural monopolies. "Did McGill's advocacy of separate transmission facilities for the unregulated company imply AT&T would walk away from the obsolescing AT&T network?" we asked. That one question soured McGill on our interview.

BOC executives were also unhappy with Brown's compromise. "Corporate tells us they'll help themselves to terminals [customer-premises equipment] and enhanced services, and you guys can sit by and fiddle around with dial tone," carped the Cincinnati Bell president. Added the general manager at Diamond State, "And local network switches." Ironically, "dial tone"—in the form of a local loop to the residence—would turn out to be a hugely valuable asset for many years.

The New-New Shape of Things to Come

More congressional and legal meandering followed in the first year of the Reagan Administration. Then, unexpectedly, on January 8, 1982, AT&T and the Justice Department agreed on a deceptively simple, twenty-five-page consent decree. This time, the organizational split would be a horizontal one, having been flipped from the prior year's vertical divide between regulated networks and unregulated equipment.

The BOCs were to be split off from Ma Bell and consolidated into seven regional holding companies. Now that the local loop was no longer under monopoly control, AT&T, Western Electric, and Bell Labs were free to enter a newly deregulated market—though with some separations between regulated and deregulated portions of the business. Bravo, Charlie Brown! Most observers thought he had won the day through a mixture of charm and an apparent willingness to refrain from fighting the inevitable. AT&T was given until January 1, 1984, to implement the new organization, necessitating the fourth gut-rattling restructuring in a decade.

Unix still represented an enormous opportunity for AT&T, but Ma Bell was engaged elsewhere. McGill's crew had introduced two relabeled computer offerings. The 6300 PC, manufactured and supported by Olivetti, offered minimal product differentiation from the industry norm and correspondingly slim margins. The 7300 workstation, originally with a proprietary operating system, was rebranded from Convergent Technology. Both offerings were sensible enough, so long as Computer Inquiry II prohibited Bell Labs and Western Electric from developing products for unregulated markets. But neither would dent the enterprise market. Meanwhile, Unix and the 3B microprocessor were largely ignored, in part because of the regulatory walls.

Intermittently during those years, AT&T had considered acquiring a minicomputer company—though that sector was peaking. It bought a minority interest in partner Olivetti, and rumors of the acquisition of EDS, Wang, or, most seductively, Digital Equipment, surfaced repeatedly, despite denials from both Charlie Brown and a DEC spokesman, who told the *Wall Street Journal* (February 10, 1986): "This thing comes up with some frequency, but there's no truth to it."

The story resurfaced again, though, in *The Ultimate Entrepreneur,* a biography of Digital founder Ken Olsen written by Glenn Rifkin and George Harrar. By this account, Archie McGill had concluded in 1983 that a union with DEC would give AT&T the perfect entry into the computer business. "McGill decided to play matchmaker behind the scenes," the authors wrote. "He introduced several DEC managers and then Olsen himself to senior AT&T executives, including James Olson who later became chairman. Olsen and Olson began a series of discussions about bringing the two companies together. It tore at

Ken Olsen's heartfelt belief on going it alone, but there were clear advantages to a merger. On their own, the future of both companies seemed uncertain. AT&T was heading into the unknown waters of deregulation; DEC had just lost its executive core and was struggling to stay competitive at both the high and low ends. But together, with the resources of a $40 billion company, AT&T-DEC could stand up to IBM."[1]

No doubt there were high-level meetings. AT&T was DEC's largest customer in those years, and DEC's massive and ultimately successful reorganization had prompted significant attrition in its executive ranks and embarrassing order-fulfillment gaffes that further bruised revenues. Nonetheless, the alleged McGill role seems improbable, given the lack of any survivable advantage in a merger between the world's leading minicomputer company and its most troubled telecom. It's difficult to imagine Olsen and McGill in the same room, given the huge difference in temperaments and outlooks. Finally, Arch himself was already under pressure, with weakening clout and little credibility within AT&T's management ranks.

After the consent decree was signed, McGill's marketing department finally expanded its portfolio to include sales activities for the now-unregulated "American Bell," later rechristened AT&T Information Systems (ATTIS). The results for 1982 were pathetic (perhaps understandably, given the turmoil) as ATTIS lost $1.2 billion. In March 1983, McGill resigned, later telling the *Wall Street Journal* (February 1, 1984) his "job of alerting AT&T to the competitive world was done." Even then, he remained pointlessly abrasive. "Mr. McGill adds: AT&T has had a difficult time understanding that the customer is its reason for being. Employees' allegiances have always been to their function as an engineer or marketer. Marketing faced a tough mental and cultural barrier."

AT&T's critics saw the end of Arch's twelve-year reign as a defeat for the forces of the future and for the customer. We were considerably less charitable: "Marketing maven Arch McGill was hoisted aboard to teach sales and competitiveness. The next ten years were marked (or obscured) by a blizzard of press releases, much tooth-grinding about IBM, general paralysis in product development, and the Mickey Mouse phone. In fairness, he and AT&T generally were not entirely to blame for this inertia. Equally debilitating were the agonizing years of indecision in Washington, where the FCC, Congress, and the courts groggily debated the future of the Bell System." On another occasion, we added: "McGill was credited with waking up the sleepy utility, but he downgraded the company's natural assets. And helped orchestrate the most destructive intracorporate politicking these amateur industry historians have ever observed. At one point during the commotion, a senior IBMer jokingly called McGill his company's Trojan Horse."

The NCR Benchmark of Unix Power

A telling measure of AT&T's underachievement was its contrast with NCR, a BUNCH survivor and most unlikely early mover to Unix and the Unix business model.

At the turn of the century, The Cash enjoyed a strong position in banking and retailing, thanks to the relentless capitalist John Patterson (with considerable help from Tom Watson). But as electromechanics gave way to electronics and computers, NCR stagnated. Then, in 1971, came China-born marketer and savior William S. Anderson, who revived NCR after quickly jettisoning the cash-register business. (Contrast NCR's assertive turn away from electromechanicals with Teletype's soft swoon.) Ferocious rounds of plant closings and downsizings—10,000 employees were let go from the hometown manufacturing centers alone—changed the cost structure and dissolved the old-guard management's "Dayton mentality."

Chuck Exley took over as president in 1976, after being recruited from Burroughs, and was named CEO in 1983. We interviewed him two years later. Chuck was a smoky-grey Midwestern industrialist with neither the sweater warmth of the DEC executives nor the boyish charms of the Sunsters. But after a grudging glass of pre-luncheon sherry, he surprised us by opening up and talking about how far the company had come. There were twenty-two, mostly new, plants, four semiconductor facilities, and a thoroughly modernized business base of almost $2.6 billion, 55 percent of which came from computers and terminals, 28 percent from various "services," 15 percent from maintenance, and just 2 percent from what was left of the cash-register business. Most important, the company had retained nearly all of its traditional retail and banking customers and was moving to additional markets.

Encouraged by our interviews, we wrote that year: "Exley himself is hugely impressive. But is he so much better than the organization? Or does it matter, given NCR entrenchment in its traditional markets?"

Chuck Exley didn't disappoint. Over the next few years, NCR executed a radical turn to proprietary microprocessors, Unix, and an even leaner business model. Already by 1983, when Chuck was named CEO, NCR had built a general-purpose Unix box on a Motorola microprocessor alongside its own proprietary, 32-bit processors. To our picky questions on why Unix, Exley explained presciently that new Unix-based engineering applications were already opening up attractive future markets. But whether Unix could really handle commercial applications would remain controversial in the computer industry for another five years.

Exley also persevered on having the engineering group adopt "open interfaces," allowing the engineers to incorporate printers and storage devices manufactured by other suppliers whenever NCR's own offerings were not at least 20 percent better. Noting that NCR held a leadership position on industry-wide standards, Hugh Lynch, the head of the general purpose systems division, opined that "pluralism represents the power of the industry."

In 1979, NCR had become the fifth-largest computer company, with nearly $4 billion in revenue. Growth remained well behind the new breed such as Sun. But Exley doubled all other major metrics. The growth in return on capital went from 8 percent to 16 percent, net profit from 3.6 percent to 7.7 percent, and R&D from 3 percent to 7.3 percent. And some clever acquisitions were made along the way, including Comten, whose box for IBM networking inserted NCR into IBM accounts; the box was better than Armonk's own offering.

In sharp contrast to AT&T's forced retreat, NCR best exemplified a company upending an outdated business model.

New Team in Basking Ridge

In 1983, AT&T still had time to build a market on Unix. Sun Microsystems had appeared just the year before, with Unix as its primary operating system. Most Unix users were academics who delighted in its openness and interactive capabilities. But many engineering applications still hadn't been converted from DEC or IBM operating systems. And the interest shown by builders of commercial software wasn't enough to give Unix a clear lead.

At our autumn visit to AT&T headquarters in Basking Ridge, New Jersey, we found enormous enthusiasm, competent managers, and a general recognition that AT&T was starting the race well behind the pack. At that point, 65 percent of AT&T's gross revenues still depended directly or indirectly on long-distance service. Another 15 percent came from rentals of network equipment inherited from the BOCs. Only 15 percent came from unregulated sales, and most of that was network switches to the BOCs. ATTIS had four segments:

- Large business systems (mainly PBXs) remained a mess, as revenues plummeted while market share dwindled to 44 percent. Though System 75 and System 85 PBXs had replaced the ill-conceived Dimension system, sales to new sites was growing less than 10 percent annually, and competition for replacement installations was ferocious. We considered it a breakthrough when our hosts finally admitted that AT&T's manufacturing, R&D, sales, and administration costs were too high. "Facing direct thrusts from IBM, Northern Telecom, and the Japanese is tough," allowed Ed Goldstein, now corporate vice president for strategy. Union wage rates were far higher than at the nonunionized competitors, and 30 percent higher than those of offshore PBX competitors. Achieving the 20 percent cost cuts mandated by Chairman Brown "won't be fast or painless," Goldstein told us (not that we had expected anything else). The most hopeful news was that the coddled cows sheltered by deButts were at last coming under the knife.

- Consumer and general business systems included key stations and handsets whose revenues were rapidly approaching the trivial.

- Services for field maintenance to existing customers were holding their own.

- Computer systems was now headed by former IBMer Jim Edwards, a much calmer, more circumspect executive than Archie McGill. His lieutenant was Jack Scanlon, a highly regarded, long-term AT&T manager.

Was it too late to reverse the steep slide? Our hosts spied promise on the horizon. AT&T market research had defined an $83 billion market with four segments—voice, data, text, and image. By their calculations, voice equipment represented just 9 percent of new equipment sales in 1983 across the industry, with annual growth under 10 percent. Conversely, new data equipment held 76 percent of the market in telecommunications gear and was growing by 30 percent a year. Unfortunately, AT&T data products covered the requirements of just 23 percent of this fast-growing market and would need to reach 50 percent by 1988, explained executive vice president Bob Casale. More encouragement came on the news that, after years of regulatory and managerial dithering, AT&T's 3B microprocessor was finally being marketed, though not widely as we learned later. Elsewhere, partner Olivetti's 6300 PC offered a slightly faster microprocessor and graphics than did IBM—though it generally underwhelmed us. Rumors of acquisitions persisted.

The ATTIS sales force now counted 2,500 account executives and 2,500 technical consultants; their mission was to sell the entire product line to *Fortune* 2,000 customers. Unfortunately, even after years of McGill badgering, the representatives still weren't computer-competent enough to brave meetings with IT executives, preferring comfortable noodling with low-level telecom managers. Senior ATTIS executives remained optimistic, however, that extensive training and aggressive recruiting, both from competitors and on campus, would improve the sales force's prospects. Maybe, but the training and recruiting should have begun ten years earlier.

Scanlon gave a less-than-pretty overview of product progress. Two new thrusts involved upgrading dumb terminals from the DataSpeed IV, a product whose market impact was decidedly minimal. An IBM lookalike knocked as "unexciting" by Scanlon was nevertheless "targeted at a very large market among the *Fortune* 2000." IBM wasn't expected to retaliate with price-cutting, given its dominant market share (and its non-response to the Xerox typewriter against Selectric). Finally, AT&T had rediscovered the modem market, previously ignored but actually "growing 20 percent a year and a pretty good cash cow," noted Edwards. Good news, but taken together, all the products mentioned still added less than 3 percent to AT&T's overall revenues.

Elsewhere, wheels spun with little traction. Sales of the 3B computer were almost exclusively inside the former Bell System, bringing in total revenues of just $600 million in 1983. Value-added resellers accounted for a few new sales, but the enterprise customers covered by the ATTIS account executives chipped in almost nothing. "Probably that's because most of those salesmen are either Bell-heads or bushy tails at this point," joked Scanlon, meaning they were lifelong telephone reps or college kids.

The 6300 PC acquired from Olivetti was sold mostly through retailers, with little penetration of enterprise accounts. "Until now, we've been looking at the *Fortune* 2,000 market from the perspective of the PC retailer," Edwards told us. "That's upside down! I've got to redirect our emphasis," he added emphatically. Admitting that the 6300 was an unabashed IBM clone, he insisted that AT&T had "learned from the Japanese. If necessary, buy the business," he intoned. "Certainly, we shouldn't let IBM beat us on price. For the short term, we're delighted to sell PCs as long as the System 75 and System 85 PBXs are manufacturing-bound. Over the long term, we simply expect the 6300 to help our reps understand the computer business." The hard truth was that Edwards didn't have a computer sales force then and never would.

Changing of the Guard

On September 1, 1986, the pragmatic James Olson replaced Charlie Brown as AT&T's chief executive officer. Much of the strategy had matured, but oft-shuffled AT&T was still an organization under heavy stress. From the deButts years of fighting to hold back the inevitable through the Brown years of accepting deregulation with grace, Olson was now embarked on a mission to put the worst lunacies of the past (like the half-baked assaults on deregulation) far behind the company while developing a credible business strategy for the future. Cheered the *Wall Street Journal* on November 12, 1987, "for the first time since the breakup of the Bell System, AT&T is presenting coherent strategies that, if executed well, could make it into the technical powerhouse it always thought it could be."

Leading with AT&T's core strengths, Olson's new strategy came in three parts: (1) Cherish the voice business "that got us here," and improve it with massive investments in fiber and software; (2) Do something about data networks; and (3) Pursue international business.

Though there were plans for massive cost-cutting and head-count reduction at ATTIS, Olson insisted the computer business wouldn't be abandoned—just revamped to emphasize networking. That made great sense. "AT&T isn't a computer company making a frontal assault on International Business Machines Corp.," an AT&T vice president was quoted as saying in the *Wall Street Journal* on November 25, 1986.

Sam Wilcoxxen, the business markets VP, ruefully remembered the years of reacting to politicians, judges, and regulators rather than to the market. "That consumed and almost paralyzed our management for fifteen years," he told us. "By the mid-seventies, Computer Inquiry II had deregulated parts of our business, but only by interposing an iron curtain between the fundamental power of the network and our customer-premises equipment. In 1982 came divestiture; for a full year, all our energies were spent unraveling history—pulling apart $154 million in assets, 1 million employees, 2,400 buildings, and so on. Then, last year's long-distance balloting [whereby consumers chose their long-distance carrier] was the greatest toss-up of market share ever seen. Fortunately, we came out better than we had anticipated. And now we're finally seeing some relief from the worst restrictions of Computer Inquiry II, as well." All that had been a huge distraction. The future could be better.

Not surprisingly, substantial investments were under way in the backbone network. A four-year plan to install 11,000 route-miles of fiber was finished in two years and then expanded to a target of 20,000 miles. At the same time, improvements in laser technology permitted fairly low-cost enhancements to capacity. Costs were dropping as well. One inadvertent bonanza came when the court's Modified Final Decree in the antitrust case mandated that AT&T vacate any building it operated jointly with the BOCs. Since most had been occupied by network switches that proved redundant under the new network technology, abandonment represented an accounting boon.

A far less favorable situation prevailed in customer-premises equipment, especially PBXs, which were weighted down by high manufacturing costs, low quality, and uncompetitive functionality. But restructurings were finally under way. The labor costs of some products were cut to 5 percent of the total from 12 percent; antiquated plants were closed, and a $3 billion write-off taken; Bell Labs' R&D expenditures were cut from previously unsustainable and often unproductive levels; and product quality was being restored after the era of recklessly outsourcing both product design and manufacturing. Especially damaging was the cordless telephone debacle; customer returns soared to 30 percent before being righted to a barely tolerable 8 percent. The company's reputation as a quality producer suffered for years.

Guiding data systems and the ragged entry of AT&T into the computer market was the senior VP for marketing, Vittorio Cassoni, a transplant from Olivetti. When we met in late 1986, Cassoni drew intricate arrow-and-target charts projecting AT&T's undeniable trajectory to industry dominance. But, in truth, the hopelessly ragged product line he had inherited weighed heavily on his chances of realizing this trajectory. The only profitable product was the 6300 PC, but just 190,000 were sold in 1986—and mostly through third parties. The 6300 couldn't begin to compensate for massive losses elsewhere. Meanwhile, the inventory of 7300 Unix workstations acquired from Convergent had been deemed "too pricey for the MS-DOS set, absent enough demand yet for Unix." The 3B microprocessor was alive, but just barely, selling in the low thousands to a few government agencies and the education market. The Unix system, having slipped the bounds of AT&T, was now controlled by the University of California at Berkeley and other forward-thinking enclaves.

Unix is the future, Cassoni had tooted brightly. "One can't base a whole business strategy on proprietary hardware architecture—that gets six months' lead time, no more." So AT&T would continue marketing the 6300 but leave the product side to Olivetti. It would continue to push an IBM-lookalike dumb terminal simply to keep the sales force engaged in computing. And, despite the fact that the Unix train was already leaving the station, AT&T would now plunge ahead, engaging 658 programmers in developing a range of functions necessary to make this lab animal industrial strength.

Cassoni was smart, but we weren't convinced. By 1987, it was probably too late for AT&T to compete profitably on the raw Unix, given the raft of savvy competitors led by Sun, NCR, and HP—and with IBM and DEC sniffing around the edges. Might the whole computer business be swept to the sidelines by a determined new CEO? That wouldn't happen. if only because the Olivetti relationship was integral to AT&T's broader strategy for its core business in Europe, insisted Al Stark in an informal conversation.

Burdened by New Leadership

On April 18, 1988, Jim Olson suddenly and unexpectedly died of colorectal cancer just four weeks after its diagnosis. Our old friend Al Stark called Naomi to say he was totally shocked; that Olson had been perfectly framed for the job and that without him, the future was uncertain. Appointed CEO the next day was Bob Allen, a leader prone to bouts of strategic myopia and, unlike the pragmatic Olson, inclined to back computing at any cost. With Allen now occupying the corner suite, AT&T announced a deal to acquire 20 percent of Sun and replace the 3B microprocessor with Sun's engine in return for Sun's beefed-up commitment to AT&T's Unix V.4 system.

It was a wonderful deal for both AT&T and Sun. But other Unix supporters—notably HP, IBM, and DEC—deduced (correctly) that Unix was no longer "open" (i.e., neutral), and they formed the Open Software Foundation to cooperate on an industry-wide offering. The rivals' response threatened to quash AT&T's hopes of capitalizing on its authorship of Unix, so the deal with Sun was axed instead. But even that didn't quell the suspicions. Salvos of hostile press releases between the two camps followed, despite promises of a summit meeting to end the hostilities. But if any meetings took place, they did nothing to heal the rift.

Back in the telecommunications arena, AT&T's three-year campaign to frighten off MCI and Sprint with veiled threats and intermittent pricing volleys fell flat, leaving Long Lines' market share stuck below 70 percent for the first time in the twentieth century. Revenues were flat "due to price adjustments made somewhat reluctantly," assured John Smart, the president of business communications services. "Now we're determined to stiffen our resistance," he told us. Did Smart mean resistance to further price cuts or to further market-share erosion? Or both? Or neither?

The clearest signal from the AT&T forces was the planned cut in headquarters' head count, to 25,500 employees from 33,000. The only good news was AT&T's plan to convert the entire network from analog to digital—twenty years ahead of schedule! "A few years ago," Smart recalled, "our target was the year 2010. Then last year, we decided to finish by 1991; now we'll finish in August or September 1990." A good thing, too, because by now, MCI and Sprint had won enough market credibility to capture business by pricing just 5 percent below AT&T, versus the previously offered discount of 15 percent and the 25 percent demanded by their earliest customers. Price was the be-all and end-all. No amount of public posturing would stay AT&T's collapse.

Perhaps Allen's desperation over declining market share in networking and premises equipment was responsible for the next bombshell. In 1990, the chief killed industry-wide cooperation on Unix by announcing AT&T's intention to acquire NCR and thereby enter the server business itself. By then, Chuck Exley had navigated the BUNCH survivor through a twisting trail of transitions from mainframes and mechanicals to seven product tiers, all running on Intel micros and Unix and ranging from PCs to workstations to multiprocessor minis. Pricing at the high end was $10,000 per MIPS, well below the going rate at IBM or even DEC and HP.

Exley acknowledged that redirecting the one-time cash-register king hadn't been easy: "It's horrendously difficult to change. And the huge tasks of training and retraining continue," he told me. Exley was ahead of almost everyone in the industry. No one was smarter or tougher—as his 1991 coup in getting AT&T to pay $7.4 billion for NCR, or $1.4 billion over the original offer, would prove.

At a luncheon we attended in Dayton, Ohio, in late 1990, the blue-vested Exley took a long pull on his cigar and mused, "Bob Allen thinks he can persuade me to stay on [as a vice chairman leading a computer business], but when they shoot their way in here, I'll be long gone." And on the spring day when the final (and giddily predictable) shareholder vote was counted, Chuck honored a prior commitment to meet with the RB in San Francisco. After a great presentation, he sat quietly, apparently without regrets. He was, as predicted, "long gone."

Sometimes, even a great CEO can't save a company from the stupidity of a desperate acquirer with too much money. Paradoxically, the NCR acquisition actually ended any AT&T hope for a Unix hegemony. Sun quickly moved to create Solaris, its own semiproprietary

Unix flavor. HP, IBM, and DEC followed similar routes. With all that, the entire equipment business drew barely a paragraph in AT&T's 1990 annual report, beginning with "the relatively flat state of AT&T's other businesses. Its share of the PBX market has fallen to 30 percent; expansion of the central office equipment business depends on foreign alliances, and computer revenues are insignificant at best." The great hope that year was the newly constructed credit-card business, from which AT&T got a nice bounce before it was sold to Citibank.

Except for his acquisition of McCaw Cellular, Allen may have been the most counterproductive CEO in AT&T's spotty leadership history; only John Akers, his contemporary at IBM, comes close. Yet, Allen would cling to his job for several more years until forced out by the incoming Mike Armstrong. The new CEO was the successful chief executive of Hughes Electronics, a position he won after being ousted from a senior IBM role by Akers. As the first AT&T CEO to know anything about computers, Armstrong soon divested NCR at a multibillion-dollar loss, along with remnants of the once-proud Western Electric (renamed Lucent). The regurgitated NCR was left in a severely weakened state after racking up $3.6 billion in cumulative losses. Its revenues in 2005 were not much better than they were in 1983, and the gain was mostly derived from Teradata data-warehouse boxes, retail systems, and service. AT&T shrank to a sickly shadow of its formerly robust self, having benefited not at all from its computing assets—no matter what the marketers proclaimed. Unix in wiser hands helped crush the minicomputer sector.

Looking back, AT&T's failed product strategy is not so surprising—no matter the punditry over a convergence between computing and communications. To begin with, AT&T never fielded a capable line of computers, just as IBM never developed a credible voice network offering despite the acquisition of the Rolm PBX company or Satellite Business Systems. In fact, the two sectors showed far more divergence than synergy before cell phones and the Voice over Internet Protocol.

Chapter 10

THE PERILS OF INCUMBENCY:

Sun and Oracle Take Over the Neighborhood

Choosing the moment to make the daring leap from a successful technology to something new and more competitive requires the keen timing of the trapeze artist choosing when to leave his trapeze. Except there's no nimble-handed catcher for the business leader. So the more stable the old business model, the flimsier seems the new—making it all the easier to just "wait and see." Success can be a killer once the wheels of change begin to turn. Two competitive pairings—Tandem Computer versus Sun Microsystems and Cullinet versus Oracle—illustrate the perils of incumbency.

Tandem was formed in 1974, eight years before Sun, as the last significant minicomputer company built on a proprietary operating system. And what a system it was. Designed never to fail or lose even a single transaction, Tandem's NonStop computer met almost instant acceptance from an intensely demanding group of banking and brokerage clients, including the Securities Industry Automation Corporation (SIAC), which provided IT to both the New York and American Stock exchanges. Over several years, NonStop became integral to the operation of the financial markets.

Sun appeared in 1982, one of the first and certainly most successful companies to start with Unix as its only operating system. For cofounder and CEO Scott McNealy, Unix's "openness" provided at least three strategic advantages: (1) It drew engineering and scientific applications from third-party software suppliers; (2) it supported Sun's sales proposition to customers by delivering lower switching costs than competitors' "closed" proprietary systems offered; and (3) Unix smoothed the transition for customers each time Sun upgraded its microprocessor, the SPARC (for Scalable Processor ARChitecture). In the early years, Sun doubled its price/performance ratio every year or two, versus every five years for DEC or IBM.

Meanwhile, Cullinet Software, which entered the database market in the early 1970s (seven years before Oracle), grew into the world's second-largest software vendor (after Lotus) in just ten years. Central to Cullinet's growth was the rampant success of the IBM 4300 minicomputer, which underpinned half the company's revenues. Oracle was started around the new relational database but at first had difficulty gaining traction against well-entrenched competition. Up against Cullinet, Applied Data Research (ADR), and Cincom in the software segment, Oracle also faced hardware majors IBM, DEC, and HP that fielded their own databases.

But Oracle was not without its charms, the first being ease of use. Its relational structure allowed a user to retrieve information quickly and easily. The second advantage was portability across most mainstream minicomputers. Three years after Oracle reached volume shipments, Cullinet was crushed.

In Tandem with Treybig

I first met Jimmy Treybig, Tandem's founder and CEO, in late 1977, just after the company floated its initial public stock offering. Tandem was then still cozy enough that each box on the assembly line carried a small cardboard plaque commemorating the customer's name and national flag. The Research Board was studying microprocessors, and since Tandem was relatively new, I assumed it was microprocessor-based. The slightly beer-bellied Jimmy was slouched back in his chair, cowboy boots propped on his desk. But when I mentioned microprocessors, he jumped up to take me on a rambling tour of the NonStops on the assembly floor. "You must know microprocessor part numbers. You see any of 'em here?"

Our meeting was short, and that year's RB report about the computer industry contained nothing about Tandem. But within two years, the company was soaring: Sales more than doubled, to $54 million from $24 million the year earlier, driven indisputably by product differentiation accentuated, as Jimmy put it, through "the leverage of our architecture." Unlike many of the failing minicomputer companies, Tandem's R&D investment, which averaged 10 percent of revenues, was dedicated solely to one processor and operating system. "This industry is no longer manufacturing- and capital-intensive," Treybig told me when we met again in 1979. "It is changing to an IQ business."

Marketing? Didn't need much. The product's unique capabilities—reliability, security, data integrity, and field upgradeability—were eagerly sought by banks, brokerages, oil companies, and the defense agencies. Field service? Didn't need much of that, either, "since the NonStop system keeps running until our engineer arrives." As for supplier relations, Jimmy had that base covered, too: "We have no shortages because we don't castrate our suppliers. We always buy what we've said we'll buy, and I never argue about pennies." Management quality was a nonissue because he didn't hire managers. "I can hire outstanding people who don't need management," Treybig bragged. Viva soaring growth and wide-open margins! The company's most serious problem was the 20 percent growth in head count per quarter. In organizational terms, he explained, "that means 20 percent of our people have been here less than six weeks."

Four years later, Tandem's ebullient outlook prompted Jimmy to fly the entire management team to Paris. Left to greet us that day in 1983 was Dr. Jerry Held, the director of strategic planning. A genuinely capable strategist, Held showed us slides listing the five most critical exogenous factors for the company over the next five years:

- IBM unleashed from antitrust concerns;
- AT&T divested of its operating companies;
- Competition from the Japanese;
- Proliferation of PCs; and
- Rapid growth of home information services.

Not a bad list, but, in hindsight, not the most relevant to Tandem. Here was another example of "insufficient understanding" by those closest to the looming threat of a destructive technology.

Held also saw the industry truncating into three sectors: (1) large-capacity database computers, with IBM, Tandem, and the Japanese as the only competitors; (2) intermediate processors connecting networks and computers, which would be left to the surviving minis; and (3) interactive workstations produced by a few minicomputer companies and maybe others. "Apple may survive," he told me, "and Wang. The Japanese may enter. Almost all the smaller contenders will fail." Held was correct only about IBM and, arguably, Apple. He completely overlooked Unix, sensibly because AT&T seemed to be floundering with a cult product for engineers, while Sun was only in its second, still-difficult year and NCR appeared an aberration. At a Research Board meeting the following April, NCR's vice president of technology asked how many of our members were building commercial applications on Unix. Only one hand went up, and even that person admitted to me afterward that his company didn't actually have any Unix projects. He just thought the speaker shouldn't feel rejected.

In the Land of the Sun

It's difficult for me to write about Scott McNealy, in part because Naomi joined Sun's board of directors after we left the RB, and partly because Scott himself is an amalgam of wisecracking smart-ass (his favorite self-depiction), unparalleled leader, strategic visionary, financial detailer, personal loyalist, best CEO golfer, and ferocious hockey player.

His father had been the vice chairman of American Motors and, many thought, the anointed successor to the CEO. At one point, he unsuccessfully pressed the board of directors to persevere as a fully integrated car company rather than being hollowed out by subcontracting most of its engineering and manufacturing functions. The board vigorously disagreed, effectively ending the elder McNealy's career. In later years, some people admitted that McNealy was probably right. The danger of allowing a company to be hollowed out could not have been lost on the son.

Scott graduated from Harvard ("majoring in golf," he jokes), then went on to the Stanford Business School. He joined three other extraordinary men—Vinod Khosla, William Nelson "Bill" Joy, and Andreas "Andy" Bechtolsheim—in founding Sun Microsystems, which

McNealy first served as vice president of manufacturing. Though not officially one of Sun's founders, John Doerr funded the start-up through Kleiner Perkins Caulfield & Byers, itself the premier venture capital firm in computing, communications, and biotechnology. All five men became leaders of Silicon Valley.

After leaving Sun in 1985, Khosla performed brilliantly as a venture capitalist and lead partner at Kleiner Perkins. But Vinod has never forgotten his Sun experience and continually lectures the CEOs of start-ups he funds on the importance of attracting a management team full of future CEOs "like we had at Sun." As far as I know, Vinod is seldom satisfied with the results. Bill Joy, the software genius who designed the Unix Internet interface (TCP/IP stack) and Java, among other inventions, stayed at Sun until 2003. Andy Bechtolsheim, who led Sun's microprocessor effort, later founded Granite Systems and became an angel investor in Google, before returning to Sun in 2004 to lead a major hardware initiative. Doerr, who briefly served as Sun's acting CEO, remained a director long after becoming the managing partner of KPCB.

I first met Scott one evening in July 1986, in a noisy restaurant-cum-singles bar, where the RB's lead researcher, Cathy Loup, and I were introduced by Carol Bartz, then Sun's VP of field operations and subsequently CEO of Autodesk and Yahoo. From the first handshake, Scott embarked on a characteristically dizzying ramble about Unix, distributed computing, industry standards, the competition, technology, customers, and the world in general. Building a company image was one of McNealy's priorities, as he looked toward the day when the purchase decision would shift from engineers buying "onesie-twosies" to senior executives buying hundreds. So Sun was spending $600,000 to develop a logo. "Where's your logo?" he barked, squinting through the gloom at my business card. I was too cynical, never mind jet-lagged, to conclude anything more than that Scott was probably nuts.

I changed my mind a day later after Scott walked me through his 140-page report on business metrics, complete with voluminous financial analyses and comparisons with competitors (especially workstation-maker Apollo) and role models (high-margin Cray), which provided the platform for his monthly management review. We met at the company's Santa Clara, California, headquarters, so I was also introduced to several Sun executives, which reinforced my positive impression; strong subordinates are the leading indicators of CEO quality in my experience.

As Sun's technology VP, Andy Bechtolsheim nearly drowned us with a fire-hose description of projections in computer hardware, complete with napkin scrawls "you can keep."

The company's basic strategy wrapped together Moore's Law, Unix portability, and emerging standards, which meant it expected to double the capacity of its $20,000 workstation every eighteen months, reaching 50 MIPS in five years. That amounted to a price/performance trajectory three times steeper than the conventional four-year product cycles then maintained by DEC and even HP. Unix would attract more applications and whisk their migration to increasingly powerful processors. Ethernet would link to Digital Equipment and others through an "open standard," while destroying archcompetitor Apollo's advantage in proprietary networks. And all this on a business model that gave Sun a 10 percent or better cost advantage, below the minicomputer makers' expectations.

Just four years old, Sun had already streaked to $200 million in revenues, headlined by a 1983 breakneck win at ComputerVision, an order that Vinod Khosla personally snatched from industry leader Apollo, essentially by camping unbidden in the prospect's lobby. Market focus was moving beyond computer-aided design to electronic-publishing, medical-imaging, seismic-mapping, telephone company, and Wall Street securities-trading applications (firms like Salomon Brothers always wanted the best and fastest for their traders). The customer base was moving away from the original resellers, who had been attracted by Sun's dazzling cost performance, and toward end users, who now accounted for 60 percent of Sun's business.

Scott was focused on the future. "Quality execution is our top priority; IBM never puts good companies out of business," he liked to say. His laserlike focus was in sharp contrast to the distracted minicomputer CEOs of the time, whose companies were falling in droves to IBM's 4300 and S/38. In October, we invited McNealy to address the RB at a meeting in Detroit hosted by Chrysler CIO Nick Simonds. Scott spoke mainly about Sun's entries in the computer-aided design space, but seemed delighted to learn that Wall Street firms like Salomon Brothers probably had more Sun devices than did Chrysler's design center.

Our analyses also took us to Apollo in Chelmsford, Massachusetts, that year. It was just then beginning a painful transition to Unix from its own pioneering operating system, causing us to end our report by noting, "Sometimes a head start can become a headache." In the same vein, Apollo's management was rightly convinced that its idiosyncratic network was better than Ethernet. But who cared? By then, its market share had shrunk to 35 percent, and Sun, with over 30 percent, was closing fast. One immediate problem for Apollo was that revenues depended on three OEM customers whose sales downturns in 1985 had forced Apollo to take a major write-down for obsolescent inventory and substantial excess manufacturing capacity. Though the imbalances had been righted by 1986, we nevertheless concluded: "The company may have trouble regaining its dominance. The real question is whether current product and service directions can do more than merely help Apollo stay even against its competitors."

The company was subsequently acquired by Hewlett-Packard for just $476 million; its technology was essentially left to wither. McNealy was jubilant over what he correctly perceived as a huge strategic error by HP CEO John Young. Apollo had been the competitor most feared by Sun. Now it was gone, unable to make the transition to the open operating-system technology and cost model in time to save itself.

At Tandem, the Victory Parade Passes

Tandem's finest hour, viewed from the perspective of the global economy, came in October 1987, when the stock market crashed. The unprecedented volume spikes would likely have choked conventional systems, with potentially staggering financial consequences worldwide. The SIAC President and RB member Charles McQuade told the group that he'd been called by the White House to warn that if the system failed, the markets would assume the computer failure was contrived to cover up a market panic that could then ignite a crash rivaling 1929 proportions.

But, meanwhile, Sun was no longer flying under the radar and had, in fact, emerged as the hottest property in Silicon Valley. "Growth rates have teetered between astounding and off-the-cliff for the past several years," we wrote, our optimism buttressed by the constant Valley bad-mouthing, a sure sign of Sun's rise.

On the day Naomi and I visited, Scott's thirty-third birthday was being celebrated with a special breakfast of "McNealy McMuffins" in the cafeteria, which was festooned with thousands of ribbons and balloons. Adding oomph to the celebration was the introduction of SPARC, Sun's first RISC microprocessor (a more efficient design than its rival CISC). SPARC opened with 10 MIPS ready to market, 25 MIPS already in prototype, and a 40-MIPS follow-on in design. And in another strategic coup, SPARC birthed the idea of a "fabless" microprocessor, with Sun retaining microprocessor design while leaving fabrication to the impossibly expensive foundries built by Texas Instruments, Fujitsu, and others. Across the continent in Maynard, Massachusetts, Digital's halting development of a 30 MIPS proprietary mainframe now seemed irrelevant.

Unix was just then expanding from its engineering-scientific base into new territory. A year later, however, business interest was still weak. "Would Unix gain the data integrity and systems reliability necessary for commercial applications?" we asked in 1988. Definitely "yes," said Sun's McNealy, though he had no other horse to ride. Definitely "no," insisted Joel Birnbaum, HP's legendary vice president of research, possibly trying to protect the market for his company's long-delayed operating system.

Despite the ambiguity, Tandem's total silence on Unix was rapidly becoming less defensible as new players moved into the high-volume transaction market. Encore and Sequent had harnessed Unix atop twenty or thirty microprocessors at capacity prices far below those of IBM mainframes and Tandem NonStops. True, the contraptions were prone to failure and data loss, but many applications could survive occasional failures and even lost data since they weren't dealing with cash transactions. At the Radisson Hotel chain, a reservation system costing just $200,000 and serving sixty-five operators, responded to an operator's request in only two seconds (dizzying at the time). At American Airlines, a trial hotel system suffered no hardware breakdowns and only nine minutes of software outage in four months of operation. Admittedly, it mattered little if hotel-reservation systems were down for nine minutes or a couple of hours, or even if a few room reservations were lost. These weren't brokerage-stock trades or bank-fund transfers, after all. In many environments, Unix rigged with parallel processors was now good enough to challenge Tandem—unless Jimmy Treybig could slash his prices.

But Tandem wasn't moving. Luckily, Jimmy got an accidental reprieve when AT&T's proposed alliance with Sun disrupted the industry's progress toward an industry-wide operating system by threatening to make Bell Labs' Unix and Sun's SPARC the de facto standard. The deal made sense, given Sun's emphasis on proprietary hardware, and would simultaneously make Unix a volume leader. Unfortunately, the always-combative McNealy publicly blurted that SPARC would be married to Unix just like Intel was to Microsoft, a collaboration of major consequence. Judging that their own RISC programs were now threatened, DEC, HP, and IBM united into a temporary alliance-of-convenience under the banner "Free Unix!" The Open Software Foundation was formed next, its acronym OSF, which the wisecracking McNealy dubbed, "Oppose Scott Forever." In the end, the AT&T offer was scratched, and neither camp ever regained volume dominance, effectively handing the workstation business to Microsoft. McNealy's irrepressible disregard for diplomacy had unleashed a disruptive counterforce, and not for the last time.

ATTIS head Bob Kavner then floated the idea of spinning off the $100 million Unix activity as a separate entity, with AT&T owning 60 percent, the employees owning 10 percent, and other computer vendors owning the rest. But after repeated confabs between AT&T and the major computer companies, CEO Bob Allen made his shocking 1990 announcement: AT&T intended to acquire NCR, which already had a strong position in Unix.

Industry cooperation came to a halt. Jimmy Treybig even suggested that AT&T's endless noodling about industry ownership of Unix had simply been a ruse to identify the most likely acquisition target. Negotiations collapsed. Kavner tried to draw back DEC, HP, and IBM by spinning off Unix into a stand-alone entity called Unix System Laboratories (USL). When that failed, USL was sold to Novell in 1992 for a stock swap valued at $300 million, a handsome multiple on USL's roughly $80 million of revenues, but far below Bell Labs' prior investments and hoped-for returns.

Sun was now free to pursue its own Unix brand, Solaris, following similar excursions by DEC, HP, and IBM, leading me to ask Scott whether the Solaris functional extensions weren't making Unix less and less of an industry standard. He laughed, observing that "programmers swallow those extensions like fishhooks in a Twinkie. I can't help it if your CIOs can't control their own programmers." As I came to realize over the years, standards were a vehicle for third-place and fourth-place contenders questing for higher ground. But market leaders sought differentiation (often invisible) to raise customer-switching costs and protect their positions.

"Unix is a puzzlement," we wrote that year. Nevertheless, we finally detected real acceptance for commercial applications among enterprises like American Airlines, Hartford Insurance, Honeywell, J. C. Penney, Kmart, and Kraft General Foods. American, for instance, no longer used a mainframe for crew scheduling, having switched to several Unix processors. Penney developed an international merchandise buying system using Unix, and Kmart changed from IBM Series/1 to Unix servers for in-store computers. True, issues of economics, data lost in the buffers, and disaster-recovery weaknesses were still unresolved, but they were being addressed.

Still, the level of infighting, paranoia, and doubt among Unix suppliers had never been higher. The Open Software Foundation was already unraveling, as DEC, HP, and IBM edged back to their own brands despite their joint $100 million investment. In October 1990, *Business Week* commented tartly, "[The alliance is] lacking the ingredient that made OSF a credible threat in the first place: the backing of the industry giants that paid for it." Sure enough, DEC and IBM were developing their AIX and Ultrix operating systems on the off chance that customers would continue to prefer their proprietary systems. HP used AT&T Unix on its workstation, but resorted to its own version elsewhere.

The industry executives we interviewed—from New York to Silicon Valley to Tokyo—couldn't stop talking about a December 6, 1990, article that appeared in the *Wall Street Journal*: "The problem is that computer companies have jumped into the market faster than the UNIX pie has grown," it judged. "Moreover, in the rush to sell UNIX systems, manufacturers have overlooked a fundamental point in economics: Makers of standard products have few means of differentiating themselves from rivals, forcing them to compete on price. Computers that run UNIX have rapidly become commodity items."

All the same, supporting Unix had become disturbingly expensive. IBM privately admitted spending $150 million annually on Unix maintenance for systems with total sales of just $200 million, meaning it was losing money once sales and other costs were considered. HP and Sun, both of which were spending $100 million, admitted they either had to make cuts or spread costs through alliances. Said DEC's David Stone, "Open systems are a club that customers use to beat the profitability out of their system suppliers."

DEC, HP, and IBM were spending tens of millions of dollars on OSF, plus thirty-five dollars per license to AT&T. Non-OSF members paid nothing to the alliance but more per license. That expense might have been acceptable when Unix rode $100,000 servers, but not when it was competing against Intel and Microsoft. Worried one workstation vendor to us: "No vendor can charge $300 for Unix on a $3,000 workstation, especially when Microsoft charges under $100 for its operating system." Unix fees to OSF would have to be slashed to eight dollars per copy, and each company could spend no more than another twenty-five dollars per copy on enhancements.

Tandem's ambivalence about Unix in such a climate was understandable, but ultimately fatal. "This could be the final playoffs," allowed Jimmy Treybig, during our visit "The most sensible strategy today is to assume the industry is narrowing, then concentrate on your fundamental competitive advantages. For Tandem, it's throughput, reliability, network management," areas where R&D could add high-margin value while the company absorbed industry standards everywhere else.

Yet neither the foresighted Jimmy nor his well-positioned board of directors acted decisively on his grim forecast for the industry. True, Tandem had begun implementing a new RISC microprocessor from MIPS Inc., but Treybig remained suspicious of Unix on strategic as well as technical grounds. Clear signs of its acceptance in commercial computing from both software suppliers and large customers weren't enough to sway Jimmy. "AT&T always rapes anyone who uses Unix," he told me. Bob Allen's assault on NCR had convinced him that computer companies should make another operating system the industry standard. "Unix is only a good idea in good times," he insisted. "When sales turn down, it's a terrible idea." From a technical perspective, Jimmy thought the throughput and price-performance improvements demanded by the market required an operating system built specifically to optimize the underlying hardware. Nor would he budge on the need for Tandem's own proprietary database, dismissing Oracle and Sybase. By now, Tandem's cost model looked paunchy, even in comparison to IBM or DEC. The highflier of 1987 was rapidly losing altitude three years later.

A Hot Sun Makes Rivals Sweat

Sun's revenues flew past Tandem's in 1990 and kept on going—from $2.4 billion to $3.6 billion by 1992—largely at the expense of Digital, HP, and the remaining workstation vendors. Scott McNealy gave us a characteristically staccato pitch, streaking through his claims of a 10:1 price/performance advantage over traditional computer makers and a 75 percent share of units sold in the RISC market (only 60 percent, grumped industry scorekeeper IDC). Sun would sell more RISC boxes in the next two months than IBM had shipped in its history, he crowed. Unix would become safe for commercial systems, including transaction processing, with AT&T's latest System V, Release 4, he assured us. But he claimed he wasn't technical enough to answer questions about how soon obvious gaps would be remedied. And when queried about the lack of business packages, such as a dowdy old accounting application like general ledger, the wunderkind exclaimed that no one had ever asked.

Scott wasn't worried about anyone in 1992 as he described the future of the computer industry by drawing a matrix of nine circles on his office whiteboard. The left-hand column was for hardware, the center column for software, and the rightmost column contained the names of the companies marketing those products. Then he filled in the circles. The top row was Pentium, then Windows, and finally "Wintel" for Intel & Microsoft—or "General & Motors" in Scott's estimation. The second row contained Sun's SPARC microprocessor, Unix, and Sun Microsystems. "We're Ford," he declared with breathtaking self-confidence. The bottom row listed PS/2 (or Power), OS/2, and IBM, which this son of the former American Motors vice chairman likened to "Chrysler." Was he nuts? "What about DEC, Hewlett-Packard, Wang, and a dozen other companies still larger than Sun?" we blurted.

All doomed, he assured us with cheerful finality. DEC and HP couldn't make up their minds on "open software" versus their own proprietary systems, he pointed out, leaving Sun in the lead on Unix— but also opening the race for volume to Microsoft. Additionally, DEC was visibly wobbling, while HP was choking on the undigested and unsuccessful Apollo acquisition, raising rumors about CEO John Young's future. "What about the Japanese?" I asked. "They're over," he said unblinkingly.

The only competition in McNealy's sights was IBM's new Unix computer based on its Power microprocessor. Some people loathed Scott's two-fisted bashing of the opposition, especially Microsoft. But even when he was wrong, his prognosis was always interesting. Second only to Microsoft in volume, Unix did dominate the industry but divided among several brands, including the AT&T original. And, clearly, Scott overestimated the survivability of IBM's OS/2 and underestimated the market appeal of its mainframes and AS/400 minis. But he was largely correct on the market factors that would exile his CEO counterparts at DEC, HP, and IBM just two years later.

By then, Sun led the industry in its installed base of high-performance workstations. Its RISC (fabricated by Texas Instruments and Fujitsu) also led in unit-sales volumes. SPARC was now being implemented by Amdahl for mainframe-scale servers, ICL for department servers, plus Cray, Hal Ltd., NEC, Hyundai, Tadpole, Toshiba, and Unisys.

There might have been more if Scott weren't so addicted to verbal pyrotechnics and so suspicious of potential competitors like Fujitsu's investment in potential competitor Hal. Many potential allies remembered how Scott first encouraged workstation SPARC clones and then crushed them: "We soon realized these parasites weren't adding any value but merely followed our salespeople to undercut their prices. So we had to kill them," incautiously admitted a senior Sun exec. Add that to McNealy's 1988 euphoria about having Sun and AT&T combine to disadvantage the other Unix brands. All that was hardly conducive to an *entente cordiale* against the Intel/Microsoft axis.

McNealy worried more than one potential ally. Visiting Fujitsu in Tokyo in 1992, we sensed a certain tension about Scott, especially after Sunnyvale faxed Tokyo a pile of memos that inadvertently included a two-page Sun potboiler entitled "What We Should Do in Japan."

"Ha ha ha," laughed President Sekizawa, simultaneously conveying considerable annoyance—through a circumspect translator—at McNealy-san's unwillingness to share the ownership and profits of SPARC design.

Back home, Sun was making far too little progress extending its penetration beyond telephone companies, research labs, and brokerage houses. Commercial customers represented 70 percent of Unix's business, yet the company derived barely 30 percent of its overall revenues from the commercial sector—even when federal government agencies, which accounted for 24 percent of Sun's business, were classified as "commercial." So the company tried to reorient half of its field reps toward commercial prospects. Reorienting a sales force is hard to do in any company, and Sun was no exception. People recruited from faltering Data General, for instance, were extremely and usefully aggressive, but they weren't exactly a battering ram of entry into mainstream business accounts.

To ramp up sales, the company decentralized into five major business units. The Sun Microsystems Computer arm under Ed Zander sold and supported complete systems, with half its 8,000 people in the field. SPARC Technology, which had 600 employees, designed the microprocessor and then sold and supported the raw engine. The SunSoft subsidiary, with its 2,000 employees, developed and marketed Solaris. Another 2,300 people were engaged in field support and telemarketing units. It was a formidable crew.

Masked Anxiety

Across the Valley at Tandem in 1992, Jimmy bounced to greet us. "We feel excited!" He wasn't convincing. Just two years earlier, he had asserted his reluctance to move to Unix. "Half our sales and 80 percent of our new accounts come through packagers. But so far, they are staying with Guardian [the Tandem OS] as often as they choose Unix." This dependence on packagers dependent on Guardian would soon be another instance of an asset becoming an anchor. Meanwhile, the company had finished installing the RISC engine acquired from MIPS Inc., which he reckoned would boost Tandem's two-to-one price/performance advantage over IBM mainframes to five-to-one (it did, but not for long). At the same time, five full percentage points had been shaved from an impossibly flush gross margin of 64 percent. Moreover, manufacturing head-count had been cut almost in half, to 470 from 900. Treybig reckoned Tandem's price per transaction needed to be within 15 percent of what workstations like Sun's could deliver. Coming soon, he told me, was a new product with twice the power for one-third the price. "Wouldn't that cannibalize Tandem's existing business?" I wondered. Nope, replied Jimmy, because lower prices would stimulate demand.

But signs of harder times ahead were difficult to miss. Treybig had taken a half-step toward open systems, but too late. Tandem's new Unix clone was missing a gene or two; it lagged the proprietary system on essentials like fault tolerance and other integrity features, making it essentially uncompetitive. So, what was the point? Meanwhile, Oracle's distribution of licenses by platform (see Table 10.1) showed that Unix had reached the tipping point, and its lead was growing. Tandem would soon follow DEC's spiral on more paths than one.

Table 10.1 Oracle Distribution by Operating System

	UNIX	DEC/VMS	Other
1990	36%	42%	22%
1991	47	28	25
1992	57	18	25
1993	61	14	26

Source: Oracle

Tandem's gross margins (Table 10.2) and percentage of revenues spent on selling, general, and administrative expense (Table 20.1) still seemed uncompetitive. "Cut the sales force," we advised. Jimmy's usually crinkly smile turned sad. He had already refocused the sales reps on banks and brokers, where the sales cycle could be as short as six weeks versus ten months elsewhere. Even so, he had doubtless heard the warning already from his board of directors, and especially its strong-minded, industry-rooted chairman, Tom Perkins, the founder and managing partner of the famed venture-capital firm Kleiner Perkins Caufield & Byers. But by the time he finally resumed cost-cutting, it was too late.

Within a year, Tandem's SG&A expense had been cut to 34 percent of 1994 revenues on its way to the targeted 29 percent. Pretty good on its face, but DEC and IBM, both with brand-new CEOs struggling for survival, had already dropped theirs to around 25 percent, about the same as Sun. Tandem cut prices, offering twice the capacity for half the cost, and advertising a 75 percent discount on extra memory, disks, and software.

Tandem's computer sales jumped almost threefold when we visited. "No one had ever before revived a dying computer line enough to grow at double-digit rates," crowed Jimmy. Trouble was, total revenues remained nearly flat as IBM's new CEO Louis Gerstner initiated massive price cuts on mainframes. Then, too, customers encountered newly assessed charges for field services. The services were free on Tandem boxes costing $2 million, but customers at the $600,000 level felt the pain.

We closed our report by noting that Tandem had lagged the industry in moving to Unix. Now the blood was in the water, its scent noticeable to customer and competitor alike. Potential new customers shied away, concerned about the company's viability and the lack of Unix-like portability should an exit be required.

More gloom descended on Tandem in 1996, as revenues fell from $2.3 billion to $1.9 billion (about the level achieved in 1991) and red ink colored the financials despite the cost-cutting. Jimmy Treybig was soon ousted by Perkins, his longtime friend from their HP days, and a year later, the one-time industry meteor was bought by PC maker Compaq.

In 2003, Jimmy was driving me to the airport after a visit to one of his investment company's dazzling computer-security start-ups when he suddenly offered an admission that "Naomi and you were right about moving much sooner to Unix." He couldn't remember the cost structure, but he reckoned it had been competitive. Maybe against Akers's IBM, I mused silently, but not against the new breed.

Heading Skyward

Sun's trajectory when compared to Tandem's was striking. Even in a down year for the industry, its growth in 1992 was a heady 30 percent, while gross margins had been honed to a fine-edged

41 percent, which still provided a 6 percent profit and allowed for spending 15 percent of revenues on R&D. The one disappointment was Sun's continuing difficulty in broadening its customer base. At least 70 percent of revenues still came from the technical space, and at least 75 percent of the sales reps were still technically oriented. "Barely a third of them could even make a commercial presentation to CIOs," allowed sales VP Joe Roebuck. But management (excepting McNealy) accepted this state of affairs without complaint. "We must be active in technical markets, where we have feet on the street," rationalized J. Phillip Samper, former Vice Chairman at Eastman Kodak, now at Sun as McNealy's sounding board and "CEO coach." To reach beyond that shrinking circle, Sun would get help from its Unix ally Amdahl, Phil declared (blindly, we muttered). To this day, the gap persists.

Sun continued to flourish through 1995, despite slower revenue growth and savage hits from Microsoft, as Moore's Law pushed the Intel chips used in PCs to workstation capacity. Unit sales of Microsoft's Windows NT increased 80 percent in 1997, against a 7 percent decline for all of the Unix variants combined. Over the next few years, Sun's workstation business eroded.

In response, Scott exhibited the steadfastness characteristic of all top leaders in computing. He was firmly convinced that Sun should continue to field both its own SPARC microprocessor design and its own Solaris brand of Unix. Perhaps remembering his father's stand against the hollowing out that doomed American Motors, he scoffed at the idea that the company should move to a PC business dependent on Microsoft and Intel, though that's what Hewlett-Packard was doing. At various points in the discussion, Scott stood nearly alone in opposition to the market-grounded views of Sun's field organization.

Just three years later, McNealy's eight-year-old prognostications about the future shape of the computer industry seemed prescient. Solaris installed on a 64-bit SPARC opened a sizable advantage over both IBM AIX and HP-UX. By 1999, Sun rode the surge in telephone-company servers and Internet portals: "We're the dot in dot-com," the Sunsters burbled convincingly. In that difficult time, Sun could maintain its prices and even fatten its gross margins, while the traditionalists were reduced to subsistence diets.

Table 10.2 Comparative Gross Margins

	1990	1992	1994	1997
Sun	42.3	45.3	41.3`	49.8
Tandem	59.3	54.7		
HP	47.2	44.2	38.1	34.0
IBM	55.5	45.6	39.9	39.0
Compaq	42.8	29.1	25.1	27.5
Dell	28.2	31.7	15.1	22.0

Source: Company Financials

In software, the only adversary was Microsoft, cheered McNealy: "Solaris revenues grew almost 15 percent, IBM AIX growth was single-digit; HP-UX was off our radar." Such optimism shattered, however, when the e-commerce bubble imploded in March 2000. Where did that leave Sun? In 2006, Scott was replaced as CEO by Jonathon Schwarz. Sun then assimilated industry-standard X86 microprocessors from AMD and Intel (while retaining SPARC) and released Solaris to the open-source world. But the company was unable to offset the lost revenues with enough service business. And in 2009, Sun was acquired by Oracle, not IBM—a bittersweet ending.

Cullinet Is Trampled by Oracle

Cullinane Corporation, formed in 1968 with private financing, proceeded to develop or acquire a few simple data-retrieval packages. Five years later, those products were running out of market steam when Naomi identified the company as a potential distributor and acquirer of the IDMS database system developed by our client, the B. F. Goodrich Chemical Company. Naomi saw that Cullinane needed a new product and concluded, after considerable reference checking, that the founder and CEO, John Cullinane, was both ambitious and honest. Goodrich agreed with our recommendation, and the parties gathered in our office townhouse to negotiate the contract, which all of us happily believed could eventually bring Goodrich $1 million. Our prognostications fell far short.

By 1978, the newly renamed Cullinet achieved revenues of $9 million, and the company launched an IPO that sold out in forty minutes. Revenues reached $20 million in 1980, $40 million in 1982, and then, in the next two years, quadrupled to $170 million—this in a company comprising 1,500 people. Only Lotus was larger in revenues among the software independents, but the trend toward independent software vendors (ISVs) was unmistakable, and ADR furthered it by raking in revenues that skyrocketed to $130 million from $17 million on the strength of programming tools and an acquired database.

Cullinet's growth piggybacked on IBM's enormously successful 4300 minicomputer, which eventually accounted for half its IDMS revenues. The revenue mix was a mulligan stew: 30 percent from existing IBM customers, 20 percent from conversions of BUNCH die-hards to IBM, 15 percent from "cohabitation" from IBM mainframe "DB2" database users deploying the smaller IDMS on remote computers, and the rest from international and maintenance renewals.

Buoyed by Cullinet's enormous success, John Cullinane began a 1985 presentation to the RB by chortling that the members might all share vicariously in his experience of accumulating wealth and hobnobbing with the Kennedys in philanthropic glory. But when the stock price hit thirty-two dollars, John relaxed his management grip. It was a terrible mistake. In just three years, the one-time ISV leader all but vanished, and newcomer Oracle moved to the fore.

Oracle Speaks

Larry Ellison, Oracle's cofounder and CEO, is an enigma—brilliant, charismatic, adventurous, changeable, technically intuitive, and ambitiously driven, with an uncanny knack for making enemies not only among competitors but among many of his fellow leaders in Silicon Valley, whom Ellison seems to hold in genial contempt anyway. But to declare an interest, long after the events recounted here: In November 2005, Naomi joined the Oracle board of directors.

With two partners and two thousand dollars, Ellison started his company in 1977, after reading and rereading an IBM paper on relational systems—and after working on a related project for the CIA. Oracle, then known as Relational Software, shipped its first rickety database in 1979. At our initial meeting in early 1980, the tiny company had a still-shaky product and a short customer list limited to defense agencies plus Bank of America. We navigated our rental car off a fog-shrouded highway in Silicon Valley and pulled up to a newly constructed pop-up building. Inside we met Ellison, his cofounder and partner Bob Miner, a few other associates, and the usual beautiful assistants.

At the time, databases hardly looked like a growth sector. Prospective sales were squeezed between powerful hardware vendors Digital, Hewlett-Packard, IBM, and Tandem, plus a few dominant ISVs led by ADR, Cincom, and Cullinet. But Ellison offered two powerful new capabilities. First was portability. For the technophiles in any crowd, Larry would explain that "Oracle operates on almost anything from a PDP 11/34 to an IBM 3033, because it is programmed in C and takes only 256k of real memory." By contrast, older databases from other independent software vendors operated only on IBM's mainframe architecture, while those from the hardware leaders operated only on the hardware companies' own computers.

Oracle's second unique capability concerned ease of use. The older databases, such as IDMS, were designed to streamline computer throughput on routine transactions. But their "hierarchical" orientation made the retrieval of random information extremely slow. Relational databases, however, emphasized retrieval (partly by using the SQL user language, which IBM let slip into the public domain). "The relational database structure simply reduces all possible data structures and situations to a series of two-dimensional tables," summarized Larry during our first visit. After that, the company focused its inventive talent on optimizing the understructure of file arrangement. Before long, benchmarks conducted by the Navy concluded that (when it worked) Oracle's product was considerably faster than old-fashioned databases in answering random information inquiries.

Oracle boomed while John Cullinane relaxed his hold on management. Its revenues had doubled (or nearly so) every year since 1984, going from $12 million to $25, to $55, $138, $282, and over $500 million in 1989, with most of that growth coming from selling database products worldwide. Portability remained "the font of all strategy," we wrote, noting support for eighty different computer platforms, including those of DEC, Honeywell, IBM, OS/2, Prime, Siemens, and Unix in its many manifestations. (Not all worked equally well—IBM mainframes, least of all.) New features were added sparingly, with bonuses reportedly paid to developers based on market acceptance. "So the incentive is to select features not on programming elegance but on what customers want to buy," explained Larry.

When we met with Bob Miner, a famously low-key and self-effacing man (who, sadly, died of cancer in 1994), he first confirmed the perils of frivolous diversity, tossing out unnecessary features. Then he sketched the company's 160-person development organization. There were just twenty people working on the core database, he told us, explaining that "more than that wouldn't help." Miner's words echoed those of Fred Brooks, the father of the OS/360, who argued convincingly in his guide to program management, *The Mythical Man-Month*,[1] that large project teams were counterproductive. Besides the core twenty, Oracle had ten programmers working on languages, thirty on user interfaces, and a separate group that fitted the product to the various operating systems. There were fifty programmers for the Unix brands, thirty for IBM, and ten each for DEC and the Apple Macintosh. By contrast, the North American sales force comprised roughly 900 people; international operations had 1,600.

Incumbent Implosion

Meanwhile, at Cullinet, caretaker managers embarked on a downward path of superficial product development and delusional acquisitions. Cullinet also began developing a set of so-called fourth-generation applications for human resources, financial record keeping (a McCormick and Dodge rewrite), and manufacturing (from Rath and Strong). Most of this fourth generation was filled with bugs, and none was very successful. Worse, those efforts drained funding from the core database; a supposedly "relational" version, the IDMS/R, wasn't relational at all. And, finally and fatally, the Cullinet offerings remained largely limited to the smaller IBM mainframes.

In 1986, IDMS orders slowed and profit plunged, to $15 million from $25 million. The following year, Cullinet lost key managers and technologists, while Oracle's revenues reached $500 million and outperformed the databases of DEC and IBM—even on their own minicomputers. Even the newer competition was falling back against Oracle's relentless sales "animals." Relational Technology (Ingres) reached $120 million on multiple platforms, while Sybase climbed to $50 million on DEC computers and Unix variations, including Sun's.

By 1988, John Cullinane had retaken control of his company and made massive staff cuts. But it was too late; the game was essentially over. That year, we wrote: "Software boutiques with portable databases like Oracle, Relational Technology, and Sybase sit in the catbird seat. For customers using proprietary operating systems from DEC or IBM, here's a state-of-the-art database and applications tools. Or for customers ready for the plunge to Unix, here's the same database and development tools—with no more conversion effort than a "recompile" to translate the programmer's original code into the machine instructions of a new and different computer. Consistency without commitment. Bingo."

Only a year later, Cullinet was sold for just $330 million, or about four dollars a share, to Computer Associates. Its eulogists were both angry and regretful. Michael Stonebraker, long the leading academic/entrepreneur on databases and the developer of the rational pioneer Ingres, summarized his thoughts in a slide entitled "On the Fall of Cullinet," which said:

- Asleep when the paradigm shift occurred.
- Had ample warning.
- Allowed the relational start-ups to prosper.
- Ultimately had to go to the home for retired software.

Cullinet had squandered its lead, while Oracle's portability with relational technology proved a wonderful fit with customers, just as Larry Ellison had explained to us a decade earlier.

But barely a year after Cullinet disappeared, the wheels fell off the Oracle sales juggernaut. In March 1990, the company shocked investors by writing off sales the reps claimed as booked, though they were never actually closed. In *The Difference Between God and Larry Ellison,* author Mike Wilson says shareholders "dumped Oracle stock as if it were sludge."[2] There were investor lawsuits and charges of insider trades. In September, bad hit worse as quarterly sales fell by $30 million, the accountants discovered a $10 million error in the recording of commissions, and the company reported a loss of twenty-seven cents per share, significantly worse even than the twenty cents bandied about just a few weeks earlier. Ellison promised publicly that the company would make up the deficit by year-end.

Part of the problem, as Wilson described in his sometimes vivid 1998 account, was that salespeople were prebooking revenues on future or conditional sales over the weak objections of corporate accountants. "By August 1990, it was apparent that Oracle was never going to collect a substantial part of its receivables," Wilson concluded. "Some customers had already returned the software because it didn't work, some had gone out of business before their payments ever came due, and some had side letters saying they could get out of their deals. Oracle had no choice but to restate its financial results for the previous three quarters—a major embarrassment."[3]

By October 31, the stock had slid to just over five dollars a share from twenty-eight dollars in August, and four hundred people had been fired in Oracle's first downsizing. Among those dumped was Gary Kennedy, the hyper head of sales, whose techniques for consistently doubling annual revenues had included groin-wrenching quota-setting sessions and rewards paid, literally, in gold coins. Ellison expressed shock at the excesses, but no one doubted that he'd set the tempo. In fact, hyperaggressive sales tactics were the only way to match the pace of what some described as Bill Gates's equally wicked "Kingdom of the North" in Redmond, Washington.

Larry came back to work from sailing and surfing, fully engaged, displaying his congenital optimism and drive. Recruited almost immediately was Jeff Henley, who had occupied top financial posts at Pacific Financial and elsewhere and who could bring muscle and credibility to Oracle's downtrodden financial folks. Equally critical was Ray Lane, who was recruited in 1992 from Booz-Allen, where he had been the senior VP. Lane, who would be named president in 1994, was a highly regarded and trustworthy executive, just what Oracle needed to lend weight to its product announcements and, perhaps more important, build a multibillion-dollar consulting practice.

But Oracle's unforgiving license negotiations with customers continued unabated. Regularly, an RB member would call the Research Board to intervene. Naomi would call Larry, who would invariably respond that he was "shocked, simply shocked. I'll have to ask Ray and get back to you." And Ray would fix the problem—though apparently treating each offense as an isolated incident, unable to get past Larry to the cultural root of the problems.

In 2000, Ray Lane left Oracle to join Kleiner Perkins, amid the typical shenanigans Larry used to push people out the door without actually firing them. Ray felt the remote and impersonal push totally inappropriate given the company-saving contributions he'd made. There were also sizable differences over money. But in 2006, Larry made one of his rare public presentations at a meeting of the CIO Strategy Exchange we held at Kleiner. Ray was there, of course. The two met after the session, and the relationship regained some measure of cordiality.

The Wilson book chronicles Larry's optimism, vision, and endless rows with industry leaders, Oracle executives, wives, mistresses, investors, and even a yacht broker—with Larry himself remaining strangely disengaged from reality in every instance. After all that, the book was noted on the Oracle Web site as recommended reading. Clever feint? Genuine admiration? No one doubts that Ellison is unpredictable.

Larry's mind is eclectic and ever contradictory. Lunch at his home followed the usual script. He was late, of course, but gracious as always. Then a tour of the garden with its small ceremonial house on the side of the carp pond and huge rocks imported from Japan. "Japanese structures like these are more approachable than Christian churches," he declared. "But didn't the light of Gothic cathedrals more easily evoke the man-to-God relationship?" I responded. And Larry was off on one of his characteristic expositions. Then came lunch in a sparsely decorated Japanese-style room. On the kitchen counter, an incongruously bucolic scene of an orange cat curled sleeping in a wooden salad bowl.

Our formal interview began with a discussion of the technical vagaries of the "two-phase commit" needed to synchronize database updates across parallel processors. Then, after an explanation of why recent results had gone soft financially, Larry turned to strategy. Like his longtime competitor Bill Gates, Ellison has always been convinced that the enemy is just over the next hill. And now that enemy was Microsoft, which might shrink-wrap its version of the Sybase database to offer a low-cost product that would chew up Oracle revenues, beginning at the low end. To fend off a Cullinet-like collapse, Larry had begun developing a curiously interleaved, multilevel strategy that broke away from Andy Grove's layered model. At the end of our visit, Larry told us he'd just bought a very large yacht to take his kids on a vacation cruise, laughing at himself over the price. Walking us to the gate, he bowed stiffly as we drove off.

Oracle's strategy evolved over the next several years into three interlocking layers (database, applications, and consulting) that are expanding even as I write. At the core is the relational database that Larry pioneered and turned into a product, emulating concepts originated at IBM. Its portability drew more customers than any other database, thereby attracting the package developers who hooked their wares to Oracle before doing the same for its smaller competitors. Larry feared that Microsoft would one day build a database product that could match Oracle in the number of transactions processed per second. At that point, Microsoft would cut its prices to commodity levels. Certainly, that was Bill's boast (though twenty years later, the high-end competition is IBM, not Microsoft).

So Oracle added a layer of business applications in accounting, manufacturing, and enterprise-resource planning (ERP). Observers warned that competing against PeopleSoft, SAP, Siebel, and other software vendors would drive those vendors to other databases. Larry's response was simple: The applications business would give Oracle an upstream profit source as it matched Microsoft's database pricing. Sales were slowed by bugs and also, perhaps, by customer suspicion of Oracle, but by 1994, we were hearing generally satisfied customer response from heavyweights (and RB members) like Alcoa, American Home Products, Federal Express, and Honeywell. Still, problems persisted.

The third layer of Larry's strategy was consulting. He couldn't help but notice that corporate installations of complex systems cost hundreds of millions of dollars, 80 percent of which went to the large consulting firms that then integrated new applications with client business processes and older, long-lived legacy systems. Worse yet, in their quest for greater profits, the consultants often seemed to expand and lengthen a project to the detriment of the software provider's revenues and reputation.

The software providers were furious over the situation. During one interview, SAP founder and co-CEO Hasso Plattner raged around his office decrying just such practices in a fecund mixture of English and German. The common consultant practice of stretching out each project made SAP's product look unduly clumsy and complicated, he complained to me. But Hasso shied away from forming his own installation teams lest the consulting firms retaliate by no longer recommending SAP to their clients. Instead, he tried to make his software more modular and hence installable, no mean feat considering the strength of technocratic resistance in Walldorf, Germany. ("Maybe an outsider like you could write our software group a letter, suggesting they write more modular offerings," he joked.) SAP continued to lead the industry, in part because it had a richer product and perhaps because its business practices drew less customer fury. But that was before Oracle bought PeopleSoft and Siebel.

Building a consulting business that can actually implement an application in a reasonable time and at a profit isn't easy. Oracle's first attempts flopped. But with the inestimable assistance of Ray Lane, Larry persevered—partly to protect his applications business from the consultants and partly to protect his core database business from Microsoft. "At some point, I could conceivably give away the database product and rely on applications and consulting for the profits," he pointed out in 1994 while visiting our office.

Larry's penchant for hyping new technologies that never really reached the market provides more fodder for his critics. The NCube parallel processor was one example, though the concept is widely utilized today. So was Larry's thin-client network computer, which seemed truly promising and, better yet, took a swipe at Microsoft. Much of the cost, weight, and battery life of a laptop was then related to the disk on which Microsoft's operating system depends for storing programs and information. The network computer assumed that programs and data would be stored instead on the Internet. The diskless appliance could be built more cheaply five hundred dollars), and with greater reliability and ease of use, than today's PC. Predictably, the Billy Club mounted a ferocious defense, arguing that no one would write a memo or work a spreadsheet clumsily and unreliably housed on an Internet server. Then, as it turned out, PCs themselves came to cost five hundred dollars, momentarily mooting the debate.

Premature though his timing, the accuracy of Larry's prediction was proved by Google's efforts to drive e-mail, word processing, and spreadsheets from the laptop PC to the Internet. Microsoft itself is now introducing its cloud as well. Hardware cost is no longer the motivator; more important are ideas of global information sharing and collaboration among a mobile workforce.

Best Wishes

After Naomi and I sold the Research Board to the Gartner Group, I was asked to attend Gartner's annual event in Orlando, Florida. Interviews with industry leaders are held in large auditoriums and then beamed to other sites, so that all 10,000 of the client-company representatives can participate. I was seated in the front row of the main auditorium to hear Cisco CEO John Chambers at one session and Larry at the second. Typically, Larry's private plane was late (he was probably flying in with some beautiful woman, smirked the cognoscenti). Larry stepped from the wings of the stage looking slightly disoriented in the bright lights. Two Gartner analysts, armed with clipboards of questions, fired away. Larry serenely ignored the questions to speak about the state of IT, Oracle, and the world.

At the end, he spotted me and flashed a huge grin. Walking me, arm around my shoulder, to the side of the stage and away from his Gartner hosts, he said, "I hope you really made them pay for the RB." I was touched, though the thought crossed my mind that, however fair the price, we probably got less than the price of his yacht and two-week vacation.

Chapter 11

SELF-ACCELERATING ECONOMIES OF SCALE:

Apple, Microsoft, and Dell

Volume wins. And volume is often driven initially by consumer crowds, not business buyers, as shown in the success of Apple, Microsoft, and Dell. And with applications or services like Google or Facebook or iPhone, volume attracts still more consumers and then more applications in a relentless virtuous circle. This chapter is really about volume and the consumer as the driver of technologies that eventually seep into the business enterprise.

Just months before the Macintosh burst on the scene, *Fortune* (May 1983) forecast compounded growth of 50 percent for the overall industry through 1987: "Now the less well-known business of selling the software that brings these machines to life is poised to become just as magical." Heeding the call, venture capitalists showered $180 million on the top ninety start-ups.

"Talent, innovation, wealth, the American Dream ... or a contemporary South Sea bubble?" we worried. The near-term results weren't pretty and did nothing to lessen our fears. And just one year later, in August 1984, *Business Week* reported the existence of 250 word-processing packages, 200 databases, and 150 different spreadsheets. But savage consolidation had already begun. Just twenty products accounted for half the industry's revenues.

Leading the pack with a 14 percent market share was Lotus 1-2-3, a top seller for 107 weeks. Number two was Microsoft Word, on the top-seller list for sixty-six weeks, followed by SideKick (Borland's notepad and calendar application) and Ashton-Tate's dBASE III database, a

123-week stalwart whose run was winding down. Novell's networking nodes were also high on the list.

Competition and innovation seemed stymied, though, as Apple CEO John Sculley declared at a major industry trade show in November: "The PC industry appears to be, at least momentarily, trapped in a gigantic rut" *(San Jose Mercury,* November 1984). Venture capitalists were losing interest, Sculley continued, and the (un)happy cottagers were now spending more time in litigation or in debates over standards than they were dedicating to new-product development.

At that point, Microsoft already held 90 percent of the 16-bit operating-system market, with also-rans Digital Research, Pick, and Bell Labs' Unix variant trailing far behind. And by 1990, the market leaders for 2000 had already been established (see Table 11.1), and of the leaders before then, all but Lotus were doomed.

Table 11.1 Changing Leadership

Year	Company	Revenue (Millions)
1980	1. Informatics	$126
	2. Dun & Bradstreet	121
	3. ASK Computer Systems	65
	4. American Management	59
	5. Management Science	54
1985	1. AGS	$250
	2. Lotus	226
	3. Informatics	192
	4. Cullinet	170
	5. Management Science	152
1990	1. Computer Associates	$1,308
	2. Microsoft	1,214
	3. Oracle	971
	4. Lotus	685
	5. Novell	539
1995	1. Microsoft	$7,419
	2. Oracle	3,777
	3. Computer Associates	3,196
	4. Novell	1,986
	5. SAP	1,887

Year	Company	Revenue (Millions)
2000	1. Microsoft	$23,000
	2. IBM Software	12,600
	3. Oracle	10,100
	4. Computer Associates	6,100
	5. SAP	5,900

Source: Company Financials

The Consumer Tides

The impact of unanticipated consequences often equals or exceeds the impact of the technology itself. As one example, IBM's introduction of its System/360 beat down the old BUNCH competitors, but its compatibility across models and product generations simultaneously created new armies of competitors in plug-compatible mainframes, peripherals, software, and leasing companies. The newcomers were much more potent and their products more beneficial to the customer than what traditional suppliers had offered.

The PC hugely expanded the consumer market and redefined the information technology sector. Since then, consumer-friendly operating systems, games, networks, Web technologies, and tools for collaboration (wikis and blogs) and search (Google) have almost always surpassed their business-oriented counterparts in volume even in the enterprise market.

Price and human factors ranging from flashier graphics to simpler commands and even stylish outer appearance are the keys to success in the consumer market. Proficiency in holding down costs and extending human factors isn't easy for old-timers to replicate. Comparing Xerox and IBM to Apple, Dell, and Microsoft points up the difficulties incumbent companies face in trying to counter the upstarts in new markets.

The Apple Falls on Xerox

We first met Xerox vice president David Liddle in 1980, when we interviewed staff members at the company's Palo Alto Research

Center (PARC) for a report on human interfaces. Dave is a large man, prematurely balding, with pate and chin sometimes assertively shaven, sometimes benignly fringed, and with a Mel Brooks eye for the IT sector's more ludicrous vulnerabilities. Someone should publish a book of his one-liners.

A team including PARC had just developed the Star workstation, the first commercial office system to replace complex commands, difficult to memorize by the typical human, with the graphical user interface, or GUI (pronounced "gooey"). Simple on-screen icons such as a printer or a wastebasket replaced IBM word-processor commands like "SYSXARCH" that had brought secretaries to tears. "Xerox's earlier experience with word processors taught us some expensive lessons when training costs swamped costs of the basic hardware," one PARCer told us.

Hardware was about to become almost secondary, according to a wide swath of Silicon Valley smarties. So Star had a good chance to succeed, despite its $20,000 price tag (still competitive against contemporary word processors). But Xerox was a study in ambivalence in which East and West never met. Its hugely talented PARC scientists generally scorned the Rochester, New York, headquarters, convinced that Rochester was too preoccupied with saving the high-end copier business from the Japanese to focus on turning PARC inventions into viable revenue streams. So the Ethernet protocol invented by PARCer Bob Metcalf would benefit 3Com (which Metcalf later founded), Digital Equipment, and eventually the entire industry—but not Xerox. Similarly, the icon-heavy human interface effort led by Dave Liddle benefited Apple, Microsoft, and eventually the entire industry—but not Xerox.

The science behind Star's human interfaces lay less in design methodology than in testing, we were told by the slightly built, extremely clever team leader, Charles Irby. Sure, PARC's brain trust had batted around any number of interesting concepts like "progressive disclosure" (i.e., presenting the user with no more information than needed for the next task). But "human factors design is more art than science," Irby informed us. "You can't feed a set of requirements into a black box and crank out a single optimum solution." Instead, PARC emphasized rigorous testing orchestrated by an independent unit of six behavioral scientists. "We needed a group who could evaluate our design assumptions objectively," Irby explained. Thereafter, armies of temporary workers typed away on a prototype to validate design decisions. Any vendor hoping to spread its systems broadly across the populace would have been wise to adopt a similar approach.

Eventually, Steve Jobs introduced a Mac that used many Star-like interfaces, but Jobs pushed well beyond Star with a more natural overall user experience at one-fourth the cost. Apple expanded the parameters of the Xerox design as has every computer designer, always expanding on prior generations of technology no matter where invented. Microsoft then copied Jobs's design to create its Windows product.

Apple burst into bloom in the mid-1970s when two teenage Steves—Jobs and Wozniak—emerged from the garage with their first two hundred boxes. From that point, whined their quickly out-legged and envious competitors, the Steves' greatest coup wasn't their amazing electronic wizardry but their recruiting of charismatic top management. Mike Markkula, for instance, a former Intel executive who retired in his thirties—partly on the bonanza reaped from Intel shares—signed on as chairman. Michael Scott, a manufacturing director from National Semiconductor, took the president's seat. Advertising magician Regis McKenna transformed a simple piece of fruit into one of the greatest brands of the half-century; not since Adam took a bite had the apple gotten so much attention. In the executive vice president slot was Floyd Kvamme, previously president of National's mainframe business and later a partner at Kleiner Perkins.

The Apple II, released in 1977, was a well-built machine that benefited from terrific marketing and a fair degree of reach in the new consumer market. The Apple III, which came out in 1980, was a disaster—months late and bug-infested when it finally did arrive. "At least ten different problems surfaced," recalled Markkula during our first visit in 1982. "None of them was individually significant, but, cumulatively, they caused 30 percent of the units to fail in the field. We thought the stores were mature enough to handle the problems, but they weren't."

It took McKenna a full year to restore Apple's polish in the public's eye. Scott vacated the president's seat (not happily), Markkula took over as CEO, and Jobs assumed the chairmanship. Somehow, Apple launched its initial public offering in 1981 anyway. And by 1982, its kiddie-corps image notwithstanding, Apple's management team could "clean the clocks" of any other company in the valley, Mike Markkula bragged to his unconvinced visitors.

Meanwhile, there were ferocious skirmishes with the distribution channels. Wholesalers sued when Apple tried to bypass them to reach the stores directly. The stores were jostled when Apple tried to bypass them to reach the largest enterprises directly (and the chains slowed acceptance of Apple products until the clouds cleared). Apple received another jolt when direct-mail retailers slashed prices, simultaneously doing away with the instruction and support needed by first-time buyers.

More lawsuits, and a bloody flag was waved by the ever-quotable Steve Jobs: "What we're doing is state-of-the-art in antitrust law." "Was this the right moment and arena from which to pursue new legal concepts, particularly for a struggling pioneer?" we wondered.

There are endless anecdotes about Steve Jobs's temper and invective as well as his creativity. His recorded outbursts against employees often seemed unnecessary and counterproductive—though many of those on the receiving end stayed for years. Then there was the story—possibly apocryphal, but widely told—of how Jobs soured a possible deal for distribution of the Mac when he exploded in rage upon learning that a visiting computer exec didn't know how to operate a PC. The story is useful if for no other reason than that it reveals the tone of the industry at the time.

In 1983, Steve received a partnership offer from Vittorio Cassoni, AT&T's senior marketing VP for the computer business, and two other executives. Cassoni was the clever, if sometimes edgy, Olivetti executive brought to the United States to bring order and profit to a struggling computer business saddled with the obsolete 7300 minicomputer and the 6300 PC clone bought from his company. A barely computer-literate sales force completed the bleak picture. A hot product like the Mac could have been a definite asset.

Apple also stood to gain from the deal, given AT&T's authorship of the Unix operating system, the 3B microprocessor, and a sizable field organization. At the time, AT&T was still seen as a potential competitor in the computer sector. A business magazine cover at the time pictured two football helmets, noseguard to noseguard—one marked IBM, the other AT&T—signifying the onset of a bloody battle for supremacy in all aspects of IT as computers and communications converged. Convergence was a hot topic among the big three Japanese firms—Fujitsu, Hitachi, and especially NEC—as well, but, as it turned out, convergence was twenty-five years into the future.

Against this hopeful backdrop, Cassoni and two other AT&T executives flew six hours in their corporate jet from New Jersey to California. Interested in a deal that could leverage distribution of the Mac, Jobs decided to inaugurate the session by having the visitors experience the superiority of the Mac user experience over the IBM/Microsoft alternative. Unfortunately, one of the three VPs announced excitedly that he'd never before worked on a PC. Not so unusual at the time; few senior executives, even CIOs, used a PC. But Jobs, or so the story goes, let loose a tirade of disbelief that a VP of computer strategy had never experienced a personal computer. And refused to continue the meeting with anyone so unserious. So the three visitors were dismissed without discussion and sent on their way for the aimless six-hour flight home.

An army of critics denounced Steve's response as a childish tantrum, but, in retrospect, he was intuitively right. AT&T would never be a factor in personal computing nor, for that matter, computing of any kind, as its shaky hold on Unix attested. (Nor was IBM ever a factor in communications.) From today's perspective, the whole idea that competition between AT&T and IBM would frame the computer industry seems ludicrous. But that's not the way the marketplace saw it at the time.

We first met Steve Jobs just three days before Apple's 1983 introduction of the Macintosh, and even then, only at the urging of Apple's executive VP, Floyd Kvamme. We weren't much jollied by the thought of meeting yet another thirty-year-old, know-it-all millionaire. The unhappy saga of the three rejected AT&T executives came later. Still, the always-intuitive Naomi might have feared that Steve would ask about her PC experiences, and I certainly would have failed the bonus-point questions. But, eventually, we came to regard Jobs as the Thomas Edison of elegant computing and user-friendly innovation.

This day Steve was charming, even glowing, amid the exuberant chaos, empty cartons, anarchist cartoons, and crumpled work papers that festooned the narrow aisles in the pre-announcement excitement. We sat on the only two chairs in his tiny office as Steve perched on the edge of his cluttered desk, munching a pita bread while politely listening to our PC skepticism. Then he leapt to a whiteboard and began sketching a visual analogy: By the 1890s, the telegraph was already fifty years old, and 25,000 people worked as trained operators. Someone may have suggested putting a telegraph key on every office desk to expand communications, Steve said, but it was impractical and time-consuming to teach everyone Morse Code.

About the same time, though, the telephone was invented. The function was the same—communications —but now anyone could talk or even sing to anyone else, no training required. In just ten years, 200,000 telephones were installed. Steve Jobs was selling to people who could use the telephone; Digital, IBM, and the others were still targeting the telegraph operators. Price and ease of use, he concluded, carried implications for sales approach, customer training, and field maintenance similar to those experienced previously by the makers of electromechanical calculators.

"So far," he pointed out, "personal computers have captured just 5 percent of the potential market—the early adapters who willingly take ten hours to study the word-processor's instruction manual. The entire industry knows how to make cheaper hardware, but reading the manuals is still expensive and oppressive. That has to change if PCs are going to reach 25 million office workers. Traditional vendors may think this problem can be solved through their existing field organizations," Jobs observed, "but the sheer volumes of new users will fracture their capabilities."

To Steve, the new technology demanded mass-volume distribution channels rather than the sturdy-shoed sales force and sleepover customer-training facilities offered by the traditionalists. For DEC, IBM, HP, and Wang, the field repair force was a source of profit and a means of maintaining an ongoing customer presence. That, and the inherent complexity of their equipment, made all four very slow to let stores push their products. Not Steve: "We don't want 10,000 more employees selling, delivering, and hand-holding; that would destroy our organization's creativity. Let IBM send in two high-priced guys to install the box, do the teaching, adjust the secretary's chair, and then come back to fix the box when it breaks. Our stuff can be coached in half an hour, even by telephone, and if a component breaks, send it back to the store."

The Mac made a huge splash. But almost fatally, in 1985, John Sculley took the CEO role. Sculley's success at deluding Steve Jobs into believing that a software marketer would make a great technology CEO was surpassed only by Sculley's success in deluding himself. In fairness, revenues grew smartly in Sculley's first years, just as they did for the PC sector generally, but market share atrophied, stranding Mac on retailers' back shelves.

After his removal from Apple, Steve formed NeXT, a radically designed workstation complete with elegant magnesium housing and an even more elegant operating system. There, his constant creativity was again on display. Naomi and I began a visit in 1987 marveling at the NeXT hardware's sleek (and expensive) design, and then we followed Steve into a small auditorium. It was completely empty except for a NeXT computer wired to two external audio speakers and three folding chairs placed before the hardware. We all sat as a charming Mozart concerto began to play, activated by Steve to demonstrate yet another part of the PC-user experience. Had he set it up knowing our technical cynicism and appealing instead to our prejudices to counter our skepticism? "But what could stereophonic sound add to personal computing?" I wondered. "It doesn't matter," Steve replied jauntily, many years before the iPod. In any case, NeXT never gained traction and was sold to Apple with Steve's triumphant reentry in 1997.

Microsoft Takes On the Establishment

The story of how Microsoft bested the big, blue giant has been told and retold. Bill Gates and Steve Ballmer like to recall how frightened they were at the prospect of going into battle against their gargantuan former ally. It's hard to believe, though, given that Microsoft had already leveraged its volume to beat its strongest, newest, and presumably most innovative software competitors—Borland, Lotus, Novell, and WordPerfect.

In 1990, the five top PC software makers were quite comparable in scale, reported *Datamation* on June 15, 1991. Microsoft had $821 million of revenue and a 95 percent market share in PC operating systems; Lotus dominated in spreadsheets, with a 65 percent market share and $556 million of revenue; Novell ruled local networks, with an 89 percent market share and $282 million of revenue; WordPerfect led word processing, with a 60 percent share and $281 million; and Ashton-Tate had a 44 percent share in databases, with $265 million of revenue. Today, all but Microsoft are gone or diminished, casualties of Gates and Ballmer's ambitions—even though the also-rans were once headed by astute executives who had built their companies, fully appreciated the new market realities, understood their products, and were focused competitors. Still, their undoing at the hands of the Redmond pair was even more savage than IBM's.

Microsoft's success was considered immorally ruthless in many quarters ("cunningly relentless," we might have said instead). There was a strategy for every major competitor, and the Billy Club played its hand very well. Not so the competitors, whose strategies had glaring flaws.

Microsoft came into being in 1975, after Bill left Harvard at the end of his freshman year to join his former instructor, Paul Allen, in a tiny PC software company writing Basic language compilers. Bill's Harvard pal and eventual alter ego, Steve Ballmer, joined the company after graduation and a brief stint at Procter & Gamble. Gates and Ballmer were a supersmart, superenergetic duo who played off each other almost like a vaudeville comedy team—but without the humor.

Bill, who is of average height and relatively slight, earnestly tries to convince his visitors of the technical, hence business, superiority of the Microsoft approach in a relentless monotone of logical argument punctuated by high-pitched exclamations of emphasis. All the while, he folds his arms across his stomach and rocks briskly. Steve is a large, tall, intimidating jock who blusters, snorts, stands too close, and generally overwhelms a visitor with the business, hence technical, superiority of the Microsoft approach through an equally relentless stream of gut impressions illustrated by endless chalk diagrams.

It was often hard to tell where the arguments of one ended and the other began, though the end result was clearly a single, coherent strategy. Neither man was ever fully at rest, driven by their awareness of just how few technology firms survive the thirty-year working lives of their founders. "I understand the challenge," Bill told Naomi in 1994, as Microsoft neared its twentieth anniversary, "and I doubt anything we do can extend Microsoft's life by more than a decade or so." That fear proved unfounded. Indeed, it was hard to conceive of this brash upstart approaching middle age. When Naomi introduced Bill to the CIO Strategy Exchange in 2005, she misspoke that Microsoft was now twenty years old. "Actually, it's thirty," Bill corrected.

Smart and aggressive themselves, Gates and Ballmer brought together a core group of equally sharp executives, largely outsiders, at each stage of the company's development, puncturing the myth of the company as dangerously inward-looking. One of the earliest such recruits was Jon Shirley, the business phenomenon of the early PC evolution who came over from Tandy Radio Shack in 1983. Jon was named president and CEO as the company was moving beyond its highly successful 16-bit operating system into other products and eventually became a company director. We knew Mike Maples, the head of development (and the company's resident grown-up), from his days at IBM, where he was highly regarded as a minicomputer strategist with a sophisticated view of the PC revolution. Chief operating officer Bob Herbold, a former Procter & Gamble marketing executive, CIO (and RB member), with a PhD in computer science, was responsible for bringing order and reason to Microsoft's marketing, manufacturing, finance, human resources, and internal IT—all areas outside the attention spans of Bill and Steve. Bob later became the trusted, white-haired TV spokesman for Microsoft in the early years of the troubles with the Justice Department.

In our opinion, Microsoft had the strongest management team in the computer industry. "Yuppie thugs," quipped Dave Liddle, with his usual wit. "Thugs" was too strong, but it was true that this group could quickly form a formidable phalanx behind their leader. Blurted Ballmer in 1992 to explain Microsoft's advantage over more collegial competitors, "When Bill tells us what to do, there's no blah, blah, blah; we just do it."

WordPerfect: Not Perfect Enough

To break WordPerfect's hold on the word-processing market, Microsoft "listened to its customers" and offered a pricing-and-support package comprising Windows, Excel, and Word. It wasn't illegal, and enterprise customers gratefully accepted the opportunity for single sourcing. In a frantic response, WordPerfect pushed back on two fronts. First, it floated the idea that its product commanded a significant advantage because it operated not just on the Windows system, but also on Mac, OS/2, and Unix. But that argument was almost a non sequitur, since the market for OS/2 and desktop Unix was close to collapse and Mac already offered Microsoft Word. Then WordPerfect turned to its army of eleven million licensees in hopes of finding enough stand-alone typists who had no interest in Microsoft's spreadsheet but did care about further innovation. An internal-strategy document denounced "those who claim that high-end word processors ... already provide far more functionality than the average user can use or understand. We believe people expect continued innovation and improvement," it bravely continued.

Designating its plan for 1993 as the "Year of Explosion," WordPerfect boasted of supporting electronic mail, color photos, charts, video, sound, and multimedia in an advertising blitz featuring a world-class cycling team. The largest enterprises were oblivious, and most individual buyers weren't impressed enough to keep them from flocking to Word, especially when a new PC came with the Windows suite bundled inside. That left WordPerfect with nothing more than a dwindling number of law firms, despite its technical superiority. Soon, WordPerfect was acquired by its also-struggling Utah neighbor, Novell, before being shipped off to Canada's Corel, where it resides today.

Borland Bows to Bill

Borland Software was the leader in tools and databases, with 1989 revenues of $400 million, when Microsoft attacked. The combination of Microsoft's pricing power and Borland's own mistakes brought it down.

Philippe Kahn had founded Borland in 1982 to market his tightly coded Turbo Pascal language, which sold by mail for fifty dollars a copy, far below the Microsoft equivalent. Microsoft's QuickBASIC eventually knocked out the Borland product, but by then, the company had acquired two leading database companies, Paradox and Ashton-Tate (the distributor of dBASE), giving it a seemingly unassailable 70 percent market share. Kahn began to lose his advantage when he decided to rewrite the company's packages into the trendy new programming discipline dubbed "object oriented." Late to market and outgunned by Microsoft, Borland watched its share of the database market slide from 70 percent to a still-dominant 64 percent. Then Kahn started a price war—perhaps inadvertently—in the spreadsheet market led by Lotus and Microsoft. Gates responded, eventually cutting prices on Microsoft's database product (originally acquired from Sybase) to ninety-nine dollars. Borland's revenues went into free fall, sticking the company with a $110 million loss. Mourned a Borland executive when we visited in 1992: "Originally, the PC industry was controlled by end users. Now it's all central corporate purchases by buyers who care mainly about price."

On the day of our visit, Borland had begun jettisoning employees, the first cuts in its history; 350 people, mostly in sales, were let go out of 2,200 total. Rising just down the road was a brand-new world headquarters that might never be occupied. Worse yet, the money poured into construction might have helped weather further price wars or make new acquisitions instead. The mood was somber, with several moist eyes as we met with the executive committee in the conference room that day. Even the typically energetic and effervescent Kahn was muted, though he soon tried to organize a vendor group to institute a lawsuit against Microsoft.

Back in Redmond, Bill was jubilant, chattering about key Borland technicians ready to decamp to Microsoft—with his active encouragement, of course. Doubtless, their exit would hasten the rival's demise. Immoral? Hardly. Hardball? Certainly.

Years later, we held an RB anniversary dinner at the Asian Art Museum in San Francisco to which we invited several industry CEOs, including both Bill Gates and Philippe Kahn. Naomi, worried that Philippe might confront Bill with some unpleasantness, cautioned me to seat Kahn at a table near the door so that I could corral him the moment he entered. It was unnecessary; Philippe told me lots about his new company, and the conversation moved smartly beyond IT.

Novell Derailed by Retrospective Strategy

Novell had been the early wunderkind in the PC local area network segment. In 1992, it still held 60 percent of the LAN market and was growing at 45 percent annually. But there were thunderheads on the horizon: 87 percent of its revenues, including those related to service, were derived from local networking, even as the need to convert communications protocols from one vendor's scheme to the next was being displaced by widespread acceptance of Ethernet as the industry standard. Microsoft decided to make its initial offerings exactly compatible, but cheaper, allowing customers to buy one or two Microsoft network devices or "nodes," thus gradually displacing the aging Novell gear. The "cuckoo egg in the robin's nest," we dubbed the strategy, as the more powerful hatchling unceremoniously shoved its foster siblings over the side.

Unfortunately, CEO Ray Noorda's obsession with Microsoft, his personal death star, seemed to distract him from forming a future product strategy. "Embalmer and the Pearly Gates," he caustically and endlessly skewered Ballmer and Gates. Instead of looking to the future, Noorda appeared determined to compete against Microsoft by becoming Microsoft—except that he chose to acquire largely moribund companies that provided more anchor than sail.

For example, seeking a desktop operating system to compete against Microsoft Windows, Noorda acquired Digital Research, the one-time PC leader that had badly missed the turn to IBM and 16-bit microprocessors almost a decade earlier. In 1992, the Digital operating system accounted for just 6 percent of Novell's revenues, while swallowing up 20 percent of the development staff. Looking for a server system to compete against Microsoft NT, Noorda traded $300 million of Novell stock to AT&T for its Unix System Labs, which had just $80 million of license revenues.

Continuing this wrongheaded strategy, Ray went looking for desktop applications and came back with two. He picked up WordPerfect and its word-processing program, and then, in an act of charity toward the even more disadvantaged Borland, he bought the Quatro Pro spreadsheet program. "We'll compete with Microsoft along 85 percent of its product lines," Ray boasted to us. Our take was that the Novellettes would soon come home, either with their shields or on them. In all, Noorda's forward strategy held a near-perfect grip on the distant past.

If Bill Gates's strategy was to infuriate his adversary into irrationality, it was a brilliant success. Noorda was belatedly replaced, first, by Bob Frankenburg, a Hewlett-Packard executive, and later by Eric Schmidt, who had previously been Sun's chief technology officer and later became the CEO of Google. Over the years, Novell introduced and acquired several meritorious products, most notably the SUSE "distribution" or flavor of the Linux operating system. But it never regained its earlier prominence, though currently very active in open-source software.

Lotus Flowers and Then Fades

Microsoft swept to victory in the spreadsheet race on the ego-driven refusal of Lotus Development's CEO, Jim Manzi, to write his products for the Windows system rather than futilely clinging to OS/2 and Unix. Both, of course, lost out to Microsoft on the PC desktop.

"I screwed up," Manzi admitted in 1990, when we questioned him about criticism of his strategy from Lotus founder Mitch Kapor. But, at that moment, Lotus was still selling 100,000 new copies per month and could anticipate further growth, given that its cumulative sales represented only 20 percent of the potential PC market. "That's because only 20 percent of PC owners actually pay for Lotus 1-2-3," riposted Bill Gates a few weeks later, "but 80 percent of owners say they're already using spreadsheets." In other words, the market was saturated with illegal copies.

Two years later, Manzi's company no longer held a dominant position. It was clearly losing share in spreadsheets, and the meter registering sales of its new Samna word-processing package barely fluttered. By then, Lotus was especially vulnerable to defections by customers attracted to Microsoft's cut-rate packages of products. For a large-enterprise buy, Manzi told us, the Microsoft bid "was $250,000 less than [Lotus's] lowest offer." And, ultimately, Jim was reduced to touting his product as the "last best hope of free people everywhere" against those devils from Redmond. No one cared, and Lotus's market position gradually eroded.

But unlike more hapless Microsoft competitors, Manzi and uber-inventor Ray Ozzie had taken advantage of the good times and healthy funding temporarily provided by Lotus 1-2-3 to develop Notes. This was a collaboration system sold successfully to many businesses that combined e-mail with group calendaring, contact names and coordinates, and common information files. By 1992, this exciting new product was the company's hope for the future. Two years later, Microsoft Exchange still hadn't caught up—perhaps the only application category in which the Billy Club had been bested.

"We look like fools," snapped Bill, dispensing with the merry quips he characteristically shot at his less-capable competitors. By 1995, the Notes user base had grown to 1.5 million customers spread across 5,500 organizations, enough to support a fancy share price of sixty dollars (for a $3.5 billion total market cap) that IBM paid in cash to acquire the company. Many years later, major enterprises were still enthusiastic users of the product.

Fortune shone less brightly on two other Manzi ideas, however; quick-turnaround consulting and a CD containing eight million business names, telephones, and demographics went nowhere. But at least the CEO couldn't be faulted for lingering in the past.

Netscape Leads the Antitrust Forces

The combat against Netscape was considerably nastier than the others with Microsoft, which engaged in a full slate of bluster, massive investment, exclusive and exclusionary deals with the PC makers, Apple, and AOL, all capped by an internal e-mail containing the phrase "cut off Netscape's air supply."

Our most memorable visit to Redmond came on December 19, 1997, on the morning after Bill realized the threat of antitrust action was entirely serious. One unshaven and unwashed executive after another came into our meeting room. The management team looked as if it had been closeted all night trying to frame a suitable response. Most rushed out after a few minutes. Chief scientist Nathan Myhrvold had apparently been asked to spend more time than usual with the visitors, so he distracted us with future technology, answering our questions with what seemed to us amazing civility and patience.

Finally, Bill arrived looking equally unkempt, and launched a nonstop, breathless rant. We decided not to take notes in deference to his disheveled state of mind. But I recollected angry, high-pitched diatribes about Joel Klein, the assistant attorney general who headed the Justice Department's antitrust division; the technological ignorance displayed by the government; and the popular resentment against successful people who have made lots of money.

"It wasn't ever for the money," Gates insisted. "We never thought about the money. All the money was going to be donated to charity anyway." At that point, the mega-billion-dollar Bill and Melinda Gates Foundation had yet to be launched, Bill previously arguing that he was too busy building Microsoft and would tend to charity later. But in light of the magnificent works now supported by the Gates Foundation, his comment seems genuine. And, after all, Bill was raised in a family concerned with good causes, his mother having been a leader in Seattle's charitable works.

Several years later, and after Microsoft had lost its appeal of the court judgment, we were asked to visit Klein and his antitrust staff in Washington to discuss potential remedies. The legal minds were very sharp, but the business remedies were often shortsighted or unworkable. One involved placing a permanent watchdog over Microsoft's practices, which we thought bureaucratically impractical for the fast-moving technology sector and a company that represented an American technology treasure.

A second remedy envisioned breaking Microsoft into three parts, each marketing its own operating system and office applications. This idea we found dangerously diversionary for America's entire computer industry, since the three would embark upon a years-long fight to the death to minimal advantage, just as DEC, HP, IBM, Sun, et al had fought over the fragmented Unix space. Years of deliberation, strategizing, and coding would be wastefully expended on trying to predict which company—and which version of Windows—would be the ultimate winner.

The only remedy left was to split off the operating-system part of Microsoft from the applications part, with both having access to the all-important Internet browser market. We thought this alternative infinitely superior to the others, and, coincidentally, that was the path the Department of Justice chose to follow.

Months later, two good friends and influential industry leaders called to say that corporate executives were unwilling to take a stand because of their own issues with the Feds. They asked that I write an affidavit supporting the two-part split, given that the only other parties willing to put their thoughts in writing were from academia. No lawyer, and dubious about the economic validity of the antitrust argument, given the early appearance of Linux, I nevertheless agreed to write a short statement saying that competition would best be served by freeing Microsoft's industry-dominant office applications to operate on Unix and Linux, while industry-dominant Windows was open to attracting office applications that competed with Office. Big mistake! My hastily written three-pager drew no kudos and was even savaged as "pathetic" on the Internet. Word later circulated that Bill had been personally offended by my "rudeness." It took a while, but we were able to work with him again. In 2001, the first year of the Bush administration, the judgment was considerably softened. And Netscape was sold to AOL for $4.2 billion.

Dell Leads; Compaq Falters

Analytically stolid is Michael Dell—a curious attribute in an industry of high-voltage rock stars. Accepting our invitation to address the CIO Strategy Exchange, he stood patiently for almost two hours without seeming to shift from one foot to another. And unemotionally explained how his company had forced the industry to accept his vision that PCs were commodities with the tiny markups appropriate to commodities. His was a partial departure from Andy Grove's layered view of PC distribution. Rather than relying on retailers, Dell created a supply chain that rolls from parts suppliers, through the PC assembly plant, and then directly to the customer.

Several years earlier, Compaq CEO Eckhard Pfeiffer had squeezed the older business model by targeting gross margins of only 23 percent and cutting R&D, closing factories, and generally changing the company's product focus from highest function to lowest cost. "If our margins start to improve, we cut prices again," Pfeiffer said. Market share was his game, and he played it well enough to win for a time. Most of the smaller PC companies were simply crushed, while even top-tier players like HP, IBM, and Sun were eventually forced to respond. Soon the Compaq model also affected the minicomputer companies. We called that "trickling price cross elasticities," meaning that the market's preference for lower-priced PCs would soon affect the pricing of higher-capacity minicomputers as well.

Then Pfeiffer made two serious mistakes. First, he was too cautious in replicating the Dell model of selling directly to consumers, but he had good reason. Any serious attempt to bypass the retail chains would have brought immediate retaliation in the form of reduced shelf space and lower sales for several years. Second, Pfeiffer veered into a ruinous $50-billion-or-bust revenue strategy that led him to acquire, first, staggering Tandem and, second, collapsing DEC, with little idea of what to do with his trophies once he got them. Sure, Compaq leapfrogged to the magical $50 billion mark, making it second only to IBM. But then what?

In a March 1998 presentation to the RB, Pfeiffer could not explain how or why his trophies were a good fit, and instead referred repeatedly to the $50 billion combined size and to secret and/or evolving plans to gain maximum value for Compaq's nearly $10 billion outlay. Thereafter, its PC market-share growth stalled; the cost structures burdening DEC and Tandem were not effectively addressed. Pfeiffer was soon replaced by Michael Cappellas, who then negotiated Compaq's sale to HP.

If Pfeiffer squeezed the business model, Dell broke it—by producing and shipping directly to customers who ordered over the telephone, thereby cutting out stores and other distribution channels. Dell thus gained instant perspective on what customers were buying, rather than waiting a week or two for store sales reports. The model also gave Dell a three-part pricing advantage over its competitors, including HP and IBM, which couldn't escape their indirect channels. The company was able to charge less because it: (1) avoided the channel markup, (2) escaped inventory buildup at its distributors, and (3) cut sales and administrative costs to just 10 percent of revenues.

Many were the benefits of this approach. To begin with, Dell's annual inventory-turn rate of thirty-five times was twice that of HP or Compaq, so the business needed less working capital. Dell also escaped the write-offs suffered when distributors shipped back inventoried PCs made obsolete by a significant technology shift, such as the introduction of more powerful microprocessors. Later, Dell used the Internet to cut sales and overhead to just 8 percent (leaving 2 percent for R&D).

"The Internet was heaven's gift to Michael," said CFO Tom Meridith. "He's a visionary, but he didn't predict the Web." That's true, but his telephone-based direct sales model clearly let Dell capitalize on electronic commerce while competitors dug themselves out of their traditional distribution channels. It would take a full decade for HP to narrow Dell's advantage, helped markedly by the shift from commodity desktops to fashionable laptops.

Requiem for the Overweights

The minicomputer companies couldn't have survived even had they incorporated microprocessors into their product lines. In the end, they were crushed by the new breed's volume-based business models, as evidenced by the contrast in 1998 revenues per employee: around $768,000 for Dell versus $665,000 for Compaq, trailed by $291,000 for IBM and only $236,000 for DEC. Four years later, the contrast between the PC rivals had widened: $912,000 for Dell versus just $474,000 for now-bloated Compaq. Hewlett-Packard's productivity had improved from $351,000 to $562,000 (to lead Compaq) over those four years.

After just fifteen years, the minicomputer era was over. The sector's requiem was written by Lou Gerstner: "After UNIX cracked the foundation, the PC makers came along swinging wrecking balls."[1] Only IBM and HP still exist today. But the larger lesson for entrepreneurs is to avoid hitching your plan to a new technology likely to be transient because it isn't accompanied by a radically new business model.

Chapter 12

CHOOSING THE WRONG WAR:

IBM Takes On Microsoft

Armonk lost the war with Redmond before it began. The PC was ultimately a consumer business in which IBM had as few viable prospects as Caterpillar Tractor would have against Ferrari in Formula One racing events.

In the early nineties, my e-mail was stuffed with messages from client-company technical staffs expressing their outrage at the world's unwillingness to acknowledge IBM's superiority. Many aficionados judged the OS/2 far superior to Microsoft's offer, especially from a networking perspective. But it didn't matter. As I replied to my outraged correspondents, "You might be right, but the kids want something they can buy in stores with the most games. And their moms and dads want the same system in their offices that they use in their homes."

The game was over—or it soon would be. I didn't need a crystal ball. CIOs from even the truest blue accounts would bow to employee demands for compatibility between the software they used at work and at home. Volume always wins; OS/2 would lose. End of story. The only wonder is how little IBM understood the terrain in terms of price point, human interfaces, and the independent software vendors.

The accelerated development of an IBM PC had been personally authorized by CEO Frank Cary back in 1980. Boca Raton, Florida, was chosen as the development site, to allow the PC team to escape the rigidity of IBM's culture. With that freedom, Phillip "Don" Estridge delivered a successful product in thirteen months with just a dozen people using standard components and third-party operating systems.

And IBM beat DEC, HP, and Wang to market with a general-purpose PC that produced around $1 billion of revenue in its first year. Cary got his hoped-for product with an effort that captured the IBM corporate imagination.

The blue-suiters were amazed and ecstatic. The new design methodology had cut through the multilayered blankets of "consensus and concurrence" to deliver a product as quickly as the Japanese. Of course, grumpy old dogs like our friend Jack Reilly growled that the boys in Boca hadn't really developed anything—they'd just snapped together available parts and put the contraption in a box without much differentiation or margin. Reilly's observation was ignored amid the celebrations. But both old dogs and young missed the more important point that snapping together components was exactly the essence of the PC business. As such, the market would ultimately belong to the most efficient snapper with the least inventory, lowest sales costs, and greatest appearance of mass customization. And that would be the unencumbered Michael Dell, who was just sixteen years old when Estridge was cheered as the "father of the IBM PC."

But what really impeded IBM's dream and strategy for a new product line was Microsoft. Countless books and films have told the story of how IBM, under the stewardship of John Akers, fumbled its opening advantage, losing to a band of brilliant computer nerds, and would have totally imploded were it not for Lou Gerstner and his service businesses. The weakness in these histories is their relentless focus on the PC to the near exclusion of everything else that was going on in the IT industry and at IBM itself in the late eighties and early nineties. In fact, until the 2005 sale of its remaining PC business to Lenovo, IBM remained among the five largest in a market where half the revenue still goes into a collection of small fry designated "all other." In short, no single PC vendor has come close to the market share IBM holds in its other business lines. The sun didn't rise and fall on PCs, whatever the enthusiasms of the time.

First Score of the Match

"Snapping pictures" was how IBM product strategists Mike Maples and Lucy Fjeldstadt enthusiastically described Armonk's new rapid-fire product generation in 1981. The PC style would become the development model for the midrange computer as well. "Almost everything below mainframe scale is blurring into personal computers," pronounced Maples and Fjeldstadt. "And if we are turning into a personal computer company, then the midrange division should act like one" by speeding up and making fewer components itself.

Ned Lautenbach was then vice president of the division, which included not just the PC but several minicomputers. He framed the IBM contribution to personal computing with no small amount of introspection: "We were able to get some synergy from an earlier product [i.e., the Datamaster], but the important fact is that we designed the finest personal computer in the industry using largely purchased components. Of course, it has our own circuit board design, new ergonomic [i.e., Selectric] keyboard, documentation at IBM quality levels, and superior packaging [cables and cover]." Admittedly, there wasn't much differentiation from competitors' products, allowed Lautenbach, in response to our questions. "The real innovation in this product plan was how we approached the marketplace—channels of distribution [i.e., retail stores], which were new to us," he said.

IBM was still riding high on a string of successes in the PC sector (asterisked for one exception, the $400 million investment in Intel, which it sold too soon in 1986, for $625 million). Akers described the PC to us as IBM's most important new venture and the brute cure for whatever ailed a large and sclerotic company: "Before we announced the Personal Computer, critics said we were late to market. Not any longer, so obviously we had a strong product. The key point in our strategy was flexibility. We took quite mundane technologies and combined them cleverly to create an attractive, very cost-effective product. In the future, we'll strengthen our competitive lead by offering connectivity to other IBM processors, use more of our own technology where appropriate, plus perhaps an IBM operating system and all the applications code harvested from third-party developers." The chief undoubtedly saw the PC as strategic to both IBM and his own legacy, gushing "the PC gave us access to accounts we had never penetrated before [loyalists of other mainframe or minicomputer manufacturers]. And, conversely, when a manufacturer can't compete in personal computers, then sales of its larger systems will ultimately be jeopardized as well." Like the Viet Nam War's domino theory?

The PC introduction had made IBM seem less buttoned-down, almost fun, in fact, particularly when a Chaplinesque tramp appeared in its advertising campaign. It was a welcome contrast to the grim image of Big Blue as the malignant Big Brother flashed in Apple ads. But IBM's real expertise in the consumer market was hopelessly inadequate, though that was where the ultimate winner would be decided, and its clunky human interfaces couldn't begin to match Xerox and later Apple.

In March 1981, we also discussed user interfaces with Dr. Lewis Branscomb, IBM's brilliant chief scientist, and several other Armonk luminaries. Their response was leaden. To start, they bounded off on pointless tirades about the uselessness of European ergonomic standards. "Flicker-free screens?" ranted one of our hosts. "How do you define 'flicker free'? Under what environmental conditions? And for what user population? And at what level of fatigue?" A moment later, the "corporate coordinator of human factors" veered further afield by blasting government action, union action, congressional hearings, and impractical European regulations.

After a bit of graceless pirouetting, our hosts were steered back to the topic. Yes, they would need better human factors to appeal to wider audiences who were intimidated by technology and wouldn't read manuals. But then Branscomb offered a wholly inadequate and irrelevant assessment of the human-interface shortfall. First, IBM needed an end-to-end systems view, he said: "Before designing a bank tellers' terminal, start with the customer coming in the door and then ask whether the teller is necessary at all." Next came programmer productivity, followed by training publications, "admittedly, the one area where we've gotten slack." Branscomb had badly missed the point and sadly lagged the times.

IBM seemed mired with the monks in the Dark Ages on making its systems easy to use without extensive training or tedious manuals. "Human factors? I guess someone will figure out how to make money on that sometime," offhandedly remarked a top sales executive. No surprise, then, when the company handed off the human factors discussion to marketing, which rolled out magazine ads to address the topic.

Curiously enough, IBM actually had a world-class human factors lab tucked out of sight in a copse of live oaks doglegged off the highway near San Jose. We had inadvertently stumbled on it a few months earlier and visited several times thereafter. Presiding was Dr. Richard Hirsh. His unit had long tested IBM terminal keyboards, but its scientists and methodologies were capable of capturing far broader insights on man-machine interactions. Unfortunately, few of IBM's product divisions showed much interest. Several years later, when Dr. Hirsh was going into retirement, he stopped by our New York office to thank me for being almost the only person to bring his lab's work to the attention of Armonk senior management. What a blunder to waste such an asset, especially when IBM hoped to establish a lead in the software-interface side of a business largely targeted at the consumer segment.

A Volley from Midcourt

IBM decided that the PC should help to unify its line of incompatible midrange computers. On October 25, 1984, came a multivolume strategy statement that was indecipherable without the patient guidance of Bill Lowe. (Bill had been IBM's original choice to run the Boca PC project, but he was pulled away early on to oversee the Rochester lab after its manager died suddenly. Now he was responsible for orchestrating IBM's fragmented midrange offerings.) The objective, as Bill explained, was to devise a "seamless front" of commands and functions that would work across the mainframe, midrange, and personal computer segments. An architectural blanket would define a set of consistent, largely IBM-only network interfaces, as well as a set of "functionally consistent," but not necessarily equivalent, user interfaces. "It's like the rental car you pick up at the airport," Bill explained. Because almost every car adheres to a certain design, "you always know where the steering wheel, brake, and accelerator are located." You may still have to poke around for the window-washer switch, but you can always drive the car. Likewise, the same instruction would answer a database query on any of IBM's minicomputers; though under the covers, each mini's operating system might actually handle queries differently.

In December came IBM's third reorganization in as many years. The PC was removed from the midrange division and elevated to its own entry systems division under Don Estridge. Don's new role was buttressed by official confirmation that "the Personal Computer is the set of intelligent workstations on which we will focus our office support."

Having the PC cloak the idiosyncrasies of IBM's different minicomputers made sense for business buyers. But it also took the company farther away from the consumer market. A PC designed to provide consistent network and user interfaces among disparate IBM midrange and mainframe computers would obviously need IBM-specific software, both to mask the differences and to provide a much higher level of network performance and reliability than consumers would ever need or pay for.

A year later, after John Akers got wind that we were working on a minicomputer report, he insisted we interview Don Estridge. The request was totally reasonable, given the PC's role in the strategy to unify the minicomputer lines. But even so, getting the Boca bunch to set a specific date was incredibly difficult, despite the best effort of our liaison Sam Albert, who could usually set up a meeting with anyone at IBM. The PC folks were concentrating on markets outside the enterprise, we speculated.

We flew down to Florida for a ninety-minute meeting on January 23, 1985, long after we had started writing the final report, and got the sense no one quite knew why we were there. In the forty minutes actually allotted to us, Estridge basically confirmed what we knew about the October 25 strategy. His entry systems division's PCs would handle presentation services (i.e., the human interface); midrange computers would route traffic and handle error recovery; and hosts—midrange or mainframes—would maintain the enterprise databases. The architecture would prevent IBM product divisions from stepping on each other with overlapping functions. And knowing the plan, customers could proceed with greater confidence on their own development of new systems, hoped Estridge.

Twenty years later—with Unix, Linux, and mainframe Web servers at the top, Cisco routers in the middle, and PCs for the user—it all sounds remarkably prescient. Beyond that, Estridge seemed annoyingly messianic. My now-yellowed notes reveal mostly pontifications about a new product-development model, several referrals to his "twelve disciples," and repeated admonitions on the need for trust and openness.

Perhaps Estridge had been preoccupied. Shortly after our meeting, IBM made a nervous foray into the consumer market with the PCjr., a low-cost computer with too little capacity and a dopey small-key "chiclet" keyboard that flopped in the retail stores against the better-designed competition. The debacle should have warned IBM management away from a dependence on consumer products, but it didn't. In any case, Estridge was soon moved into what IBMers called the "penalty box" and pushed into some vague job in corporate manufacturing, while Bill Lowe was brought back to resume the work he'd started in 1981.

Tragically, on August 2 of that year, Estridge and his wife were killed in a crash at the Dallas-Fort Worth Airport. Subsequent views of his capabilities were mixed. Akers would say during the Estridge family's litigation against the airline that Don could eventually have been named CEO. Other observers took this as posthumous kindness rather than reality. A more balanced assessment came from Kleiner Perkins partners John Doerr and Floyd Kvamme, who eagerly if unsuccessfully recruited him as CEO of fledgling Sun Microsystems. After he declined, the job was pushed on an uneasy Scott McNealy, who performed marvelously in the post. But the episode reflects the judgment of two experienced CEO evaluators after a very close look at Don's capabilities.

IBM Loses Points with Consumers

When Lowe returned, the PC effort had just five software engineers, mostly acting as contract officers, he told us. By 1986, 1,500 IBMers were building the OS/2 as an extended industrial-strength offering with the control and reliability valued by large corporate customers. About 120 Microsoft people were working on the joint venture, thus reassuring cottage-software companies that they wouldn't be blued and bleached out of existence at some random date. But the Billy Club was moving in another direction.

In an apparent gaffe, IBM actually widened the divide by ceding to Microsoft the royalties received for their jointly developed operating system on all non-IBM PCs. A sale of an IBM clone would thereafter bring Microsoft the same amount of revenue as it would receive from the sale of an IBM original. That fateful concession permanently drove a wedge between each side's incentives, to IBM's massive and irrecoverable disadvantage. From then on, Microsoft listened more often to PC makers when extending its product and less to IBM. Repeated attempts to renegotiate the deal came to naught.

IBM continued to suffer ominous defeats in the consumer sector. The quality assumptions, pricing models, and human interfaces relevant to the business market just didn't work with consumers. They were far less likely to buy the more expensive IBM PC purely on the strength of its brand. Enterprise CIOs, on the other hand, were responsible for creating secure and reliable productivity environments for tens of thousands of employees. Which meant that they accorded far more weight to software quality than they did to consumer buzz.

But what impressed the CIOs seemed a weakness to PC-oriented observers smitten with Microsoft's entrepreneurial whizbang. For example, Paul Carroll, a *Wall Street Journal* reporter who accurately chronicled IBM's troubles in his 1993 book *Big Blues: The Unmaking of IBM,* seemed unfazed by Microsoft's spotty software-development practices: "The Microsoft programmers weren't big on following the accepted rules on programming. They used whatever tricks they could to get some feature to run fast. Never mind that the poor programmer who in later years tried to update the operating system might get confused and wreak unintentional havoc. The Microsoft group didn't bother documenting their work much. One programmer inserted the initials of his friends as headers.... The Microsoft programmers didn't go in much for testing either. They thought they did, but their testing wasn't up to the standards IBM had developed in its mainframe work over the years."[1]

That attitude would be a double-edged sword with negative implications for Microsoft's future. In our visits to Redmond, company executives openly admitted that half the bugs in any new software release were left for the first customers to discover. In contrast, IBM engineers were strongly encouraged to hold back the release of any new software until the estimated number of bugs remaining was less than the estimated number still latent in a piece of software released five years before. Clear and consistent documentation was just another important part of IBM's quality story—at least in its traditional markets.

The popular wisdom also favored Microsoft over IBM on the efficiency of their program code. Recounts Carroll, for example, "One of the biggest fights the IBM and Microsoft developers had came when a Microsoft developer took a piece of IBM code that required 33,000 characters of space and rewrote it in 200 characters, 1/160th of the original space."[2] The episode makes the IBMers seem muddily stupid. Certainly, Microsoft had the advantage in attracting brilliant computer-science graduates steeped in the latest programming techniques from the best universities. But IBM had years of experience tightening program "path lengths," that is, the number of instructions in the path to complete any routine. For example, its airline control program, which underlay the reservation systems of many leading airlines, processed more transactions per second in 1980 than has any Microsoft product thirty years later. And Microsoft's NT operating system, which was originally targeted at 8 million bytes of code, actually reached the market with 20 million. Such program bloat would impede PC performance and complicate software maintenance for several years.

Mike Maples was correctly philosophical with us: "We faced Hobson's choice—either delay release for a year or go to market with what we had and learn from early-user experience. We chose the latter." Good strategy, great product, but not necessarily a model of disciplined or efficient programming.

Bus to Nowhere

Not surprising, but ultimately irrelevant, Lowe began building IBM engineering capabilities to develop differentiable and more profitable hardware extensions. What may have been his biggest loss involved the PC "bus" or data pathway between processor and memory and between the processor and various peripheral devices. For two years, Lowe tried to reestablish the IBM lead with a non-standard "Micro-Channel Architecture," which was faster than the older standard but not entirely compatible.

At the same time, he tried to introduce the PS/2, a new line of personal computers based on the micro-channel, which not only failed but, worse yet, delayed IBM's move from the 16-bit Intel 286 microprocessor to the much faster 32-bit 386. IBM's slack year gave Compaq and other fast followers an enormous boost, raising their PC market shares as IBM's fell precipitously, to below 40 percent. Buoyed by his company's new stature, Compaq CEO Rod Canion led a successful revolt by "the gang of nine" PC makers against the Micro-Channel, permanently ending IBM's leadership in PC design.

But Canion was soon smacked as well. Within the year, a closet product-development team secretly organized by Compaq Chairman Ben Rosen demonstrated that the company could and should revamp its cost structure to compete against the commoditized clones. Eckhard Pfeiffer replaced Canion, who might better have tended to his company's cost structure rather than politicking around the industry. Pfeiffer quickly figured out a way to cut product costs and, more important, slash gross margins to 23 percent, a move that probably damaged IBM more than the micro-channel loss.

IBM continued to straddle the consumer and business markets. For his part, Lowe remained fixated on software targeted at the corporate market, both as a way to grow margins and because the IBM history and culture resisted dependence on Microsoft. After all, IBM had always supplied its own proprietary operating systems.

The OS/2 version featuring the graphical user interface still hadn't been shipped by late 1988, delayed perhaps by the frictions with Microsoft. And Bill Lowe, having been beaten on a significant promotion by Dick Gerstner, left IBM for Xerox. When Gerstner subsequently contracted Lyme disease, control of the PC business fell to Jimmy Cannavino, a polarizing figure who was viewed very positively by some and with near contempt by others—often at the same time and from surprising sources.

Cannavino had joined IBM as a high-school-educated repairman of tabulating gear in Chicago, and his exploits were near legendary. We'd first met him as a product planner for the mainframe division and found him full of useful facts and charming blather. But years later, as head of the PC business, he began our interview by threatening to make sure I never interviewed anyone at IBM again if I didn't report exactly what he said. I stopped taking notes, disregarded everything he told me, and made sure I never interviewed him again. In fairness, it was a time of considerable stress for Jimmy, though others witnessed quite similar behavior in calmer times. In that sense, Jimmy and Bill Gates were clearly an awful fit. Cannavino's testosteronics reflected the IBM way and were much admired by Akers and several other top IBM executives. But they were totally ineffectual for an ongoing negotiation with Gates and Ballmer or the new breed outside the blind alleys in Armonk.

Over the next three years, the IBM-Microsoft association would be a series of lulls and reengagements centered around their fundamental incompatibilities. "Their relationship is somewhere between prenuptial agreement and final divorce," clucked a Valley smarty at the time. By 1990, any pretense of cooperation had withered. Microsoft openly sought a decisive victory over OS/2. Its new Windows operating system promised features that were then advanced for the PC, notably the ability to run two or more programs at once. The company hoped to preempt IBM's desktop efforts and still leave itself room to raise prices by a hundred dollars per copy.

IBM fought back by rushing a new version of its OS/2 to market within a year. "If you compare the [Microsoft] Win32 description to the [IBM] Release 2.0, you'll find there is no difference," trumpeted Joe Guglielmi, vice president and master marketer, in a desperate telephone call just as I was giving our RB report a last read before distribution. To gather allies, Joe busily offered joint distribution deals to independent software developers, notably Borland and Lotus. Jabbered Guglielmi, "We have more control over markets than we have yet made clear."

What hubris! Ultimately, Armonk would have no control over the PC market at all—and customers, not the Billy Club, would punish Lotus. By releasing the 32-bit version of its spreadsheet program for OS/2 a year ahead of the Windows version, Lotus ceded the market lead to Microsoft Excel.

By the time of our 1992 visit, Microsoft had a clever three-tier strategy: (1) "CE," a low-end operating system for use on smart telephones and fax machines; (2) Windows, for desktops scheduled for 1993/94; and (3) the new NT operating system, an assault on Unix being targeted at the enterprise market, where corporate customers were thought to have an "obsessive concern" for security, reliability, and network management. The new NT system was already six months late and would be later still. But an earlier version had already been shipped to 30,000 independent software developers.

"It's very impressive for 200 developers writing 3.5 million lines of new code over four years," observed Paul Maritz, the senior VP for systems, displaying considerable satisfaction. He was probably right. Certainly, IBM hadn't yet delivered a competitive alternative, even though it had seven times as many people working on it.

IBM was wobbling, but its PC adventure wasn't dead. Large customers liked its operating system for a variety of networking and reliability features. Even Microsoft was ready to concede IBM some advantage in the high-end corporate set, allowed Maples, knowing the business market from his tenure at IBM. "At that level of [high-end throughput] operations, we at Microsoft don't even know what we don't know. We have just two designers trying to architect an eventual market response. That answer may not satisfy everyone," he said, "but Microsoft prefers to approach the opportunity from its position as a PC software company. We don't have to be a $60 billion company [like IBM] to succeed." Maples meant that he didn't have to drag along hardware to be profitable and that the home was probably a better launch pad than the corporate office for the market dominance Bill coveted. He was dead accurate, as it turned out.

Still, Cannavino and Gates kept fencing for position, with Jimmy alternately making nice and propping up OS/2 to disengage from Microsoft, and Bill trying to keep IBM as an ally-cum-channel to build Windows. IBM pursued several other personal computer approaches, such as a user interface called Top View and a consumer network dubbed Prodigy/Trintex that it developed in partnership with Sears. Both were expensive flops and trivial sideshows given IBM's revenues and an industry bet of this magnitude.

OS/2 flopped like a decked fish. In mid-1992, software boss Lee Reiswig visited us with the news that IBM would ship two million copies of its marvel, but not even half were used, most being nothing more than freebies distributed to enterprises. Estimates of development costs ranged from $200 million to $500 million, which portended a significant potential write-off.

The game was in its final moments. Microsoft had scored on volume; IBM wasn't even on the same court. "IBM brags that PROFS [its mainframe office product] has 350,000 users, but our stuff has 10 million," snapped Gates. "They're nowhere." The comparisons of installed base and current-year shipments (shown in Table 12.1) supported his brag.

Table 12.1   1992 Operating Systems (millions)

	Installed Base	Shipments
DOS	105	15
Windows	20	10
Mac	10	3
OS/2	2	n.a.
All UNIX	2.2	1.7

Volume drives serial victories, as we've seen. The more copies sold, the lower a vendor can drop prices and, hence, attract even more users. More users draw more software from independent vendors, and more software draws still more users to the majority operating system.

Mike Maples scored the match for us: "Windows is shipped with 85 percent of all PCs in the United States; close to that in Europe and Japan. There are three aisles of software packages in the PC store for Windows titles, one each for DOS and Mac, none for OS/2."

This would be John Akers's last year, but OS/2 developers would soldier on, perhaps embarrassed to admit final and total defeat. Microsoft's fiscal 1993 revenues were then around $3.7 billion, or about 6 percent of IBM's $64.5 billion (with a $5 billion loss). But on February 6, 1993, investors placed Microsoft's value at $35.5 billion, over 80 percent of the $43.7 billion attributed to its gargantuan competitor.

Reiswig visited us again in 1994, this time with headier news about Warp, as IBM marketers had helplessly renamed the OS/2 version to suggest a spaceship future. Warp had shipped four million copies that year, and six to ten million were expected for 1995. Another version of OS/2 was in the works based on the kernel (nucleus of an operating system that manages the systems resources) developed at Carnegie Mellon University and also used by Apple. The two PC operating systems could capture 25 percent of the market, putting IBM ahead of Apple in the share race, Reiswig hoped. Forty percent of large businesses were already working with OS/2, he told us.

We were suspicious. There had been deafening silence on OS/2 not just from most "enterprise" CIOs on the Research Board but from key PC software firms. Wasn't this just "shelfware," shipped but neither bought nor used? Reiswig insisted that IBM could use its $11 billion software business to keep investing in OS/2, and, besides that, the newly installed CEO Lou Gerstner was personally behind the effort.

In Redmond, Bill was quick to drown any doubts about NT's acceptance. "NT is happening. True, I predicted we'd sell one million copies the first year. But what's doing better? Not OS/2, not AS/400. Not HP Unix, despite an admirable rearguard action. And not Sun, except in a few scientific areas." Arriving soon would be Intel's Pentium microprocessor, and the workstation business formerly dominated by Unix would soon open to Microsoft as well. "What's the difference between a $2,500 personal computer and a $25,000 workstation?" crowed Bill. "We've already gotten most of the Sun applications vendors to port their packages to NT. We're still weak in a few scientific disciplines, but I keep asking … how are we doing in attracting the package for thermal physics?" Steve Ballmer had a slightly different take on the match. "In server systems, we still celebrate every win, unlike desktop applications, where we lose so seldom that we memorialize the losses."

Gerstner, who had spent time at Nabisco and American Express, was probably the only person at IBM who understood much about consumer markets. And as he recalled in his autobiography, "We came to the OS/2 v. Windows confrontation with a product that was technically superior and a cultural inability to understand why we were getting flogged in the marketplace. First, the buyers were individual consumers, not senior technology officers. Consumers didn't care much about advanced, but arcane, technical capability. They wanted a PC that was easy to use, with a lot of handy applications. And as with any consumer product—from automobiles to bubble gum to credit cards to cookies—marketing and merchandising mattered. Second, Microsoft had all the software developers locked up, so all the best applications ran on Windows. Microsoft's terms and conditions with the PC manufacturers made it impossible for them to do anything but deliver Windows—ready to go, preloaded, on every PC they sold."[3]

In March 1995, Lou Gerstner told a plenary session of the Research Board that IBM would leave the desktop market to Windows and NT, and that OS/2 would henceforth be limited to the server market. But from the Boca Raton and Austin, Texas, software labs came press stories promising a fight to the death that confounded customers about IBM's real intentions.

Enterprise Customers End the Game

On October 12, the match finally ended, and the spectators left the stadium—at least as we saw it. At a sectional meeting of the RB, our guest, John Thompson, then IBM's head of software and later the company's vice chairman, met with twenty CIOs in the Rainbow Room at Rockefeller Center in New York City. Across the table from him, coincidently side by side, were three "true blue" CIOs from IBM's most loyal and innovative accounts. Bob Hinds of Caterpillar had been one of the first CIOs to bring a business focus to IT, refusing to provide any product or service not explicitly funded by the users. Norm Vincent of State Farm had installed thousands of Series 1 minicomputers for State Farm's field agencies with ongoing help from our good friend, Jack Reilly. (Norm's open-mindedness was evident from his sponsorship of a pioneering effort to integrate the ill-fated Go notepad computer into the company's field operations.) Frank Erbrick of UPS was midway into a Herculean effort to bring his company's technology up to par with bitter rival FedEx. Together, they represented tens of millions of dollars in mainframe, midrange, and other purchases.

"We're going to discontinue OS/2 in our agencies because our agents want to use the same system at work that they do at home," announced Vincent. "We're taking the same direction based on pressure from our dealers," added Hinds. "We're dropping OS/2, too," said Erbrick. Thompson was visibly shocked. The business user could not be separated from the home user, since work brought from the office had to be finished at home on the PC chosen by teenagers. IBM's hope of a business-oriented PC operating system was doomed.

Later, we heard that Thompson had berated his staff for failing to brief him on the wholesale swing to Microsoft. Naomi and I wondered if he would turn up the following week to address the second Research Board section. We should have known Thompson would come; he is hardly the fearful sort.

In the end, the contest was one that IBM was totally unsuited to enter—never mind, win. Decades of IBM culture, good and bad, had thrown up too many roadblocks along the way. In one sense, here was a classic confrontation between conflicting management philosophies: consumer versus business; shortest time to market versus highest reliability and lowest life-cycle costs. Microsoft worked to turn out a steady stream of products even at some reduction in quality, while IBM drove to obtain maximum quality despite the extra time needed for testing and documentation. Each one could succeed in its appropriate market space, but there were collateral consequences. For Microsoft, the emphasis on speed to market left a reputation for defective quality that retards success in the profitable high-end server space to this day (witness the recurring string of security holes in Windows).

As Gerstner wrote: "The pro-OS/2 argument was based on technical superiority. I can say without bias that many people outside IBM believed OS/2 was the better product. The anti-Windows argument was that the legendary Microsoft hype machine was using clever marketing and wily PR to foist an inferior product on consumers, take greater control of the industry, and, in the process, destroy IBM.

"What my colleagues seemed unwilling or unable to accept was that the war was already over and was a resounding defeat—90 percent market share for Windows to OS/2's 5 percent or 6 percent…. The OS/2 decision created immense emotional distress in the company. Thousands of IBMers of all stripes—technical, marketing, and strategy—had been engaged in this struggle. They believed in their product and in the cause for which they were fighting. The doomsday scenario of IBM's losing its role in the industry because it didn't make PC operating systems proved to be little more than an emotional reaction, but I still get letters from a small number of OS/2 diehards."[4]

The repositioning was complete by the time of our 1997 visit. Gerstner was ebullient about the robust software business he'd started. "There was no software company four years ago," he noted. "We gave software away in fat hardware prices. Now IBM is the second-largest software business in the world [$12.8 billion vs. Microsoft's $13.1 billion]." But OS/2 was, indeed, finished. "We absolutely had to stop fighting the religious wars against Microsoft. We lost. Every survey showed our products were better, but their market share was 80 percent. So now we're focused on groupware, database, transaction processing, systems management, and tools." To that end, Gerstner acquired Lotus and Tivoli, paying $743 million for the latter, a network-management company with just $50 million in revenues and $5.5 million in profits. IBM watchers scoffed, but, after all, this was much less than IBM squandered on OS/2 and perhaps not so high in a time of "irrational exuberance."

From the reflection in our rearview mirror, we remain convinced that John Akers misdirected the company's capabilities and attention to the PC, nearly excluding more pressing problems in mainframes, midrange products, and cost structure. Perhaps the PC looked either more important or more tractable than other issues. Perhaps Akers hoped the PC would do for his legacy what the System/360 did for Tom Watson Jr.'s —or what the surge in competitiveness did for Frank Cary's.

In any case, Akers's tenure didn't suffer because of a lack of attention paid to the PC. Nor, as noted previously, was IBM Microsoft's only, or even most-bloodied, target.

Chapter 13

POWERING TO THE APOGEE:

Ken Olsen at DEC

Digital Equipment is the poster child for technology's boom and bust, and its founder/CEO Ken Olsen the brilliant strategist who lost his touch. Almost every ingredient of success, apogee, and subsequent decline is evident in the next two chapters. Success is difficult and slow, failure a sharp downward spiral. What's especially apparent is how easily an asset becomes an anchor. DEC's asset was the VAX product line, which stretched from desktop to mainframe. No other computer vendor had anything similar. But asset became anchor when VAX helped slow management's response to Unix and Microsoft.

We last visited the company in 1993, midway through the death spiral that toppled Olsen and ended with DEC's being acquired by then-PC giant Compaq Computer. Naomi and I lunched that day in Maynard, Massachusetts, in a cozy sitting room with former COO Jack Smith, the holder of badge No. 10 as one of Ken's first hires. It was Jack's last day before retirement.

White-haired and with a ring of Boston Irish in his speech, Jack reminisced about the shuttered New England mill towns of the 1960s, where "often the only business still open was the saloon." Ken, DEC cofounder Harlan Anderson, and Ken's brother Stan, among others, had reversed that decline, bringing new jobs to down-at-the-heels towns in Massachusetts and surrounding areas. DEC's headquarters were located in Maynard's former woolen mill, with its lovely red-brick exterior and broad-boarded floors streaked dark with the oils and sweat of century-old weaving processes. Once the mill made horse blankets for the Union Army. Families had worked there for five generations, or so we were told by more than one secretary who was probably the last in her line to work at "the Mill."

DEC's part in that tradition was about to end. The speed of its collapse caught many by surprise, the symptoms of decline masked by the weakness of its traditional competitors. Across New England, factory towns were shuttering again, as the minicomputer competitors faltered and the locus of technology moved west to Silicon Valley.

The Early Years: "Pushing the Iron"

Digital Equipment Corporation was founded in 1957 by a band of MIT engineers from Project Whirlwind, the pioneering effort to develop the first real-time computer for the Air Force, still using vacuum tubes. In return for 70 percent of the company, Ken Olsen and Harlan Anderson coaxed $70,000 in venture capital from American Research & Development and its founder, General Georges Doriot, a legendary lecturer at the Harvard Business School. For her 1981 book *The Computer Establishment*, Katherine Davis Fishman spoke to both Olsen and Doriot. As Ken recalled, "When we made our first proposal to ARD, Doriot told us our profit projection of 5 percent wasn't enough, that we'd better raise it to 10 percent, and he said to promise quick results, because most of the men on his board of directors were over 80."[1]

After two years spent building electronic components, the still-tiny DEC put together its first computer, calling it a "programmed data processor," or PDP-1, avoiding the word "computer" to calm investors and avoid retaliation by the always-dangerous IBM. "We told Ken not to emphasize computers," Doriot told Fishman. "Here were IBM, Burroughs, RCA in that business. To have two young men come over to older men and talk of competing with them didn't sound quite modest.... [Ken] has a full understanding of the market two or three years out, he knows how to take the available techniques and use them imaginatively, and his ideas are not so advanced that they're dangerous." Noting that DEC's first-year sales exceeded expectations by 50 percent and its profits by 200 percent, Doriot concluded, "I think DEC needed less counseling from us than most of the companies we've been connected with."[2]

In 1965, the 12-bit PDP-8 was introduced and quickly became the darling of the academicians and government scientists who drove the progress in interactive computing during those Cold War years. Priced initially at $18,000 apiece, 50,000 PDP-8s were sold over the next fifteen years. The more powerful 16-bit PDP-11 was launched in 1970, playing catch-up against a slew of minicomputer competitors, especially Data General, which had been formed a few years earlier by DEC breakaways, to the lasting enmity of Ken Olsen.

Nevertheless, the PDP-11 was a marvel and was followed by an escalating line of compatible models that eventually sold 250,000 units. Along the way came the high-end, 36-bit PDP-10, a multiuser, interactive, time-sharing machine developed in parallel with (but separately from) the PDP-11. Together, the PDP lines launched the company on a 40 percent annual growth trajectory, with revenues crossing the $1 billion mark in 1972. DEC now had 41 percent of the minicomputer business and 38,000 employees.

For its first two decades, DEC "pushed the iron," meaning it built components and computers with minimal applications software, mainly for OEMs to embed in their final products. Two culturally distinct hemispheres existed at DEC, we wrote: "The hard technology side (central engineering and manufacturing) was visibly preferred by Ken and his alter ego, the VP Engineering, Gordon Bell, and all the inner circle. The soft technology side (sales and service) drew much less interest from those who mattered, unless an issue (such as remote diagnostics for field service) was highly susceptible to an engineering solution."

Linking the two hemispheres were the powerful "product divisions" established in DEC's formative years around markets, distribution channel, and industry segment. Their fundamental mission was to push sales of the company's products within their designated market slot. Conventional product-marketing functions were augmented by the division managers' skill in wheedling special features from engineering (sometimes through Ken's personal intervention). Sector-specific software was built by DEC's own sizable programming teams or by universities, software firms, or favored customers with whom it cooperated.

There could be up to twenty product divisions—the numbers and names changed from time to time to reflect market opportunity. First came OEM (half the business) and then components (the traditional business and the first segment to come under attack from the semiconductor houses). After that came the different market segments like laboratory, process control, education, telecommunications (mostly AT&T), and points in between. The financial sector was left to IBM and Wang, to Ken's eventual regret.

Learning to Dance with Business Customers

In DEC's engineering culture, business applications were treated as stepchildren and were thus often unsuccessful. Not until 1972—a year after distributed applications using its equipment had been developed at Continental Can, Dow Chemical, and elsewhere—did DEC create the business systems division under Irwin "Jake" Jacobs. The System 300 and 500 were introduced expressly for the business community a year later.

At our first visit in 1974, the group had fifty-nine salespeople and only forty software-support engineers. Jake claimed that $500,000 was being spent to develop software that would appeal to EDP (electronic data processing) shops. But DEC's indifference to business customers was still apparent when Jake blurted to a computer conference that summer: "Minicomputers are just like any other computers … except you don't get any vendor support." Another signal was DEC's slow-footedness in adding to its machines Cobol, then the dominant programming language for business applications. Not surprising, business sales amounted to only $30 million, or just 7 percent of DEC's total annual revenues.

Nineteen-seventy-four was also the year of DEC's first-ever quarterly decline, after five years of skyrocketing results. Blinded by the flash of fingerlings hatched since 1968, many on Wall Street concluded that DEC's glow had faded. True, it had lost share to the newcomers, but the dirge was premature: DEC would remain atop the minicomputer industry for another fifteen years. "Steady Grey" just below IBM's "Big Blue" was the way we characterized their one-two placement over those years. And on the numbers, DEC looked strong, indeed: The company had cumulatively installed 20,000 PDP-8s and 15,000 PDP-11s, numbers large enough to draw Armonk's attention (though absolutely minuscule compared to later counts of PCs and Unix servers).

By 1976, the hottest hot button was office automation, and Wang, along with other minicomputer-based entrants, was hustling the first movers toward the exits. Here was another chance for DEC in the business market, we speculated. So we went to visit Jack Gilmore, VP Business Systems and an experienced technology executive whose operation was creating a secretarial workstation by wrapping PDP boxes in a veneer of text editing and rudimentary data communications.

"Powerful and expensive," we opined, plus there were only twenty field people. "So what?" countered Gilmore, contending that even twenty was too many. Better to confine training and implementation support to a combination of videotape and floppy disk, he said. No on-site human intervention needed. "Hand-holding is never worthwhile. We can offer good hardware/software value, and the office manager can determine its use." Good luck, we sniped, seeing his rationale as nothing more than a reflection of DEC's traditional biases. But Gilmore's dictum against hand-holding would be the right one for the PC business.

These were the home-enthusiast years for the PC; sales were sparse and applications sparser. Amid the press-and-pundit euphoria in 1977 over PC-driven recipe collections and lawn sprinklers, Ken Olsen growled incautiously and infamously that "there is no need for a computer in the home," a remark that draws squeals of disbelief to this day. Ken later insisted that he was talking not about PCs, but about embedding microprocessors to make the home "intelligent." "I didn't think anyone wanted a record of what they'd taken from the refrigerator in the middle of the night," he told me. Or, as he recollected in *World Business* magazine (May 28, 2002) twenty-five years later: "I said, 'I don't think we want our personal lives run by the computer.'"

Until 1979, our visits to DEC hadn't attracted top-management attention. Who needed scribblers serving the hostile corporate data processing community? But more new entrants were crowding into the sector, putting pressure on DEC. Its annual revenue growth had slowed to 25 percent. Not bad by normal standards, but behind HP's 30 percent-plus trajectory. So, thinking the time was right to seek broader access, Naomi contacted someone with the ephemeral title of VP corporate operations. "Mail room and the nurse," I grumped as we drove through the snow from Boston's Logan Airport to Maynard.

Not for the first time, Naomi was right. Vice President Win Hindle was, to a very real degree, DEC's organizing principal, Ken's amanuensis, and the decisive entry point to the entire corporation. The first time this New England Brahmin greeted us, it was with courtly charm in the colonially furnished sitting room where we would spend many interesting hours over the next fifteen years. But our first exposure to DEC's top tier lasted only thirty minutes before we had to retrace our route back to Logan through the already graying slush. We were invited back a few weeks later, though, this time scooting via DEC helicopter over MIT to Maynard. A steady stream of DEC executives paraded through the sitting room that day, with the CEO the last to be interviewed.

Ken Olsen was a giant—in physical stature, presence, ethics, and (generally) vision. A man with sharp insights, a wonderful chuckle, and an improbably large and unevenly shaped head. When we complimented him for an especially good quarterly earnings report, he graciously responded, "Sometimes our success merely reflects the weakness of our competitors." That remark would come to haunt him in the future.

A Stormy Ride to the Future

Before our first visit, the Grand Dragon (as the boss was widely known) had navigated the company partway through a stormy transition from multiple computer lines to a single new 32-bit hardware architecture (VAX) and operating system (VMS). The new line would span a "two orders of magnitude" range in which the high-end hummer had one hundred times the operating capacity of the smallest box. Many existing products were left orphaned or dead. (The PDP-11 was eventually stripped down to a microprocessor targeted at the OEM market, with no further development funding.)

In *The Ultimate Entrepreneur*, the Rifkin-Harrar biography of Olsen, Ken is alternately described as moralistic, overbearing, abusive, charismatic, and involved in every decision, though his skills were said to lay more in the physical world of circuit packaging than in the abstract world of computer architecture. For that, there was Gordon Bell, who credits himself in the book with having personally guided VAX development without much input or interference from

Olsen. "'Ken had absolutely no role, as president or engineer, in VAX, beginning with its inception,' Bell says. 'He must clearly be given credit as president, though, for letting it come into being.'"[3] How kind of Bell. Clearly his earlier relationship with the CEO had soured.

Yet later, the authors write: "Olsen neither favored nor rejected the proposal in the initial meetings. In his typical fashion, he pushed hard to expose the core of the issue. He sparred with Bell about whether the plan represented a true corporate strategy or just a simple product change. 'Ken's harangues were always very painful,' Bell says, 'but also useful to me, because then I could go off and address the issues on his mind.'"[4]

Once convinced by Bell that his strategy for DEC was all-inclusive, Olsen allowed the decision-making process to advance. The authors continued: "The issues got aired and a consensus developed. But Olsen worried. The company would be betting billions in development costs and potential lost revenue on this scheme. DEC would be heading into areas where it had little experience, such as building its own microprocessors, building large disk storage units, and writing software to run on networks. Could Digital market this plan? he wondered. Could it afford to be wrong? Despite all the reasons against it, Bell's strategy was formally approved by the board of directors in December 1978. 'I took no active part in forming the strategy,' Olsen admits. 'But once it got going, it was my job to say we're one company, this is the strategy. If you don't like it, get out.' He proved once more why he has stayed so long on the top of his company. He saw the new parade starting to march, and he simply got out in front and started waving his baton."

In that last, wholly gratuitous potshot, the otherwise meticulous authors show a breathtaking disregard for the essence of corporate leadership. Certainly, no one would have criticized Tom Watson for not understanding integrated circuit design when he made his industry-smashing decision to bet the company on System/360. Olsen was doing the CEO's job, and doing it admirably.

As for Gordon Bell, he was a brilliant man whose sometimes fuzzy digressions into the anthropological implications of computing were hard for us to comprehend. Neither Naomi nor I would ever have credited Bell with having the business gravitas to translate an excellent technical concept into a financial triumph. Moreover, he was "infuriated" about everything and anything related to Olsen, spending much of the next decade in continual and often silly tirades against his one-time partner and boss. Doubtless, Rifkin and Harrar had inside sources other than a discordant Bell, but they are not in evidence throughout these passages.

The transition to VAX required enormous effort. But an even more massive change was under way to reshape the DEC organization. Reining in the product groups, whose independence was once central to the company's success, was now vital to maintaining a disciplined product line. Otherwise, each product group would scheme continuously to unravel hard-won product coherence. In short, the freewheeling product groups had become gangrenous and now required amputation.

Underestimating the Resistance Within

Unfortunately, Ken was too optimistic about the time required for such radical surgery to heal. So were we, naively assessing the product groups as having "received considerable attention in the trade press, though their real clout over line divisions now seems modest." How could we have been so mistaken? In fact, the rearguard actions of disgruntled old-line leaders would slow or subvert the impact of the new organizational model for the next half-decade.

Over the years, the product groups had accumulated an array of potent prerogatives, including semiautonomous advertising budgets, technical-support allocations for favored customers, and even control of finished-goods inventory. By the late 1970s, those prerogatives had become disturbingly pernicious.

To start, the groups' inventory estimates were often wrong. Too-high estimates meant the company would be burdened by obsolescence, while those that were too low led to misallocation of equipment. And the problem was compounded by the fact that disparate divisions served different parts of a customer's operation. So equipment needed for a customer's process-control operation might be on back order with one DEC unit, while that same customer's labs got whatever they needed from a different one. Moreover, the different product groups fielded their own account representatives and could exercise considerable autonomy in contract negotiation, confounding the efforts of a sister group or trampling the already hapless sales force.

What a mess! While sector-specific clout had its place in university departments or isolated laboratories, it caused consternation and confusion among major enterprises whose buyers spanned several DEC pigeonholes. Product-group allocations of scarce technical resources were entirely self-serving and without regard for the revenue potential of a company's account as a whole. In fact, 70 percent of all joint-development projects with customers were contracted without involvement of the DEC sales reps or customer CIOs.

The irony was that this assortment of product groups was only affordable so long as the company maintained the plump gross margins protected by high switching costs. The compatibility and commoditization afforded by the PC and Unix would unalterably crush those margins. As formulated, the groups had become a burdensome anachronism for a company of DEC's maturity and scale.

Restructuring the Company

On the 1979 organization chart, Ken placed himself clearly at the center of every major decision and specified twelve direct reports. The formerly unbounded product groups were corralled into three divisions, losing some of their functions to the corporate staff and the now more powerful (or so we thought) line divisions. There were three staff VPs for corporate operations, corporate marketing, and corporate planning. Then came six line divisions, including finance, personnel, manufacturing, engineering, sales, and customer service.

Manufacturing, with 23,000 employees and twenty-eight plants around the world, would be run by Jack Smith, who, as noted earlier, was DEC badge holder No. 10. The excellence of Jack's organization was a source of considerable pride in those years. Engineering was the province of Gordon Bell.

DEC's weakest area was sales and international. Pundits thought the weakness stemmed from a compensation plan based solely on salary, with zero commission on sales to heighten incentive. We agreed. Zero commission had been appropriate during the early "missionary" days when customers had to be shown the promise of minicomputers and DEC stood nearly alone. But with the technology's widespread acceptance and dozens of competitors, a new approach was required.

No such weakness was apparent in customer service, headed by Jack Shields, a highly analytic, smartly goateed, one-time truck driver. Shields had joined DEC right out of the Navy in 1961, and even though he lacked a college education, his stellar performance eventually won him consideration as a likely candidate for the CEO slot. (In fact, a college degree was hardly a prerequisite for success in the computer industry. Witness the careers of Michael Dell, Larry Ellison, Bill Gates, Steve Jobs, and DEC's own Jack Smith—not a college degree among them.)

The three surviving product groups were technical, component, and commercial, with a layer of oversight management added to temper their excesses. Nonetheless, product-group leaders retained direct access to their customers, creating considerable confusion and disarray just when DEC needed what we called a "single face to the customer."

The technical products group accounted for 33 percent of total revenues, and its engineering, laboratory, education, medicine, government, and OEM relationships had been DEC's mainstays five years before. Heading up this contentious crew was the master diplomat, Win Hindle, though even he couldn't staunch the one-off project requests floated to Ken.

Now the group was under siege from commodity microprocessors, other minicomputer makers, and the first defections to Unix, especially in the engineering and scientific community. In the OEM segment, which once contributed half of DEC's revenues, Olsen and the other Maynard executives had hoped to hold the medium-volume customers who wanted to avoid rewriting their process applications. And reluctantly concede the million-device volume markets to the semiconductor foundries. They were disappointed. Within five years, the OEM segment lost two-thirds of its business.

The computer products group, under the leadership of Stan Olsen, provided 22 percent of total revenues with its microprocessors, dumb (i.e., nonprogrammable) terminals, and word-processing devices. This varied array of products should have been the basis of a vigorous PC launch. Instead, the effort became mired in ferocious politics, and DEC was never able to sustain a serious market position in PCs, despite a series of wobbly ad campaigns.

The commercial products group, under Julius Marcus, also provided 22 percent of revenues. (Field maintenance and other services accounted for the remaining 23 percent). Half of commercial sales came from process-control applications, mostly for the petrochemical sector. A third came from AT&T. DEC's disdain for commercial applications made growing this segment fast enough to compensate for losses elsewhere a slog. The evidence of that disdain was everywhere.

Scrutinizing the Product Line

To begin with, the new VAX/VMS system was inexplicably introduced without the software tools commonly used for business systems, and the database was both too slow and too fragile. When DEC's new networking system failed to gain market traction, it was downplayed in favor of the IBM standard. A critical transaction-processing system delayed for the PDP-11 was delayed again for VAX.

Then there was pointless and embarrassing product overlap. The PDP-2020 was a perversely idiosyncratic 36-bit computer introduced by the large-systems product group just as DEC was centralizing its wares on the 32-bit VAX. Trilled the 1978 annual report: "There has also been a growing appreciation among smaller businessmen that, at last, there is a mainframe system they too can afford."

Industry analysts who questioned the apparent overlap between the 2020 and VAX were reassured that "VAX is a [scientific] Fortran machine, while 2020 is a [commercial] mainframe." But didn't that distinction exactly contradict the official view that VAX could and should handle everything? Absolutely. Nevertheless, Win Hindle expressed the hope that the 2020 might appeal to time-sharing services, dismissing mainframe ambitions as "an overly optimistic delusion." Andy Knowles, the VP for corporate marketing, called the advertising campaign "misplaced and misleading." The embarrassing discord may have given Olsen just the reason he needed to dismantle the large-systems product group in the next reorganization.

The good news for 1979 was the coherence and compatibility of the VAX product line from top to bottom. Software compatibility brought economies of scale for DEC, its customers, and the all-important independent software firms, which could now develop and pitch just one version of their product to every DEC customer.

"In the long run, companies with good architecture will finish in front of those with just marketing," was the management mantra. An integrated product line, central to Ken's strategy for the next several years, could certainly help explain his inability to grasp the importance of what many DECsters called "me-too" operating systems like Unix. Curiously, neither HP nor IBM exhibited a comparable level of software compatibility at that time, a particularly glaring shortcoming for IBM. Yet both survived the competition from Unix and the PC. Curiously, DEC did not.

The struggle to centralize the fractious business units around a single computer line left many employees feeling wounded and angry. Some of DEC's brightest lights departed in the strife, seemingly leaving the company less open to new technologies and business models. Moreover, the struggle to contain those problematic product groups would distract Ken from shrinking DEC's gross margins to the fighting weight demanded by Unix compatibility and lower switching costs for customers.

Yet, in 1979, Steady Grey held a three-part distinction, we noted: "It was then twice the age and twice the size of other mini makers, yet still dominated by the founding engineer. In fact, at $1.8 billion and an annual 25 percent growth rate, DEC is fast becoming the second-largest computer manufacturer in the world," overtaking NCR and gaining on IBM.

A Bungled Assault on the Office Market

We began our study of office automation in 1980 against the backdrop of a discordantly successful Wang Labs and a host of word-processing companies. Once again, I drove through the snow to talk to DECsters, this time to Merrimack, New Hampshire, seat of the office-automation activity still headed by Jack Gilmore. With Win Hindle's blessing and DEC's newfound interest in large-enterprise accounts, the atmosphere was decidedly less frosty than in 1976.

Jack's view of the world was intriguing at the time and mostly accurate more than a quarter-century later. DEC's own product-development plans seemed reasonably on target as well. No obvious failing blocked Steady Grey from capturing a segment of the office market from its strong base in engineering or distributed processing. Gilmore even spouted the same pseudo-anthropological lessons emanating from the office-automation centers at Xerox and IBM. For example, problem e-mail users fit into three classes, he told top researcher Cathy Loup and me: "blabbermouths" spread the word on every small personal achievement; "jungle fighters" spread complaints and criticisms; and "power users" blanket e-mail like confetti on sister departments, often unproductively. However, Jack's modest estimates of 15 percent productivity improvement now look to be "New England conservative."

He then talked about an office market evolving in three stages:

- First stage: Pure word processing would find market acceptance fueled by secretarial efficiency and eighteen-month product life cycles. "In 1976, they predicted 73,000 units and $1.5 billion in revenues in 1981," he said. "But the industry actually topped that in 1979."

- Second stage: Word processing would be wrapped into electronic mail. DEC started with CCA's Comet system and then developed its own, amid shrieks of "not invented here" from the trade press and mutterings about a lawsuit from CCA. DEC was firmly in the second stage, Gilmore assured us.

- Third stage: Gilmore accurately anticipated the addition of spell-checkers, work-flow managers, collaboration, and calendar coordination. A DEC engineer had already built a spell-checker with six thousand words, enough to cover 90 percent of the vocabulary in most business correspondence, he said. A new office information system was planned that would include e-mail, text editing, and, eventually, graphics and typesetting interfaces—though DEC's commands were still too arcane, our researchers judged.

We'd been enthusiastic until, as we folded our papers to leave, Gilmore unexpectedly announced that his product group would be disbanded or absorbed by the vertical product groups, still the bane of most large customers because of their tendency to fragment DEC's representation and bypass the IT function. Two months later, *Electronic News* (February 1981) reported that Jack Gilmore had been reassigned. The DEC spokesman was quoted as saying "that he did not know Mr. Gilmore's new title." The company would make many more assaults on the office market, but its failure to follow through in 1980 may have killed the opportunity.

Puzzlements in Personal Computing

Meanwhile, the PC line was also exhibiting considerable disarray: The DECmate PC, based on the PDP-8 microprocessor, was not a glowing success. Nor was an improbable upgrade kit intended to convert DEC terminals into PCs running Larry Kildare's rudimentary operating system, the CP/M.

For a 1981 study on personal computing, we met with Win Hindle and Andy Knowles, formerly VP for corporate marketing, who now headed a new "small systems" group. Knowles was responsible for a plethora of terminals, word processors, commercial OEM products, and, of course, personal computers. Ken Olsen's brother Stan was gone, victim perhaps of the unsuccessful forays into PCs and word processing. Or perhaps Stan was the loser in a power shift.

According to a May 1982 piece in *Business Week,* Stan "became convinced that word processing could become DEC's stepping-stone into the low-cost end of the computer market.... But when the word processor finally came out in 1976, it was a flop." Then, too, related *BW,* Stan's efforts were thwarted by Knowles, "described by several insiders as a 'vicious infighter.'" Stan, "frustrated by his inability to get consensus among engineering and other departments ... resigned." The article offered an insight into the dirtier undercarriage of the Steady Grey vehicle. Ken later told us that "one of the most difficult acts in my career was firing my brother."

In our meeting, Win benignly insisted that the future looked bright. "Heavy bread" had been invested in five-inch magnetic disks, added Andy. More important was the glittery array of technical gizmos lined up for the National Computer Conference. DEC would offer high-resolution display, an ergonomic keyboard, the new disk, an integrated modem and Ethernet connection, and "snap-together" installation that "your secretary could master."

But after that, the picture became clouded. For starters, the plan lacked the coherence in either hardware or operating system to draw the independent software vendors. DEC would field three microprocessors—the PDP-8, the PDP-11, and an "industry standard" (presumably Intel with a PC operating system). The two PDP's would sport only their native operating systems, leaving Unix out of the picture. Knowles justified this inward-looking plan by peremptorily dismissing the two PC operating systems as poorly designed. And Unix was essentially nonstandard, he sniffed: "There are at least fourteen different versions of Unix."

No doubt, Ken agreed, as later evidenced by his famously misunderstood "snake oil" assessment regarding Unix made publicly in 1984 and afterwards. However, he was talking about sales claims of effortless applications portability from one brand to another—not about the operating system *per se.* He was right, but that didn't prevent his detractors from having a field day. And being right didn't keep him from missing the main point: The different versions of Unix resembled each other closely enough to attract the independent software firms that were developing engineering and laboratory applications; it was much easier to extend their product's reach from one Unix to another than from DEC's proprietary operating system to HP or the other minicomputer companies. Unix soon caught the attention of the scientists and engineers who had once flocked to the PDP-8.

In that context, Andy Knowles missed the point, as well: "Although we aren't depending on the me-too operating systems, we're not too worried about attracting independent software developers. If this new hardware is successful, the software firms will swarm to it." Happily, the new packages would simply add to the wealth of applications packages that had propelled the PDP-8 and PDP-11 in the past. Andy was seriously mistaken, but that was understandable. After all, that year's industry leaders—Apple, Commodore, and Tandy—all had their own operating systems. IBM was mud-wrestling with Microsoft, while pioneers like Altos and Vector Graphic that incorporated the me-too operating systems were tottering. In hindsight, DEC's directions were wrong, but so were those of many traditional industry leaders. There was still time to recover; both IBM and HP would do that.

Mapping Future Strategy

By 1982, with many of the organizational battles apparently over, the company was focused on the future. And the growing clout of the two Jacks clearly signaled the direction of DEC's newly consolidated organization. Jack Shields was in charge not just of field engineering (with 13,000 employees worldwide versus 9,000 in 1979), but also sales, consulting, software services, and education. Jack Smith added engineering (held jointly with Gordon Bell) to his manufacturing duties and was busily pairing the development groups with specific manufacturing plants to shorten new-product introduction cycles.

Considerable progress had been made in corralling the product groups, although profiles provided by two VPs that year still suggested considerable resources and reach. The laboratory data products group plowed DEC's traditional heartland. Out of two hundred employees, there were a dozen PhDs and fifty-five hardware and software engineers (mostly the latter) who partnered with favored customers to build applications that could sell more DEC-platform products. As an example of the program's reach, much of the pharmaceutical industry eventually adapted VAX-based molecular models originally built at the DuPont labs. "We maintain close alliances with our chosen pioneers, remain alert to their needs, and make offers they can't refuse, such as special software, occasional [free] hardware, and extra support," explained the division VP. But despite DEC's longtime presence, the laboratory market was already highly competitive, and many high-performance players were flooding in.

Meanwhile, the one hundred thirty-five people in the manufacturing, distribution, and control group were focused on process control, materials planning, and robotics. The group's sixty-two engineers were building factory-floor and robotic programming systems, while other developers were working on a text editor specifically for factory foremen. Twenty-five technical specialists were assisting, or sometimes bypassing, the field sales reps, and there were twenty-five liaisons to third-party software firms and another twelve dedicated to DEC's own factories.

Yet the product divisions had lost their self-defeating prerogatives, starting with product inventory allocation. From now on, "we'll allocate processors by customer, certainly not by product group,"

Shields confirmed. Nor could the product groups allocate technical specialists to favored accounts; instead, those resources were shifted to the field organization. And their individual, often discordant marketing campaigns were supposed to give way to cooperative campaigns with the encouragement of new performance metrics that shared credit for revenue gains. No longer did they control communications, either, because product marketing was moved to manufacturing under Jack Smith. And, finally, the negotiation of nonstandard contract clauses was a thing of the past. "While special clauses make the departmental customer look good, our atrocious administration of those clauses always confuses and irritates the MIS [management information systems] executive," judged Bob Hughes, an ex-IBMer heading commercial accounts.

The favored hard-technology hemisphere hadn't gone untouched either. Until then, central engineering had been led solely by Gordon Bell, a world-class computer master with less competence or interest in complex management. By his lights, Bell would always know as much as did the product manager. That worked when the company offered a product line with several unconnected, midrange processors like PDP-8s, PDP-11s, and terminals. But once VAX spanned workstations to mainframes, expertise was required in several different circuitry and heat-dissipation technologies. Besides, DEC had added disk storage, networking, and, most important, semiconductor components. It was time for a different organizational approach.

Jack Smith was given joint management responsibility with Bell over central engineering for at least two reasons: to achieve more discipline in product development along with greater focus on product "buildability" and lower manufacturing costs. Plant managers were forced to compare manufacturing productivity against that of competitors, said Smith. "They've stopped measuring their performance exclusively against their own previous results and begun comparing our underlying cost trends with those of 'direct competitors,'" notably neighbors Data General and Wang, plus IBM.

Equally pragmatic was DEC's decision on whether to make or buy products and their components. "We won't build unless we eventually expect to be a world-class supplier; otherwise, you can't hold any advantage over buying outside," explained the VP for manufacturing technology, Dick Clayton. No fuzzy ideology here; DEC bought machined metal parts, most plastics, small disk drives, and even small printers from Japan. "Our engineers had to swallow their pride, once they took the printer apart and considered the price," Clayton said. The "not-invented-here" bias later attributed to Ken was not in evidence.

Engineers at DEC's world-class semiconductor fabrication facility exhibited a similarly practical bent, working to shorten the design cycle and reduce the manpower required per circuit design in each succeeding chip generation. But its products were always embedded in DEC computers. Selling to outside buyers was extremely difficult absent the volumes enjoyed by the semiconductor firms, admitted the facility's impressive boss, Jeff Kalb. "With our extremely short product life cycles, just when you're up the learning curve, it's time to throw out the design as obsolete. So our price/performance will never be better than 80 percent of the volume microprocessors," and probably not that, he said.

As we were leaving, Jack Smith gave us a glowing account of communications connectivity and architectural compatibility. Then he awarded us two handsome charts—one suitable for framing, the other wall-sized. Arrayed on the charts were all the DEC processors, harmonizing around an E-shaped network arrangement in shades of blue to connote compatibility. Only DEC's "Rainbow" PC—using Intel processors and me-too operating systems—was isolated in its whiteness.

Achieving the Apogee

From the distance of years, the elegant product order pressed by Ken now seems too orderly for a period of radical transition and innovation in hardware, software, and business models. After all, 1982 was the year Sun Microsystems was founded, launching Unix as the operating system for the entire computer industry. But at the time, DEC seemed in very strong shape, both managerially and in its product line.

Six months later, on May 2, 1983, *Business Week* published a major cover story subtitled "Will Digital Equipment Corp.'s Massive Overhaul Pay Off?" It confirmed and expanded on what we'd learned. Win had asked if we'd speak to the reporters, thus releasing us from our usual self-imposed restriction about talking to the press. He worried that the changes were too complex to be readily communicated. We agreed to his request and were subsequently quoted making some remarks that were perceived as being highly positive in Maynard: "If DEC can prove an adept marketer, 'it will have no major weaknesses,' declares Ernest von Simson…. 'Now with just one salesman calling on a large customer, DEC should be able to do a better job of capturing [large accounts],' according to Naomi O. Seligman."

Ken received very positive marks on "three key pieces of this restructuring only now falling into place." On management: "Olsen is streamlining an overgrown corporate bureaucracy and decentralizing decision-making." On products: They "can communicate easily with each other." On marketing: He "is working hard to develop closer ties with customers, organize new distribution channels, and launch more innovative promotions."

BW concluded: "Olsen, whose genial public demeanor has concealed a frenetic, hard-driving management style, refuses to be as sanguine about DEC's prospects as his executives and shareholders. 'I'm never satisfied—when you get satisfied, you're in trouble,' he says. However, he acknowledges with a grin, 'Well maybe fleetingly—for just a moment, I do think we're exactly where I'd like us to be.'" Ken was fifty-seven, at the height of his influence over both his company and the IT sector generally. Within a decade, it would all come tumbling down, with Ken Olsen ousted from the company he founded and took to the apogee of prominence in the computer industry.

Chapter 14

TUMBLING TO COLLAPSE:

The Palace Guard Ousts Olsen

"I don't want to be the next Ken Olsen," several CEOs have told me in recent years. They mean that they don't want to miss the next great thing. But what they should want is the good sense to leave before they lose the company's cadre of strong lieutenants or do something that cripples their ability to object. To lose or weaken the firm's best eyes and brains in a rapidly changing business milieu is a fast track to oblivion.

Congratulations on the *BusinessWeek* plaudits were premature, as DEC's post-reorganization blues persisted, and the mind-set at the top seemed unchanged. One telling incident occurred at a sales force pep rally in which middle management made an impassioned presentation on the value of spending more time developing personal relationships with senior customer executives. Barely a moment later, Ken rose to reassert his belief that those "loyal" engineers would always be DEC's best friends. If the audience wasn't confused, the customer might well be.

Besides, even if Ken couldn't imagine it, the not-so-"loyal" engineers would soon abandon DEC for Unix and then Windows. Unfortunately, Ken's imagination also failed him when it came to envisioning the customer as a consumer using computer systems for games, word processing, and, eventually, accessing the Internet.

Apart from customer defections, potentially serious problems were roiling engineering. Sharing the top job, a demotion of sorts, was a psychological blow to the always volatile Gordon Bell, who "began thinking about leaving," according to Rifkin and Harrar: "He couldn't thrive without a challenge, and the VAX was now becoming a process, just carrying out the plan. The creation was over. More important, stress was wearing Bell down. He felt at times as if he were carrying both engineering and Olsen. 'Running engineering was never that hard for me,' Bell says. 'It was doing it with Ken on my back that made life pretty miserable, because I simply didn't respect his engineering judgment on anything except packaging.'

"The combative, but synergistic, relationship Bell and Olsen had shared for the past decade was collapsing," the authors wrote. "Bell believes Olsen grew frightened of him because he understood the 'nooks and crannies of engineering.' Bell says, 'I used to keep management on their toes by simply being able to challenge any manager to know more than I did about a project.' Olsen, by putting Smith in a co-leadership role with Bell, apparently intended to see engineering as a process rather than as a content-oriented job."[1]

New Roads Not Taken?

Strangely, Bell had given us a quite different, less self-righteous perspective in 1982, six years before the Rifkin-Harrar account was published. Gordon was easily DEC's most expressive futurist. At the top of his R&D priorities list that year was man-machine interface, or how people might interact with their computers more intuitively and with less training. Although Bell listed a host of possible interfaces, he seemed convinced that speech recognition was finally ready for a stunning entrance after hovering on the horizon for fifteen years.

Naomi and I agreed, partly because we also assumed that many executives and non-engineering professionals would forever scorn keyboards as a secretarial accoutrement. So speech recognition would be critical to advancing the widespread acceptance of computers. A year later, Steve Jobs introduced the Mac, basically ending the question. Today, the notion that voice recognition could ever become a general-purpose replacement for the keyboard seems absurd.

But apart from man-machine interface, Bell hardly pushed rampant innovation during our 1982 interview. To the contrary, he provided a lengthy exposition of his past few years as what he called an "internal city planner," ensuring not only architectural homogeneity but systems interconnectivity as well. "We don't need more research," he told us. "I love research, but we already have more ideas than we can exploit." Ken was obviously not the only person taking a process perspective on engineering. Or was Bell merely echoing the party line until he could make a respectable exit?

Nor did we receive any industry-bending ideas from Sam Fuller, the head of advanced corporate research. Sam was a highly intelligent, quasi-academic with excellent connections in leading universities and government labs—the wellspring of DEC success since its earliest days at MIT. "We don't have to duplicate their excellent work," Fuller explained. "So we act as a halfway house, proving the feasibility of academic research concepts that may appear in commercial projects three to eight years later." A great idea since the technology platforms preferred by engineering and science students were inevitably drawn into the businesses that employed them. A bad idea once the universities led the parade to Unix.

After agreeing with Bell on new human interfaces, Fuller's second topic was artificial intelligence, another long-playing R&D dream, he allowed. "Artificial intelligence is the buzzword of the eighties, but most of the buzzers haven't done any real work yet," he said. DEC had perfected a system to configure customer orders so that computers were shipped with the right boards and cables—previously a significant source of errors and customer dissatisfaction. Fuller expected similar applications to follow. But twenty years later, this would be classified a mechanical expert system rather than AI.

The third item on Fuller's agenda was the "scientific workstation" being built by a small lab in Palo Alto. Featured was a still-sketchy basket of artificial intelligence applications, advanced human interfaces, and a highly experimental processor architecture. Those objectives would be considered ambitious, he reckoned, even against those Japan Inc. was exploring in the joint venture ballyhooed as the Fifth Generation Project. (More on this later.)

Finally, we discussed a small project to build a "workbench" of programmer tools based on Unix and specifications developed at the still-prolific Bell Labs. Fuller was convinced that Digital could gain, or avoid losing, a competitive advantage by displaying a more avuncular attitude toward Unix. By today's lights, that was an extraordinary understatement. After all, Unix creator AT&T was DEC's largest customer, and Unix was already gaining popularity in the same universities that had launched the early PDPs.

How could DEC have focused on dead-end technology dreams that minimized both Unix and the PC? It's hard to believe that Gordon Bell's intuition was so dulled by his supposed state of depression that he couldn't sense the waters darkening as twin hurricanes roared toward DEC's path.

First Defections

In March 1983, Bell suffered a serious heart attack. When he returned to work, wrote Rifkin and Harrar, "the fire was gone. Bell stopped his combative, frontal attacks on engineering issues. He still emotionally engaged himself in company issues and the VAX strategy in particular. But he no longer showed the will to fight the constant, wearying battles. With Smith running Engineering as Gordon's equal and Olsen very much controlling the corporate direction, Bell felt overwhelmed. Neither Olsen nor Smith understood the architectural complexities of computers. And DEC's decision-making process was slowing down as the company grew."[2]

More to the point, the computer industry was about to embark on a roller-coaster ride, a moment of decision similar to that when Frank Cary replaced Tom Watson Jr. at IBM. Watson had birthed the VAX-like System/360, creating new competitors, which Cary met by decentralizing to wrench the company into greater innovation. The difference at Digital Equipment's moment of decision was that no one stepped forward to break the VAX-only mold. And it's not clear that Bell had the managerial means even if he'd had the opportunity.

Shortly afterward, Gordon Bell announced his intention to join Data General founder and DEC defector Henry Burkhardt in a venture called Encore Computer. Encore, a parallel-processing company, did not succeed. Eventually, the truly brilliant Gordon Bell found a home as a senior researcher at Microsoft.

Bell was hurt that Ken Olsen did not urge him to stay, but begging defectors to stick around would have made Olsen or any other reasonably capable CEO appear weak. "It's not [Bell's] kind of world anymore," Ken told *Computerworld.* "It used to be a lot of disconnected projects.

Now we're organized and scheduled and planned. He couldn't tolerate it. He's fun, exciting, charismatic, but he doesn't fit into a disciplined organized environment. We're not his kind of company anymore."[3] In our view, Olsen's assessment of Bell made more sense than Bell's diatribes about Olsen. Olsen was CEO, not Bell's codeveloper.

Reports continued of a dogged rearguard action by the product groups to deter and possibly derail top management's decision to reduce the groups' prerogatives. A telling example came from the product division organized around DEC's high-end time-sharing computers. Serious delays in the development schedule for the DECsystem10 (plus overlap with VAX) finally convinced Olsen to kill the line despite dire insider warnings of massive customer defections. An armed detective sat in the front row during the DECsystem10 announcement in case a furious fan rushed the podium, or so we were told (perhaps apocryphally). In fact, 80 percent of the DECsystem customers stayed with DEC.

Olsen was right to cancel the DECsystem10, notwithstanding unconfirmed reports of a cabal plotting to have him declared mentally incompetent to continue as CEO. At some point in all the maneuvering, backbiting, and smoke-blowing, he must have forcibly intervened, because erstwhile cronies fell by the wayside and other managers defected.

That autumn, the overall business also came under pressure. In a particularly troublesome quarter, sales volumes declined despite an increase in customer orders because the product groups' still fragmented order-entry systems couldn't provide manufacturing with a coordinated demand schedule. (Inventory control was still passing from those groups to central control.) Quarterly earnings fell by 75 percent, prompting the stock price to lose 20 percent in just one afternoon.

Unscrambling the Thought Lines

In November 1983, Naomi and I met with a subdued Ken Olsen and Win Hindle, putting a game face to a threatening situation. The sales force was settling down after yet another reorganization. The embarrassing and costly disarray in order processing and financial-reporting systems was slowly being repaired. Most of the holes left by defecting management were being filled, but some of the defections hurt, allowed Win. VAX was doing very well; personal computers were proceeding according to plan.

We were working on a Research Board report entitled "Computing in the 1990s." Like An Wang, Ken Olsen was uncomfortable predicting more than two or three years ahead. "Brilliant ideas never come from long-range strategic planners," he began. Often, the big ideas—like the now-ubiquitous credit card—are recognized only well after they've taken root. "So," he continued, "I would rather emphasize an organization that encourages diversity, hence creativity, than try to predict what that creativity will produce." His reticence was either genuine or merely an attempt to heed his own famous dictum that announcing a strategy means losing the strategy (by forewarning the competition).

Ken was noticeably at odds with most of Sam Fuller's technology projections from a year earlier. Creative notions about new user interfaces drew snorts of disbelief: Keyboards would dominate; non-keyboard devices would be employed "only for specialized applications and for oddball situations pursued by start-ups," he pronounced. But DEC had a new device, he told us, that "reads" e-mail or whatever through a voice-synthesizing technology. "That's DEC talk for sizzle," quipped Win. E-mail drew Ken's ambiguous approval. "My memos are read in offices around the world in minutes," he told us. "Of course, I don't have time to see many responses, so my secretary gives me a summary. And sometimes I don't have time to read that."

Ken was dismissive of artificial intelligence. "I've always been suspicious of anything so popular. But maybe it's just an extension of what we're doing in expert systems. And maybe AI will consume lots of machine cycles," he grinned. And the "highfalutin claims" about robotics and human intelligence that were coming from the Japanese Fifth Generation project were simply "ridiculous," he judged. "What the industry needs instead are efficient automation devices that do the same things over and over until they're reprogrammed." Score another point for the Grand Dragon's vision as much of the Fifth Generation project evaporated.

For the near term, he was preoccupied with networks and high-end processors, both of which have remained the bedrock of technology development in the decades since that interview—though the underlying technical assumptions have changed.

Olsen was excited about DEC's networking prospects: "Our vision is the integrated computer network serving the customer's entire organization. Unfortunately, IBM has the same vision, and we know they have been targeting our markets." He saw local networks as an important battleground. "Our Ethernet versus IBM's 'token-passing' network; it's a battle IBM can ill afford to lose … so it should be fun. Meanwhile, we'll maintain the VAX architectural discipline to preserve connectivity across all our products. Few other companies can pull that off, maybe just DEC and IBM." And VAX capacity would stretch heavenward: "Gigantic" machines would be introduced, he told us. As for parallelism, he was dubious but open-minded, saying DEC was "too ignorant to attempt linking up thousands of VAXes, but the universities love mucking around for us."

We didn't observe any great company-saving ideas that Olsen was blocking. To the contrary, networking and high-end machines were exactly the right prescription.

What had surprised Ken the most in the 1980s? "The success of the 'me-too' operating software. I don't know how we could have foreseen it, but we're now supporting MS/DOS and Unix. Most changes come slowly when you're watching," he declared. "For example, semiconductor development obviously had a profound impact; nonetheless, it's been a slower process than outsiders realize."

Looking back, where was Ken wrong? Least importantly, about the role of PCs for executives: "Nonsense," he said. "No one runs a business with color pie charts. Management takes analysis, work, and worry." True, but he missed the wider reality: The ratio of people to computers, as Ken's neighbor An Wang foresaw, would soon match the ratio of people to telephones, opening a gigantic market for PCs. Exiting the consumer sector was probably the right thing to do, as IBM discovered. "Marketing has always been our strength," he insisted, ignoring our apoplectic expressions. And, then, taking a dig at IBM, he continued, "If you know the names of your customers and you know your product, you don't need Charlie Chaplin" (a reference to IBM's consumer-PC ads featuring Chaplin's tramp).

Ken's worst mistake, bar none, was his belated and then halfhearted support of MS/DOS and Unix. This was the year Sun beat Apollo with its first defining sale to ComputerVision, and NCR was well on its way to adopting the Unix business model. By downplaying me-too operating systems and, more important, the margin pressures they would unleash, Ken was foreshortening the company's ability to react. But in this, he was not more myopic than his East Coast competitors.

Grinding into Decline

When we returned in 1985, the organizational wars had ended, but not without serious losses. Gone from the organization chart, besides Gordon Bell, were all three product group VPs, whom we had interviewed in 1982, plus Dick Clayton, VP of manufacturing technology, and Bernie LaCroute, the group manager for networking, who left to become COO of Sun, DEC's ultimate nemesis.

Olsen was still bitter: "I probably owe society a book warning about spoiled entrepreneurs, about friends who once worked for me," he mused over an otherwise delightful lunch around the conference table in his airy office. "An entrepreneur might like to jaw about innovation, but he's the last person to delegate so others can innovate. And the quality of his judgment is too easily subverted by wealth and destroyed by flattery. Like preachers or scientists, an entrepreneur always benefits from the assumption he's honest when, too often, they're not."

It was an extraordinary reflection from an extraordinary man whose defining imprint on the company he'd cofounded twenty-five years earlier had not faded. The Grand Dragon was still triumphant, but his company was downshifting to an incremental pace just as the new players were accelerating.

The slowing began with the organization. All six line functions—manufacturing, engineering, marketing, sales and service, finance, and personnel—now reported to Ken (with Win's box for staff operations glued alongside). All pretty normal until one noticed that Jack Smith filled the first three boxes, making him seem to be the chief operating officer and Ken's heir apparent.

Jack was "a man of uncommon good sense," we'd noted admiringly in 1982. But he was not creative or innovative, characteristics that were especially critical since the other three direct reports were Jack Shields for field sales and services with little technology or product experience, the Personnel VP, and finally the new CFO. Jim Osterhoff was excellent and sensible but recruited from Ford Tractor, hardly a fast-paced technological environment.

At least the product groups were reduced in number and prerogatives. Control over inventories had been centralized. But the central coordination of advertising was moving slowly, despite pressure from the budget committee. Changing a once-successful company is always harder to accomplish than anyone believes at the start.

We discerned little radical progress in reducing the cost structure. Finance Chief Jim Osterhoff described a series of ratcheting steps that would prove far too incremental to combat the destructive new business models just over the horizon. Accounts receivable outstanding had shrunk to seventy-five days from eighty-three. Inventory turns improved slightly to 2.3 per year from 2.1 after the consolidation of inventories stocks previously held by individual product divisions. (Jack Smith vaguely suggested four or five turns per year as a reasonable target, but even that would prove far too little.) Manufacturing head count was down to 28,000 from 31,000 over the past several years; the engineering numbers were just about right, though tinkering could "get more from the dollars we spend"; the sales staff should grow to meet the opportunity. If there was a continuing problem, it was the size of the staffs remaining even after the restructuring. "We've got to do more business, but less with ourselves," Osterhoff quipped.

The inadequacy of these actions was already evident. Profit margins had dropped to a skinny 5 percent compared to 18 percent just four years earlier. "Was the price pressure permanent?" we asked. Given the plight of traditional competitors, "yes" would have been the easy answer. But Osterhoff set off on a possibly true but not terribly relevant explanation of why the computing sector differed markedly from other industries: "Usually, the salesmen like low prices, and the engineers want higher prices. Here, the engineering community dominates and views lower prices for higher performance as their personal gold star." What he didn't mention was that the computing sector's margin assumptions were under permanent assault.

Equally disquieting to us was the dangerously comfortable "5-5-5 rule" offered by research VP Sam Fuller. "Looking at any number of historical precedents," he declared, "it typically takes five years for any new idea to become viable, five more years for the viable idea to reach the market, and another five for the product to ramp up to a billion-dollar business." Following that scenario, DEC should stay in strong shape for at least another five to ten years on nothing more than a steady diet of pragmatic business improvements.

"Incrementalism at its worst!" we huffed. The 5-5-5 rule would prove fatally inapplicable to changes in industry-wide business models and cost structures.

Slow and Steady Product Development

The big news on this visit was DEC's attempt to move up-market against the ravaging Unix crowd by building mainframes with exotic bipolar circuitry and high-performance cooling. We found VP Bob Glorioso hard at work on a machine designed to attack IBM's strongholds, especially insurance and banking. We were in a curious position. We had previously suggested to Ken that DEC not concede these markets to IBM, but that was before we realized the full extent of IBM's achievements in design, testing, and ceramic packaging. "Had DEC missed the window of opportunity?" we wondered.

Again, the pace was not encouraging. Glorioso explained that DEC's much-delayed 8600 "mainframe" had been embarrassingly underwhelming for three reasons: the challenge presented by high-speed, high-heat chip technology; the one-time "complexity barrier" of designing large-scale machines; and the company's preoccupation with the personal computer. "Digital didn't try hard enough at the high end," Glorioso told us. "Every resource was thrown at the PC. We wasted lots of talent." That preoccupation hadn't been obvious to Naomi and me —just the opposite, in fact.

All of that was past history, he assured us. Now there was greater focus on competing against IBM on mainframes, blessed specifically by Ken. Hard at work on the follow-on mainframe 9000 was a hundred-person engineering team, including "all the players who worked on the 8600, totally enabled by their experience—and very smart," according to Glorioso. They would pursue faster custom-circuit chips, possibly fabricated by an outside foundry, and new cooling, possibly water-cooled just like the IBM mainframes. The new cooling and packaging might use technology acquired from Gene and Carlton Amdahl's now-defunct Acsys/Trilogy.

Glorioso seemed reasonably aware of the technical hurdles in Steady Grey's race against Big Blue. But we worried that Ken might have bet the company on fighting the last war. There would be profound changes in mainframe technology and pricing within a decade.

RISC processors still drew few accolades. Semiconductor VP Jeff Kalb was convinced that RISC development would take three or four years. So its threefold expected power gain would barely match what could be gained by simply moving VAX along the trajectory promised by Moore's Law. "So we should be reluctant to turn away from VAX, particularly if an excursion into RISC would deflect our resources from the more important future technology—parallel processing." Kalb may have been right about RISC.

Sam Fuller, the R&D chief, concurred about the future of parallelism, but he thought DEC should simultaneously make the transition to RISC, given that the software would have to be converted anyway. The Grand Dragon wasn't enthusiastic about either idea. Ken had grown bored with RISC after three in-house prototypes yielded only marginal results, though RISC was being vigorously pursued by Sun and HP and would eventually give them a sizable advantage, especially in the Unix workstation market. Always skeptical about the future of parallelism, Ken thought it couldn't succeed without practical answers to questions such as: "How will you know if one of those processors fails?" On both ideas, the CEO became the blocker.

Kalb eventually grew tired of fighting with Ken, and left DEC to become CEO of Maspar, a parallel-processor company that ultimately failed in part because its nonstandard instruction set required customers to rewrite their software. It wasn't the problem Ken had foreseen and worried about, but his rejection of parallel processing was probably the right call at the time. It would take another decade or more until Amazon, IBM, Intel, Sun, and emblematically, Google (with its million processors), moved forward with the concept.

Our other product discussions were orderly and mundane. On the product front, storage system VP Grant Saviers was totally abreast of industry trends toward smaller and denser discs. Networking VP "B. J." Johnson was a delightfully smart man pushing all the right standards. For local connections, DEC was already the largest supplier of standard Ethernet. And in networking, DEC would move its own DECnet to the X400 standard being laboriously worked out by the International Organization for Standardization (OSI): "DECnet won't be much more than a marketing name after that. We've told the Europeans OSI is good for them and equally good—and potentially profitable—for us." Win Hindle was less sanguine about the pace at which these government bureaucrats could reach consensus. His view was the right one. OSI was flattened by the Internet protocol completed by Sun's Bill Joy, removing any opportunity for DEC.

Marketing Missteps and Organizational Rifts

War stories about the recent organizational rifts and Ken's continuing contempt for marketing excesses occupied a large part of our 1985 conversations with Olsen. "Digital has a long way to go in organizing our message and putting it across," he started, before dismissing "marketing gloss as it's tossed around by trade performers. I won't advertise unless we have something to say."

Gone were prior flights of fancy. "We goofed even going into the personal computer retail market," judged Olsen. "Probably we could have won, but victory would have destroyed us as a company." Doubtless he was referring to the marketing hyperbole and easy attitudes toward product quality rampant among the PCers. Marketing had too often missed the mark outside of DEC's comfortable preserves in laboratory and manufacturing. "We've probably mistaken great products for good marketing in the past," Olsen admitted. "And I take personal responsibility for our neglect of the financial-services sector. Previously, it was just a target of opportunity. Given the historic cultural differences, perhaps our stupidity was unavoidable. Now we're organizing to do better." In our view, he was probably a decade late in that realization.

We ended our visit with Win Hindle, who was bursting with optimism. Yes, DEC had lost key people, including Gordon Bell, but his erratic genius no longer fit the company anyway. And the existing roster of top executives, including Smith, Shields, Saviers, Kalb, Johnson, Glorioso, Fuller, and the others, would continue to lead the company forward. Win was equally positive about the product lineup based on a single architecture as opposed to the fragmented structure at HP and IBM, and DEC's leadership in Ethernet, processor clustering, and disks. DEC would make exciting announcements in workstations next year, he promised.

What was Hindle's primary concern? "Marketing, as Ken Olsen reminds us three times a week. And we're not yet good at convincing senior executives in large companies. But we've got plenty of excellent products—and interconnectivity. We've got our organizational act together. And we're working extremely well together at the top. Of course, Ken is still an inspirational rabble-rouser; he'll always be more of a natural leader than a traditional manager."

In sum, from now on the company would focus on one strategy, one product architecture, and investment only where DEC had differentiable strengths. Ambivalence reigned with respect to the PC and its me-too operating systems. "Follow the crowd, and you have nothing to offer," proclaimed Ken that day.

Everything sounded great to us—and most other observers—in 1985. But, as we would come to realize, DEC was too tightly focused. The single VAX architecture fostered a stasis, but Olsen didn't follow Cary's decentralization to escape System/360. Despite implementing a flavor of Unix on VAX and planning on a software layer that would let VMS work on RISC, the original VAX/VMS configuration would remain DEC's core strategy until Ken was ousted in 1992.

The same sort of paralysis was apparent in the management ranks. Ken was now past sixty, the retirement age at both HP and IBM. But apart from Jack Smith, there was no obvious successor. Jack Shields, Grant Saviers, Jeff Kalb, and Bob Glorioso would all become CEOs, but at companies smaller than DEC. Probably none of them could have wrenched DEC around as Lou Gerstner did at IBM.

Transition or Crisis?

Calamity was just around the corner, but in 1985, we still judged DEC's reaffirmation of focus a totally sensible strategy. Perhaps we were distracted by the pileup of wreckage in the minicomputer sector. Just six months earlier, once-vibrant Datapoint had been dismembered by Asher Edelman, and three months after that, John Cunningham abandoned the dying Wangs (both Doctor and company). The other leaders had problems as well. Elsewhere, Data General was struggling with poor marketing and worse management structure. At IBM, Akers's excessive focus on the PC and his indecisiveness elsewhere left holes in its midrange line. HP was freighted with John Young's simultaneous gambles on RISC, Unix, and a new management team.

Our report on the minicomputer sector was entitled "Transition or Crisis." The March 1986 plenary meeting was held in New York around the huge directors' table in the brightly skylighted cupola of Equitable Life's offices. Presenting were Ken Olsen, An and Fred Wang, IBM's Jack Kuehler, and Edson deCastro leading a Data General contingent. It was the last time enough East Coast computer companies would still exist to fill a two-day meeting.

By 1986, the RISC processor and Unix were being widely installed in engineering workstations by Sun, HP, and IBM. Only Digital hadn't adopted RISC. Regardless of the soundness of their reasoning, Olsen's and Kalb's decision left DEC looking ridiculous in price/performance comparisons with Sun's hot boxes.

The industry had entered a period of savage consolidation, a fire first fanned by Unix and soon to be intensified by Windows. We were struck by the similarities to the early automobile industry, which counted 181 different competitors in the U.S. market between 1895 and 1926, and many more that died before ever producing a thing. By 2000, only two survived as independent American players. Computing followed that model, often forcing survivors to self-amputate gangrenous limbs. The inability of proud patriarchs at Data General, DEC, and Wang to saw off body parts doomed them in the end.

We were lulled into complacency by reflecting on a piece in *Fortune* from November 1932 that celebrated big-name survivors of the Great Depression—names like AT&T, GE, and United Technology—whose grim statistics would have augured otherwise. "A surprising number of the great corporations whose names were investors' charms in 1928 and wisecrackers' laughs in 1929 have not only remained in business but give every sign of ability to remain in business indefinitely." Sure, IBM and DEC had big problems, but still we wrote: "Size can help sustain hard times and management gaffes. Market position is worth a lot. By those lights, IBM and DEC will probably remain in the computer industry's top tier come the year 2000 just as their competitors predict." Those competitors were half-wrong, and so were we.

The Downhill Run Accelerates

In 1987, DEC still looked like it might survive, partly because its competitors' flaws were so visible. The American majors were struggling. The European minicomputer makers like Bull and Nixdorf were going nowhere, while the much-feared Japanese were reduced to hitching a ride on the coattails of IBM's mainframe operating systems.

One curious side note was the paper alliance between DEC and the shriveling Apple under John Sculley's leadership. The announcement came complete with John and Ken in happy-couple smiles for the trade press. Powerful alternatives to the old guard were afoot, Sculley assured us, scrawling portentously on his office whiteboard "MAC + DEC > IBM." The alliance made sense for Apple, hoping to compete against Microsoft and Unix by piggybacking on Steady Grey's sales force. But the advantage to DEC was harder to fathom. And Ken was definitely bemused, saying only that DEC "might help Apple connect to our equipment, but no more."

Five years after Bell's departure, VAX was still considered a master stroke, especially in comparison to the perennial mess at IBM. Remembered Olsen, "I'm given credit for the strategy, but I didn't formulate it." Having just one architecture allowed DEC's engineering cadre to concentrate on stretching VAX from microprocessor to mainframe—though the hoped-for DEC mainframe was still lodged in the birth canal, unable to follow IBM across the speed/heat divide by replacing air cooling with water.

"I was surprised how hard our engineers had to work to implement liquid-cooled machines," admitted Olsen to us privately, and the struggle wasn't over. The first product release was announced at just 20 MIPS—well below mainframe capacity—and wasn't expected to double for almost five years. Still, it remained Ken's pet project, targeted at his favorite market opportunities in financial services, and headed by his favorite young executive, Bob Glorioso. "If this business were just about minicomputers, I'd be too bored to keep working," he told us by way of explanation.

Despite disappointments over the 9000 schedule and scale, DEC continued to gain sales and market share, leading us to conclude that strategy formulation in the computer business was shaped by two issues: "First, that the pressures we're witnessing will force industry consolidation or a serious shakeout over the next ten years. Second, that the successes of the past decade owe more to the losers' blunders than to the winners' managerial perfections. Thus, Digital was given an extraordinary window of opportunity when IBM dawdled over its midrange spread. With all that—plus Ken Olsen's bloody single-mindedness—the winner for the decade is Digital."

We got no argument from the Grand Dragon himself: "The thing that surprises me most in the last few years is our unexpected strength against IBM," Ken told us with as much realism as modesty. The best judgment on the other faltering industry leaders came from Fred Wang: "Both HP and [Wang] were burned by our idiosyncratic experimentations."

But both men were looking at the situation from the rearview mirror and the wrong coast. As we wrote: "Sun is Silicon Valley's hottest property these days. Growth rates have teetered between astounding and off-the-cliff for the past several years. It sets the pace in workstation price/performance—all on Unix and industry standards." More daunting, Sun's business model provided a 10 percentage-point cost advantage over the minicomputer model. Its RISC processor would match DEC's workstations in performance and top Glorioso's mainframes within the year, before doubling again the year after. The Sunsters ravaged DEC's workstation market just as the semiconductor companies had already savaged its OEM business.

Year-old complaints about capacity limitations at the high end of DEC's product line were barely being addressed. After a brief visit in 1988, we wrote: "Product development is in the doldrums. Database presentations are platitudinous, processor plans lackluster." About the new 30-MIP transaction processor, we concluded: "After two years' delay (and counting), the new machine seemed almost pathetically irrelevant given the industry pace." In comparison to IBM's mainframes, the 9000 was nothing but a minicomputer further limited because it ran only with DEC's proprietary operating system.

By then, a pincer assault of Unix and Microsoft Windows threatened total absorption of the low-end workstation market, where DEC had once been the heartthrob of a generation of engineers. A compelling example centered on DEC's own office systems group, which was building its wares to work with the entire spectrum of PC and Unix operating systems. "The group strategy conceded the war for workstation is over, and VMS lost," we noted. "Future success depends on staying ahead of the standard in operating systems." Unfortunately, DEC's image-processing line possessed no such clarity of vision; its team was still developing for VMS as well as Unix and, potentially, Microsoft.

All the flavors of Unix weren't exactly the same plain vanilla, but they were close enough. That hissing noise emanating from all across the computer industry was the sound of gross margins leaking air. Proprietary computer systems commanded 60 percent gross margins versus 50 percent for Unix boxes, and Compaq would soon target 23 percent for complete PC systems. The net result was a minicomputer business devastated at the low end and sucked dry at the top.

The Cracks Become Visible

By 1989, serious cracks were visible at Digital Equipment. The 9000 was flattening out at 30 MIPS, and DEC's database was far inferior to Oracle's, even when both ran on VAX systems. At the same moment, Maynard was losing its previous competitive advantage against HP as the fruits of Young's strategic gambles on RISC and Unix reached the market to enormous customer enthusiasm. Olsen had failed to move the company forward in the window of opportunity that HP was now closing. More managers defected. On October 3, Jack Shields left behind the 70,000 employees he oversaw in field sales and service for the thankless, and ultimately fruitless, task of trying to resuscitate Prime Computer.

His departure raised new speculation about succession. The *Wall Street Journal* pointed out on October 4, 1989, that "Mr. Olsen has always avoided anointing any successor, noting he is healthy and plans to continue running the company for the foreseeable future." Then it quoted an analyst: "Olsen believes he's good for another ten years of running the company. When Olsen goes for succession planning, he'll skip a generation [of managers] and go down twenty years from his age."

On the product front, the office-gear strategy hadn't evolved in the ten years since the hasty departure of its product manager—except that PCs were now welcome. DEC's database was still much too pokey; our questions on customer complaints had been stonewalled two years earlier. Now the project manager finally admitted, "We weren't ready for the full difficulty of moving from the forgiving world of information retrieval and decision support to the demanding, transaction-heavy world of office automation." Momentum had been lost.

The remedy? Some software had been improved, narrowing the performance gap against IBM and Oracle, we were told. But to reach parity, processor speeds would need significant juicing, but any such upgrade depended on the long-delayed 9000.

And where, after all this time, was Ken's mainframe? Glorioso was noticeably reticent and defensive when we visited. Not a whiff of concrete performance estimates, just blather about "exciting" new packaging that could quadruple the capability for heat dissipation and cooling. We didn't buy the happy talk. Later, we got a call telling us "not to worry; the VAX 9000 order rate is within the projected range." "So, what else could be expected from desperate customers after a two-year dance?" we wondered.

Our conclusions were more dour than ever before: "DEC percolates a sense of being caught in a wrenching transition on sales force, organization, database understructures, and processor technology. From which one hopes the company will burst as from a springtime chrysalis. DEC is an excellent company. But it's passing through a series of crucial transitions that customers could wish had been navigated two years earlier, when the competition was still weaker."

Eight months later, in July 1990, Ken wrote Naomi and me to say: "We are pleased at the way the VAX 9000 is going now; we have what we think will be a significant success; and we plan to continue that product for a long time. We also see new technologies that make it even more exciting." Even then, DEC's high-end computer was still based on the VMS proprietary operating system.

Despite his own enthusiasm, customers weren't responding in kind, complained Ken. He thought he might order his sales force to ignore the holdouts. "However, the question of which customers we should serve is still up in the air. We are now getting the impression that users, like your members, have become very conservative. After years of exploring the revolution that desktop computing would do to an organization, exploring the wondrous claims of standardized operating systems that would solve everyone's problems for very little money, and after years of swapping IS managers, many of the companies are becoming conservative and are seriously considering a ten-year commitment to IBM and showing little stomach for exploring new ideas. If this is the way large computing and the large corporations are going, we might very well leave it to IBM, without competition, because we feel there is enough market in other areas. I'd like to meet with you and hear your views and advice as to how we might help with your Board members."

When we called Win Hindle, he acknowledged that Ken had written the obscurely intentioned letter himself, and asked to visit us in New York. After we talked, I opined to Win that Ken had been right so often that no one would contradict him. In this period of savage dislocation, he should retire. Naomi and I then agreed, at Win's request, to go to Maynard and tell Ken what we thought to his face. A few days later, after carefully preparing what we would say to maximize the message and minimize the flutter, we boarded the Digital helicopter in New York.

Upon arrival, Ken, Win, Naomi, and I conversed for several hours on a dozen points, especially our belief that Ken should retire and our feeling that, however excellent at operations, Jack Smith lacked the strategic sense necessary to be CEO. We also described the general deterioration of DEC's position, including client reports that the desperate sales force had begun making claims that sometimes bordered on the unethical. This topic, as we might have guessed, engaged Ken more forcefully than anything else.

Later, as Ken walked us back to the helipad, I joked that I hoped he would still let us use the helicopter despite our critique. He responded, "You two have always been honest with us, and you're welcome back to Maynard anytime."

It was vintage Olsen. But we never returned to see Ken. By then, Steady Grey was clearly on the sidelines, having entered a downward spiral—though it was initially masked by the bloat in low-margin maintenance and service revenues (see Table 14.1). Revenues per employee were awful. The workstation battle was over, and Sun had won. McNealy didn't even mention DEC that year in his survey of the competition, worried only about IBM's recently announced RISC-based Unix machine.

Table 14.1   Service and Maintenance as Percentage of Total Revenue

	1989	1990	1991
Digital	35.7%	37.1%	40.3%
HP	21.0	22.8	23.7
IBM	16.0	16.0	20.0

Table 14.2 **Revenues per Employee ($1,000)**

	1989	1990	1991
Digital	104	115	122
HP	144	163	181
IBM	185	188	213

Source: Company Financials

Reacting to business commoditization would have required heroic efforts by someone with no sentimental attachment to the past.

Olsen Is Ousted by Former Compatriots

Unfortunately, Ken didn't take our advice to retire. After posting a 1991 loss of $617 million and debt of $2.8 billion, he was forced out on July 16, 1992, when Digital Equipment announced that Ken Olsen would be relinquishing the CEO post, effective October 1, but would remain as a director. (By coincidence, that same day, John Young announced his retirement from Hewlett-Packard at age sixty.) A few days later, Ken told his engineers he had been fired, and in September, he resigned his directorship as well.

Ken attributed the bitter ending of his legendary thirty-five years at the helm of the world's most successful minicomputer company to his unwillingness to make the deep personnel cuts demanded by the board of directors (14,000 had been let go already). And the official history, as told on the Digital Web site, graciously concurred, saying that "the man who had forever epitomized the heart and soul of DEC" could not bring himself to let thousands of workers go.

Ken remembered his fall somewhat differently, as he told *World Business* (May 28, 2002): "Of course I look back at things I could have done differently. I'm more conscious of things I did wrong after 35 years than the things I did right. But the thing I lost at Digital was this overwhelming movement in one part of the company that speed was all that mattered. Forget all the services that made your business; just sell one fast product. That started when I was there and I lost control, starting about three years before I was deposed."

Observers and the press blamed Ken himself: "There has been an unbelievable cry from executives and people who recently left the company who felt the company could not turn around without him leaving," commented Glenn Rifkin, coauthor of *The Ultimate Entrepreneur* in the *Washington Post on* July 17. Sadly, that explanation rang true to us.

The New Order

The new CEO, Bob Palmer, was known, sometimes viciously, as the "guy with the good suit"—good suits now having replaced shaggy sweaters as appropriate attire for executives at "the Mill." But Steady Grey needed more than a clothing upgrade. Revenue growth for 1992 slipped into negative territory, well behind the low double-digit increases posted by Amdahl, Intel, Apple, HP, and Sun. Even IBM managed a slight gain in revenues that year. The market didn't react kindly to DEC's decline, taking the shares down to a price where total market capitalization equaled just 40 percent of revenues versus roughly 100 percent for Apple, HP, and Sun.

Palmer had joined the company in 1985 as the vice president for semiconductor operations and was promoted to VP for manufacturing and logistics in 1990. Now, as CEO, he was most intent on returning the company to profitability through the three objectives he outlined when we met in 1994:

- Restructure the field organization as "customer business units," with full profit-and-loss responsibility to keep everyone focused on hard selling;

- Rationalize the product line, focusing on the 64-bit Alpha microprocessor (he was right that Alpha was much ahead of Intel Pentium, but 64-bit capacity processors wouldn't find a volume market for another ten years); and

- Reverse Olsen's operating-system priorities, putting Microsoft's NT at the top, Unix second, and DEC's own VMS last; to make the once-glorious VMS price competitive against Unix, its development budget was cut, inadvertently accelerating its demise.

Based purely on volume, the best hope for Alpha was Microsoft NT, the self-confident and shiny new CEO insisted. With Alpha's 64-bit power and DEC's global networking capabilities, a powerful new axis could be formed. The smiling-couple photos of Bob Palmer and Bill Gates appeared in the trade press, but Redmond didn't seem to care much for the new union. The Micro-hardies were obviously interested more in global sales presence than global networks. Snapped one to us, "Digital knows how to lose money selling their own products. So they might as well lose money selling ours." Ironically, Microsoft wouldn't get a 64-bit Intel processor for many years, leaving Sun with the bubble market for high-volume Web sites that temporarily peaked in 2000.

Simultaneously, Palmer placed enormous emphasis on building a PC business. His objective of "fifth place by '95" (just a year away) was not impossible, given the weakness of everyone below Compaq, IBM, and Apple (future leaders HP and Dell were tied in seventh place). Continuing the numerical juxtapositions, the market-share target was "7 percent in '97," which would represent a tripling of its then-current share. A difficult objective given DEC's weak sales presence among business customers and its even weaker position among the retailers—and, in fact, it never happened. By 1997, DEC was still not among the top five PC makers, and only Compaq and IBM had market shares above 6 percent.

Unlike his predecessor, Palmer's quest for profitability did not exclude downsizing. He immediately closed factories and cut another 30,000 employees, many in Europe. But DEC was still too far from the new business model to right itself. On Black Friday, April 15, 1994, the company stunned the world (and its own CEO) by announcing a third-quarter loss of $183 million. Like HP, its gross margins had shrunk by 20 percentage points, but DEC was much slower to react and nearly collapsed before its gross margins bottomed out at 28 percent. The outlook was bleak, even assuming margins could be muscled back to 38 percent. "Our SG&A burden alone was 35 percent, and our R&D at 12 percent," VP Enrico Pesatori told us. "The best we could hope for was a permanent 10 percent loss," he said.

Pesatori, who had been recruited from Zenith Data Systems to head the computer business, tried to simplify the organization, cut the sales force, and rely more heavily on indirect channels. Now, only the largest thousand accounts would receive direct representation, with an emphasis on the financial, telecommunications, and manufacturing sectors.

"Financial?" we asked with discernible surprise.

Yes, "DEC has great customer loyalty in banking," we were told. That was news to us.

Meanwhile, 7,000 once-loyal accounts were tossed to the resellers, raising howls of frustration and more defections from the customer base. R&D was cut to 8 percent, in part by closing the small labs that had once built special software for favored European accounts, thereby further reducing customer loyalty. Understandably, sales followed. The company that once numbered 126,000 employees now had just half that number, and a third of those 63,000 resided in Europe.

In 1995, the company experienced its first back-to-back profitable quarters in four years, but profit was no longer synonymous with competitive leadership. By mid-1997, DEC could finally announce that Alpha would be the first processor to work with the newest version of Microsoft NT. Full stop. Sales were so slow that Palmer decided to institute an antitrust suit against Intel, which promptly settled by agreeing to buy DEC's once leading-edge Hudson semiconductor facility. "Maybe Gordon Moore would like to house his library at Hudson," snipped the cruel Intel-ites.

The following year, DEC was sold to Compaq for $9.6 billion. At a London analysts' conference (*CMP Techwire*, January 27, 1998), Compaq CEO Eckhard Pfeiffer was quick to criticize Olsen, who, by then, was six years gone from the company. "There has been a strong Ken Olsen spirit—not invented here—although that has changed over time," and "in terms of efficiency, a lot needs to happen at Digital."

Suggesting that Olsen had become disconnected from reality, Pfeiffer said, "You have to be very, very awake every day and watch what's happening to you in the industry. You must never be in denial, and you must always evaluate and be prepared to change quickly."

Poor Eckhard wouldn't or couldn't follow his own advice. Unable to change quickly enough against Dell and incapable of utilizing DEC's "rich technology," notably the Alpha, Pfeiffer himself would join Olsen in forced retirement within the year.

Pfeiffer was replaced by Compaq CIO Michael Cappellas, and both Compaq and DEC were later subsumed in the merger Cappellas engineered with Hewlett-Packard.

The last time I saw Ken Olsen was in a New York restaurant. "You fired me," he said, tongue in cheek. He recounted the management revolt that ended his career and told me how many of his oldest friends had turned against him in the end. I'd hear that story again and again from computer executives in the years to come. The last time I saw Win was after he'd been named ethics officer—a designation intended to confer continuity, which actually would have been wholly superfluous over the prior quarter-century. But on Win's retirement in June 1994, Naomi and I received a letter from him, announcing his retirement and continuing in part:

> "The objectivity of your analysis and the care you put into your observations are unique in the industry. It is no wonder to me you have such loyal members.
>
> "I also value the fun you have in your work and the good-natured humor you bring to otherwise dry subjects. Even as the recipient of your "steady grey" label, we respected your reason for pinning that title on us. Every one of my colleagues has always been eager to talk with you because of the balanced perspective you bring to every meeting.
>
> "I will miss our conversations. You have always responded to questions with clarity and warmth. More than anyone I can think of outside our company, you have seen Digital's strengths as well as the gaps. Thank you for caring and helping us by pointing to our shortcomings and celebrating our contributions ..."

A very high compliment from a most principled man!

Chapter 15

FIELD FORCE AND COUNTERFORCE:

DEC, HP, and IBM in Battle Mode

Many CEOs would agree—sometimes grudgingly—that the field force is their most potent and productive asset. Great sales reps, properly trained and motivated, can push a mediocre product beyond its expected trajectory. Or ease the company through major delays of frontline products, as Hewlett-Packard's sales force held the customer base during a multiyear delay in its new RISC minicomputers. Competent field engineers backed by diagnostics and repair technology can prevent customer defections over software bugs and hardware burnouts.

But the field force also has its dark side. On occasion, sales executives will block the introduction of radically new products, as IBM's sales force tried to block Tom Watson Jr.'s transition to tape from punch cards.

New sales representation models can encounter similar resistance even when a change in technology chops away at gross margins. Though a failure to increase sales productivity can be disastrous, flexibility is not the dominant characteristic of most field organizations. A comparison of the IBM, DEC, and HP sales organizations, with a side tour to Data General, will help illustrate the problems.

IBM's sales reps were considered its crown jewels since the modern company's formation under Tom Watson Sr. around 1924. Account executives were tall, aggressive, and able to burst through (or at least wheedle past) any customer company's receptionist blockade to get to the CEO. So if an IT executive rejected the IBM offering in favor of a product clone, the matter didn't end there. The account exec could quietly suggest to the CEO that "your guy isn't quite up to the job anymore." Or so it seemed to many IT execs caught in the crosshairs.

DEC had the opposite profile. Its sales reps were salaried engineers who received no commissions, which Ken Olsen feared would lead to overselling by the "ninnies of the field" (as we speculated Ken viewed his reps). The DEC sales force's preferred audience was the software-minded scientific, engineering, and process-control community. DEC reps avoided commercial data processing departments, believing them to be bureaucratic and biased in favor of IBM. Similarly, the size of Olsen's field-maintenance organization was tightly constrained on the expectation that the target customer would be self-sufficient, while "those ignorant end users would suck us dry."

Little wonder that IT executives called Digital Equipment "idiosyncratic" and "quirky." The organization produced great hardware, they agreed, but it seemed impenetrable, and no one returned telephone calls. It came as little surprise that enterprise-market analysts like us were largely ignored by DEC's top management through the 1970s.

Data General Leads the Way

We drew a much warmer welcome at Data General (DG) in neighboring Southboro, Massachusetts, in 1975. DG was, in many ways, the mirror image of DEC. Founded in 1968 by DEC refugees Edson deCastro and Henry Burkhardt (both key to PDP-11's development), the company assembled its first "Nova" mini in a Hudson, Massachusetts, storefront. Within the first year, employment grew from ten to ninety, and doubled every year thereafter to reach 3,300 people at our visit.

Unit sales rocketed from 110 in 1969 to 690 in 1970, doubled in both 1971 and 1972, and then bounced from 9,000 to 14,000 in 1974. Data General ranked second only to the much-older DEC in cumulative installations. Revenues blossomed to $30.3 million in 1972, $53.3 million in 1973, and $83 million in 1974.

Formed just as minicomputer-based distributed processing was gaining currency, Data General found it easier to navigate the business market than DEC, even though the OEMs made up 70 percent of its box sales (accounting for just 35 percent of revenues, however). One positive was its cadre of commissioned and admirably aggressive sales reps, who were no more like the IBM blue-suiters than they were like the DECsters. Our assessment at the time "may be harsh and is certainly not universal, but the first-time buyer's initial problem may be in evaluating the offerings of a colorless salesman in a somewhat shabby suit, looking nervous around the eyes. Again, this is a problem for all of the minicomputer vendors."

DG and DEC maintained a distracting rivalry, fueled in part by the personal animus between CEOs Olsen and deCastro. True, DG's management team seemed more colorful alongside DEC's grey "conservatism." Heading sales was Herb Richmond, a man of epic antics (like the time he hurled a harpoon across the room at a sales convention), whose office was a greenhouse of dense plantings, trellised from the ceiling, that barely covered a full-length poster of a nude male in all his frontal glory. The poster was intended to convey some marketing message, now sadly forgotten.

While DEC reps were warned to stay clear of EDP executives, their Data General counterparts were encouraged to engage them in sympathetic and supportive dialogue. During our meeting, we were given a nineteen-point overhead foil entitled "End User Selling … Sophisticated Market," which included a host of practical prescriptions ranging from "play on the DP manager's curiosity about minis" to "become client bridge" and "don't threaten computer-center revenue."

In the end, DG captured its share of commercial distributed-computing sales, partially through its aggressive selling approach and partially through its technical ability to attract high-profile designers of the most elegant minicomputer systems, like Southern Railway. Significantly, many DG reps were recruited several years later by the fledgling Sun, from whence they pummeled DEC.

Hewlett-Packard Reps Earn Elite Status

Hewlett-Packard's productivity-leading field force developed its excellence through a combination of recruiting, focus, and management support. All three were rooted in the original measurement and instrumentation business and the Bill-and-Dave (Hewlett and Packard, respectively) philosophy of resolving practical engineering problems.

HP's primary market was discrete manufacturing (e.g., the assemblers of components or parts), where the company's own advanced practices in manufacturing computers, disks, and instruments could be turned into customer relationships. So the manufacturing sector received 85 percent of marketing dollars, 95 percent of applications development, and 50 percent of sales effort. "Fraught with opportunity" was a favorite phrase used by computing-head Paul Ely to bridle attempts to mount more than guerilla forays into other sectors. So financial services, for instance, got no more than sales-rep "trolling," Ely would explain. "If the banks and insurance companies discover us, that's fine.... But we'll discover the manufacturing companies," he observed for us.

Down the road, we would sometimes disagree with Ely's approach. The "discrete" manufacturing cherished by HP was moving offshore, and much of the high-end workstation business used to model parts and assemblies would be lost, first to Sun and later to the PC. But on our annual survey asking CIOs to force rank the top ten IT vendors on sales and service, HP regularly outscored DEC, IBM, Wang, and all the other computer companies—a strength that would carry the company through the troubled times ahead.

HP field service achieved top marks from customers by making embedded diagnostic tools a primary objective, from product design through manufacturing. Beyond that, the field staff were almost all college graduates, trained to "fix everything," while the other mini makers hired people with less education at lower salaries and then specialized their training around different devices or components. That meant the HP engineer could usually solve the problem on the first visit, while his counterpart from DEC and elsewhere had to call for assistance and a second specialist. Certainly, HP's people were initially more expensive. But a first-visit fix built more customer loyalty than did waiting for the screwdriver monkey to call in a specialist. First-visit fixes were probably more cost effective as well.

A Skills Imbalance at Digital Equipment

By 1979, the crush of minicomputer competition had begun squeezing DEC's business model. Falling sales and tightening margins in the engineering, scientific, and product-embedded OEM markets raised top management's interest in shifting some sales reps to the enterprise market. But, burdened by a twenty-five-year engineering culture, the company never effectively executed that shift despite periodic attempts to right the skills balance by hiring from IBM and, more often, the old mainframe BUNCH. "Burroughs [the B in

BUNCH] is a particularly easy mark," declared a naïve sales VP. "Could he really imagine second-tier Burroughs salespeople selling decisively against IBM's blue-suiters?" we gasped. DEC would have done better to hire gunslingers from arch foe Data General (as Sun did). But Ken Olsen might have felt uncomfortable having them around.

Field engineering under senior VP Jack Shields was in stronger shape: 9,000 field engineers fixed hardware, 2,000 supported software, and another 1,400 were in customer training. DEC was still notorious for slow response times, but Shields had definite plans to improve both performance and profitability. The cornerstone of his game plan was technology, proudly displayed in a photo of the new Digital Diagnosis Center gracing DEC's annual report. This facility could remotely isolate hardware failures to the subassembly level on 1,500 high-end PDP-11s. Now, DEC could diagnose instances of operator error or "no problem found" messages without actually dispatching a repair person to the scene. And even when a visit was required, prior isolation of the problem allowed the dispatch of a more narrowly trained (hence, cheaper) and more productive specialist; tests showed that a specialist typically finished a job in half the time required by a generalist.

Shields diverged from the IBM policy on software repairs. Whereas IBM vice president Jack Kuehler was convinced that, eventually, all software repairs could be made remotely by specialists, Shields advocated "a spectrum of offerings" and thought the choice of on-site visits should be left to the customer's discretion. Sure, software maintenance could be performed remotely, Shields said, "but we'll let IBM force that on its customers while we continue to offer on-site software support from our field offices to anyone willing to pay. We'll let IBM pave the way."

Plummeting prices for workstations and small servers would gut notions of on-site hardware repair, however, just as surely as they had for calculators and word processors. Remote software repair represented the more promising long-term business opportunity. Fortunately, Shields discovered that symptoms of hardware failure were often caused by outdated operating systems. After a sharp intramural turf tussle, the software-repair people were moved into field services. Most software bugs and questions were remedied by telephone, using just 2 percent of the entire support staff.

By our visit in 1982, Shields had assumed responsibility for sales as well, reflecting great strides on his two objectives: "First, provide the highest-quality service and be recognized for it; second, maintain our current contribution to corporate profits." Disciplined management combined with automation to produce unambiguous wins. Customer surveys rating satisfaction from 1 (boo) to 10 (bravo) had improved from a snakebit 4 to 7.8. Equally important, field service was flashing great economics: Total costs had not increased more than 2 percent a year, while the cost per call had declined by nine dollars the previous year—and this despite an 18 percent increase in the cost per person.

In his new role, Shields focused on unifying account representation. Previously, different salespeople from each powerful product group visited different customer departments without coordination. So the VP for customer manufacturing received different representatives, technical support levels, and even contract terms than those offered to the VPs for engineering or research. DEC saw this fragmentation as responsive, but it annoyed the customer's IT executive.

At first, coordinated representation was expanded from only the twenty largest customers (or "national accounts") to the top three hundred accounts. The move won almost immediate acclaim from the large enterprises we knew. At last, the account field managers had authority over sales reps and technical resources, a major power shift. Shields even contemplated worldwide account managers, but he let IBM lead the frustrating battles over national autonomy against the powerful country managers in France, Germany, and elsewhere.

Shields suffered an important defeat, however, in his campaign to change DEC's idiosyncratic compensation plan from straight salary to base salary plus commission. No matter, he insisted; there were other compensation levers. Besides, paying only straight salaries lubricated organizational change, since the field reps' livelihoods weren't threatened by reassignment from favored accounts. But absent commissions, the reps also couldn't be dragged from dying markets in engineering to emerging markets in enterprise business. Far more muscle was required to redirect their attentions, and time was very short. "Too many Digital salesmen are still noodling in the lab, machine shop, or cubbyhole of a fellow engineer," we scolded. "In fact, some of the old guard may not be retrainable, after all."

Despite the energy shortfall, Shields remained confident. The least productive 10 percent of the staff had been terminated, and new representatives were being hired, some with experience in enterprise sales. "We have incredibly good people," he said. "Our task now is to value them, train them, and expect them to perform." Less optimistically, ex-IBMer Bob Hughes, now DEC's marketing head, cautioned us that another year would pass before the account managers really knew their customers and the product groups adjusted to their new relationships with field sales. Instead, the sales force only became more lackluster. Continuing rearguard actions by the product groups to derail the new organizational regimes ultimately disadvantaged both DEC and its CEO, hastening their demise.

Interestingly, DEC led the industry in incubating service businesses, under the assumption that the computer industry was reaching a new stage. "As hardware becomes a commodity, only those manufacturers with the most enduring applications and attractive services will really prosper," said Don Busiek, manager of the new software services unit. "For strategic reasons, we're trying to build this organization very fast." He predated Lou Gerstner's rescue of IBM by almost a decade, but his words were nearly identical. DEC was on the right thought track, despite insidious inside carping that Shields was moving too quickly.

Shields was also pioneering three new sources of field revenues: software repair, consulting, and applications development:

- Software repair (700 employees) was an Atlanta-based hotline focused on word processors, where most apparent failures were caused by user error. Want to know how to underline? Either read the manual or (for twenty dollars a month) call Atlanta. Revenue was growing by 80 percent a year, though from a small base. The Atlanta unit provided 40 percent of software-service revenues using just 17 percent of the staff. Over the next twenty years, its approach would be widely emulated.

- Consulting (3,300 employees) provided 60 percent of booming software-service revenues, up 80 percent from a year earlier. But this was where Shields diverged most radically from the DEC culture of providing nearly free customer support. Once he resigned, Olsen would sharply constrict this unseemly business.

- Applications development had already been attempted by most hardware manufacturers, but with generally pitiful results. Fully aware of the problems, Busiek wanted to distribute third-party software rather than build his own. The best future channel might be electronic, he presciently opined: "Customers could examine the merchandise electronically. To buy, they'd simply enter an account number, and we would mail the package the next day … or download it directly to their personal computer."

In 1982, a decade before DEC's collapse, the company hardly lacked good ideas for the future.

A Missed Opportunity to Polish IBM's Crown Jewels

That same year, IBM's crown-jewel sales organization was experiencing flutters of its own, as we learned from VP George Conrades. We had been introduced to George a few years earlier by our good friend Jack Reilly, then head of sales for IBM's Series/1 minicomputer product division. George was a golden boy and future star, but Naomi thought he looked twelve years old and would never be successful. She shared her opinions with Jack, and Jack told George. Conrades good-humoredly never let Naomi forget that rare lapse in her generally impeccable intuition. He ultimately recruited her to the board of Akamai, where he served as CEO and later chairman.

At the time, though, George was head of IBM's national accounts division and working to refocus the sales force on IBM's largest customers and away from the small banks and mom-and-pop retailers that they once relied on to top up their quarterly revenues. "These days, the sales branch can no longer meet its sales quota by prospecting in new little companies," he explained. "National account managers have nowhere else to turn but their existing customers."

With the antitrust threat finally fading after thirteen years, IBM was returning to its most aggressive tactics and targeting 18 percent annual revenue growth. Key to the campaign was reaching beyond the "glass house," or the management information systems department (MIS), to the end-user population. The idea was to build demand. Teach end users how to apply computing, the theory went, and they would push MIS gatekeepers into buying more computers. That meant calling on 5,000 purchasing sites and 500,000 potential product delivery points for the small band of companies that represented 80 percent of IBM's total revenues.

As we wrote at the time: "From a [customer] perspective, the best outcome of this reorientation would be a cooperative band of knowledgeable, credible, and articulate missionaries, persuading customers to swallow their suspicions and take the plunge to improve productivity through information technology. The worst (and unacceptable) outcome would be coveys of flushed roosters spewing inappropriate solutions at an increasingly suspicious customer management. The prognosis is mixed."

IBM's investment in field people was substantial; many large enterprises had six to ten headquarters offices filled with blue-suiters on one mission or another. But the reps weren't ready for the new environment, grumped Jack Reilly. "Too many of our salespeople have become captives in the glass house. They've forgotten how to work hard enough to build end-user contacts over the long pull."

Relearning those skills wouldn't be easy, especially in the immediate turmoil caused by changing representation on 30 percent of the largest accounts and 90 percent of the intermediates. "We've just thrown 100,000 people in the air, you know," observed a seasoned sales executive, a trifle uneasily. Looking back, this would have been the ideal moment to cut 30 percent of the field staff. Highly unlikely on Akers's watch—and, indeed, it didn't happen.

A Floundering DEC Draws Competitors

During a visit to DEC in 1985, Win Hindle, vice president for corporate operations, kept insisting the field force was making progress toward becoming a power in commercial accounts. But from the outside, Sales still looked to be floundering, scoffed competitors—notably Hewlett-Packard's Paul Ely: "Several years ago, I thought it impossible HP could ever leapfrog DEC in scale. Today, that is not totally unlikely." Ely's newfound optimism sprang from several factors, including DEC's slowness in adopting Unix and embracing the PC and, most important, the lethargy of its sales reps. "Digital's sales force has no enthusiasm or understanding for customer hand-holding," Ely said during our interview. "They haven't yet learned that marketing has a technology of its own; we spent five years learning it. DEC has at least given us a short-term wedge. Some of our growth will be at their expense." And it was.

DEC's sales force was still in painful transition, while field engineering continued to make progress. Jack Shields now had a dozen direct reports, and field service was profitable on the basis of remote diagnoses and other technologies—even as the ratio of service fees to equipment prices declined. A very healthy situation that might help explain why customer-satisfaction ratings continued to climb from 7.8 in 1982 to 8.2 three years later.

The consulting business grew to 5,000 professionals generating $500 million a year. Maybe the trend toward complex networks of computers created an opportunity for designing, installing, and balancing these colossi, Jack theorized. In fact, the successful consulting practice was already raising Ken's concerns that DEC was charging customers to fix shortcomings in its own products.

Meanwhile, there were discouraging shortfalls in the national account program, which was originally intended to displace DEC's fragmented sales approaches in major accounts with a single account team: "After three years of effort, we're only now able to expand from forty to a few hundred national accounts," confessed Shields. "We've had to replace some account managers, and we'll have to replace more. No matter. We're developing account managers who grasp that future sales are dependent on understanding the customer's business strategy." Brave words, but difficult to achieve. By now, the transition from decentralization around the product groups to centralization around major accounts had been stalled for several years.

Also irksome, in our view, was the establishment of seventeen applications centers (fifteen to a hundred people each) to develop industry-specific applications software. The Hartford, Connecticut, center would build software for the insurance sector; Detroit would build for automotive; Santa Clara for semiconductors; and Southern California for aerospace. In reality, the applications-center concept was an eerie admission of DEC's inability to attract third-party developers, in large part because its customer base was relatively small next to Microsoft and the Unix camp. And it would fail—as did comparable activities established by HP, IBM, and Wang. Earlier ideas for exciting new software-distribution channels had already vanished.

The Blue-Suiters Go Pale

In September 1985, Jack Rogers, the head of IBM's sales and services, consolidated twenty-five regional offices into thirteen area offices and then merged the account group selling to the 2,000 largest accounts with the group selling to smaller businesses. However, staff cuts were too gentle, and the number of marketing people actually increased, admitted the official announcement.

Clump! The exercise merely thickened the management layers and accentuated the bureaucracy. Without separate sales forces for office products and the Series/1 minicomputers, the already ineffectual blue-suiters were expected to sell more product lines. Never mind opening new opportunities, the reps were instead "running around selling typewriters," complained George Dinardo, the irrepressible CIO of Mellon Bank, to the *Wall Street Journal* (September 13, 1985).

Meanwhile, IBM's senior management, almost all of whom were ex-salespeople, believed that having "blue-suiters" camped in customer offices could boost sales by establishing close rapport with senior IT executives. To the contrary, we soon learned, the gap between the IBMers and their largest customers was actually widening. On a rainy November morning, we hosted a meeting between Jack Rogers and ten top CIOs requested by IBM. The intent was to surface ideas on how IBM could work more productively with its largest accounts. Our offices would provide neutral territory.

Besides Rogers, those present from IBM included the VPs for the eastern and western regions, along with RB members including Irv Sitkin from Aetna, Max Hopper from American Airlines, Ray Cairns from DuPont, Bob Capone from J. C. Penney, Bob Musser from Mobil, and others. These men were leaders at some of IBM's fifty top accounts.

After a round of preliminary to-and-fros, Rogers attempted to move the discussion by asking the CIOs to describe the last time they'd received expert counseling from their IBM account executive on business or technology questions. Total silence for a minute or two, as though no one quite understood the question. "I never meet with my IBM account executive," blurted Bob Capone. "Do any of you guys meet with account executives?" Only one charitable fellow said that he had done so, perhaps recalling that an IBM executive sat on his company's board of directors, we surmised.

There was stunned silence from the IBMers, which I found difficult to understand. After all, these were nominally the top sales executives from one of the world's top sales organizations. Shouldn't they have been able to respond smartly even in extremis? Instead, the meeting ended dismally within the hour.

Later, Naomi and I speculated that the IBMers might have prepared for the meeting by reading call reports their account executives had written about visits to these CIOs. If so, one had to wonder if any such meetings had actually taken place. At minimum, there were serious disconnects between headquarters, the field, and the actual customers.

Clearly, the staff levels allocated to major customers during Akers's own field career were now counterproductive. No longer would CIOs assign entire office suites to hordes of customer reps and systems engineers. Selling solutions to end users, as envisioned by Conrades, hadn't happened.

The following February, Rogers was bumped up to head corporate services and replaced by Ed Lucente, who had previously managed the dogs and cats like typewriters and copiers in John Akers's product organization. Ed was another IBMer with a tough-guy reputation. Nevertheless, nothing much changed. The sales situation at IBM wasn't improving at all, confirmed *Fortune* in January 1987: "[Akers's] *mea culpa*, corporate-variety, jars the senses, because it conflicts so sharply with the conventional wisdom about IBM. Almost everything written about the company, including 1982's *In Search of Excellence*, pictured the salespeople as practically living with the customer, sharing in his every strategic decision. But no, says Akers, the sales force got away from that, in part, it appears, because business only a few years ago was so terrific that selling became a breeze. A recent survey IBM took of its sales reps suggests just how complacent they became: Amazingly, they have been spending only 30 percent of their time with their customers. Akers says the marketing problems are fixable—in time. He has the pressure on. 'I am certainly demonstrating impatience,' he declares. 'I am certainly demonstrating lack of satisfaction.'"

Impatience was a curious response from Akers, given that just five years earlier he himself had been president of North American sales.

Even then, IBM's system of incentives, rewards, and metrics was totally ingrown and unproductive, he'd been told. Internal studies proved that half the people awarded trips to the annual sales meeting in Hawaii didn't even have sales quotas, never mind that they didn't sell. Branch managers received more points for filling out Equal Employment Opportunity Commission (EEOC) documents and ramrodding sales-expense reports than for any revenues achieved by their sales reps. Bureaucracy was rampant, with layers of management occupying fancy offices in plush IBM-owned real estate. One reason the issue wasn't forcefully addressed was the general euphoria reflected in the 18 percent growth targets.

New Heads, Same Old Drift

Jack Shields tired of waiting for Ken Olsen to announce retirement plans and left Digital in 1989 to become CEO at Prime Computer. Without a powerful protector, the sales force was hammered for nutty gaffes like charging customers $200,000 to fix DEC's own software, or for a new warranty policy that angered customers by raising prices an average of 8 percent. "Shields placed too much stress on revenue targets for his organization," groused one senior DEC executive. Actually, Shields's profitability targets looked less like flaws and more like lifelines. By then, the computer market had split into a few aggressive competitors and a dozen starving firms willing to sell anything at any price. The era of Ken's uncommissioned engineer noodling with his favorite customers had clearly passed.

Despite a new head of field operations, sales remained sluggish and the reps hopelessly adrift. Part of the problem was strengthened competition: "[Shields's successor] is not responsible for the resurgence of IBM and Hewlett-Packard," observed an International Data Corporation analyst. (*Boston Globe,* October 4, 1989) "But he's being held responsible for a lack of policies to combat them"). A lack of competitive computers against RISC hummers from Sun and HP was a critical factor.

Several desperate and ultimately irrelevant organizational restructurings followed. Six hundred employees and several layers of management were removed in one such restructuring. Then came an ill-starred effort to organize around industry segments, which fell apart after ninety days and was replaced by a less ambitious effort to reorganize by account (a program that was supposed to have been completed two years earlier). Bob Hughes, now the sales boss, reckoned that changing the Maynard culture would take another two years—up from the one year he had projected seven years earlier. The field's resistance was grinding down the company. Efforts to improve the communications links between sales teams, headquarters staff, and product divisions also withered. Within a year, customers were questioning the ethics of embattled reps who would allegedly make any promise for a sale. It was time for a massive downsizing.

Selling the Sales Office

Meanwhile, over in Armonk, George Conrades had become senior vice president for North American sales and, by 1990, was reportedly among the top five candidates to succeed Akers. IBM was still spending much higher percentages of revenue on sales than any of its near competition. If anything, the atmosphere had actually soured since Jack Rogers's truncated meeting with RB members five years earlier. The role of influencing the customer's purchase decisions had passed from old Tom Watson's crown jewels to IT consulting giants like Arthur Andersen and Electronic Data Systems (EDS). Big-company CIOs were pushing back on the number of IBMers uselessly taking up their office space. "How about letting the customer fill out an order form, preferably electronically and definitely at a discount to reflect 'reduced representation'?" they suggested at RB meetings.

Conrades was smart and vigorous and working hard to effect changes in sales-cost structure and to ventilate the stifling culture. Management layers were removed until just two or so remained between headquarters and the seventy geographic "trading areas" he'd formed. When local managers were given responsibility for profit as well as revenues, they began cutting costs, starting with their fancy real estate. "Before, the branch manager was really concerned about the parking place for his BMW in front of the marble headquarters. Now he wants to sell the damn building," cheered George.

The poster boy for the new ethic was Duke Mitchell, a New Jersey trading-area manager. When we visited, Duke was ensconced in new office space in a converted warehouse. The new digs featured a huge bullpen that had been tarted up by painting the ventilation pipes in a psychedelic Peter Max palette. To keep field reps in the field, there were no permanent space nor desk assignments. Upon arriving, the rep logged into a system that made a one-day desk assignment, to which it automatically routed phone calls. When we visited, less than 20 percent of the desks were occupied. "I want them in the customers' offices, not here," barked Duke. Was it the way of the future or a halfway house? We couldn't tell, but it was definitely an imaginative and aggressive attempt at changing a powerful mind-set.

Much more was necessary, however. The product divisions were in full cry over a $6 billion field staff that was not yielding additional revenues. Margins were plummeting, and sales reps still weren't aggressively opening up new opportunities when they had a mainframe order to shepherd through the customer's procurement cycle. Too many remained more interested in perks than customers.

As at DEC, it was time for a massive downsizing. Most immediately at risk were the systems engineers who helped customers on issues of new-technology implementation. "The guys in the product divisions want me to remove SEs from their profitability numerator, basically by firing them," said Conrades. "But they have their feet nailed to the loading-dock floor; they have to be at the customer's site to compensate for problems in the usability and installability of our products." The prerequisite was product quality.

Longer term, Conrades hoped systems engineers could be converted into revenue-generating consultants in specialty areas like image processing, multimedia, and manufacturing, where deep knowledge would make them profitable. "We don't have to invent anything," he said. "In every area, there's a technology or methodology within IBM that will blow you away. We just haven't yet packaged those methodologies, as Andersen has." But, unlike Andersen and other consultants, Conrades continued, the IBMers "would only pull IBM products along, never someone else's," turning every consulting opportunity into a potential double sale.

Conrades's graphic was an arrow, with the point representing IBM's consulting practice, the feathers IBM products, and the shaft IBM's organizational ability to work together. "Next, we could make people responsible for developing their own skills and then paying them in relation to their bookings," he suggested. It was good thinking to preserve IBM's full-employment policy, but, in practical terms, it was more quest than campaign so long as IBM's consulting skills were an industry joke. George was realistic: "My existing delivery system is an anachronism. By 1995, we'll have the right one, or there won't be one," he warned us.

Actually, the end came much sooner. Conrades was demoted and chose early retirement the following year. The general view was that an increasingly embattled John Akers had removed a potential competitor. And, indeed, George soon reappeared as a dynamic and highly effective CEO, first at BBN and later at Akamai, both Boston-area high-tech firms.

It's hardly fair to say that IBM hadn't been creative during his watch. Unfortunately, the only real answer for IBM and its traditional competitors was drastic shrinkage. Finally, though, IBM decided to crack the outdated full-employment policy rather than continuing to struggle against IBM's sales culture. Massive firings were left to George's successor.

In Retrospect

For a full decade, the computer industry's two largest and most successful firms, DEC and IBM, labored fruitlessly to change the business culture, knowledge base, customer focus, and energy levels of their huge and expensive field forces. All of it was hopeless wheel-spinning, absent the ability to confront the reality that the two fundamental problems were external. First, many customers no longer relied on their sales reps to identify and implement the latest technology as they had when IBM walked arm in arm with CEOs and DEC noodled with leading scientists and engineers. Now, good discounts with favorable terms on an expedited delivery schedule were what they demanded. Second, gross margins were permanently flattened as the star walkers reduced the customers' costs of switching to an alternate supplier. Had DEC and IBM recognized and reacted to the new reality, their histories might have been much different.

Chapter 16

DISTRACTED BY COMPETITION:

IBM Battles Fujitsu and Hitachi

Not infrequently, company leaders fail to meet new and potent competition because of an outdated obsession with protagonists from the past. For almost two decades, America's IT sector was preoccupied by visions of cheap Japanese computers swarming the marketplace; they would beat us in computers as they had in automobiles, motorcycles, VCRs, watches, and cameras. In 1982, just 5.1 million automobiles rolled off U.S. assembly lines compared to Japan's 6.9 million. And America's pathetic export level of just 353,000 cars trailed far behind Japan's 3.8 million—not to mention Germany, France, and even Spain, which exported 495,000 cars.

"Once again, the alarm is being sounded across the U.S. EDP countryside, warning of the imminent invasion of the U.S. market by the Japanese," mused *Datamation* in January 1973. Nearly nine years later, *BusinessWeek* devoted its December 1981 issue to the coming onslaught. Particularly endangered was U.S. dominance in PCs, because "the Japanese traditionally have low costs for components such as semiconductors and keyboards."

Sure enough, Japanese exports of data-processing equipment in the first six months of 1983 tripled, to $819 million from $274 million a year earlier. Most of the increase represented printers, floppy disks, modems, and fax units. But there was also $300 million in mainframes and mainframe components bought from Fujitsu and Hitachi, respectively, by Amdahl and National Advanced Systems (NAS), a National Semiconductor subsidiary formed to sell and support computers after Itel exited the business.

In addition, Japan's government-sponsored Fifth Generation Project promised huge advances in parallel processing, artificial intelligence, automated language translation, robotics, and other future stuff, drawing near-hysterical responses from American pundits and academics. So Armonk, led by John Akers, was most probably obsessed with Japan Inc., too—especially its Fujitsu and Hitachi components with their IBM-compatible mainframes.

Xenophobia as Strategy

Old-timer Fujitsu had been formed in 1935 as a spin-off of Fuji Electric, itself a joint venture of the Zaibatsu conglomerate Furukawa Electric and the German telecommunications-equipment supplier Siemens. Fujitsu launched its computer business in 1953 with the Facom 100 model—"only seven years after ENIAC," we were pointedly reminded at our first visit there. By 1970, under the guidance of Japan's "Mr. Computer," Toshio Ikeda, Fujitsu was second only to IBM in the Japanese market. Nine years later, it was No. 1, driven by an aggressive sales campaign heavily spiced with a "buy Japanese" flavor. Of course, Americans were no strangers to the nativistic card, either.

Fujitsu became a favorite target of America's business press because of its aggressive stance at home and its high-profile connection to Amdahl in the United States. For example, *Forbes* (June 9, 1980) commented on AT&T's rejection of a Fujitsu fiber-optics contract: "It is heartening too that we seem ready to defend our leadership. AT&T chose last month to Buy American rather than honor a loaded low-ball bid from Fujitsu on advanced fiber optics work. Congress and the FCC applauded the action. The gauntlet is picked up. This time things will be different."

Business Week (May 19, 1980) followed the trend with a cover story photo of a scowling Fujitsu Chairman Taiyu Kobayashi, cropped to make him appear particularly menacing. Two years later, *Fortune* (May 22, 1982) carried a fairly innocuous remark from the company's president, Takuma Yamamoto, explaining his company's lead over IBM in the Japanese market. "'At IBM, they don't commit themselves to specific delivery dates. It seems they act superior to their customers."

Even though the Fujitsu president was correct about IBM's unexpected mainframe backlog, *Fortune* was somehow moved to riposte,

"Yamamoto had best avoid hubris himself.... Fujitsu earned only a paltry $85 million worldwide on sales of $2.7 billion." ("A thin-margin strategy to build market share against an overweight competitor?" we countered.)

Hitachi elicited much warmer press reviews in the United States, in part because its U.S. ventures were less confrontational. This GE look-alike had emerged in 1910 from Namihai Odaira's motor-repair shop in Hitachi, a copper-mining town. The company received a major boost when World War I shipping blockades forced Japan to become more self-sufficient. By the 1930s, Hitachi's product line had expanded to include everything from washing machines to railroad engines.

In 1951, computer development began at its Central Research Laboratory, which had worked on radar in wartime. The first commercial HITAC 3000 computer was introduced in 1959. A year later, Hitachi completed a reservation system for the National Railroad, a considerable software achievement at the time. By 1978, it was a preeminent international supplier of computers, and *Fortune* (September 25, 1978) wrote: "Hitachi has emerged with few scars and the fattest pretax margin in the computer industry—about 10 percent. That is largely because of a subtle strategist named Katsushige Mita," who had become Hitachi's president by the time we visited. Purred even Fujitsu-basher *Forbes* (July 23, 1979): "Here's a look inside the company that many observers insist is Japan's best-run—and hardest running."

In December 1979, Hitachi made its first deal with National Semiconductor's NAS subsidiary. The arrangement was generally harmonious, in contrast to Fujitsu's deal with Amdahl. NAS sold Hitachi's high-end mainframe on a nonexclusive basis and gave up any intention to produce its own. As for duration, "frankly, it's indefinite," replied Tadeo Usui, Hitachi VP and general manager, in response to our question. Confirmed National Semiconductor CEO Charlie Sporck in a separate interview: "The Hitachi arrangement will last as long as it serves a purpose for both parties. Legal glue isn't the issue."

Hitachi was soaring. For the fiscal year ending March 1981, overseas sales climbed 35 percent, while Hitachi America's revenues topped $250 million, up 25 percent over the prior year and 322 percent over four years. Semiconductors and consumer electronics led the march, but the computer business had grown stronger as well. In May 1982, Hitachi made its debut on the New York Stock Exchange.

But the Welcome Wagon hit a speed bump a month after the Big Board listing, and from this apogee, Hitachi began a downward slide. On June 22, 1982, six Hitachi employees were arrested by FBI agents in the office of a phony consulting firm and charged with conspiring to steal IBM trade secrets. Hitachi countered that its employees had been unfairly entrapped. The details were messy, however: The materials allegedly used in Hitachi planning sessions were clearly marked and included ten loose-leaf notebooks page-stamped "IBM confidential."

A wide swath of Hitachi managers was involved, even the general manager of its Kanagawa Processor Works, who was accused of personally participating in conversations with FBI undercover agents. Eventually, the evidentiary trail led far beyond the ten notebooks to include seventy-five secret meetings, sixty-five hours of audio tapes, thirty-five hours of videotapes, $600,000 or more in payments, and a trophy snapshot of a Hitachi engineer draped over IBM's newest disk drives.

After mutual posturing, the issue was settled with Hitachi paying IBM an estimated $300 million for the unauthorized use of its software, plus monthly license fees of around $3 million. Hitachi was also required to submit its new products to IBM for examination prior to market release. National Advanced Systems was fined $3 million and ordered to submit its pending computer products for IBM's examination as well. There was also lurid industry scuttlebutt of a stormy meeting at which IBM's CEO Frank Cary and president John Opel personally berated Charlie Sporck and NAS president David Martin on their partner's malfeasance as if they were wayward teenagers. Sporck was unlikely to have bent to such chest-thumping.

Fujitsu was implicated in similar activities but managed to escape with a private penalty and no public exposure in the Japanese press. Interestingly, it didn't take long for IBM to reconcile with Hitachi, which years later agreed to buy IBM's disk-hardware business and resell its mainframes. The relationship with Fujitsu, though, was permanently frosted, and the two entered a long-standing arbitration over access to IBM software. Over lunch in late 1985, Jack Kuehler told us, "We don't get in the same room with Fujitsu without our lawyers present. But we'll make an agreement with Hitachi over the telephone."

By then, 59 percent of Fujitsu's annual revenues came from computers, 23 percent from components, and only 18 percent from telecommunications, the company's roots. But exports represented just 23 percent of total revenues, far short of the 30 percent predicted by Kobayashi just three years earlier.

The stumbles on Fujitsu's multiyear journey through the American market had been numerous and embarrassing. To begin, Fujitsu's 1970 deal with Automation Sciences to market the Facom 230 against the low (and vulnerable) end of IBM's System/360 line was intended to bring in $100 million in revenues in five years. But the deal unraveled in just two years' time. A Massachusetts word-processing shop acquired by the Japanese company in 1980 was largely defunct by 1981. Fujitsu's U.S. components group sold only a thousand PCs, despite offering a basket of extra features and a symphony of radio jingles. At least two minicomputer introductions in that period also failed.

A 1980 joint venture with TRW Inc. (originally Thompson Ramo Woolridge) had the TRW vice chairman, J. Sidney Webb, who was also the new venture's president, bragging to *Business Week* (May 1980) that "Japanese hardware and U.S. distribution and software know-how constitute the best fit I can imagine. I'm like a kid in a candy store looking at all that Fujitsu hardware. I think we're going to sell a helluva lot of computers." Nothing much happened except in point-of-sales devices. Webb retired, and just months before our arrival, Fujitsu announced it would buy out TRW's share of the venture, with President Yamamoto explaining to *Business Week* (March 14, 1984): "Today, we are finding the small computer market very difficult to handle…. It's better for us to have a one-sided business-decision process, especially in such a fast-moving business."

Journey to the Land of the Rising Sun

In 1984, we prepared for the first of our visits to the Japanese computer companies. Naomi decided she'd go along, though she had been warned that a woman would be expected to remain silent at the meetings (which she did). We spent three days each with friendly Hitachi and suspicious Fujitsu, followed by meetings with Nippon

Electric, Oki, and other key players, including people from the Ministry of International Trade and Industry (MITI).

Between the Hitachi and Fujitsu visits, we made a courtesy call on George Conrades, then head of IBM's Far East area. George arranged a sushi lunch in a Tokyo hotel suite so that we wouldn't be seen going into his office and possibly fingered as IBM spies. The meeting was uneventful, with George describing how he'd been sent to help IBM Japan regain its No. 1 domestic-market position lost to Fujitsu. We chuckled as we entered and exited via separate elevators. But, as we would soon discover, we had naively and massively underestimated the bitter suspicion Fujitsu held for both Western journalists and IBM. Later, we wondered if we'd been observed or even followed that day.

Our introduction to Fujitsu had been arranged through Amdahl CEO Gene White. Given that the two companies had evolved a multipart deal that included Fujitsu as a major shareholder, mainframe-component supplier, disk OEM, and collaborator on communications boxes, we expected a reasonably pleasant and informative visit. Instead, our initial reception in Tokyo ranged somewhere between frosty and hostile, with continued uncertainty and repeated agenda changes deliberately signaling our dubious worth. When we arrived to meet Shiro Yoshikawa, executive director of Fujitsu's international operations group, with responsibility for Fujitsu America and the Amdahl relationship, and his deputy, Michio Naruto, our two contingents sat on opposite sides of an oval table.

Gazing across the miniature intertwined Japanese and American friendship flags perched on the table, Naruto-san opened the meeting through an interpreter. "Welcome. We will discuss Fujitsu technology with you. Refrain from asking questions about Fujitsu strategy on direct entry to the U.S. market or on our relationship with Amdahl. Finally, let me announce that we wanted to decline this meeting. It's only because of Mr. Gene White's sponsorship that Fujitsu consented." Then, breaking into emphatic English: "We are forced to meet." Smile. Nothing enigmatic here.

Over the next two days, we visited product engineers, factories, and the R&D operation. The technology was impressive, despite the constant chatter of our guides. We thought Fujitsu would certainly make headway in the disk market and keep pace or surpass IBM in mainframe hardware. During our tour of the Atsugi lab, the director emphasized the facility's advanced work in high-heat circuitry for mainframes. His engineers had moved beyond silicon to something called HEMT (for High Electron Mobility Transistor), which was 40 percent faster than the equally exotic Josephson Junction.

We concluded that Fujitsu's march into the international mainframe market could be slowed only by IBM's legal defense of its operating system.

The second day's luncheon was spiced with more commentary from Naruto-san: "Fujitsu doesn't want to meet anyone. Besides, we have nothing to sell in the United States—at present. Amdahl is an entirely separate company. The U.S. press often misquotes us; sometimes our proprietary data is even leaked to the U.S. government and to competitors. Besides, management time is too precious."

The atmosphere grew even darker over the obligatory farewell dinner. The architecturally exquisite restaurant was surrounded by a large but carefully hidden garden, astonishing in space-starved Tokyo. The internationalists Yoshikawa and Naruto were again our hosts, accompanied by two junior executives who served as translators. We were in a private tatami room, complete with geishas kneeling beside each diner—including Naomi, to each woman's visible embarrassment. Another woman played a traditional stringed instrument whose sounds, we were told, "are of small birds clustering among the waves." The food was excellent and the hospitality delightful, with Yoshikawa-san offering well-honed strings of cultural insights, jokes, and even a song. Then, he fashioned an origami shape or two, one of which resembled a phallus-like teeter-totter, that he handed to Naomi before leaving for another commitment.

Captivated by the performance, we expected to adjourn to our hotel. But, instead, Naruto unleashed another stream of admonitions and accusations. Among the highlights:

- "The questions you submitted were intended to ferret out Fujitsu strategy." We'd submitted the same questions to Hitachi and NEC, but we nodded pleasantly and apologized again for Western ignorance.

- "Fujitsu insists you write on only one subject—our commitment to advance technology." We said we understood that commitment.

- "Fujitsu doesn't need you to help define its strategy." We expressed cheerful amazement that our host would even consider such an approach to strategy formulation. Besides, we repeated, we don't work for vendors.

- "All consulting firms must be highly sensitive to IBM interests to survive. They can't make a living otherwise." Now, it was our turn. We politely declined Naruto-san's help with our business strategy, and told him we made our living by specifically not working for IBM—or any other vendor.

- "Amdahl management thinks the Japanese are very stupid. But they will learn we are stubborn farmers." "What the hell did that mean?" we wondered silently.

- "The Research Board members are not particularly welcome here, because Fujitsu has no direct presence in the United States among such customers." Was this a statement of fact or pique given the sorry outcomes of Fujitsu's multiple efforts to establish a market position in word processors, PCs, and minicomputers?

Then Naruto unexpectedly promised to visit us during his next trip to New York. Naomi responded charmingly that such a visit might help build mutual confidence. He rushed out, leaving the two junior marketers nearly pale with embarrassment, explaining the prior scene as a consequence of two age-old traditions: tightly knit rural families and closed villages "in which any stranger is viewed suspiciously since he might be a tax collector." No question, we were strangers.

But Naruto was also highly strategic and intelligent, as we learned later. That evening's orchestrated outburst was clearly meant to send a message, perhaps to IBM or maybe Amdahl—or even to other parts of Fujitsu. Our visit may have embarrassed international operations by emphasizing how little penetration they'd made into the U.S. market. If nothing else, we'd gotten a glimpse of a very angry IBM adversary that would demand as much of John Akers's focus as did the PC and Microsoft.

Cordial Hitachi

By contrast, our Hitachi meetings were extraordinarily amiable. The company was the twenty-eighth-largest in the world and Japan's third-largest. Its annual revenues were $19.4 billion, and it had 162,000 employees and 20,000 products, including nuclear power plants, locomotives, refrigerators, escalators, television cameras, supercomputers, and, of course, IBM-compatible mainframes.

Three dominant strategies were widely articulated during our tours. First, like Japan as a whole, the company would relentlessly exit declining businesses such as electric motors to enter growth sectors such as electronics. Profit potential triggered these decisions, not revenue or market share. Second, Hitachi emphasized engineering; seventeen of its twenty-nine top executives held engineering degrees. Hitachi also had Japan's largest R&D budget, with $994 million spread among seven laboratories and ten thousand employees. Finally, the company relied on direct communication without marketing fluff, which, doubtless, contributed to notorious gaffes but also explained the success of foreign partnerships.

In the months prior to our visit, Hitachi's president, Katsushige Mita, had been busy doing damage control after the FBI sting. At a meeting with the Japanese press the preceding January, he acknowledged the terms of the settlement but denied "any top-management involvement in the theft of IBM trade secrets," as *Electronic News* had reported on January 30, 1984. At least four high-level demotions were subsequently revealed, including that of Mita's successor as general manager of the Kanagawa Processor Works.

The shamed management seemed to withdraw from view, observed *The New York Times* later that year. "Psychologically, at least, the company has not recovered despite growing computer exports. Mr. Mita, for instance, who was once talkative with the press, has not granted an interview to foreign reporters since the IBM incident.... 'He has had enough of the IBM incident,' explains a public relations person." His embarrassed silence extended not just to reporters. After a barrage of questions about IBM at Hitachi's annual stockholders' meeting, "finally Mr. Mita could take it no longer," the *Times* revealed on July 15, 1984. "He interrupted a persistent questioner and asked for an end to the discussion. 'We did our utmost to solve the problem and punished ourselves, including myself … We would like to do our best from now on too.' A round of applause erupted, silencing the questioner."

With an introduction from Charlie Sporck and the accompaniment of Dave Turner, National's canny liaison to Hitachi, we encountered no problems with arrangements and agendas. We visited the Kanagawa works, the Odawara works (which produced peripherals, including disks), the Central Research Labs, and the supercomputer installation at Tokyo University. In every case, the semiconductor and manufacturing technology (but perhaps not packaging) was on a par with IBM.

After the tours came an audience with Mita and top management. He opened by emphasizing product quality and profits (raising good-natured laughter from the group). When he was general manager of the Kanagawa works, he told us, there had been occasional complaints about quality until the company invested $100 million in simulation testing. At that point, customer problems dramatically dropped. "However, we are not gods! We are human beings and have sometimes made mistakes." An awkward sadness descended on the group.

Now it was time for questions. Since women weren't supposed to speak in polite company, Naomi, normally the outside partner, was reduced to passing me scribbled notes (a stoicism that rewarded her with a Michimoto pearl necklace). Slightly disconcerted, I began with our standard and innocuous formal questions, now made somewhat ominous by the wholly unexpected dustup at Fujitsu: "From your perspective, Mr. President, what are Hitachi's primary strategic strengths or directions?"

Mita responded: "First, our emphasis on advanced technology, which you have probably observed during your tour of our disk facility at Odawara. Hitachi carries 31,000 patents and is spending over $1 billion, or 7 percent of revenues, on R&D. At the same time, Japanese software could not possibly be competitive in the United States, so it would be self-defeating to depart from the world of IBM-compatibility there.

"Most important," Mita went on, "Hitachi remains dedicated to product reliability. Reliance on uninterrupted operations is increasingly critical to the economy. Therefore, profitability must be secondary to reliability."

The president closed by underscoring the inherent synergy in Hitachi's broad mix of electronic businesses—semiconductors, telecommunications products (just merged into the computer group), and consumer products—to help share the burden of semiconductor research and chip fabrication. He then excused himself from the meeting. He had spoken only in Japanese.

Now was the moment for the gift-giving ceremony, but I had followed the Japanese custom of leaving our present in an inconspicuous corner. Naomi suddenly hissed, "Give him the present! Give him the damn present." I stumbled across the room to retrieve our clever lithograph that superimposed nineteenth-century Japanese paintings onto scenes of New York. Would he appreciate this attempt at cultural convergence?

I vigorously pressed the cylinder into the president's hands, only to hear him whisper in nearly flawless English, "It is not the Japanese custom to open your present here." Mita's gesture was so quiet and graceful that I was hardly embarrassed. Five years later, ending an interview with another Hitachi executive, two subordinates immediately began tearing off the wrapping of a colonial silver bowl. We demurred that "unwrapping is not your custom." "No, but it's yours," shot back the executive, with visible good cheer.

Softness in Software

Curiously, none of the Japanese computer companies ever achieved an end-product presence in the American market, except perhaps in disks and laptops. The explanation was not hardware prowess but software productivity, and our visit gave us much to ponder on that score. For instance, at a Fujitsu software factory, we found two thousand systems software engineers (a group that had doubled in recent years, we learned), 60 percent with recent college degrees in mathematics or physics but none in computer science—since such programs didn't yet exist in Japan. They sat in floor-wide, eight-hundred-person bullpens, outfitted uniformly in smocks and billed caps.

Fujitsu also had twelve thousand applications developers in thirty-seven separate applications subsidiaries. Each new recruit received six months of training plus another six months of apprenticeship with an experienced programmer. "How did all this training affect programmer productivity?" we asked, with a cautious glance at the ever-alert Naruto. We'd read Japanese press reports that domestic output per man day was 15 percent higher than in the United States. "At least 15 percent, I hope," replied the director, because Fujitsu's teams were all so young (i.e., energetic) and fresh from the university (i.e., equipped with current techniques). "The U.S. has too many tired middle-aged programmers."

Moreover, Japanese lifetime employment encourages people to remain with the employer for the seven years our host reckoned it takes to become productive. "I couldn't have confidence in those American programmers who change jobs every few years," the lab director went on. If he really believed all that, he had probably not visited Microsoft, Sun, or the rest of Silicon Valley, I guessed. But even IBM was probably ahead of Fujitsu in programmer tools. One indicator was the ratio of terminals to programmers; Fujitsu had one terminal per 2.7 programmers, versus the 1:1 ratio common in the United States.

At Hitachi, we spoke about software with a group executive, Dr. Takeo Miura, who was built like a barrel with military-cropped grey hair. The brilliant "Bear" (as he was called internally) was well ahead of Fujitsu in his deep understanding of the issues confronting the Japanese computer industry. "Our computer business is already growing 20 percent annually," he told us, "but exports are only 15 percent of revenues [the same as Fujitsu's] and must be enlarged to match the 30 percent Hitachi realizes from exports as a whole. Future growth will depend on integrating our communications and local networks for factory, home, and office automation."

Despite major projects to build applications for the Japanese finance and distribution markets (where Hitachi was entrenched), "software for the U.S. market must be developed in that market by Americans," Miura related. As for operating systems, Hitachi had its own for the Japanese market. Elsewhere, Hitachi would retain its commitment to IBM-compatibility, at least "at the user level; since the IBM standard is an international standard like English, it's impossible to fight."

At Tokyo University, we met Professor Akito Arima, director of the computer center, who began by describing the institution's advanced work in building a network linking seven campuses. He quickly turned to Japan's shortfall in software, saying its "weakest point" was the Japanese societal attitude esteeming electronics engineers but not software developers. His explanation was that "information" (i.e., software logic) was cheap and little valued in Japan. "We cannot sell knowledge [intellectual property] here. In that respect, we are far behind the United States."

At Oki Electric Industry, we encountered similar reluctance. This $3.5 billion company exported mobile telephones, memory chips, and especially small printers. But over a fine French luncheon, the general manager for overseas operations said Oki needed a world-standard operating system for its product line. "It would be far too risky for Oki to develop its own." Minicomputer companies in the U.S. far smaller than Oki had done just that and achieved early market success, we noted at the time. Admittedly, most would fail with the advent of Unix.

At the Japan Information Services Industry Association (JISIA), we learned that 299 of its 350 member firms had revenues of $1 million or less, and only 26 had revenues over $25 million (far smaller than software firms in the United States). Most of the work was on-site custom programming for the computer companies. Packaged software applications were still insignificant in 1984: "A custom-made suit is still preferred in Japan," observed the JISIA president.

The president also described Japanese public attitudes toward the entrepreneurship driving the American computer industry. "A young Japanese person cannot be proud of himself if he just works for money and self-fulfillment. Rather, he must work for an organization of high repute—the largest corporations, trading companies, or government. So big organizations attract the best engineers; smaller ones settle for graduates in shipbuilding or English literature." Certainly, there were exceptions we visited, including the software firm Ascii Ltd., whose atypical foresight and technical prowess were cemented by its close relationship with Microsoft.

At MITI, we found an organization both less omnipotent than the American press feared and more competent, forceful, and fortified with greater resources than our own Commerce Department. Its people were top graduates of Japan's most prestigious universities. In the past, the agency had successfully pursued a national economic plan to redirect investments from dying industries to new sectors. But now corporate resistance had weakened the program, though the industrial coordination remained much greater than America could muster.

From the director of data processing promotion, we learned of a program to encourage the development of commercial packages, including tax incentives, loans, and a promotional registry. So far, there were only 4,500 packages in the registry compared to 100,000 in the United States—and the shortfall extended to programmers. According to MITI's figures, Japan had 340,000 programmers, or systems engineers, in various categories, two-thirds of whom worked for user companies. That figure met just 38 percent of Japan's requirements, and the gap with the United States was widening. "In the United States, 70 percent of all elementary and secondary schools already use personal computers; in Japan, just 100 of our 40,000 schools own even a single personal computer. And of those, sixty are used solely for administrative processing." (Today, Japanese schools are much more "wired" than their American counterparts.)

The director of the electronics policy division described efforts to build export markets through the same three-stage process that had succeeded so well with consumer electronics: start with an overseas beachhead, study the market, grow. But unlike consumer products, he observed, computers required technical-support organizations and software—and software carried such strong cultural overtones that it had to be homegrown.

Japan's best near-term prospect, the director said, was a virgin market "like AT&T, where Japanese companies can integrate our midrange computers with telecommunications." We were unconvinced, having watched AT&T, over the past decade, devote its managerial energies in a Sisyphean battle against deregulation rather than Unix. No matter, closed our host, checking his wristwatch: "There is entirely too much competition in the Japanese computer segment for the domestic market alone. It's completely out of control." MITI would later encourage Hitachi and Fujitsu to merge their mainframe activities. But the Ministry didn't prevail, whatever America's exaggerated assessment of its clout.

MITI was also the coordinating agency for Japan's Fifth Generation Project. Despite hysterical finger-wagging from the U.S. press and several noteworthy American academics, results were meager. Government funding had been cut back, as we learned. The caliber of scientists contributing to the effort was far from top rung, admitted a

Hitachi middle manager. The best scientists were too busy at home, diligently pursuing language translation, speech recognition, and image processing for their own companies. Japan would ultimately fail to export software except, famously, the closed routines embedded in games, telephones, and so forth.

Japan could only enter the international computer market using someone else's publicly available operating system. It was still too early for Unix. Operating systems from the minicomputer companies like DEC were protected by patents and by gross margins lean enough to hold off cloning as an unattractive strategy. Only the IBM mainframe operating system, partially in the public domain, offered substantial total revenues and still-rich margins for Japanese plug compatibles. That left IBM and Akers fighting essentially alone against competition from Japan Inc.'s two hardware-rich pinnacles, Fujitsu and Hitachi.

But the Japanese competition would prove merely a temporary distraction in the face of more serious threats from other quarters.

CHAPTER 17

NAVIGATING THE WAVES AT IBM:

Akers Runs Aground, and Gerstner Takes the Helm

Seldom can a CEO recruited from inside a company navigate disruptive change in an industry's business model. "More companies fail because of strong cultures than weak strategies," observed Richard Foster. Someone steeped in the culture can't crack the culture. Wang, Digital Equipment, and IBM all proved the point. It took outsider Louis Gerstner to rescue IBM from the mistake-ridden reign of the consummate insider, John Akers.

We first met John over lunch at IBM's Armonk, New York, headquarters in 1982. "Gentleman Johnny," as we privately called him, appeared physically fit, with a slightly ruddy complexion and a shorter stature than the prototypical IBM senior executive. A Yale graduate and former Navy fighter pilot, Akers spent his first twenty years at IBM's "crown jewel" sales division, becoming its president at age thirty-nine, before being named to head the midrange computing group. For a corporation that had always honored salespeople, he was a logical choice for CEO. And it didn't hurt that he'd once been Frank Cary's administrative assistant.

Our meeting began on a strangely nervous note when he showed us a cartoon urging caution with consultants that someone had "slipped under my office door." He then proceeded to give Naomi and me a long, informed, and comprehensive rundown of IBM's most fundamental strategic requirements for the next decade.

IBM had to develop products more quickly, he told us: "Too many four-year development projects have produced still another system the world didn't need." He also praised the swifter time-to-market models employed by the minicomputer companies and the Japanese. Though wrong about the Japanese (outside of consumer products, they were actually very sluggish), Akers definitely reflected the popular wisdom: "[The Japanese] announce something every six months; if customers don't respond, they change it. Six months may be too short for real product development, but we certainly need granularity [i.e., regular frequency] in our midrange product announcement rhythm."

Ahead of their contemporaries at Digital or Wang, the IBM executives had already begun to appreciate the profound changes in product development and business model initiated by the new PC companies. "Today, IBM has more humility," said Akers. "We can't possibly address all the market opportunities. So I no longer care where we acquire technology if it's cost-effective." So, too, with software: "Unfortunately, our determined self-reliance in the 1970s means that the software available for intermediate-scale processors hasn't grown much in five years. We missed all the sales potential of third-party software developers, particularly in the engineering/scientific markets." Later, a divisional product VP chimed in: "Not one of the four most popular operating systems on the market today was developed by a hardware vendor."

Armonk was beginning to feel the margin pinch. "Part of our plan involves tighter pricing," said Akers. "We can no longer be comfortable with any substantial delta [i.e., difference] between our prices and those of competitors." Good thinking. Too little action, unfortunately.

The Opel-Akers Interregnum

In February 1983, when CEO John Opel assumed the chairmanship from the retiring Frank Cary, Akers was named president and chief operating officer, cementing the line of succession. The antitrust suit had been dismissed as "without merit" by the incoming Reagan Justice Department. At almost the same moment, Opel ignited a short-term booster engine for revenue growth with a new mainframe-pricing policy designed to tilt customers toward purchase rather than lease.

By some accounts, Opel was worried that a competitor like Amdahl might leapfrog IBM technology and encourage customers to cancel their IBM leases and return the now severely devalued equipment. Given how little technological improvement there was between the upcoming IBM 3090 mainframe and the predecessor 3081, his was a legitimate concern.

Even so, the new pricing policy was probably unnecessary, given the impending expiration of an investment tax credit that would have encouraged a flurry of near-term purchases anyway. Between the new pricing, the tax credit, Kuehler's new 4300 minicomputer, and the advent of the IBM personal computer, revenues soared from $29 billion in Opel's first year as CEO in 1981, to $46 billion in 1984, while earnings doubled to $6.6 billion. Hubris was only natural, as when Cary told associates that revenues would top $100 billion by 1990. More than twenty years later, the world was still waiting.

Inflated revenue projections were less damaging than actual revenues bloated by cannibalistic maneuvers, however. Equipment purchases ballooned short-term financial results at the expense of leasing's predictable revenue stream. They also increased the uncontrolled inventory of secondhand mainframes, which were sold at sharply discounted prices, thus putting a drag on new-product pricing. Opel's burst of revenues from sales—not rentals—represented a mortgage on the future. Nevertheless, IBM's next two years were glorious.

For at least the next decade, Armonk opined, the race was won. "The mainframe is where the real muscle lies. The only worry is getting too greedy," noted an IBM executive. These were blowout years for big iron, but the rise of the PC also boosted sales. IBM's stock price topped $162 a share.

Akers came to the plenary meeting of the Research Board held in San Francisco in March 1983, just a month after being named president. Naomi had convinced him that only he could answer the still-remaining important questions related to convergence of the midrange product line. Here was an opportunity for the new president to expound his principles and hopes for IBM to fifty of its most important customers.

John answered none of the open questions, giving, instead, a remarkably detached and wispy presentation that ended with a member's question about the new CEO's greatest concerns. "Our factories are sold out. The antitrust suit is almost settled. So my only real concern is security for my family," Akers glibly answered. After uttering a few more platitudes, he dashed off to locate his personal bodyguard.

"We were sheep," loudly whispered CIGNA CIO Allan Loren of his colleagues' failure to challenge Akers's opt-out presentation. (Loren would later become the CEO of Dun & Bradstreet.) But, in retrospect, the presentation was the message, for Gentleman Johnny would remain strangely detached as the CEO at IBM, apparently more driven than driver. His tenure at the top would be largely dictated by inbred traditions rather than responsive to the external tumult that was roiling IBM.

Gentleman Johnny Takes the Helm

Akers was named CEO in February 1985, with Opel remaining as chairman. Insiders completed the roster: Paul Rizzo as vice chairman for worldwide sales, Allen Krowe as CFO, and Jack Kuehler the senior VP for all IBM products.

Outsiders, including us, wondered if Gentleman Johnny's lifetime in sales, bolstered by his two-year finishing school experience overseeing midrange products, had adequately prepared him for the tough battles faced by a CEO.

But why worry? Frank Cary had already beaten back the challenges raised by leasing companies, plug-compatible mainframes and peripherals, minicomputers, the Justice Department, and a striking level of organizational dysfunction. Then, too, John Opel had capitalized on IBM's technological assets with a stunningly successful sales and pricing campaign. What looked to be a sunny interlude in IBM's history might need nothing more than a sunny public presence at the top. So why not anoint a charming fellow with impeccable sales credentials?

Through no fault of Akers, IBM's fortunes began their plunge into long-term decline that very year. The newly introduced 3090 represented only a half-step on five-year-old investments in technology. It contained a few architectural tricks, but no advances in circuit density, packaging, or much else—and only the traditional doubling in price/performance. All in all, an amazingly uncompetitive response that resuscitated Amdahl and its cohorts. The midrange muddle was no closer to final resolution than when Akers took over the minicomputer group four years earlier. The ballyhooed PC business headed by Don Estridge suffered from the embarrassing withdrawal of the consumer-targeted PCjr, with its rubbery "chiclet" keys and underpowered processor.

Akers's first year ended with weak profit results and was followed by another sizable drop in 1986. Mainframe sales were much softer than anticipated, first because customers had overbought ahead of the tax-credit expiration, but also because they were unwilling to replace their just-purchased equipment with the lackluster 3090 and, most important, because the new Unix competitors were offering much better price/performance.

Why didn't IBM simply cut the costs of its sales operations so that it could reduce prices? Halfhearted moves in that direction did little to offset the margin pressures from minicomputers, PCs, Unix and Microsoft. The pressures were publicly visible—in the front page of the September 13, 1985, *Wall Street Journal*, no less: "Margins before sales, administrative, research, and marketing expenses are 60 percent to 80 percent on mainframes but only 45 percent to 50 percent on medium and small computers," confirmed its report.

At one point, Akers met the grim news of falling mainframe sales and market share by asking a close aide, "Do we really have to discuss such bad news before breakfast?" Perhaps, he continued, sales would bounce back as they had when he was branch manager in Boston. A weak opening bid in a tough game that demanded purposeful strength.

Meanwhile, Unix and the PC continued to squeeze IBM's gross margins. Two years had passed since Steve Jobs ended the chapter on customer hand-holding by the traditional computer companies (and the traditional calculator companies before them). Market trends should have augured substantial increases in R&D spending on customer self-support, accompanied by sharp cuts in field staff. Neither was done. Akers lacked the certitude expected of CEOs, especially in such tumultuous times.

IBM missed its 1986 forecasts, instead turning in flat revenues and declining profits. In October, Allen Krowe, the senior vice president for finance, was reassigned to head the minicomputer and communications divisions; he was replaced as CFO by Frank Metz. Press pundits wondered if Krowe had been too bullish on future growth or just too abrasive. "In my opinion, Krowe got shot," an anonymous former IBM employee told the *Wall Street Journal* (October 20, 1986). A letter to the *Journal's* editor over Akers's signature fired back: "As a corporate executive now responsible for a major part of our product line, Allen is taking on a key assignment of obvious significance. Further, it is because of his long track record of performance that he has earned this challenging position and on October 28 [1986] been elected to the IBM board of directors." The letter of October 29 was forceful and true, but not enough to quell the speculation.

In November 1986, we spent considerable time with Krowe discussing minicomputer strategy. He was greyer than at our 1979 interviews (so were we), but his smarts, decisiveness, and commitment were still clearly intact. Yes, management had missed the impending downturn after the artificial order rush brought on by the previous year's expiring tax credit, but so did everyone else, he told us. It was at that point, Allen said, that he persuaded Akers to let him become the "lightning rod" for missing earlier growth projections. "John didn't deserve that burden [along] with his responsibility for guiding the entire corporation of 400,000 people." Krowe then took the low end of IBM's product line, without objection, from Jack Kuehler, the senior VP overseeing all of IBM's products. "Jack's product line went from Abraham to Zebra. Finally, he said, 'let's split it up.'" A close Kuehler lieutenant confirmed that "Jack was terribly overextended. His formal meeting schedule alone stretched from 7:00 a.m. to 7:00 p.m."

Krowe's take on the revenue shortfall differed from the press's traumatic perception. The bonanza years were exaggerated by high inflation, he explained: "Remove inflation, and our real growth was 8 percent during the period. And at current inflation rates, our growth rate is about 6.5 percent now." More troublesome, in Krowe's opinion, were the declining rates of MIPS shipments, doubly painful as competition forced down prices. "For fifteen years, we shipped 40 percent more MIPS every year [yielding 20 percent annual revenue growth after 20 percent price/performance gains]. Then, in 1985, growth dropped to 36 percent and, in 1986, to 32 percent"—but those declines excluded gains elsewhere. Over the previous five years, Krowe said, IBM had shipped twice the capacity in PCs as in every other product in its history.

We were unsettled by the PC remark from the usually straightforward Krowe. PC capacities were grossly inflated and at profit margins far below those commanded—and lost—in mainframes. And there was no way to reverse slowing mainframe growth without a significant reduction in IBM's assumptions about gross margins and price, something Akers knew but did nothing about.

A Revenue Problem?

The shadows were deepening, but there was still a bit of daylight left. The year 1987 began with a January *Fortune* cover story by Carol Loomis, a first-rate business journalist, that opened with a bit of hopeful chat from the CEO: "'There have been only six chief executives of IBM,' noted John F. Akers, the sixth. 'I hope that when my tour is over, people will look back and say, he deserved to be among them.' Ahead are eight years to make it; behind are the two worst years ever to greet a new IBM chief executive. Already battle-scarred, Akers must still win a war if he is to earn the place in history he covets."

Then came a clearheaded view of the situation. "IBM, to quote the short, unsweet summary of one of its top executives, has 'a revenue problem'—too few dollars coming in because too few computers are going out. It also has a cost problem that is specially its own: an absolute unwillingness to lay off employees. These facts, simple yet enormous, have taken IBM's stock down by more than 20 percent since April, a period in which the market as a whole rose by about 4 percent. These facts have launched IBM on a wrenching campaign to cut what costs it can and to relocate the thousands of employees ...

"IBM's revenues rose hardly at all in 1986," Loomis continued, "making their worst showing in 40 years. Still they totaled around $50 billion. Profits were down in 1986 for the second year in a row, the first double dip since the 1930s, and were down a lot. But IBM probably still earned close to $5 billion, more than any other company in the world. Its 1986 return may be only 14 percent, a sharp slide from its recent returns of more than 20 percent. But 14 percent is better than most companies can claim. Blurted Akers with spirit, 'Many executives would love to swap their problems for the problems we have.'"

"Nonsense," Loomis should have countered. The company was clearly milking an old technology base and even older sales concepts. The stock was down, profits were down, and revenues were flat, while other parts of the industry were racing ahead. Instead, the writer remained remarkably deferential: "Akers, a decisive, non-bureaucratic executive ... says IBM got out of touch with its customers. It persisted in trying to sell them products when what they wanted was solutions— help in getting their thousands of computers to talk to each other, help in wringing both productivity gains and competitive advantage out of their investments in data-processing equipment."

Actually, IBM's most pressing problem wasn't selling solutions but cutting heads—and it wasn't happening. While two soft years had certainly gotten the attention of IBM management, attention hadn't yet turned to alarm, she observed: "All these financial maneuvers will help earnings. But the possibilities for really major surgery on costs are missing because of IBM's dedication to the concept called full employment, which for 45 years has cushioned the company work force.... Walton Burdick, chief of human resources at IBM, says he cannot imagine what it would take to make the company abandon the full-employment concept. 'Let's put it this way: It would take something far beyond what we've experienced in the past 45 years.'"

In fact, Akers had already begun downsizing the company but through a rich early-retirement package that attracted many of IBM's best performers. Our friend and liaison, Sam Albert, took the package and the opportunity to set up shop outside Armonk's walls as the premier "IBM watcher." Many others confirmed the observation made succinctly by *Wall Street Journal* reporter Paul Carroll: "Of the 10,000 people who took the severance packages, 8,000 were rated 'one.' There were just 22,000 people so rated in the U.S. workforce of 220,000 at the time. So Akers's program cleared out more than one-third of his best people in the United States."[1]

Allen Krowe offered us a more soothing spin: "We haven't resorted to pink slips like other companies. That approach permanently changes the way people feel about the company." But downsizing by any name is serious. "We took out $700 million in expenses in 1985, another $350 million in 1986, and a final $350 million was planned for 1987." Such actions punched a hole in old Tom Watson's full-employment policy, but they still weren't enough.

A year later, Krowe himself took early retirement to become the CFO at Texaco, eliciting another blizzard of ill-deserved press razzberries. Reuters described Krowe (September 29, 1988) as: "Widely seen as the victim of a shakeup at the computer company two years ago." The *Los Angeles Times* stated (September 28, 1988): "Krowe was widely blamed for pushing IBM to gear up for large revenue gains that never materialized." In a sense, that's right. After delivery delays for the 3033 in 1976 opened the door for Amdahl to fill unmet customer demand,

Cary determined that plant capacity should allow for an early burst of orders just after announcement, even if overcapacity resulted later in the product cycle. That couldn't be blamed on Krowe.

Despite the huff and puff, the global employee count of 373,000 for 1990 was only slightly less than the 404,000 reported in the *Fortune* piece three years earlier. IBM's financial image took a dead-cat bounce, from a 10 percent rise in revenues to $69 billion with $6 billion in profits, from its new mainframe family and the new RISC/Unix System 6000. But more fundamentally, the situation hadn't improved, warned *Business Horizons* in its year-end issue. Selling, general, and administrative expense (SG&A) swallowed up a tubby 34 percent of revenues versus 29 percent for the hardly lean mini makers and 25 percent for the workstation set, which the reporter correctly judged as the trend of the future. The asset base of $77.7 billion was so unproductive that IBM drew just 81 cents in revenue per dollar of capital, and revenue per person badly lagged the newer players.

On the brighter side, the article credited IBM with scale, worldwide presence, and a top credit rating. Incredibly, the author judged the probability of 2000 revenues topping $110 billion at 90 percent, giving even odds on their reaching $170 billion. Both projections were impossibly airy, especially as industry prices and margins eroded to the low levels commanded by commodities. As the *Business Horizons* observer had implied in the first place, the next years would be bloody, with IBM growth lagging the industry, including the equally troubled DEC (Table 17.1)

Table 17.1 Key Operating Revenues

	Revenue Growth 1988-92 (%)	Revenue per Employee 1990 (1000s)
Sun Micro	45.8%	$215
Compaq	40.3	370
Apple	19.6	437
Hewlett-Packard	16.1	144
Amdahl	12.3	262
Digital	7.6	104
IBM	5.5	185

Source: Company Financials

New People and Priorities

George Conrades, once considered a candidate to succeed Akers, was hurried out the door and replaced in 1991 as senior vice president for North American sales by Bob LaBant, a less-seasoned executive but a better buddy to John Akers. Abandoning much-needed culture change for less time-consuming ax wielding, Bob decimated the field organization amid a wider downsizing that lopped off 20 percent of IBM's employees, leaving the head count at 301,000. Not all was the result of firings. A significant reduction was achieved by spinning off the printer business in what many observers saw as a harbinger of survival. But, no doubt, the full-employment concept had been permanently skewered.

LaBant was triumphant when we visited late in the year. The field force was 17 percent lighter, and middle management had lost 31 percent of its members, with more rollbacks planned. Bob claimed to have expanded his direct reports to twenty-one as against the traditional three or four, while the general manager of the New Jersey trading area now had seventeen. Soon, management would represent just 7 percent of the field population, down from 11 percent overseeing a much larger force previously. Bottom line: IBM's SG&A expense had shrunk to 21.4 percent of revenue from 26 percent, with 20 percent on the horizon. Soon, a rejuvenated Old Blue could spin around the dance floor with a much younger crowd.

But the PC competitors weren't standing still, having cut their sales-cost benchmark well below 20 percent of revenues. Eckhard Pfeiffer replaced Compaq's founder and CEO Rod Canion in 1991 and proceeded to drive the company from its self-styled "BMW" image toward a commodity business. Factories were consolidated and closed, reducing fixed-asset value even as the number of manufactured units tripled. Sales costs were driven below 15 percent of revenues. (A decade later, Michael Dell would upend the model again, driving sales costs toward 5 percent on a wholly commoditized product line.)

In truth, IBM simply couldn't cut its costs quickly enough to keep pace with the new-breed Unix vendors, let alone the personal computer makers. Management's brave efforts were far too late to yield a sustainable or profitable result. "Finally, the field force may be positioned for a turnaround," we wrote. "An earlier start was stalled because Akers stonewalled his managers' repeated warnings of the coming shift in product mix and margins."

By now, we opined, Akers should have zeroed in on four priorities:

- Keeping forward momentum in mainframes by investing in the technology necessary to remain remotely price competitive against the new servers;
- Rationalizing the minicomputer business into two or three offerings;
- Cutting operating expenses in line with the new industry business model;
- Boosting IBM's already enviable position in personal computer hardware.

Instead, Akers focused IBM's best talent on the Japanese threat (already beaten) and Microsoft (probably unbeatable), leaving the other priorities marinating in passivity while naming second-raters to leadership positions. He had forced out top people like George Conrades and Mike Armstrong, who could have provided the motive force for decisive action.

IBM announced its first quarterly loss in October 1992, and the board of directors cut Akers's salary by 40 percent, leaving him with $2 million. Nothing improved. By year-end, the buzzards were circling.

At our last lunch with Jack Kuehler, he acknowledged that the mainframe business was in free fall, chopping his hand in a steep downward plane to illustrate the trajectory. It was late autumn, and halfhearted snow spackled the grounds outside Armonk. The gloom was pervasive.

Outside the glass wall of the small, private dining room where we three lunched, a man stood silently staring into the distance. A guard, I supposed, wondering at what I perceived to be a new level of paranoia at IBM. Actually, the man was a smoker driven outdoors by the new government policy prohibiting the use of tobacco in office buildings. It seemed a very long time since we'd interviewed the brilliant Dr. Bertram, as he puffed triumphantly on his large cigar from behind his desk. Black Jack had died a year earlier, following a five-year illness.

Mainframe revenues were down a bone-rattling 10 percent as the result of both horrendous near-term economic conditions (particularly in Europe) and savage price wars. A robust secondhand market helped to expand excess capacity by several notches, inflated still more by a wave of customer data-center consolidations that also curbed demand to some degree. But it was the high-end minicomputer companies (notably HP) that took the biggest bite out of mainframe sales, taking advantage of their less expensive technologies and lower gross margins to initiate "rightsizing" programs aimed at moving customer applications away from the IBM, Amdahl, and Hitachi behemoths.

When Kuehler stood to leave, he appeared blearily diminished from our previous meetings. "Say a prayer for us," he asked before bolting from the room, leaving Naomi and me alone with the empty plates and dreggy coffee cups.

Jack had told us that the only bright spot for IBM was the new AS/400 minicomputer. But it wouldn't be enough. Akers's departure was imminent, and tens of thousands of employees would follow.

Akers Exits, and the Search Begins

That year's loss hit $8 billion, a whopper. As Lou Gerstner would later recount from his first day at IBM: "[Vice Chairman Paul Rizzo] said that mainframe revenue had dropped from $13 billion in 1990 to a projection of less than $7 billion in 1993, and that if it did not level off in the next year or so, all would be lost."[2]

By the beginning of 1993, IBM shares had lost an estimated $77 billion of their value since the peak in 1987. John Akers resigned at the insistence of IBM's directors after a lengthy board meeting, on January 26. After exiting Armonk, Akers would join Frank Lorenzo as a director in Lorenzo's Continental Airlines. Following the disgraced Akers out the door was Frank Metz, the CFO widely described as "the nicest guy going," but an executive not really a match for IBM's vastness and complexity. Bob LaBant, who had replaced George Conrades, also joined the exodus.

The search committee was headed by Jim Burke, former CEO of Johnson & Johnson and a role model for crisis management after an anonymous nutcase injected poison into Tylenol capsules. Most of the CEO candidates discussed in the press were fairly obvious: Larry Bossidy of Allied Signal (later Honeywell); Jack Welch of GE; Charles Exley, retired legend from NCR; and Ross Perot, founder of EDS and a third-party presidential candidate. Insiders named included Jimmy Cannavino, who had headed IBM's PC efforts.

Outside observers thought the company beyond redemption. As the *Los Angeles Times* reported on February 28, 1993: "'Some who might be capable of doing the job of CEO won't want it,' said former IBM exec Kenneth Bosomworth, president of International Resource Development. 'The opinion of many of IBM's competitors is that the company is in much worse shape than the board thinks.' Today nobody will be able to turn around the $65 billion company," continued the article. "Shares may skid to $15."

One of the more ironic episodes was Jim Burke's approach to John Sculley, then CEO of Apple Computer. Burke had met Sculley when John was at PepsiCo and had been impressed by his consumer-marketing skills. Another member of the search committee knew Sculley from their days at Brown University, and a third was a neighbor of Sculley in one of New York's more golden suburbs.

For a time, it appeared Sculley was the lead contender, according to insiders we talked to. Fortunately for IBM, Sculley made the bizarre demand that his entire management team be brought over to IBM. But apart from its first-rate CFO (which IBM obviously needed), Apple's management team was largely dysfunctional. The thought of this crew managing a company of IBM's scale and complexity was ludicrous. The IBM board couldn't stomach such an outrageous proposal, and the Sculley nomination died. The irony heightened when, shortly thereafter, Sculley himself was sent packing by the one-product Apple.

Also, in January 1993, *Fortune*'s Carol Loomis revisited the CEO she'd admired as "decisive" six years earlier. Now, she reported, "John Akers took the graceful, even heroic way out by saying he would move on; thereby opening the way for the radical change in the company's leadership the company needs. Akers though, really had no choice. At this point, the board would not have let him stay. He had lost his constituencies, among them IBM's shareholders, who had watched $77 billion in market value disappear since the top in 1987 ... This first burning question about IBM today is who will be selected—who indeed can be persuaded—to take on the monumental job of running the company? The second question: Can the new boss unshroud the good things about IBM and bury the bad?"

Gerstner Rights a Sinking Ship

On March 23, the board announced the selection of Lou Gerstner as Chairman and CEO.

Gerstner had previously been CEO of Nabisco Brands, president of American Express, and a director at McKinsey & Company. In the weeks after his arrival, he calmly drew input from many industry figures, including Naomi and me. We met in IBM's New York office on 57th Street, within walking distance of our own offices on 61st Street. When we met Lou Gerstner, he struck us as round but not fat, quite compact, and very quick. He seemed open to pursue almost any idea, peppering his guests with a steady, low-key chain of questions.

Afterward, Naomi asked what I thought of IBM's newest CEO. To my surprise, even after conducting hundreds of management interviews, I realized I had no impression at all. "That's because he was interviewing and learning from you," explained my clever wife. "And he's a damn good interviewer."

At first, Gerstner, the outsider, was greeted with a cacophonous chorus of suspicion, criticism, and advice from the press and the investment community. The consensus faddishly screamed for a breakup, as fervently espoused by *Wall Street Journal* reporter Paul Carroll, who hung his argument on Gerstner's lack of IT savvy. Wrote Carroll: "The broad outlines of Akers' decentralization made enough sense that Gerstner will probably try to continue it, especially because Burke, the head of the search committee, believes so strongly in decentralizing.... But Gerstner has no particular experience in the computer industry ... So Gerstner will be able to apply only management consulting dogma to IBM. His choice by the board indicates that it doesn't think there's any grand vision out there that could revitalize IBM the way the movement into computers did in the 1950s, the way the 360 mainframe family did in the 1960s, and the way the PC did briefly in the early 1980s. Without that grand vision and without a breakthrough product, Gerstner will just be fiddling."[3]

Fortune's Carol Loomis had already set the agenda in January with her all-caps cry to "SET THE BUSINESSES FREE." The melodrama didn't end there. "The sum of the parts of IBM is greater than the whole," Loomis wrote. "Management must immediately identify its most self-sustaining businesses and give them full autonomy, selling off chunks in many cases. Vertical integration worked well in the mainframe era but that's history. Today, corporate alliances constantly shift and evolve.... A single sales organization handles the whole range of products from $99 PC software to $20 million mainframes."

The Economist (March 1993) was no more supportive of an intact IBM. "As PCs become cheaper, more powerful, and easier to link into networks, the number of customers prepared to buy from IBM will dwindle. Indeed, IBM's various businesses would be much stronger competitors if they were not hamstrung either by Big Blue's still-vast corporate overheads, or by the need not to tread on other divisions' toes. It may take a few more quarters of leaping losses to convince Mr. Gerstner of the need to break up IBM. Shareholders, their investment at an 18-year low, and their dividend halved for the second time this year, might wish that their axeman would turn visionary overnight."

All this was outrageously presumptuous and ridiculous in business terms. What the pundits missed in assessing Gerstner's experience level was his almost-intuitive grasp of the core issues, his ability to listen—often to many conflicting voices—and his decisiveness. On the subject of dismemberment, we knew from talking to enterprise CIOs that large companies wanted to buy IT systems from one, or at most two, sales reps, not individual boxes and components from many. Holding the company together was one of the two recommendations we emphasized to Gerstner the afternoon we met. The other was to aggressively apply merchant technology and pricing to mainframes.

Gerstner asked whether IBM could build a "services" business. We thought that would take time, based on our bleak assessment of IBM's internal skills. Even five years after George Conrades's assurances, the real talent remained in the labs, not the field force. And most visitors to the IBM data centers came away believing they were hopelessly overstaffed. As a result, we told Gerstner he would have to engineer a widespread overhaul before IBM would be credible as a service provider. Lou proved us wrong by correcting the staffing problems and replacing castoffs from the sales force with true professionals. Ultimately, IBM would build the world's largest computer-service business.

The new chief opted to hold IBM together. Neither an easy nor an obvious decision, Gerstner explained himself when he wrote in his autobiography: "Given IBM's scale and broad-based capabilities, and the trajectories of information technology, it would have been insane to destroy its unique competitive advantage and turn IBM into a group of individual component suppliers—more minnows in an ocean.... So keeping IBM together was the first strategic decision, and, I believe, the most important decision I ever made—not just at IBM but in my entire business career."[4]

Over a span of several years, Gerstner also reshaped the company, selling off certain product lines in which IBM was no longer competitive, while buying others to bolster its integrated offering. The communications-controller business was sold to Cisco, the disk hardware business to Hitachi. The PC business became relatively inconsequential (and perennially unprofitable) and was sold to the Chinese in 2005. In that sense, the pundits were partly right in calling for spinning off parts of the company. But IBM Global Services now accounts for half of total revenues, while software ranks second only to Microsoft. Both software and services are a strong pull for IBM offerings in mainframes, AS/400, Unix, and Linux. Meanwhile, IBM's semiconductor activities produce world-class microprocessors, which lead the industry in high-end parallel processing and simultaneously dominate the low-end game box sector.

Another major challenge was bringing IBM's fat margin cost structure in line with the prevailing business model. "Keep slashing costs," *Fortune*'s Loomis had warned in January, recommending that IBM go beyond firing employees to write off obsolescent plants and equipment. She followed up with another argument for breakup: "If a consistently profitable IBM is to emerge, it will be not only broken up into more competitive pieces but also smaller overall. In fact, IBM may be genuinely unmanageable at its present scale. Too many disparate and competing businesses contend for capital and top management's time."

Bunk! There were other, more effective organizational options to relieving IBM's choking complexity, as the new CEO would demonstrate. Clearly, IBM's cost structure had to be revamped and assets sold. The numbers looked awful in Gerstner's first four months, as mainframe revenue dropped 43 percent, dragging down gross margins by more than 10 points, to 39.5 percent from 50 percent.

He later wrote: "Our competitors were spending 31 cents to produce a dollar of revenue, we were spending 42 cents for the same end. So we made the decision to launch a massive program of expense reduction—$8.9 billion in total. Unfortunately, this necessitated, among other things, reducing our employment by 35,000 people, in addition to the 45,000 people whom John Akers had already laid off in 1992. That meant additional pain for everyone, but this was a matter of survival, not choice."[5]

Labs were consolidated, and unproductive assets were sold to raise cash, starting with the Federal Systems division, a Watson-era consultancy. But contrary to press verdicts, IBM's investments in mainframes were hardly obsolete. New fabrication equipment was needed for the new chip technology, but asset life could be extended in packaging, design automation, and development processes.

Under Gerstner's guidance, results improved rapidly. In the next fiscal year (1994), IBM achieved a 7.7 percent operating margin, compared to a negative margin in tumultuous 1993. Sales and administrative costs had been slashed from 30 percent to 25 percent of total revenues, while R&D narrowed from 9.2 percent to 6.8 percent. Gerstner had moved in the opposite direction from the pundits' strident recommendations—eschewing dismemberment for consolidation and centralization.

By the time we visited that year, all software except for operating systems reported to SVP John Thompson, all processors (except PCs) with their operating systems to SVP Nick Donofrio, and all components plus storage and networking hardware to SVP Peter Toole. Gerstner wrote that his arrangement mirrored the successful organization of Watson Jr. Fortunately, that wasn't wholly accurate since operating systems remained with their hardware processors, not bottled up under a software czar. In addition, hardware was split into PCs, processors, and peripherals, where each could face off against external competitors rather than trying to syncopate a hopelessly vulnerable pattern of product announcements (as had occurred after the System/360 was introduced).

The mainframe was under continued attack from critics who insisted that customers would prefer networks of microprocessors. A nice thought, but hopelessly unrealistic at the time. In our conversation with Gerstner, we expressed our belief that mainframes would be needed for many years, notably in insurance, banking, transportation, and complex manufacturing (for parts databases). But survival required new chip technologies and drastic price cuts, we told him.

Gerstner rightly ignored press judgments about the calcified state of IBM management. True, breaking down the culture of endless formal presentations and delayed decision-making became a focus of the new CEO. He also helped move IBM in a different direction by bringing in several excellent outsiders—executives such as Bruce Harrell (senior vice president for strategy) and a team of top staffers he'd carried to Nabisco from American Express. But Gerstner astutely retained the hidden heroes of the Akers tenure, notably the aforementioned Nick Donofrio and John Thompson, along with the brainy Irving Wladawsky-Berger, who had pushed new mainframe technology, Denny Welsh, who initiated the rise of IBM Global Services, and Sam Palmisano, who would take over Welsh's job, eventually succeeding Gerstner as CEO.

To make way for the new regime, several senior executives left. Some took big jobs elsewhere; others were mainly bureaucrats and politicos.

The Akers Legacy from a Distance

Perhaps the biggest mistake that can be laid on the shoulders of John Akers was his failure to force the changes in mainframe pricing and technology that his successor embraced to save the business. Akers paid too little attention to midrange rationalization. Instead, he let himself and the company become distracted by the PC software business. He also delayed, until his tenure was winding down, the cost reductions demanded by the new business model—and even when he did make cuts, they were too shallow.

Gerstner's own account of his meeting with his predecessor carries a strong subliminal whiff of Akers's passivity and detachment. "We were as comfortable as two people could be under the circumstances. We talked mostly about people. He was surprisingly candid about, and critical of, many of his direct reports. In reviewing my notes from the meeting, I guess I subsequently agreed with 75 percent of his appraisals. What struck me was how he could be so critical but still keep some of these executives …

"John was preoccupied that day with IBM's microelectronics business. He said the basic research unit was not affordable and needed to be downsized. He was quite concerned about IBM's software business, mainframe business, and mid-range products. As I look back at my notes, it is clear he understood most, if not all, of the business issues we tackled over the ensuing years. What's striking from my notes is the absence of any mention of culture, teamwork, customers, or leadership—the elements that turned out to be the toughest challenges at IBM ..."[6]

Why hadn't Akers replaced his subpar executives, especially when the company was clearly in trouble? And why cut microelectronics when that segment could provide a more price-competitive platform for the mainframe and was a promising business in its own right?

I think the answers lie partially in Akers's temperament and partially in the traditions of the company forged by continuous attacks from relentless competitors over two decades and three CEOs (Watson Jr., Cary, and Opel). While Akers was rising through the sales ranks, Armonk was waging multifront wars against leasing companies, peripheral makers, the Japanese, and the U.S. Justice Department. The Big Blue response had been ferocious and direct confrontation, with a willingness to do whatever it took to secure victory. Hundreds of millions of dollars were spent to hold onto large mainframe customers, and the organization itself was upended to give Armonk's battlefield commanders more maneuvering room. From these wars and organizational restructurings came both victories and a Spartan mind-set that was not always positive and that inhibited IBM throughout the Akers years.

Gerstner pinpointed the same tendency in his description of the "religious war" with Microsoft: "It was draining tens of millions of dollars, absorbing huge chunks of senior management's time, and making a mockery of our image. And in the finest IBM fashion, we were going to fight to the bitter end."[7] There had been many previous fights to the bitter end, and IBM had generally won. But John Akers engaged the corporation in a PC war fought in the consumer sector, where IBM had zero experience and competence.

Chapter 18

SQUANDERED COMPETITIVE ADVANTAGE:

IBM Mainframes and Minicomputers

Competitive advantage can be squandered by executive indecision in a surprisingly short time. A delayed decision can be far worse than a mediocre decision. In IBM's case, the delays and indecision involved its mainstream product lines in mainframes and minicomputers. In both cases, Akers's delays lost the company a significant share of the computing market that it never recovered. In mainframes, the delays involved implementing a new technology. In minicomputers, it was the five years required to consolidate the five different minicomputer families. Of course, the industry was buffeted by the standardization of operating systems and the commoditization of hardware prices. But a CEO like Tom Watson, Frank Cary, and Lou Gerstner would have weathered the blow, leaving the company in far better shape than did John Akers. In the end, his chairmanship demonstrates the destructive power of the weak or misguided CEO better than almost any other case. That IBM survived at all was more a function of size than management.

Akers became head of the midrange product group in 1981, when the need to consolidate was clear to everyone including himself. This was also the year IBM introduced its blockbuster 3081 model, with its epic technological breakthroughs in circuit density, ceramic packaging, engineering automation, and testing. What was needed for the future was a continuation of the technology track set by Black Jack Bertram. Instead, IBM introduced the lackluster 3090. Well-orchestrated price/performance improvements and uncertainty over the expiration of the tax credit created a mainframe sellout. Nevertheless, we wrote worriedly: "The Armonkishers are midway through a ten-year base technology, not a dawning as was true [last time]."

As it turned out, IBM's enormous investments of the late 1970s projected a ten-year payback. So over five years, the 3090's price/performance merely doubled. Seventy percent of the improvement came from clever circuit design rather than enhanced chip technology. Manufacturing processes were more automated but not significantly different from our previous visit to Fishkill five years earlier. All in all, turning out the new 3090 model "was a cakewalk in comparison to the previous 3081," admitted the assistant plant manager. We thought that pace dangerously complacent in view of the acceleration in IT technology. Indeed, IBM's previous advantage over the Japanese was sharply narrowed, if not totally lost. And its technology pace was substantially behind the new breed, such as Sun Microsystems.

An opportunity to regain some of the lost ground began to take shape when IBM invested $500 million in a new semiconductor facility to produce enough memory chips to avoid dependency on its Japanese rivals. "We realized [the chips] would soon be our life's blood," recalled Dr. Irving Wladawsky-Berger, the disarmingly pixyish genius who subsequently led IBM campaigns into e-commerce and open-source software (Linux). But memory-chip self-sufficiency proved unnecessary after the Japanese lost the business to the Koreans.

With the chip threat diminished by 1986, Dr. Wladawsky-Berger began suggesting that the new facility could begin the transition to a new technology that could radically reduce mainframe costs. Until then, the logic circuits used in mainframes had depended on expensive and exotic, high-powered, high-heat "bipolar" technology. But minicomputers and PCs used cheap, low-powered, low-heat technology—CMOS (pronounced "see moss") in IBM lingo, for "complementary metal-oxide semiconductor."

By 1988, the competitively sensitive idea of CMOS replacing bipolar chips in mainframes was discussed quite openly at a Research Board meeting. CMOS chips would eventually outperform bipolar technology since the extraordinary circuit-density trajectories projected by Moore's Law meant a computer could be built from many fewer chips (or even just one). In a nutshell, fewer chips meant shorter distances for the electrical pulse to travel and faster compute speeds. After that, several CMOS processors would be strapped together in parallel-processing arrangements for another huge boost in total mainframe performance. The challenge of wiring the processors together would be simplified by embedding the connections in the multilayer ceramic modules originally built to dissipate the heat of bipolar mainframes. "It's not as difficult as people think," insisted Dr. W-B in a nudge to the higher-ups; the first mainframes of the new order could make their debut in the early 1990s. So, future mainframe advances, to update Captain Hopper's prediction, would come from more but smaller oxen.

Akers wasn't nudged. In 1990, IBM introduced yet another bipolar mainframe, the Enterprise System 9000, in its self-proclaimed "largest announcement in twenty-five years." But IBM was falling behind both Hitachi and Fujitsu-supplied Amdahl. By then, both Japanese competitors held big leads in bipolar chip-circuit density, while IBM clung to its ten-year-old advantage in stuffing and stacking circuit boards—though Fujitsu was catching up there, too. As one indicator, we surmised that Fujitsu-supplied Amdahl's internal cycle times were 20 percent faster than IBM's. And Fujitsu waved another battle pennant by building mainframes with just one circuit board per processor, compared to six for IBM.

Cloudy with Showers in Japan

That year we returned to Japan, its economic bubble deflated and, coincidentally, the prospects of the Japan Inc. computer industry beginning to wobble. The Nikkei stock index had tumbled from its peak of 38,000 to 24,000 and was falling still, taking with it the cheap capital that had powered earlier technology investment. The April 14, 1990, *Japan Economic Journal* (*JEJ*) bluntly stated: "The miracle of insanely cheap capital in Japan is over. For the first time, Japanese companies will be paying the global cost of capital."

The demographics produced by Japan's low birthrate were another constraint. "Japanese companies recruiting prospective employees from next year's crop of university graduates are already under pressure," reported the *JEJ*. "The talent sweepstakes is unquestionably a seller's market in which jobs outnumber takers by a margin of three to one. The majority of Japanese firms still target only males, some even going to such lengths as adorning their brochures with photos of beautiful women in revealing bathing suits or even shots of their women employees. Others stress an easygoing office atmosphere."

Over an elegant lunch at the Hotel Okura, a Hitachi senior vice president suggested that "perhaps Japan could recruit immigrants ... so long as they didn't bring along a crime problem."

Exacerbating the shortage of tech workers was the Japanese young people's choice of academic majors and careers. The percentage of graduating engineers entering manufacturing had fallen from 65 percent in 1965 to under 50 percent by 1990, as more young people turned to financial services, where they could earn 30 percent more than they could in engineering. Most recent computer-science graduates were still hardware engineers, not computer scientists interested in programming. The shortage of programming talent reflected a lingering cultural misconception that more value would come from hardware than from software.

We spent two days each with IBM's archrivals, Hitachi and Fujitsu. Both knew international markets were turning from mainframes to other processing platforms, especially cheaper UNIX servers. That made the IBM plug-compatible market less attractive and perhaps even economically unsustainable. Yet both continued to research ever-higher-powered/higher-heat circuit materials and processes like gallium arsenide and Josephson junction (which IBM had, by this time, abandoned). Neither gave a hint of moving to ultra-high levels of circuit integration using the cheaper CMOS technology or to parallel processing for commercial computing.

At Hitachi, Dr. Takeo Miura, the wise head of its computer division, generally confirmed the weakening international prospects for mainframes and proprietary operating systems. "Over the last two years," Miura said, "the computer business in Japan has changed less dramatically than in Europe and North America, where most mainframers are struggling, as are the minicomputer suppliers who sustained themselves too long with a captive audience dependent on their proprietary operating systems." Exactly right! But even if home-market revenues looked secure, Japan's exports were weakening amid rising R&D demands in circuitry, packaging, and design automation. Also rising were the costs of maintaining Hitachi's own operating system over a relatively small customer base.

"Going to Unix represents one of the four most critical decisions we've made in the computer business," Dr. Miura went on, ranking it just ahead of Hitachi's decision to enter the overseas marketing venture with Itel and, later, National Semiconductor. But he had no illusions about Unix, citing its weaknesses in security, data integrity, and true portability, and noting its lack of Japanese applications outside health care and computer-aided design. Hitachi's main hope was to form an alliance in which HP would provide RISC architecture and market savvy. That idea never went anywhere; HP complained about the intolerably slow pace of decision-making in Tokyo, and Tokyo complained about HP's stinginess with its know-how.

Fujitsu Goes Extraterritorial

Over at Fujitsu, the skirmishing with IBM continued, though, fortunately, Naomi and I were now treated as Swiss neutrals. Since our first awkward meeting with the International Operations executive Naruto-san, we'd spent two days on a train with him and Amdahl CEO Jack Lewis visiting Fujitsu's excellent plants in northern Japan. He was, as he had once implied to us, indeed a farmer; he spoke of his work planting trees on his small farm for the eventual enjoyment of his son. At Fujitsu, he was now responsible for acquiring other computer companies and growing the parent into a behemoth of $100 billion "as a downside possibility," with $150 billion a welcome upside. His target date was 1997.

At that point in 1990, Fujitsu had acquired ICL, England's doddering mainframe company, for a heady $1.5 billion. But Amdahl, he assured us, would remain independent. And Fujitsu would be the pioneer in what we call today the "global enterprise": "We won't continue the 'single crystal' model, which allowed us to grow to $20 billion ... Fujitsu will have no defined nationality, just the nationality of all its companies ... We are ET [extra territorial]," he crowed. Unfortunately, buying up struggling computer companies from a now-dead era was no way to build an international business. But no matter, Naruta was a clever man, and he came to trust us, especially after Naomi was named as an "independent consultant" advising the arbitrators on both sides of the Fujitsu/IBM litigation over intellectual property used in operating systems. "The famous Naomi-san" is how

Naruto introduced her to the CEO at the opening of a Fujitsu facility in California some years later.

Actually, the Fujitsu/IBM litigation was an anachronism. The international competition for IBM-compatible mainframes was drawing to a close. A Hitachi executive vice president told us that the Ministry of International Trade and Industry (MITI) had asked privately if either Hitachi or Fujitsu would consider withdrawing from the mainframe market and consolidating around the survivor. That didn't happen, though the race in plug-compatible mainframes proved frustrating and ultimately self-defeating for the Japanese.

During that year's visit, a senior Fujitsu executive responded in an uncharacteristically blunt fashion to our question about the ferocious competition with IBM over plug-compatible mainframes: "We were like two giants fighting to the death on an ice floe without noticing the ice floe was melting." The fight distracted Fujitsu, causing it to miss the fleeting opportunity to become a top international player in the computer hardware business, despite the acquisition strategy. Only IBM survived in mainframes, because of its world-beating innovations in circuitry and software.

Naruto doubtless saw this trend, musing at the beginning of a meeting with us: "In the future, computer companies won't be able to make money on hardware. And they can't make money on 'open' systems like Unix." But Fujitsu didn't act on this insight.

Equally aware that competition was shifting from compatibles to commodities was IBM's mainframe-division president, Bernard Puckett, a clever man but without Jack Bertram's intensity or engineering brilliance. "For me," Puckett told us, "the turnaround began two years ago, when I announced publicly that our competitors weren't only the other mainframers and the Japanese, but [high-end Unix servers] like Sun, Sequent, etc. My people knew it already, of course, but hearing that the boss was willing to confront the new breed of servers was an important acknowledgement."

There was no indication of a similar acknowledgment from Akers, unfortunately.

The only effective competitive response would have been an immediate reduction in prices and a parallel effort to implement cheaper CMOS technology as soon as possible, Puckett reckoned. That would have profound consequences for IBM's plug-compatible competitors. "If hardware revenue is going to shrink, [Amdahl and the others] had better be developing more robust operating systems of their own to compete against our MVS [multiple virtual storage] operating system," he said. Otherwise, they'd be left with sharply shrinking hardware margins, freeing IBM to profit from its operating system, very much like Microsoft. Finally!

The first manifestations of the new parallel architecture were slated to appear somewhere around 1993, starting with machines targeted at scientific computing using AIX (the IBM variety of Unix). But, like Ken Olsen, Puckett warned us not to expect applications to move freely from one brand of Unix to another. "Open systems do not mean standard systems to a computer company," he declared. Vendors will insist on developing operating systems that best use their idiosyncratic hardware architectures. Applications can't be moved from IBM to Sun or Hewlett-Packard without modification, he insisted, and "any other claim is pure pablum."

As for mainframes, the first parallel systems would be narrowly targeted at retrieving data from huge data files, only later moving to processing commercial transactions like product orders and financial payments. For this market, three hundred to five hundred microprocessors using mainframe architecture would be strung together, explained Puckett. Though Puckett was headed in the right direction, many of the details he described never came to pass.

When the bottom fell out of the mainframe business in 1992, Puckett's two-year-old assessment about the real competition looked prescient. So what became of the answer? Where were the long-promised IBM mainframes using low-cost circuitry to beat back the aggressive minicomputer companies? Later, we learned that CEO Akers had sidelined the effort. Perhaps he or his advisors were persuaded that the mainframe market would move in IBM's favor even without a major investment in new technology, given the lack of discernible motion by the Japanese. Or perhaps he couldn't stomach the billion-dollar investment in fabrication equipment needed to move from bipolar technology to CMOS, given his commitment to personal computers.

IBM Rewrites the Rules of the Game

When our conversation the following year with new CEO Lou Gerstner turned to mainframes, we made two points. First, mainframes were not dead, pundit gloom notwithstanding. A substantial customer constituency would need the big hummers for decades. Or at least until mountains of applications code could be converted. Second, the best defense against the new Unix boxes were cheaper CMOS and savage price cuts.

Gerstner obviously heard the same advice from many quarters, including from his brother Dick, then an IBM vice president. In his autobiography, Lou recounted making the "dramatic price reduction" on mainframes and deciding to "reaffirm" the decision to move from bipolar to CMOS. "I am convinced that had we not made the decision to go with CMOS, we'd have been out of the mainframe business by 1997. In fact, the point has been proven more or less by what happened to our principal competitor at the time, Hitachi. It continued development of bigger and bigger bipolar systems, but that technology eventually ran out of gas and Hitachi is no longer in this business ..."[1]

Two years later, the new mainframe technology was clearly in evidence. IBM's plug-compatible competitors were essentially dead. Nick Donofrio, now the senior VP of the new server group, told us CMOS mainframes in ten-way couplings would reach a heretofore unimagined 800 MIPS by 1997. More important was the price. From $100,000 per MIPS a few years earlier, the price would be sawed down to $10,000, depending on software; a few years later, the price actually fell below $5,000. Bipolar was over, continued Donofrio. The last bipolar mainframes would top out at 50 MIPS; bipolar's market share would fall to just 20 percent by 1997.

Over at Amdahl, the atmosphere was delusional. The capable and candid Jack Lewis had retired; the new CEO was Joe Zempke, his longtime protégé and a former college basketball star. Joe had a standard shtick about aspiring to be a professional player until he jumped for a ball against former New York Knick Dave DeBusschere, who knocked him out cold. Like John Akers, Joe was a nice guy, considered promising in good times but simply inadequate to head a troubled company against withering competition.

Mainframe prices were in a squeeze, acknowledged Joe. With Amdahl's 1993 losses mirroring IBM's, the company cut its staff by one-third, to 5,600 people. Sales and service people now made up 60 percent of the workforce, while the product-development and manufacturing staff had shrunk to 30 percent from 50 percent. Whether the cuts signaled a greater dependence on 54 percent-owner Fujitsu or a gradual exit from the mainframe business wasn't clear.

Fujitsu, still Amdahl's chip supplier, was caught flat-footed by IBM's sudden switch to CMOS technology from bipolar and would continue on the old path for another generation. Not a problem, insisted the Amdahl mainframe product manager gamely but unconvincingly. Claiming that prices were "stabilizing" at between $14,000 and $20,000 per MIPS, he asserted that "CMOS won't have as much impact on mainframe prices as IBM says." Meanwhile, Amdahl R&D spending was in free fall, sliding from 23 percent of revenues to 13 percent, and then to 8 percent. Even the stingy Unix-server crowd spent a larger percentage of revenues on R&D. "If revenue can't fund R&D, we can't do it," warned the product manager.

For the first time in their twenty-year competition, Amdahl mainframe projections lagged behind IBM's. Total capacity would be 400 MIPS, versus 500 for IBM, by 1997, and 640 versus 800 by 1998. And support for the latest MVS upgrades would lag even further behind IBM. Ironically, Amdahl lawyers had finally won carefully constricted access to IBM software documentation several years earlier. But Amdahl's engineers now judged the documentation "too sloppy and inaccurate to provide a solid basis for new product design," we were told.

The company was desperately trying to change its product mix in the hope/fear that mainframes would represent barely one-third of total revenues by 1997, just two years away. The rest would be generated by Unix servers (perhaps on Sun's SPARC microprocessor), consulting services, and various mainframe software add-ons. A disk business previously projected to provide 25 percent of Amdahl's total revenues was now problematic and would soon be discontinued. Amdahl's new Antares software tool intrigued us, because large and complex programs could be generated using just a few programming instructions. But large customers balked, unwilling to get locked into a tool this powerful from a potentially dicey supplier. So another star slipped below the horizon.

Zempke was subsequently replaced as CEO by the head of Amdahl's consulting business—now the only remaining revenue source other than reselling Fujitsu boxes. Amdahl's stock price continued to sink until 1977, when Fujitsu bought the remaining shares and erased "Amdahl" from the subsidiary's name. The "silicon samurai" had been on the ropes since the beginning of the mainframe decline. It couldn't extend its export business as everyone expected in the mid-1980s; in fact, exports actually shrank, from 30 percent of revenues in 1985 to 24 percent in fiscal 2004.

Yet hope never disappeared: "It will not be enough to just (focus) on Japan; we will also have to make our presence known abroad," said Fujitsu's corporate VP for servers in 2005. Nevertheless, the U.S. business had shrunk, and Europe had fared not much better. In fact, the company overall had not been especially profitable. After monumental bloodletting in fiscal 2002 and 2003 and a small profit in 2004, the cumulative results over the previous fifteen years added up to a $1 billion loss on $541 billion of revenue.

Japanese competitor Hitachi remained a player in the U.S. mainframe market through the 1990s on the basis of its 80 MIPS Skyline processor, which customers bought even at a price premium because of its "headroom," that is, its capacity for applications growth. But that bright spot soon faded, and Hitachi eventually agreed to resell IBM mainframes. Gerstner summed up the era when he told us in a 1997 conversation, "When I retire, someone should give me a plaque with an inscription commemorating my decision to invest heavily in S/390, not milk it as I was advised." We agreed.

The Midrange Muddle

Inexplicably, Akers also failed to push vigorously for midrange consolidation, even though he had been directly responsible for the systems products division where all five minis were clustered. Certainly, he understood both the problem and the outlines of a solution. "It is amazing how very hard our people worked during the 1970s, but on the wrong things," he told us. "It's a Noah's Ark of product overlap ...

two of everything." Cary's injection of innovation was atrophying into a smelly kennel of old dogs.

But every dog has its friend, and the animal lovers at IBM were very powerful. Frank Cary and George Beitzel had midwifed the Series/1; Jack Kuehler personally managed the introduction of the 4300; and Allen Krowe pushed and protected the 8100. The System 34 was IBM's primary entry into the small-business market, while the System 38 represented its only redemption from the failed "Future System."

What was needed from Akers was strong and decisive action. Instead, IBM's minicomputer group meandered through five reorganizations, each one reorienting the company to a different, and ultimately toothless, minicomputer strategy. The winning strategy that finally emerged in 1988 could have been far more effective seven years earlier.

A month after the 1981 reorganization, we visited Mitch Watson, the new midrange czar. Mitch was the true-blue insider: a mathematics major as an undergrad, a sales representative and product planner at IBM, and a one-time administrative assistant to chairman and CEO, John Opel. Watson's plans and programs were, understandably, still in flux. His newest charge, the personal computer, was viewed as more of a mascot than either a threat or a priority.

The larger issue was convergence. How quickly could the five product families be merged or discontinued? Mitch offered four alternatives: (1) create an outer skin of compatibility by making applications programming languages like Cobol work identically everywhere, (2) mask the differences with a software layer of microcode while leaving the underlying hardware and software, (3) find each mini a distinct market niche, and (4) kill a couple. "That last would make some customers unhappy," allowed Watson. Yes, "but the only assurance we'll regain economies in manufacturing and field support is to simplify our product line," added the planning manager, Mike Maples.

The options were easier to imagine than execute. By a March 1982 presentation to the RB, Watson still lacked a clear statement of direction—to the annoyance of our CIO friends. Notably abusive were those who had bought scads of 8100s or Series/1s, both already drawing low whistles of imminent demise. Jack Kuehler's 4300 still drew praise, and the high-end System 38 for small-business computing remained as a harbinger of something better to come.

When we returned to IBM in November 1982, a wrenching reorganization had just split the midrange division into two peer units. "Systems," under superstar Bill Lowe (reassigned from IBM's excursion into PCs), had a two-year "center-field" horizon to rationalize the existing product line.

"Product development," under Frank Rich, another up-and-comer, had a four-year horizon for a new generation of midrange computers. Cutely code-named Fort Knox, the project's one thousand programmers, spread over three or four locations, were supposed to bring all the differing architectures together and create both a unifying hardware architecture and a new operating system.

Lowe's group was supposed to buy time for Rich's ambitious product introduction. Building a new hardware architecture and operating system simultaneously could geometrically increase the risk of delay (as when the System/360 operating system was delayed), or even kill the effort altogether. "Another instance of planning for completion in three years, but finally shipping the product in six," Rich quipped.

So, would the trick be to keep bailing water until a new boat could be built—or bailing water to postpone a painful decision? We were not won over.

Lowe's perspective on the minicomputer survivability ranking in 1982 was characteristically succinct. Only the System 34 had a clear future—as a low-end, small-business system. The old dogs, including the 8100, the Series/1, and the 4300 (DOS) operating system would get, at most, one more spin before being "stabilized," he told us. The System 38's long-term prospects were dim because it depended on the wrong chip architecture and couldn't be tightly coupled to other System 38s. Subsequent managers would give this lineup at least five more twirls over the next five years in a marathon of indecision.

View from the Top

At the December lunch with John Akers, closing out our interviews, the division chief gave us a commendably clearheaded assessment of the past decade's progress and limitations: "The decentralized organizational structure was brilliant for the early seventies, but it almost strangled us by the late seventies," he opened. "Apart from decentralization, there were other serious problems, some reaching back into our remotest corporate memory. Central to that memory was the centralized mainframe, on which IBM continued to focus long after the rest of the industry had turned to minicomputers and distributed computing [see Chapter 5].

"We lurched along with all our eggs in that one, big mainframe basket," he went on. "One of those lurches produced the 8100—a product that is only understandable when you consider our historic bias toward large computers [and their tightly connected network devices]. But the market for the 8100 turned out to be far smaller than when development began ... The Series/1 never really lived up to its promise, particularly among third-party software firms and the scientific community." The System 23 was simply chewed up by the PC, and typewriters, copiers, and underpowered word-processing machines were all herded off to the last milking shed.

Convergence wouldn't be easy, Akers admitted. "It might have been easier to cut off all but one current architecture and move to develop a single evolutionary stream. The problem is that three of our systems have real strengths, and not one is really right for the future. Nor does it make sense to declare four deaths during the uncertain business of bringing out another generation. The technicians now anticipate that with our unique, next-generation hardware, we could emulate [i.e., mimic through software] our own and even the competition's computers quite readily. But that will take time. We can't even rope in our own five architectures immediately. First, we'll capture a couple, and after eighteen months or so, a couple more." In fact, this mimicry never happened.

Wouldn't the old systems distract IBM from the more critical business of delivering a coherent and innovative product line, we wondered, especially against aggressive companies like HP and DEC? "Over one thousand engineers are already dedicated to our next system," snapped Akers. "Name me one competitor with more new product resources than that." We couldn't, but it didn't matter anyway.

As our lunch with Akers ended, he redirected our attention to something obviously more interesting than minicomputers, namely PCs—"what they are today and what they're going to become." John began by basically dismissing medium-scale processors, saying it was "debatable" whether they should be the critical focus of the day. "A coherent set of intelligent workstations is really a more important product introduction," he declared. "Personally, I think the intelligent workstation may be the most visible indication of IBM progress in small systems over the next year or two." Though we didn't understand it then, Akers had anointed the PC as IBM's primary strategic focus.

No End in Sight

A year later, much had changed—but not as expected. Akers had been promoted to president, leaving behind the midrange. Bad news: Fort Knox's one thousand programmers had been disbanded, the project falling to "scope creep," as the specifications attracted new requirements "like flypaper," we were told by Bill Rich in late 1983. In the end, the design process produced a technical monument that was probably unworkable, acknowledged Bill Lowe, who had since been "promoted" to the penalty-box role of architectural coordinator in the communications products division. "Given normal project schedules, the release of a single massive new operating system posed too many risks for a market as competitive as this one," Lowe said. He was vastly understating the problem. Today, it seems totally nutty to think that multiple teams in three locations with divided loyalties and ambitions could ever build a coherent system. And they didn't.

Also unconvincing was the basic objective, that is, one system that could absorb all five minicomputer families without requiring the customers to reprogram much or all of their applications. Instead, most of the old minis should have been killed rather than dragged screaming into a new system. Breaking the barriers to compatibility is how Tom Watson had proceeded with System/360 and how Ken Olsen won with VAX. Now consolidation came excruciatingly slowly from year to year:

- The 1983 survivability ranking held at System 36, Series/1, and 4300. System 36 would be offered as a complete working business system for customers with little internal data-processing experience ("like the Wang business"); Series/1 would be sold to customers capable of developing their own applications ("like the

DEC business"); and the 4300 would continue the mainframe 370 line "since we're IBM."

- The 1984 survivability ranking was still System 36, Series/1, and the 4300, with System 38 and 8100 receiving "reduced investment streams." System 36 remained the computer of choice for easy operation in small businesses and offices without full-time technicians. But it would not receive the necessary upgrade from 16 bit to 32 bit because "that would just gum up the works by dislocating customer applications." Sales shortfalls in the smallest 4300 were attributed simply to pricing. And at last, Unix would be supported within the next year or two, lest it provide the springboard for the next DEC or Wang. Two-year-old Sun wasn't mentioned

- The 1985 survivability ranking was System 36, enigmatic System 38, and Kuehler's own 4300 with the VM operating system. After the fourth reorganization, Kuehler was now responsible for setting the product agenda and establishing the newest survivability ranking: "I'm a 370 bigot," said Jack, admitting the obvious. Banished to the boondocks suddenly were the Series/1 along with the 8100. The three winners were now grouped into the systems product division. "The best way to make something happen is to create an appropriate organization and set of measurements," Kuehler continued. Wasn't this exactly the same line used in promising convergence under Mitch Watson five years earlier? We didn't ask. More to the point, the one thousand developers at the Rochester lab were back working on an upgrade for the System 36. Until it arrived, IBM customers seeking a new relational database were seriously advised to strap a small System 36 to a large System 38. "Pragmatic, if not elegant," pushed the IBM marketers. "Arrogant and myopic" was our response. Series/1 was tossed to the communications products division for hospice care, from whence it would be sold only as a network controller.

In a similar vein, the 4300's outdated DOS operating system was saved from extinction when the Böblingen lab refused to work on something new or disband. German labor law and the fear of adverse publicity in a major market doubtless underlay Armonk's indecision.

At Long Last, an End Point

The 1986 survivability ranking came to a truly amazing finish as Allen Krowe took over the minicomputer division. Suddenly ranked No. 1 was the System 38 follow-on, the AS/400, followed by the 4300 follow-on, the 9300, and a new Unix computer with a RISC processor. The last was targeted at the scientific and educational markets and third-party software developers. To counter the Sun/AT&T duo, IBM even joined the Corporation for Open Systems with DEC, HP, and others to cooperate on Unix. But Armonk was late to the game, given Sun's glittering success.

Two dogs were finally dispatched. The 8100's applications were to be accommodated by 9370/VM in two years. Too late! Opportunistic entrepreneurs were already offering conversion aids to DEC systems. As for the Series/1, its market had atrophied until 90 percent of its applications were owned by twenty-four customers; that dwindling segment could be hand-carried to the 9370. In the world of IBM minis, the race went to the slow. Meanwhile, the ancient and uncompetitive DOS remained enshrined in Böblingen.

Of course, the biggest surprise was the sudden flip-flop on System 36 and System 38. Now, the 36 was out and the 38 was in. The conclusion for 1986 was that System 36 would never match the capacity of DEC's minicomputer family. "When System 36 capacity expanded from fifteen to thirty simultaneous users per processor, customers just grumbled 'so what?'" recalled the product manager. "Even doubling and doubling again would have required years before we achieved radical capacity improvements." The decision not to expand System 36 to the more powerful 32 bit architecture in 1984 had probably been a mistake.

So, six wise men from the Rochester lab were locked away and tasked with the mission of deciding what to do next, "as though the future of their lab hung in the balance," recounted Steve Schwartz, the midrange division president. The result was a next-generation machine that blended the ease of use of the System 36 with the power and database of the System 38. Called the AS/400, it was introduced two years later, sold 65,000 boxes annually, and brought in $5 billion of revenues—a number that expanded to $15 billion when disks, communications devices, and maintenance were included. Suddenly, IBM's minicomputer market share was growing by 1 percent a year—

mostly at the expense of third-tier players—versus 2 percent annual increases for the newly revitalized HP, while Digital experienced a slight decline.

That surge ended with the 1992 collapse of the European market, which had provided almost half of all AS/400 sales. But by then, IBM's 220,000 installations placed it second only to DEC in systems priced between $15,000 and $1 million. Ultimately, the AS/400 would be crowned IBM's most successful minicomputer and the last successful computer anywhere with a "proprietary" (i.e., non-Unix/Linux, non-Windows) operating system.

Allen Krowe's closing remarks in our 1986 interview reflected an IBM management clearly smarting over DEC's ability to reach a broad market with just one architecture. "We want to dispel a trade press fiction," he said, without suggesting that we were the authors of this fiction—"the self-serving claim that one architecture is inevitably superior to multiple architectures. We don't think any single architecture can serve all customer needs."

Over the years, various IBM executives had emphasized that they'd achieved many of the manufacturing economies of a consolidated product line by using common circuit boards, power supplies, memory chips, and even cabinetry. But to us, the focus on common componentry overlooked the real reason for forcing a unified midrange architecture. The issue was less about cutting manufacturing cost than about building a wide enough platform to attract the maximum number of independent software developers.

In fact, the AS/400's single architecture would consolidate volume, draw more independent software applications, and drive more sales than the whole IBM kennel of minis. But it was very late. Commodity microprocessors were sucking the oxygen from every other market space. Indecision had cost IBM dearly in lost opportunity.

Chapter 19

BUILDING A GREAT BUSINESS:

Paul Ely at Hewlett-Packard

Great CEOs in the computer sector share two overriding characteristics: the vision to discern potentially disruptive forces in technology, business model, and/or their own company's organization structures; and the steadfastness to make the necessary changes even over the objections of their own executive cadre. Both Watsons, An Wang, Ken Olsen, and Lou Gerstner exhibited these characteristics, as we've seen. So did Paul Ely, who built Hewlett-Packard's successful computer business.

HP was the most energetic and farsighted of the minicomputer companies, with strong management closely attuned to technology rhythms and noticeably less dependent on a single, dominant personality like Bill Gates, Larry Ellison, Steve Jobs, and the other star walkers.

In 1939, Bill Hewlett and Dave Packard formed their partnership in "the Garage," later landmarked as the spawning pool of Silicon Valley. A coin toss determined the sequence of names atop a company led by lifelong alter egos. HP became known for superb quality, dogged innovation, and conservative economics. The philosophy built around "The HP Way" was legendary:

- Encourage entrepreneurial innovation by keeping business units small and independent, splitting off new units as necessary, limiting central control and sometimes even coordination among them.

- Emphasize R&D to provide product differentiation and strong margins.

- Focus on real customer problems by providing workable solutions rather than components.

- "No" to debt and "yes" to MBWA (management by walking around) and "next-bench" product design, which would build tools for other engineers.

All these axioms worked marvelously for the instrumentation and measurement markets that dominated the first thirty years of the company's existence. Pundits regularly named HP among America's best-managed companies and cited its laudable growth and profitability.

In 1978, Bill and Dave, then in their sixties, retired from active management without the age-defying bravado of other founders, remaining as directors for another decade. Yet they stayed active within the company and occasionally disruptive.

HP entered the IT segment in the mid-1960s hawking an instrumentation computer and, two years later, the first programmable electronic calculator. Both were competently planned and well executed, as was its next offering, the HP 2000 mini. But in 1969, the near collapse of efforts to develop the HP 3000 initiated a period that insiders later recalled as "seven years in the wilderness." The product was announced at the fall Joint Computer Conference in 1971, with first delivery promised for August 1972.

The early machines were full of problems, including the "twenty-four-day bomb," which destructively reset the internal clock after twenty-four days of continuous operation. Ultimately, the HP 3000 was withdrawn from the market in the spring of 1973. Customers were actually urged to "decommit" their orders by a young marketer, Ed McCracken. That debacle drew widespread press burns in *Computer World* and elsewhere. Worse for Bill and Dave personally, remembered a survivor, was an "unflattering" case study by the Stanford Business School, the mind spring of the Silicon Valley phenomenon. The botched launch was so awful that it even drew special mention in the 1973 annual report: "Placed on the market in 1972, the 3000's initial performance did not meet traditional Hewlett-Packard standards. The product has since been modified and its capabilities enhanced by improved software."

Gulp! A major HP product publicly fluttered to earth like a dying pigeon. Bill and Dave issued a legendary two-line memo stating unequivocally that HP would never again be embarrassed by releasing an untested, flawed computer line.

Paul Ely was brought over from the microwave division in 1973 to head the computer salvation effort. Ely was a tough manager and brilliant strategist, though perhaps temperamentally unsuited to the arm's-length, numbers-driven execution style of Hewlett and Packard. Recounted an HP chronicler on his Web history of the HP 3000, with considerable understatement, "[Ely's] management style was not necessarily a typical HP one." But few of the industry's most dynamic pioneers, including Watson, Gates, Jobs, and Ellison, could have navigated the HP Way, either.

By 1976, the electronic data products group was on a noticeable upswing; the HP 3000 and its Multi Processing Executive (MPE) operating system were fully operational and realizing strong customer acceptance, despite an already overcrowded market. Two years later, the revenues of Ely's group registered $761 million, surpassing those of its sister group, electronic test and measurement products, at $740 million. However, profits lagged those of the traditional lines by 30 percent, crimped in part by "the disappointing shipment levels of our new hand-held calculator models," noted a company press release.

First Stop: Palo Alto

We first met Ely and his management staff in 1979. For Naomi and me, HP became the gateway to Silicon Valley. We saved the West Coast third of our biennial tour until the chilly gloom of New York's December. Then, exiting the San Francisco airport, we'd exult in the warm air and fruity scents. The weather was delicious, and the people were generally intelligent, open, and quietly prosperous. Naomi and I and a researcher or two would drive gleefully south on U.S. Highway 101 until Palo Alto, where we stayed at Ricky's in the early years, later at the Garden Court. We were seldom disappointed.

By then, the HP 3000 had become the workhorse of the commercial minicomputer market, while many of the early entrants such as Computer Automation, General Automation, and ModComp were already in terminal decline. We saw clear cultural differences between HP and its larger, East Coast counterparts, beginning with the egalitarian office arrangement. Only Bill and Dave had offices, while everyone else was housed in bullpens. Our opening session with Paul and his direct reports was held in a sunny and sparsely comfortable meeting room. "Do you like it?" asked Paul. Luckily, we were slow to answer; it was the new board of directors' room, where Ely himself would take a seat the following year upon being named a director.

Several aspects of the company's positioning were compelling. To start, the emphasis on practical R&D that could be quickly translated into products differentiable from the competition. The computing groups spent an industry-high 11.5 percent of revenues on product development (versus 9 percent for HP overall), split 60 percent on software, 20 percent on disks and printers, and 20 percent on processors and semiconductors.

Because the total dollars were far below the sums DEC and IBM could allocate, Ely preached a regimen of "do a few things well," while maintaining a careful balance between technical and commercial computing. One objective was to double processor performance every two years, while dropping the price per MIPS 25 percent annually. That seemed awesomely competitive against the slower trajectories of the East Coast companies. Especially noteworthy, we thought, was Paul's assertion that "output devices like printers would eventually show the same gains that semiconductors have for the last fifteen years." Electromechanical gains? What seemed loony then is indisputable today given printing's technology advances.

"Competence not glitter," we wrote approvingly of Ely's emphasis on sound strategy formulation. As one middle manager described his job that year, "30 percent personnel supervision, 20 percent budget review, and 50 percent interaction with my peers to develop strategy." In hindsight, and whatever the merits, Ely's focus on strategy gave an early hint of the widening conceptual disharmony between his group and the company's traditionalists. As Dave Packard later explained to the *Financial Times* on July 3, 1992: "The longest planning period we have ever had was three years. We had a five-year plan and didn't pay any attention to it. Three years is as far ahead as we could see. That says a lot about this industry. It's very hard—it's not making railroad cars. You have to be flexible and roll with the punches."

Three years may have been the limit for instruments, but the computer business needed a planning perspective of at least five years.

Ely clearly saw the computer sector in an advanced state of consolidation, where he erroneously speculated that IBM, DEC, HP, and either Burroughs or Honeywell from the BUNCH, would end up as the dominant players. Each was roughly half the size of its closest competitor, so major changes in ranking were unlikely. Even so, Paul continuously plotted HP's leap into second place. Beyond that, "One new contender might move to the top rank, or ten of the little ones could survive through specialization, but no more. The field is already too crowded," he said. The semiconductor houses could be dismissed as potential competitors because their nickel-and-diming engineers were incapable of appreciating the full service required by the minicomputer business. Of course, neither Paul nor anyone else foresaw that new entrants would bring entirely new business models.

The biggest problem then, as later, was that HP's independent units invariably launched autonomous computer development efforts. Independence had been the bedrock of success in the instrument and measurement businesses. But in computing, such frivolous diversity placed HP at an intolerable disadvantage in everything from R&D to software to parts inventories to field maintenance. Competitors drew sizable efficiencies from having fewer product models.

A reorganization, announced in September 1979, would reduce product fragmentation and cut losses from the electronic calculator. There would now be three product groups:

- Technical computing, under Doug Chance, would handle the HP 1000 scientific computer, desktop systems, and semiconductor sales accounting for half of HP's computing business;
- General systems, under Ed McCracken, included the HP 3000 and represented 40 percent of the business;
- Computer peripherals, under Dick Hackborn, comprising disks and HP's world-leading printer business, represented just 10 percent of revenues in 1979, but would grow hugely.

The calculator products group was dissolved, its products swept elsewhere in the organization as competition intensified against the semiconductor houses and the Japanese.

HP Acquires Its Own Brilliant "Doctor"

HP's prospects rose measurably in 1980, when Ely recruited Dr. Joel Birnbaum, the leader of IBM's oft-thwarted 801 RISC project, as well as Jim Bell, one of DEC's top computer scientists. Joel was a large, handsome man, vaguely reminiscent of DEC's Ken Olsen in the generous dimensions of his head and breadth of his thought. Enormously imaginative and cultured (married to an opera singer), Joel had become sorely disillusioned by IBM's rampant bureaucracy under John Opel. Subsequently, he decided to join HP on the promise of a computer lab that actually brought products to market.

In our first discussions, Birnbaum emphasized two breakthrough areas. First was RISC, which would reshape the computer industry for more than a decade. The idea was simple enough in principle: Instead of including more and more machine instructions on a chip, reduce the number to those that careful testing could show were used most frequently and make all of them executable in a single machine cycle versus several. Then get a second performance boost by applying the savings in chip "real estate" to various performance accelerators (e.g., "registers" to store frequently reused data). In the end, HP's "precision architecture," or PA-RISC, had 130 instructions, not the theoretical sixteen, and leapt miles ahead of prior designs in throughput.

Birnbaum's second projection involved the convergence of voice and data communications—a rosy but elusive vision shared by Datapoint, Fujitsu, IBM, and Wang. But unlike Datapoint and Wang in their final years, HP's multiyear project on convergence was targeted not at some mythical workstation but at a "virtual network" combining the best features of circuit-switch telephone networks and packet-switch data networks, much like today's Internet. Twenty-five years later, Joel looked prophetic—though the concept was first realized as Voice over Internet Protocol, or VoIP. But Cisco and Juniper would gain the advantage of this technology over HP because of their focus on telecommunications.

For our 1981 report on the potential of personal computers, we met Paul at the muted Stanford University Club. Perhaps by virtue of geography or HP's decentralized culture, Ely was a year or two ahead of Olsen and Wang in assessing the PC's potential opportunity, limitations, and threat. (IBM had already started work under Don

Estridge.) Paul opened by describing the enthusiasm he'd encountered among early buyers after wandering into a neighborhood Byte Shop, where he had serendipitously parked his bicycle. "Was this a California phenomenon?" we wondered. Did Ken Olsen or An Wang ride bicycles to malls near their homes where they found new stores selling computers?

Paul foresaw not only the PC's potential volumes but its near-term commoditization as well. To our grousing about the lack of product differentiation among the dozen PC companies we'd visited, he responded, "There isn't any, except Apple and [the application-laced] Osborne Computer." To some degree, Paul had stumbled into a conundrum that would roil HP management for decades: How can a company famed for its culture of research and product differentiation survive a commodity market?

Fifteen years later, Dave Packard would succinctly state the problem in *The HP Way:* "With each product, HP strives, as I have said, to make a contribution to the state of the art—to add something new and different. Oddly enough, this desire, which helped us in the calculator and later in the computer field with our reduced instruction set computers (RISC), was actually a hindrance in entering the personal computer field ... many companies have arisen whose entire business is software. This is especially true for the personal computer (PC) whose owners couldn't care less about writing programs. Today, if you do not offer PCs with standard interface to the software suppliers whose products the user will buy, you will miss a large share of the market ... in today's computer world, the contribution we can make is in ease of use, speed, reliability, and above all, affordability."[1]

So Ely's group continued spending $35 million annually on R&D to create PCs the customer would value enough to pay the typical HP premium. "Wouldn't RB-scale companies pay 20 percent more for three times the reliability? How much for two times?" he'd ask us. What about easier programming through the use of "soft" (i.e., programmable function) keys so that users wouldn't have to relearn everything each time they switched between their home computer and their office mini? Our eagerly delivered brainstorms were probably wrong. In fact, Microsoft would eliminate the relearning problem by blanketing both home and office markets with Windows.

Nor did he need our input to surmise correctly that standards-based networking would be critical, and that computer stores would not displace direct sales forces no matter what the pundits thought. "I can't think why any RB-scale company would decide to buy its personal computers one at a time from a computer store unless the [CIO] had lost all control," he said.

By then, HP's congenitally idiosyncratic units had launched three different PC product lines: The computer terminals group reporting to McCracken offered the Digital Research CP/M operating system on the Intel microprocessor; the desktop computer group reporting to Chance launched Unix on a Motorola microprocessor; and the now-ghostly desktop calculator unit placed Microsoft DOS on an Intel microprocessor.

Pruning the Branches

At the outset of our 1982 study on the computer industry, we pondered the collision between HP's decentralization and Paul Ely's sensible dictate of "do a few things well," especially in a business that favored volume and compatibility. DEC had finally wrestled an equally fragmented organization into line behind VAX/VMS, and IBM was talking about cutting its minicomputer lines. But HP had too many computer product lines, none of which exhibited the scale now required by the industry. In processors, the business computer group offered a system grossly underpowered (at 16 bits) against the VAX (with 32 bits), while the technical group announced two new offerings, one underpowered and one state of the art, using the Motorola microprocessor. There were still three PC product lines.

We weren't the only ones concerned about fragmentation. *Business Week*'s December 6, 1982, cover story noted: "There are signs that HP's dramatic growth in computers is colliding with its unique entrepreneurial culture, and that the clash is threatening both. The decentralized style that HP has forged over the years—one that assigns the design and manufacturing of products to the individual divisions and gives the sales responsibility to separate marketing groups—has resulted in overlapping products, lagging development of new technology, and a piecemeal approach to key markets."

We began our HP tour that year in Boise, Idaho, visiting the peripherals group managed by Dick Hackborn, a fit and squarely-built man of enormous personal charisma, who could also become a grumbling enigma. We were intrigued by the innovative fervor emanating from the cubbyholes and the quick intelligence of his seemingly teenaged lieutenants. Hackborn was a brilliant leader who would provide and protect the continuity of HP's most important product line. He would also become a deciding factor in the CEO struggles of the next two decades.

The printer and disk businesses were booming, powered by excellent product development, careful alliances with the Japanese, and Hackborn's unconflicted support of distribution through the retail stores where the HP printer brand enjoyed a favored shelf position. That year, peripherals represented 46 percent of HP's computation sales, projected to become 63 percent within three years. "Maybe the time has come to reverse the preeminence of processors over peripherals," beamed Hackborn.

Product overlap was far less evident among printers and disks than among processors and PCs. One division made hard disks, a second made floppies. The Boise division manufactured laser printers, Vancouver produced lower-speed devices, while low-end electromechanicals had been farmed out to OEM suppliers. With those clear product-line distinctions, divisional innovation could be left uncurbed without impacting or overlapping with the products of the sister divisions. As a headquarters executive explained it later: "Peripherals are most like our original instrumentation business, the 'product sets' are naturally separable enough to encourage innovation through small autonomous development groups, which is the HP tradition." Bill and Dave would have nodded in warm agreement, as evidenced by the six full pages Packard devoted to printers in *The HP Way*; processors barely got two.

But back in Palo Alto, ruminating on the power of Boise's focus, we became ever more convinced that product fragmentation would impair HP's competitiveness in a rapidly consolidating processor market. Over dinner with Paul Ely at a local seafood restaurant, we brandished our *BusinessWeek* as a lever. There was an appetizer course of uncharacteristic and uncomfortable dodging. "Other observers" long ago noted the problem, chirped Paul, perhaps to distract us. We parried that we'd need to write something more than "might satisfy other observers." Back and forth went the verbal sparring right through the main course. Finally, over a virtuous dessert, Ely at last conceded that the HP way toward organizational change was to keep wrestling for consensus until "the need for change has become painfully obvious to all." Besides, he added, the necessary reorganization and consolidation was mostly "behind us" in PCs: All used the same keyboards, casings, and circuit boards, except for the microprocessor chip.

We were nodding over tea through our jet lag when Paul allowed that a future reorganization would combine the technical and commercial processors and also create an overall market development and applications unit.

Two weeks later, we read an HP press release confirming the unification of all PC activities under Cyril Yansouni, with the notation that "this new combined organization is intended to focus HP's marketing, engineering, and manufacturing resources on a single unified strategy." And on February 2, 1983, HP announced the formation of a new computer products group, with all midrange processors, operating systems, and semiconductor operations under Doug Chance. While Ed McCracken got the new business development group responsible for "development and strategic marketing activities," Dick Hackborn's peripherals group picked up data communications devices. Unchanged were personal computers and field operations.

For Paul Ely, this implicit centralization would mark the apogee of his HP career. Centralization was clearly the direction being taken by IBM and DEC and, equally clearly, not the HP Way. Paul probably sensed he was out of step with his CEO. He drove us back to the hotel and, while we were standing in the lobby, inexplicably insisted that we get to know John Young. We'd have only one more conversation at HP with our friend Paul Ely.

HP Gains on Its Bigger Rivals

The next day's meetings with Doug Chance, Ed McCracken, and others demonstrated that HP was indeed closing the gap with DEC and IBM in server consolidation, while moving ahead haltingly to industry standards like Unix and Ethernet. Chance was intelligent and open-faced, driving unselfconsciously through his stutter to announce that the first product consolidation joined the underpowered HP 3000 commercial system with the processor architecture of the HP 9000 technical computer.

Both Chance and Birnbaum were still decidedly cautious about RISC in 1982: "RISC architecture may not succeed," Joel told us. "And we certainly aren't going to proceed very far without extensive prototyping and testing." Echoed Doug: "RISC looks extremely promising, but we're not betting the company until we get a closer look." Whatever the speculations of IBM critics, RISC and Armonk's 801 project were not yet a sure thing.

Next, we met the leanly wired Ed McCracken, who was at once strategically ambitious yet sensibly restrained about industry-wide standards. Unix was HP's best hope of leapfrogging DEC in the technical market, he said. Standard operating systems would simultaneously be a plus for HP and devalue DEC's gold-standard VMS. How would HP prevent its products and profits from being commoditized? "By sliding Unix between a layer of applications software above and our hardware below." Well, maybe, we thought.

On Ethernet, Ed was similarly supportive and equivocal: "We are always enthusiastic when an industry standard is accepted; it helps reduce the perpetual drain of resources otherwise dedicated to refits and retrofits." Of course, HP had much less to lose than the two front-runners. Sun CEO Scott McNealy would use Unix, Ethernet, and eventually the Internet protocol to leapfrog DEC and HP in the workstation market. Standards can turn newcomers and also-rans into front-runners.

In McCracken's longer view, the computer industry was within twenty years of its own apogee. "The year 2000 could be our equivalent to 1960 for the automobile industry. We are near the point where we must be number one in very specific markets." Amid the progress on standards, consolidation, and possibly RISC, "the only bad news is that we don't yet have a gee-whiz product" to differentiate HP in the PC markets, he acknowledged.

Applications software was perhaps the best way to serve both the market and the culture. "Bill and Dave always believed the original instrumentation business was closer to providing the customer with a concrete solution than the computer business," McCracken observed.

Applications might bridge that soulless divide, and, to that end, HP had bought two small software houses. But Ed was worried these chicks might be crushed by the HP Way. "Our most difficult task was persuading them not to adopt HP's style and methodologies; then we would have learned very little." But applications would prove a dead end, not just for HP but for DEC, Wang, and the other hardware makers as well.

We visited Ely and Birnbaum for our 1983 study *Computing in the 1990s*, to speculate on research that might significantly affect the IT industry or generate a "whiz-bang" HP product. Paul responded that within his five-year planning horizon, all the major trends were obvious, except for "one or two humdingers that are completely unpredictable." One major strategic goal was to become more cost competitive against the Japanese by reducing R&D expense—but without slowing the pace of product introductions. He was now sure that RISC could drive a onetime 10:1 performance step and then double every two years, heading toward $10,000 MIPS in the 1990s.

Joel was equally optimistic. His advanced systems lab was hard at work on the precision-architecture version of RISC that would offer the greatest computing advantage. Early tests of existing applications demonstrated good performance gains from RISC by simply recompiling most programs and only reprogramming a few heavily used modules. After that, he turned to the work in his computer science lab, which included robotics, database, artificial intelligence, and graphics.

Birnbaum was most enthusiastic about expert systems: "They could be diamonds in HP's instrumentation business and blend with our personal computer strategy, as well." In fact, they did neither. Touch-sensitive screens were pioneered by HP, perhaps with an eye toward "Fitts's law," which held that the human finger was the most direct and hence "natural" interface. But touch-sensitive screens didn't much excite the PC market, though they've become commonplace on bank ATMs, automated ticket vendors, and other such devices.

Though Joel Birnbaum's projections were as farsighted and sensible as those of An Wang or anyone else, most of the glitterati described that day remain exoticisms. Few ever reached the market in any volume. Of course, Joel was likely playing to our curiosity, while keeping his focus on the RISC project so critical to HP's future. But it's worth noting that even when advanced technologies are successfully developed, their use is often short-lived as even newer technologies grab the spotlight and fickle users rush to make the switch. So, even when advanced products are feasible, the question becomes: Who will use them?

Perhaps the clearest anthropological assessment came from the clever Dr. David Liddle of (sequentially) PARC, Metaphor, and Patriot Partners, who noted that the real mystery is not how quickly things change but how slowly. The only important new PC application since spreadsheets and word processing, Liddle once said, was the browser—everything else was just function creep: "The baroque moving to the rococo," in his words. But that wasn't surprising, he added: "Just because people now have computers, it's nonsense to believe software firms can invent new tasks for them to do."

Paul was jetting in from someplace and packed for someplace else that day, so our conversation was short and soon turned to the competitive landscape. He was convinced that the game for IT market dominance was winding down and HP was winning. IBM was still the only real competitor, and Silicon Valley complaints about its cutthroat pricing were silly. "I don't really expect IBM wants this business to become a price gouge like semiconductors. That isn't IBM's style or ours."

The turmoil at DEC and torpor at Wang were also becoming visible out West. "Several years ago, I thought we would never leapfrog DEC in scale. Today, that is not totally unlikely." And "Wang isn't overwhelming competition," despite its reasonably strong sales organization.

Paul was much more interested in Apple, having intuited correctly that the Mac's advance signaled profound change. "The phenomenal success of Apple was a shock to me, and it has permanently altered this industry," Paul said, though its networking could remain a problem. "Three years ago, I didn't recognize the full criticality of personal computers to our future. Without them, we could be the Burroughs of the minicomputer business. Even if I had recognized [their criticality], HP didn't have the proper [centralized] organization to respond. The winds of change in this industry always seem sudden. The industry structure is fragile. The only healthy response is to be reactive. And our organization will continue to change—frequently and often."

The winds of change blasted Paul Ely in 1984, tearing him away from HP computing and dropping him into the relative backwater of the analytical, components, and medical groups. An extensive reorganization that created five EVP "sector chiefs" also gave the COO position—Ely's obvious next career step—to Dean Morton, an executive who was highly respected but without obviously relevant IT experience. On January 8, 1985, Paul Ely resigned to become CEO of Convergent Technologies, where he was soon joined by Cyril Yansouni, previously head of HP's PC business. Also decamping was Ed McCracken, who became CEO of Silicon Graphics. On September 23, two new group VPs were announced—Doug Chance for information systems and Lew Platt for medical and analytical systems.

Convergent developed workstations that were resold by AT&T, Burroughs, and others; its business was now clearly threatened by Unix and the PC. Paul cut five hundred jobs and developed a new strategy of selling systems complete with business applications to small companies in five vertical markets. But it was too late. In October, Convergent surprised investors with a $25.6 million loss, as revenues plunged from $117.3 million to $64.7 million, reflecting in part a massive $15 million decline in orders from AT&T alone. In August 1988, Convergent was acquired by Burroughs, with Ely named to the board of directors.

Most CEOs ousters occur after they've failed in the marketplace. Ely was ousted because he failed with the management structure and "the HP Way." The changes he steadfastly sought simply conflicted with the company's scriptures around small divisions and loyalty to the instrument and measurement businesses. Those scriptures were irrelevant to the growing IT business—but no matter. Ely was not the CEO and in no position to force cultural change on the company's senior management, including its still-active founders.

Chapter 20

CEO TUMBLES:

Hewlett-Packard's Horizontal Phase

Boards of directors have several duties, notably providing transparent assurance that the processes for financial reporting, executive compensation, and corporate governance meet the requirements of investors and regulators. But their most important responsibilities include firing the failing CEO and recruiting a replacement who can successfully lead the company for the next ten years or so. On these issues, the record of the HP Board is questionable at best.

Despite the company's placid appearance, top management was caught up in continuing turmoil, caused, in part, by constant interference from the founders (and their surrogate) for years after their formal retirement. Paul Ely, who hoisted HP into the computer business, was fired for being "abrasive," with the active connivance of John Young, the CEO. Young was forcibly but tactfully retired by the founders for bureaucratic centrism. His successor Lew Platt was ousted by the founders' surrogate. The flaw? Not abrasive or centrist enough. And the successor's successor, Carly Fiorina, was fired as being too removed from the details.

Strategic coherence and consistency suffered. Until quite recently, almost all of HP's profits came from printers and toner, the one segment of the business that was shielded from the continual perturbation. This isn't an argument for blind CEO retention, but HP's twenty-five painful years do suggest Board caution.

Naomi and I were aghast at Paul's sudden downfall. There were unverified stories of board-level politicking and intrigue. Paul had been "too abrasive" for company cohesion, relayed Ed Matthews, an RB founder with strong ties to HP. Yet here was a man who had headed an organization with arguably the strongest management team in the computer sector at the time. Under his leadership, the company's nearly disastrous HP 3000 program was salvaged, its computer revenues soared to $3 billion, and substantial progress was made towards a RISC-based computer generation and Unix.

Young launched the new computer on a trifecta gamble—simultaneously changing hardware architecture, operating system, and management team. This seemed even riskier than IBM's attempt to change hardware and operating software on the "bet-the-company" System/360 or the failed Future System.

But those lessons were apparently lost on HP's leadership. John Young was pushing a two-way gamble into a three-way improbability, especially once he widened R&D's purview to embrace measurement and instrumentation as well as computing. The complexity of managing IT development by committee would yield terrible results.

In 1985, we interviewed Young, COO Dean Morton, and John Doyle, Ely's replacement as executive VP for information systems and networks. All three were smart, first-rate executives. Doyle accompanied us on our tour of HP facilities in Idaho and Colorado. His disparagement of Paul Ely, though infrequent and indirect, was nevertheless unmistakable. "We can once again disagree without being disagreeable," he told us. "Or agree without the terminal niceness that merely signals suppressed rebellion." The disagreement apparently stemmed from the fact that the company's best computer scientists gravitated toward Birnbaum's research activity, while the traditional instrumentation and medical businesses were steadily losing ground to niche competitors with better computing capability.

John Young was a healthy, Nordic-looking man, whose occasional body flexing made him seem curiously self-conscious. From his perspective, the most significant event of the past eighteen months was the reorganization repositioning the company "from the product side to the market side." No longer was there a split between computing and HP's traditional products; now everything was reoriented around six market segments—measurement, engineering, medical, analytical, information processing (IT), and manufacturing. All HP business units would share equally in the computing advances engineered by Birnbaum's organization.

"We are who we are," intoned Morton, pointedly. And who we are is "a major designer and manufacturer of more than 10,000 measurement and computation products," noted that year's annual report, in a sequencing that glossed over computation's faster growth and larger share of revenues. HP had made a backward choice on resource allocation.

The new RISC-based computers were late, the operating systems even later. The 930 was a dead-end machine using purchased components and designed mainly to keep existing HP 3000 customers from bolting to a momentarily resurgent DEC and a youthfully vigorous Sun. The follow-on 950 would be built from microprocessors produced by HP's own semiconductor foundry and would debut the mainstream product line. Both should have been en route to the market by then.

In February 1986, HP disclosed that first deliveries of the 930 would be delayed until the fourth quarter, volume shipments until early 1987. And the mainstream 950 was delayed until late 1987. Discouraged customers might have fled in droves except for hand-holding by HP's excellent field sales representatives. Nevertheless, HP was squandering a golden opportunity while DEC and IBM remained mired in their own problems. More importantly, the streaking Sun was rapidly outdistancing HP in the Unix markets.

Investments in the software arena were disappointing, too. HP's futile ambition to produce and sell business applications ended with the sale of the two software companies discussed two years earlier. The haze enveloping HP's proprietary (MPE) operating system was even more unsettling. Members of the MPE development team sported impressive credentials, but many were new. And when we asked—repeatedly— what were quite conventional questions about code quality and error counts, we got no real answers. "What's going on?" we wrote. "Are we asking the wrong people? Or could the new code still pose problems for early users?" There was little information from the RB members, in part because HP required customers receiving early tests of the new "Spectrum" computer line to sign stringent nondisclosure agreements, promising to tell no one if there were problems.

Our suspicions about extended delays to MPE were confirmed at an April 1986 Research Board meeting in Phoenix, when Joel

Birnbaum freely admitted that while the hardware might appear on the new schedule during the fourth quarter, the reworking of the operating systems still needed another year. A Web-based history of the new machine was compiled by former HP insider and Robelle Solutions Technology software expert Bob Green. He quotes a round-table discussion among HP customers that concluded: "Most of what is printed about Spectrum is not to be trusted. Projection of Spring 1986 for a Spectrum that will reliably run existing MPE applications is not an attainable release date." In July 1986, a customer recounted: "When we arrived in Cupertino to do our first testing, we found a prototype Spectrum system crashing every few minutes and running slower than our tiny [16 bit] System 37. We were appalled. Nothing in HP's public statements had prepared us for the state of the project. The Unix version of Spectrum, on the other hand, seemed to be humming along nicely, showing that it is not a hardware problem."

Even eighteen months later, recorded Green, "HP continued to 'spin the shipment' of Spectrum without mentioning that these were not finished products." Only the nondisclosure agreements prevented Bill and Dave from being as painfully embarrassed as they had been by the HP 3000 project fifteen years earlier.

By the time of our brief visit to Joel Birnbaum a year later, HP had hunkered down. From the outside, Paul Ely's hope of possibly leapfrogging DEC appeared sadly deflated. An extremely defensive atmosphere was accentuated by the oppressive level of cops and ID badges now apparent at every entrance. Joel was no less smart and clever than before, but now he spoke in only vague platitudes. Computing was entering a final phase of "pervasiveness," he said, when its absence would be more noteworthy than its presence—rather like the hotel room without a TV or the kitchen without a clock. In that environment, innovation would flow naturally like water down a hill. "Could Gutenberg have predicted his invention would spawn a greeting-card business?" he asked. Or, in a particularly jejune remark, "The problem with envisioning the future is that no vision is ever outrageous enough."

But Joel was much better than that. And remembered twenty years later, he was ahead of the popular wisdom, especially his view of the computer's future "pervasiveness." But his very foresightedness made it doubly difficult to explain his hopelessly conservative stance on Unix in commercial computing. Will Unix be used for transaction processing? Definitely not, he said. Unix was meant for knowledge workers interacting online, but not for voluminous financial transactions— in part because it lacked the necessary data-integrity and system-availability features. Though right at the time, he was predictably wrong a few years later. Perhaps he feared that Unix would too quickly make the long-delayed MPE/XL obsolete after its difficult and bloody birth? Based solely on the barbed-wire paranoia visible everywhere, HP was caught in a downdraft.

Bill and Dave Rush from Retirement

It was at this point that Bill Hewlett and Dave Packard reentered the management picture to reinstate discipline and focus. A single manager took charge of the operating system project, displacing the committees necessitated by Young's clumsy matrix linking the labs and everything else with the six market segments. In February, HP finally released the 930 and 950 Spectrum computers, though customers were still combing bugs and performance suckers from the MPE operating system the following October.

The product was not completed until 1989, concluding an eight-year product-development cycle—long by any measure. Happily, the results were better than expected: 70 percent price/performance gains annually (versus 50 percent under the older hardware regimen). Nevertheless, revenue growth remained stunted as PCs continued siphoning demand from minis, and business investment generally remained below par. At a 1989 Research Board meeting held at Stanford University, Young had regained enough momentum to half-seriously exhort the CIOs to develop more applications and soak up the hardware expansion.

In a further effort to punch up the growth numbers, he plunged into the acquisition of Apollo Computer for $476 million. Its top twenty accounts represented a sizable opportunity, we were assured excitedly, because they didn't overlap HP's own customer base. But this onetime leader in hot-box workstations had been late moving to Unix and was losing the technology race to Sun and Silicon Graphics (where Ed McCracken was now CEO). In the end, the Apollo technology was left to wither, and the HP/Apollo combine steadily lost workstation market share—mostly to Sun (claimed Scott McNealy jubilantly). It's not clear how many Apollo accounts were actually retained long-term, though HP executives claimed a higher retention rate than they'd expected.

By any light, Young's centralization of R&D was an unmitigated failure. Clearly, the committee-laden overhead associated with shuffling people and work around an organizational matrix seriously retarded the RISC product line. And those delays helped IBM survive its midrange product muddle, while giving DEC a temporary reprieve as well. Forcing technology developed for computer systems on the instrument and measurement businesses wasn't worthwhile, either. Had HP chosen, instead, to employ the commodity technology developed in massive volumes by Intel and Motorola, lower instrument prices and greater market acceptance would have followed. The inappropriateness of Young's centralization was confirmed by then-CEO Lew Platt's 1998 decision to spin off those businesses into Avaya.

We were not alone in our judgment. As the *Wall Street Journal* reported on July 22, 1991, an unnamed HP executive confirmed delays to the operating system by the decision process: "'There was always reason for another level of review, and we just became mired in our own administrative processes. Likewise, HP lagged in PCs. Its models were late, high-priced, 'me too' copies of IBM's PC. HP's share of the world PC market was a dismal 1.2 percent of 1990 sales, according to Dataquest Inc. Its 1988 acquisition of Apollo Computer Inc. added new burdens. Melding the two concerns went at a snail's pace.'"

After noting "a hodgepodge of computer products," the article concluded: "So in the early 1980s, HP took two critical steps: It decided to make its computers conform to common standards, and in 1984, it tried to place its disparate computer operations in a single unit. The first move [by Ely] proved astute ... But the second move [by Young] proved a long-term liability. Putting all computers into one organization helped the company switch to a single architecture, but the organization became mired in its own complex decision making process involving numerous meetings among the many groups whose components went into a computer. The result was gridlock."

More telling still were the gritty recollections of Dave Packard in *The HP Way,* published shortly before his death in 1996. Under the ominous chapter heading "The Perils of Centralization," Packard records: "By 1990 we faced a crisis. Committees had taken over the decision-making process at HP, and decision cycle times had ballooned. For example, one central committee, the Computer Business Executive Committee, was intended to achieve a better focus and coordination for computer activities. Instead, it was slowing vital decisions.... In fact, the paralysis was spreading to areas of the company that had nothing to do with computers. That we were struggling was no secret; our stock had fallen to $25."[1]

An almost identical statement could have been written by a board member of the more visibly troubled IBM, and at almost exactly the same instant.

Back in managerial harness, Packard and Hewlett "began systematically to visit several HP facilities and meet with employees at all levels of the organization to find out what, really, was going on." For better or worse, it's hard to read this in any sense other than that the founders were undercutting their handpicked CEO John Young. Packard admitted as much: "Eventually, we knew what we needed to do. Too many layers of management had been built into the reorganization. We reduced them. We brought a gifted younger manager, Lew Platt, into the executive committee as chief executive. His predecessor John Young—the skilled executive who had managed the company's explosive growth through the late 1970s and 1980s—was part of the group that selected Lew. (In 1993 Lew was promoted once again, to chairman of the board of Hewlett-Packard.)"[2]

Young announced his retirement in 1992. Given the recent turmoil, one might have expected a few niggles and barbs from the business press. But in sharp contrast to the poisonous pieces targeted at DEC's Ken Olsen and IBM's John Akers, there came an almost orchestrated rhythm of highly adulatory notices. Burbled the *Financial Times* on July 17, 1992: "Mr. Young is leaving HP on a high note. His departure comes as the company is enjoying an earnings surge that has defied the computer industry slowdown. For the first half of its fiscal year, HP reported a 44 percent increase on revenues of $8bn. Although sooner than expected, Mr. Young's retirement had been planned; a succession committee was formed two years ago to choose the company's third chief executive ..."

Trilled the *Wall Street Journal* that same day: "Hewlett-Packard Co. named Lewis E. Platt president and chief executive officer, succeeding John Young who will take early retirement at the helm of the electronics concern…. While Mr. Young was known to be considering retiring, the timing of his announcement was somewhat earlier than analysts anticipated. At the same time, he is leaving the company at a point at which it has been performing better than ever, reflecting a major reorganization that Mr. Young engineered two years ago."

Young benefited mightily from press genuflections at the moment of his retirement. But cranky observers (like us) wondered about the "earliness" of his departure. Nine months after the fact (April 26, 1993), *Forbes* took a different tack in a piece that contrasted HP's changing of the guard with the sorrier situations at DEC and IBM. The difference was the personal intervention of Packard and Hewlett, *Forbes* indicated, with both then nearing eighty. "'If we didn't fix things, we'd be in the same shape as IBM is today,' said Dave. Whereas Tom Watson Jr. was impotent to end his frustration with CEO John Akers, Dave and Bill owned a fourth of the stock, controlled the board, and maintained the respect and even reverence of the engineering culture. 'If something needed to be done, we just had to get in there and do it,' Packard said. That could well serve as a motto to be posted in every corporate boardroom in America," *Forbes* concluded. It would not be the last instance of an overactive HP board.

In *Perfect Enough*, a 2003 account of the goings-on at HP by *Fast Company* editor George Anders, the author describes a meeting of the board in early 1992, a meeting called by Packard that excluded John Young. "A boardroom coup had begun," Anders writes. "Packard wanted John Young out. Other directors had been hearing for a while that HP didn't have the leadership that it needed; that it was being overtaken in the marketplace by younger companies like Microsoft and Intel. Now an angry Dave Packard was betting that a different CEO could revitalize HP. 'We need to make a change,' Packard said. 'I want it very clearly understood that this is my responsibility, and that Bill is not responsible for this.' Packard stared at his co-founder, Hewlett stared back. As fellow director Jay Keyworth remembered, an exasperated look crept over Hewlett's face. Hewlett picked up a yellow no. 2 pencil and flipped it toward the middle of the boardroom table.

As he did so, Hewlett said: 'Packard, I was there three years before you were on this one. And I'm totally there with you now.'"[3]

In the end, Naomi and I judged Young a capable CEO whose bureaucratic failings were initially masked by the printer-profit machine created by Dick Hackborn, the RISC product development fostered by Paul Ely, and the organizational rescue achieved by Lew Platt. Nevertheless, Young's efforts to coordinate R&D with the independent business units had seriously retarded his company's progress.

Lew Platt Takes the Helm in Troubled Waters

Platt was an even-featured northeasterner, totally direct as he gazed through his Coke-bottle lenses and with ethics that were never questioned. His appointment as CEO left two unhappy also-rans—Doug Chance and Dick Hackborn. Chance, who felt slighted because he had run much of the computer business while Lew was over in measurements, departed to become CEO of Wyse Technology. Hackborn, who didn't leave, was Lew's more dangerous adversary.

Dick Hackborn, a Bill-and-Dave favorite, whose printers provided most of HP's profits, met us for dinner at New York's Sign of the Dove. He told us (and, separately, many others) how he had declined Bill and Dave's entreaties to take the CEO job because he'd been unwilling to leave Boise. (Or maybe, we speculated, he was even less willing to leave his hermit's shell and face the public, the press, and Wall Street.) Even so, he was sorely disappointed, muttering that he might even quit the company. Unfortunately, for Platt at least, Hackborn was instead appointed to the board of directors, where he eventually led the uprising against Lew and spiritually headed the search committee that found Carly Fiorina.

At Platt's accession, HP was still getting a lift from its RISC architecture, especially against DEC, which was hobbling toward acquisition by Compaq. Platt was farsighted enough to lead an industry-wide margin squeeze by downsizing his sales force and restricting direct representation to the largest seven hundred accounts. Midsize customers forced to rely on resellers were outraged. But his actions helped HP contain its costs in the face of widespread price cuts (see Table 20.1). Of course, the dominance of retailers and resellers in

Hackborn's disk and printer business went a long way toward reining in HP's SG&A numbers.

Table 20.1 Sales and General Administration (percentage of revenues)

	1990	1992	1994	1996
HP	28.1	25.7	19.7	17.0
DEC	30.7	33.6	29.9	
IBM	30.0	32.9	25.4	21.2
Tandem	40.5	41.8	34.5	

Source: Company Financials

R&D was again under pressure, this time from the PC business model, which devoted, at most, 2 percent of revenues to developing new features that would differentiate their products—at least until the competition caught up again. One issue for HP was the maintenance of two operating systems. Proprietary operating systems like MPE lost both customer appeal and their premium price as Unix edged into business processing. Simultaneously, Unix development came under pressure as its portability lowered switching costs and competition lowered prices. Now only Sun, with its market share, (and perhaps IBM) could justify the $100 million annual cost of a world-class Unix lab. For workstations, the imminent release of Intel's 32-bit Pentium chip was even more worrisome. Despite its initially anemic computational capabilities, Windows would soon attract engineering/ scientific applications.

Meanwhile, Platt built up a 3,500-person professional services organization, headed by Ann Livermore, that focused on specific specialty areas where HP consultants could gain repeatable experience that could then be applied to other accounts. Among the most popular was "mainframe rightsizing," cleverly pitched to maximum advantage and minimum customer controversy. No need to displace the mainframe, the consultants advised, but no need to buy another, either. Instead, off-load portable software to HP Unix, leaving enough capacity on existing IBM iron to handle the nonportable "legacy" programs. The program was successful in drawing new sales, and Ann became a strong candidate to follow Lew in the CEO's chair.

But consulting was too labor-intensive to be an engine of HP's growth and profitability, observed longtime CFO Bob Weyman later. So services should be contained to its current 23 percent of revenues. By contrast, Digital's service revenues accounted for 46 percent of revenues—a major weakness.

HP had another banner year in 1994. Over at IBM, the new CEO Lou Gerstner was desperately buying time by simultaneously cutting prices and staff. And DEC shocked the world (and its new CEO, Bob Palmer) with its July announcement of a huge loss attributable to slow-footedness in adjusting to the industry's new cost model. HP's computer revenues were now far larger than DEC's, $20 billion versus just $13 billion—though half came from printers. Its 1994 growth of $4.7 billion equaled Sun's total revenues.

But HP was not immune to the industry-wide price and margin collapse, especially after Compaq's aggressive drive to bring gross margins down to 23 percent, and Lew Platt knew it. He was pressing to remain competitive in PCs for two reasons, he told us: First, HP could then offer its customers a complete system end-to-end, from desktop to server. Second, becoming competitive in PCs would help pull the company as a whole toward the lean-cost model set by Dell that Platt was convinced would eventually govern the entire computer business. In fact, HP's own gross margins on its Unix and MPE servers had dropped from 52 percent in 1985 to 38 percent in 1994, with a 4 percent plunge in 1992 alone. Only printers (with $6 billion in sales) kept overall 1994 profits at 10 percent of revenues.

The top line of HP's organization chart had changed markedly under Platt. Now the split was between minicomputers or servers and PCs, instead of by market segment. Heading computer systems, including servers and workstations, was Wim Roelandts, the outwardly impassive Dutchman who had previously led HP's world-class Unix development activity. Heading computer products, including PCs and printers, was Rick Balluzzo, a frantically ambitious, forty-two-year-old executive and Hackborn protégé. "Rocket" Rick was lean, twitchy, and vaguely driven, a bottle of spring water always in hand as he accompanied us to every meeting. "Minder or observer?" we wondered.

The organization was now split top to bottom; the direct sales force sold Unix to large accounts, while the indirect channels pushed PCs. There were whiffs of another imminent organizational collapse, like those of 1984 and 1990, only this time the pain would be considerably greater.

The Not So "Special" Relationship with Intel

Now came a strategic gamble, larger perhaps than even Young's trifecta. Whereas Young's strategy smothered R&D, Platt decapitated it. In signing a joint venture with Intel, Lew demoted HP's precision-architecture RISC project, reassigning its crown-jewel architectural team to work instead on Intel's 64-bit, "wide-word" microprocessor. The delivery date of Intel's new marvel was highly confidential, but winks and nods suggested 1997. Questions concerning the real value or meaning of the lash-up with Intel persisted. "Can HP survive Andy Grove?" asked one executive, pondering his company's uncertain future with Intel, whose other name for "partner" was "organ donor," according to Valley jokesters. (Andy was furious with us when we wrote that, growling it was simply press nonsense that ignored his company's excellent relations with longtime partners Microsoft and ceramics-supplier Kyocera.)

HP management remained steadfast in the face of our repeated questioning: "Going it alone would leave us no better than number three in volume [behind Intel and PowerPC from IBM and Motorola]. Now we'll be number one," promised Platt. "This deal will change the shape of the computer industry," enthused Roelandts. Rick Balluzzo exulted because HP would now transition into a commodity supplier of Intel processors and Microsoft operating systems. "If you can't compete in the PC business, you're not going to be in the computer business," he told *Fortune* (September 29, 1997). "Your business is going to look more and more like PCs over time, so you'd better get used to it."

The *Fortune* writer plainly agreed, calling Balluzzo "Platt's heir apparent" and observing, "So why worry so much about PCs? The short answer: If the computer industry has such a thing as a center, PCs are it. A computer company must sell PCs in order to supply big corporate systems, and the lucrative integration and support services that go with them. Without a thriving PC business, HP will be consigned in perpetuity to the role of a peripheral player that makes mainly, well, peripherals."

That was certainly the popular wisdom at the time. And it was true that the PC couldn't be ignored. But in no sense was the PC business an "absolute necessity," as Lou Gerstner would demonstrate at IBM.

By December 1997, prevailing market winds could no longer be deflected by the printer business alone. HP's outlook was, at best, mixed, especially against a resurgent IBM. For the fiscal year ended in October, company revenues grew just 12 percent, now having "disappointed Wall Street for the past four to six quarters," CFO Bob Weyman admitted to us. More cost cutting was needed. "In PCs, we could be as profitable as Compaq." Printer sales probably wouldn't return to the rollicking growth of prior years, though printer supplies would do well. His prognosis of a return to "high-teens" growth was readily conceivable.

Meanwhile, the microprocessor under joint development with Intel was dangerously late from the projections given earlier. As a stopgap, HP's beleaguered hardware engineers cobbled together their own 64-bit RISC processor. But we'd begun to doubt whether HP would realize the gains originally anticipated from the joint venture. In 1994, Lew Platt had insisted that HP's inside knowledge of the new architecture would give applications processed through HP compilers a definite advantage over competitors on the new platform. Also, a common compiler (which converts the programmer's work into machine instructions) would bridge the gap between HP's 32-bit computers and the new 64-bit machines under development with Intel.

Three years later, the outlook was considerably less robust. Recompilation alone would realize just 60 percent of the targeted throughput, with 80 percent no more than "a target," we were told by Albert Yu, Intel's senior vice president for the microprocessor products group.

"Did the 64-bit processor contain a special assist for HP applications?" we persisted. "I didn't say yes, and I didn't say no," revealed Albert, taking care to pause so we could record his enigmatic answer. "Yes," snapped Platt a day or two later, but unconvincingly, as it turned out. What about the special relationship with Intel, heralded in 1994? "Probably not worth much" was the consensus of our interviews among the experts at Compaq, Dell, and IBM, who had reason to give the question careful scrutiny. Intel had zero incentive to give any one PC maker an advantage that would drive the others to another (probably clone) chip maker such as AMD. A level playing field kept PC makers "scrambling, naked, and hungry," in industry parlance, and so ill-positioned to challenge Intel in any way.

Another Competitive Advantage Slips

Unix development was weakened by both Wim Roelandts's departure and budget cuts. Now Platt was forced to answer press speculation, gleefully fanned by Sun's McNealy, that HP might abandon Unix to foster a closer relationship with Intel and Microsoft. "We'd be out of our ever-lovin' minds to drop Unix. Those companies that spread these rumors reflect their small size," Lew told *Electronic News* in May 1994: "Unlike Sun, an $8 billion company, we're a $42 billion company. We're large enough and experienced enough to walk and chew gum at the same time, and our customers need both Windows NT and Unix."

But, in fact, a power struggle was clearly evident from Roelandts's departure, as Platt confirmed to us: "Previously, the Unix group had an independent marketing group that hated Microsoft. So we couldn't coherently address customers who wanted both NT and Unix-based product lines, although, initially, we were uniquely positioned to serve customers in mixed environments. Then Digital announced its 'special' relationship with Microsoft, so I asked, why not us?"

"But cementing that relationship required firing top managers in the Unix area. Yes, the resulting morale problems slowed development in high-end servers, but that's behind us," insisted Platt. "And, today, we have a unified sales and marketing organization across the product lines."

The whole episode was curious. From our conversations in the Valley, we surmised HP's "special" relationship to Intel was special mainly to the needier HP (just as Digital's special relationship with Microsoft was special only to the needier Digital). Meanwhile, HP lost momentum and credibility in high-end servers and failed to share proportionately in the surge of server sales to Web commerce over the next three years.

The weakening of HP's competitiveness probably deepened as Balluzzo prevailed in the view that the future belonged to Intel and Microsoft. That cost model placed severe pressure on many parts of the organization. The field sales organization, which had been able to hold onto the customer base despite extended product delays, sustained deep cuts for a second time. Now only the top 200 accounts would get full support. The top 500 accounts now shared 200 account executives. The next 6,500 accounts were represented by 350 lower-level representatives and some specialists. HP's sales-and-service rating among Research Board members tumbled from first place in 1995 to sixth in 1997, leading only the decomposing DEC.

Equally troublesome for the long term, Joel Birnbaum's 1,400-person R&D organization was under fire as too far removed from the market—and too expensive. How could HP's PC business compete when Dell spent under two percent of revenues on R&D and the Taiwanese "white box" PC makers spent zilch? The labs were split into three parts: enterprise systems covering both NT and UNIX and newfangled stuff like load-balancing middle ware; PCs and printers, with a budget emulating the Dell model; and a small unit for basic research.

Birnbaum was clearly uncomfortable with the new balance. "My answer to demands for R&D cuts derives from David Packard's view that we can't be successful unless we add value" through product differentiation, he told us. "The goal should be profitability, not growth; market share is an extra reward, not an objective." Unfortunately, valuing profitability over growth was swimming against the tide of popular wisdom, despite outriders like the Alex, Brown & Sons investment bank, whose analysis in May 1997 declared: "We believe HP needs ... radical new product offerings. While we commend the company for attempting to embrace networking and photo reproduction, we do not think these businesses will become catalysts for near-term growth." Few listened.

The problem was partially funding, but, more profoundly, the difficulty of coming up with something truly "differentiating." That day, Birnbaum proudly brought a mock-up to show us. A clever, coffee-cup-sized scanner with the code name Zorro was supposed to capture images from pages when randomly stroked across the surface; the images could then be e-mailed or faxed or stored on a user's hard drive. There was also talk of a tie-clip–sized printer. Intriguing, we thought. But Zorro never reached the market, and neither did the tiny printer. Ultimately, HP's only real innovation concerned desktop printers and, occasionally, software.

The Power Struggle Continues

By 1998, Balluzzo was desperate to be named CEO—even calling Naomi to suggest we lobby the directors on his behalf. Not fully understanding his ties to Hackborn, we were surprised by his chutzpah and, in any case, weren't inclined to side against Platt. When asked, instead, to settle for the top computer job, Rick jumped ship in early 1998 to become CEO at Silicon Graphics, which he moved from Unix/RISC processors to the Microsoft/Intel platform before departing yet again, this time for Microsoft. He stayed for a few years before the inevitable clash with Steve Ballmer left him at large once again.

Lew Platt was surprised by Balluzzo's sudden departure and the vituperation he slung in his wake. Over the year, Rick's dissatisfaction gelled, according to George Anders's account in *Perfect Enough*. Fanning the flames, if not pouring on gasoline, was the jungle fighter Dick Hackborn. Central to his dissatisfaction was the growing sense that HP was still spending too much or getting too little from R&D: "Platt had let HP become so decentralized and fragmented that even when someone had a great idea, 'There was never much wood behind the arrow,' as one insider put it. It had been a long time since the last big [R&D] triumphs: Dick Hackborn's laser and inkjet printers of the mid-1980s. Employees knew it, and so did Wall Street analysts."[4]

In retrospect, the implied analysis looks at once cogent and half-baked. Any discussion of "the last big triumph" should certainly have included the highly effective RISC processors, which, however delayed, captured significant market share from DEC and IBM. Even so, too few great ideas beyond RISC had ever reached the market.

Finally, the board sensed that HP was falling behind the business models of Sun and especially Dell. But Sun was booming as a result of costly R&D, oriented toward high-end, Unix-based 64-bit processors that caught the Internet wave perfectly. By contrast, HP had off-loaded processor development to Intel and lost its innovative edge in Unix.

Dell got rid of middlemen in favor of selling direct by phone and Web site to cut costs and improve customer satisfaction. It also capped R&D at 2 percent of revenues. HP couldn't figure out an effective response, and its stock barely budged in the midst of a legendary bull market. The employee count had certainly been cut, but apparently not enough. "Terminal niceness" was the pejorative used against Platt—an eerie echo of the phraseology used in a quite different context against Paul Ely.

Should HP really have abandoned its heritage and followed Dell's model? The HP Way's core strategy was based on adding value through clever product development and staying out of commodity markets. Moreover, HP couldn't bypass its retail outlets without jeopardizing the favored shelf position of its printers and taking an enormous hit in PC revenues. But Hackborn now turned his critique to HP's position on the Internet, especially in contrast to Microsoft, where he had been a director for the past four years. "'HP was missing the Internet,' he argued. Its software developers hadn't grasped the importance of the World Wide Web; its computer strategy showed limited awareness of the Internet's impact, and the company's own Web site was feeble.... Hackborn had watched admiringly in 1995 as Gates reoriented his entire company around the Internet. That took guts, Hackborn believed. That was a performance worthy of Dave Packard—stubborn, controlling, and just plain right."[5]

It's hard to know exactly what Hackborn could have meant. Yes, Bill Gates successfully protected his near monopoly in desktop operating systems by attacking Netscape and the browser market with a free product. But other parts of Microsoft, notably "Office," were little affected; and many of its other Internet ventures—such as Wallet, MoneyCentral, and most recently YouTube competitor Soapbox—remained notoriously mediocre. Perhaps he was confused by his directorships at both HP and Microsoft.

Late 1998 marked our last formal industry tour. This time, we restricted our interviews to the swift and the soaring, like Cisco, Dell, and Sun. We didn't visit Compaq, whose once-aggressive business model had fattened uncomfortably with the acquisition of DEC and Tandem. Nor did we go to IBM, whose revenue growth was strained by Gerstner's price cuts. And we omitted HP, beset as it was in the workstation market by PCs from below, by IBM's price cuts in the middle, and, at the top, by Sun's 64-bit processor humming under a fine-tuned Unix, while HP's Intel-partnered Merced/Itanium would be delayed for another five years.

The gap between the leaders and the trailers in 1998 is described in Table 20.2.

Table 20.2   1998 Indicators as Percentage or Multiple of Revenues

	Market Capitalization	R&D/Revenue	Growth/Revenue
Cisco	17.8	12.6%	33.5%
Dell	6.7	1.5	52.8
Sun	3.8	11.1	14.2
Compaq	2.6	4.3	26.8
IBM	2.1	6.2	4.4
HP	1.6	7.1	9.7

Source: Company Financials

On March 2, 1999, Lew announced both his own imminent retirement at age fifty-eight and the pending divestiture of HP's original measurement and instrumentation businesses. He was the third consecutive leader of HP's computer business to be fired, a record of executive defeat unmatched even in the turbulent computer business. And hardly the totem of bland competence we'd imagined a decade earlier.

Almost weirdly, the divestiture left HP with the same constellation of IT-related businesses that had gotten Paul Ely fired fifteen years earlier. "Sentimentally, it was a very hard decision.... I spent more than half my career in measurements," said Platt in *Time*'s June 28, 1999, edition. But measurement devices now represented just 17 percent of total revenues and had become a drag on profits and a dilution of management focus. "We fell behind in the early days of the Internet," Lew acknowledged.

The search for a new CEO bumbled along for a few months. By mid-June, *Business Week* reported three candidates: Carolyn Tickner, head of HP's printer business; Ann Livermore, head of services; and Intel's Paul Otellini, who would stay on to become president of the semiconductor giant. Suddenly, on July 17, came the surprise announcement that the CEO position would go instead to Carly Fiorina, head of Lucent's $20 billion global-services businesses. The previous October, *Fortune* had named Fiorina America's most powerful businesswoman, saying, "In an age of celebrity, it may surprise you that our No. 1 woman is someone you've never heard of." No one would overlook her again.

Meanwhile, Platt announced he would retire on December 31, replaced as nonexecutive chairman by Dick Hackborn. In September, Lew and Carly were touring Wall Street and they stopped by the Research Board. We'd sold the company to the Gartner Group by then, and Naomi had already released her office. I was within three weeks of finishing my exit project. So Lew, Naomi, and I gossiped about our next lives, while Carly conferred with the woman who briefly succeeded us. It was the end of an era for all of us. Lew went on to become the nonexecutive chairman of Boeing, where he helped the company navigate a difficult patch using his well-known ethical standard as a fulcrum in the restoration.

Now Mark Hurd leads HP, moving there from NCR, the former stomping ground of Chuck Exley, no less. Mark follows a string of executives who, in very quick succession, fell from grace for reasons that sound frivolous in the retelling. Paul Ely, who, in effect, was the CEO of Hewlett-Packard's computer business, was demoted for being too abrasive. John Young was shunted aside for being too bureaucratic. Lew Platt was fired for being too nice, and Carly Fiorina was let go for not being hands-on. Mark Hurd could be the outsider who carries HP to the scale but perhaps without the product innovation envisioned by Bill, Dave, and then Paul Ely.

Chapter 21

LIMITS OF STRATEGY?

The extreme turbulence of the computer sector in the 1980s provides an intellectual wind tunnel for testing radical survival strategies and effective leadership. What can be learned from the leading computer companies and the men who led them? Are there limits to strategy, however brilliant? Or were these CEOs diminished and even fired simply because of their own managerial inadequacies?

Yes, they were buffeted by disruptive technologies, but wouldn't more savvy CEOs have identified the threat soon enough to navigate through the turbulence? Yes, company survival depended on radically different business models, but wouldn't farther-sighted leaders have identified the turning points soon enough to lead the restructurings? And yes, such painfully massive restructurings were impeded by stiff internal resistance, but wouldn't stronger leaders have forced compliance on middle management?

Perhaps it's not so easy. The potential impact of disruptive technologies like the microprocessor can be difficult to discern even by those closest to the action—witness contemporaneous interviews with the CEOs of Intel, National Semiconductor, and Motorola. Conversely, the real distinction between disruptive and essentially transient technologies like the minicomputer is often befogged in Creative Ideology.

Besides, a technological advantage alone is not enough, as evidenced by Amdahl's futile twenty-five-year assault against IBM. Much more important is the accompanying business model. First movers trying to harness a disruptive technology to an outdated business model will fail, as did Commodore, Tandy Radio Shack, and, to some degree, Apple.

Even when the disruptive technology and its equally disruptive business model are clearly visible, the survival strategy can be nearly impossible to implement. Incumbents can be hobbled by organizational and physical assets that quickly become boat anchors. Faced with hard choices, executives can be distracted by traditional competitors doing even worse than they are. Response may be further delayed while management is still savoring a recent apogee—witness Tandem, DEC, Cullinet, Lotus, and many others. That's fatal given the mind-numbing levels of attention over a remarkably long term required to change minds and incentives in the field organizations at both DEC and IBM. Too often, the only prescription is massive downsizing, but that's something sitting CEOs find very difficult, especially if they're a founder or lifelong employee.

Ups and Downs

By definition, apogees mark the beginning of decline. When you've reached the highest point and can go no further, you may fight to hold your position, but, in terms of movement, there's no place to go but down. Thus, the same Ken Olsen who persevered with VAX/VMS was later implicated in his company's failure to move more aggressively to Unix, RISC, and the new business model. An Wang was responsible for heroic business leaps but failed to acknowledge the irresistible appeal of the Intel/Microsoft platform and the layered business model. Vic Poore, though never Datapoint's CEO, was its brilliant guiding light in distributed processing and local area networks; Poore even helped invent the microprocessor. But he didn't see that standardization in microprocessors and networking would make even his sturdiest innovations obsolete. And the list goes on.

All this is evident in *Innovation, the Attacker's Advantage*, where Richard Foster places the challenge posed by disruptive technology in a desperate perspective: "Prior success handicaps change." The recent apogee adds further disadvantage: "I don't know any comprehensive statistics that would stand up to academic scrutiny, but my feeling is leadership changes hands in seven out of ten cases when discontinuities strike. A change in technology may not be the No. 1 corporate killer, but it's certainly among the leading causes of corporate ill health."[1]

Creative Ideology

Identifying the moment for radical change is complicated by the fog of "creative ideology," a swirl of claims by IT-connected gurus that often give new technology far more credibility than it deserves. So, determining whether a new technology will truly usher in lasting, rather than transient, change in the workplace or the marketplace is never easy.

In the early days at IBM, for instance, "management by exception" cloaked the disadvantages of magnetic tape in comparison to the then-ubiquitous punch cards and the disks that would come later. Later, in its efforts to promote its impossibly expensive office computers, IBM promoted *Textverarbeitung*, which made a virtue of consolidating secretaries into typing pools. Both office systems and typists would be displaced by the PC.

"Distributed management" was another concept that disguised the fact that the minicomputer, with its proprietary operating system, was merely a way station between the vertically integrated mainframes and the layered industry supporting the PC.

First-Mover Disadvantage

Potentially disruptive technologies also carry the risk of first-mover disadvantage. Too frequently, unwitting entrepreneurs will use new technology to support old business models, putting them at a disadvantage against older competitors that have the brands and financial resources to survive the early battles. Again and again, a new industry is eventually dominated by as many old players as new.

Take an example from outside the IT sector. In the 1890s, the use of Thomas Edison's electric bulb for street lighting was delayed for decades by the fortuitous invention of the Welsbach mantle, a wick that improved gas-lamp luminance. The improved wick gave the gas companies time to find new uses for their product (in kitchen ranges, etc.) and allowed them to gain control of the fledgling electric companies. The result is clearly visible today in the "Gas and Electric" designations appended to many public utilities.

Similarly, the quick failure of two early PC leaders wasn't an accident. Tandy emulated the integrated technology model of the minicomputer, and Commodore erroneously accepted the $600 pricing model of the home-entertainment center. Of the pioneers, only Apple survives, but its cute, consumer-oriented imaging denied it a relevant share of the business market. Meanwhile, the PC market is led by a latecomer, Dell, and an early traditionalist, HP. And the Unix camp was ruled by a newcomer, Sun, and two traditionalists, HP and IBM. If Linux wins the day, some combination of latecomers and traditionalists will likely assume the leadership again.

The Burden of Assets

Incumbents can be severely burdened by outdated assumptions about field sales, support, and R&D. Management may find it difficult or impossible to make needed change, especially when support accounts for half the revenue, as at DEC and Wang. Neither Olsen nor Wang were emotionally able to jettison employees even though their companies' survival depended on it. In Wang's case, dropping its hardware products to focus only on PC-based applications would have meant cutting the company by three-quarters, at least for the interim years. Sitting CEOs, founders or not, are usually the wrong people to lead a radical restructuring, regardless of threat.

The burdens of incumbency are rooted in the peculiarities of technology. IBM executives couldn't imagine offering a computer whose operating system they didn't control. DEC's management couldn't imagine opening the successful VAX product line painfully forged after years of internal dissension. Neither Tandem nor Cullinet could have matched the offerings of Sun or Oracle without a massive rewrite of their software. The expense of such a transition was deemed too expensive when times were good, and impossible to bear once downturns gained momentum.

Organizational Resistance

There's no doubt that disruptive technology creates a schism between the future-oriented CEO and the decidedly pragmatic, and, therefore, change-resistant sales force. The resistance to change was especially visible in the sales forces of DEC and IBM in the late 1980s, but many other companies encountered the same kind of pushback. The sales staff's closeness to customers and its line of sight into the competition sorely complicate the CEO's formulation of a change strategy and his or her ability to persist in its execution.

Distracted by Competition

Technology leaders, I believe, are too easily distracted by traditional, but no longer relevant, competitors. Akers continued to focus on the Japanese mainframe makers even though a new class of servers presented a greater threat. Ken Olsen and An Wang were distracted by IBM and their Massachusetts competitors, ignoring the new competition sprouting up in California, Texas, and Redmond, Washington. They drew solace from benchmarks showing their productivity was near or slightly better than those of comfortable old adversaries that were themselves disadvantaged. Meanwhile, Sun's founders soon determined that DEC was a toothless tiger whose cost structure could never be squeezed into a competitive business model. They took that knowledge and ran with it.

Failures in Succession

Founders' succession is hugely difficult for any board of directors. Wait too long, and the most promising in-house successors will have decamped, as occurred at DEC and Wang. Wait until the business goes into a downdraft, and the founder will insist that his reputation be preserved by allowing him time to right the business. Wait until the outcry from the shareholders reaches a fever pitch, and there's a greater chance of making a slipshod choice that will itself need rectification, as at HP. The time for founder succession comes well before the decline. That's why smooth successions have occurred so seldom, with the transition from Watson Sr. to Watson Jr. at IBM being among the few exceptions. Sun's CEO transition ended with the troubled company being sold to Oracle. It remains to be seen if Dell, Oracle, and Microsoft will break the streak.

Entrepreneurial Blight?

A 1979 *Business Week* piece ascribed the problems of the first minicomputer dropouts to the managerial limitations "of the entrepreneurs who launched them." Was founders' disease the cause of their downfall? Not necessarily, though venture capitalists routinely oust the founders of fledgling companies as soon as the employee count crosses a hundred. But that abstraction ignores the countervailing truth: The most successful companies in the IT industry today were built by their founders. Look at Bill Gates at Microsoft, Larry Ellison at Oracle, Michael Dell at Dell, Steve Jobs at Apple, Scott McNealy at Sun, and Andy Grove, Bob Noyce, and Gordon Moore at Intel.

But for an earlier generation of computer executives, the picture is mixed. Akers at IBM and Young at Hewlett-Packard were professional managers, while Ken Olsen at Digital Equipment and An Wang at Wang Labs were founders. All understood the risks of a disruptive technology or, worse, a radically different business model. Indeed, Olsen and Wang were working engineers who had previously introduced their own disruptive technologies and almost upended IBM and the mainframe generation through radical cuts in gross margins. Similarly, Akers and Young had spent lifetimes fighting in the technology wars. But, despite their experiences, their responses to problems were often too slow or off the mark altogether.

That wouldn't surprise Clayton Christensen, as he studied several industry leaders' failures to adjust to change and concluded again that there were simply limits to strategy. "It wasn't the case that the leading companies' engineers tended to get stuck in a particular technological paradigm or ignored innovations that were 'not invented here.' The cause of failure could not be attributed solely to established firms' inadequate competence in new technological fields or their inability to stay atop their industry's 'technological mudslide.'" Nor was the cause a dotty management's inattention to the market, including both customers and competitors.

"Probably the most important outcome of this attempt to define the problem is that it ruled out poor management as a root cause. Again, this is not to say that good and bad management aren't key factors affecting the fortunes of firms. But as a general explanation, the managers of the companies studied here had a great track record in understanding customers' future needs, identifying which technologies could best address those needs and in investing to develop and implement them. It was only when confronted with disruptive technology that they failed. There had, therefore, to be a reason why good managers consistently made wrong decisions when faced with disruptive technological change. The reason is that *good management itself* was the root cause. Managers played the game the way it was supposed to be played."[2]

Steadfastness in Leadership

Are we missing the "critical success factor" of effective leadership, to paraphrase the academic buzz? At a summit of new-technology-company CEOs that I attended in 1997, the moderator posed the question: "Which personal characteristic do you consider most important to the success of the company?" Many responded "personal ethics"; some said "personal sensitivity to the employees"; and, of course, there were the obligatory mentions of "strategic vision."

But, on reflection, I realized that I knew several successful CEOs whose business ethics (as distinct from personal morality) had been questioned. More were considered wholly insensitive to their employees. And vision is a perishable currency until executed.

So, for me, the critical characteristic is "steadfastness"—the CEO's ability to hold the direction he's selected even while pundits, customers, and especially his direct lieutenants say he's wrong. Tom Watson Jr. introduced tape storage over the objections of top sales executives frozen by the fear of displacing the hugely profitable punch-card business. An Wang drove his company's transitional leap from prior success in desktop calculators to office computers, though his VP for sales, John Cunningham, disagreed. Ken Olsen overrode the inclinations of the powerful marketing groups to consolidate technology and organization around the VAX/VMS system. That launched DEC on a decade of market supremacy. Scott McNealy ignored the recommendations of his field representatives to become a reseller of Microsoft/Intel products. Instead of being hollowed out, Sun continued development of its microprocessor and operating system that made it the "dot" in dot-com. Lou Gerstner ignored the advice of press and pundits who wanted him to break up IBM and jettison the mainframe, which remains profitable to this day.

So, in some sense, for a CEO to remain steadfast, he or she must confront the inevitable conflict between grasping the future and holding the present.

Notes

Introduction

1. Schumpeter, Joseph A. *Capitalism, Socialism and Democracy.* New York: Harper Press, 1950, 84.

2. Ibid, 86.

3. Foster, Richard N. *Innovation: The Attacker's Advantage.* New York: Summit Books, 1983, 27.

Chapter 2

1. Watson, Thomas J. Jr., and Peter Petre. *Father, Son & Co, My Life at IBM and Beyond.* New York: Bantam Books, 1990, 187.

2. Ibid., 189.

3. Ibid., 199.

4. Fishman, Katherine D. *The Computer Establishment.* New York: Harper & Row, 1981, 31.

5. Watson and Petre, 205.

6. Ibid., 189.

7. Christensen, Clayton M. *The Innovator's Dilemma: When New Technologies Cause Great Firms to Fail.* Boston: Harvard Business School Press, 1997, 7.

8. Bashe, Charles J. et al. *IBM's Early Computers.* Cambridge, MA: The MIT Press, 1986, 190.

9. Watson and Petre, 195.

10. Ibid, 195.

11. Bashe et al., 177.

12. Ibid.

13. Watson and Petre, 194.

14. Bashe et al., 190.

15. Watson and Petre, 196.

16. Ibid, 216.

17. Ibid., 218.

18. Ibid., 180, 212, 221, 224.

19. Ibid., 290.

20. Bashe et al., 577.

21. Ibid., 476.

22. Watson and Petre, 348.

23. Ibid., 348.

24. Ibid., 347.

25. Rodgers, William. *Think: A Biography of the Watsons and IBM.* New York: Stein and Day, 1969, 285.

26. Ibid., 285.

27. *Harvard Business Review.* March/April 1980.

28. Watson and Petre, 360.

Chapter 3

1. Watson and Petre, 401.

2. Ferguson, Charles H., and Charles B. Morris. *Computer Wars: The Fall of IBM and the Future of Global Technology.* New York: Times Books, 1994, 35.

Chapter 7

1. Wang, An, with Eugene Linden. *Lessons, An Autobiography.* Reading MA: Addison Wesley, 1986, 223.

2. Ibid., 13.

3. Ibid., 165–166.

4. Ibid., 216–217.

5. Ibid., 108.

6. Ibid., 216–217.

7. Ibid., 219.

8. Ibid., 219.

9. Fishman, Katherine D., 53.

Chapter 8

1. Brooks, John. *Telephone: The First Hundred Years*. New York: Harper and Row, 1976.

Chapter 9

1. Rifkin, Glenn, and George Harrar. *The Ultimate Entrepreneur*. Chicago: Contemporary Books, 1988, 264.

Chapter 10

1. Brooks, Frederick P. *The Mythical Man-Month: Essays on Software Engineering*. Boston: Addison Wesley, 1975.

2. Wilson, Mike. *The Difference between God and Larry Ellison*. New York: Harper Business, 1998, 204.

3. Ibid., 210.

Chapter 11

1. Gerstner, Louis V., *Who Says Elephants Can't Dance*. New York: *Harper Business*, 2002, 119.

Chapter 12

1. Carroll, Paul. *Big Blues: The Unmaking of IBM*. New York: Crown Publishers, 1993, 99.

2. Ibid., 101.

3. Gerstner, 162.

4. Ibid., 138–139.

Chapter 13

1. Fishman, 211–212.

2. Ibid., 212.

3. Rifkin and Harrar, 175.

4. Ibid., 179.

Chapter 14

1. Ibid., 251–252.

2. Ibid., 252.

3. Ibid., 255

Chapter 17

1. Carroll, 161.

2. Gerstner, 15.

3. Carroll, 355.

4. Gerstner, 161.

5. Ibid., 163.

6. Ibid., 27–28.

7. Ibid., 138.

Chapter 18

1. Ibid., 45.

Chapter 19

1. Packard, David. *The HP Way: How Bill Hewlett and I Built Our Company.* New York: Harper Business, 1996, 107.

Chapter 20

1. Ibid., 149.

2. Ibid., 150.

3. Anders, George. *Perfect Enough: Carly Fiorina and the Reinvention of Hewlett-Packard.* New York: Portfolio, 2003, 24–25.

4. Ibid., 36.

5. Ibid., 38.

Chapter 21

1. Foster, 116.

2. Christensen, 97–98.

Index

Masi, Carl, 123
Massachusetts Mutual Life
Insurance Company, 53–
54, 112
Matthews, Ed, ix, 356
Mauchly, John, 2, 16–17
McCaw Cellular, 166
McColl, Hugh, 87
McCracken, Ed, 342, 345, 348,
350–352, 354, 359
McGill, Archibald, 151–154,
155–157
McGowan, William, 137–138
MCI, 136, 137–138
McKenna, Regis, 198
McKinsey & Company, 142–144,
151, 318
McNealy, Scott, 10–11, 167, 170–
175, 178–179, 183–184,
220, 351, 360, 379–380
McQuade, Charles, 173
Memorex, 30, 49, 58
Meridith, Tom, 213
Metcalf, Bob, 197
Metz, Frank, 309, 316
Micro-Channel Architecture, 222–
223
microprocessors, 5, 88–89, 91,
94–97
Microsoft, 100, 108, 195, 202–211,
214, 220–230
See also Gates, Bill
Miller, Richard, 130–131
Miller, Wiz, 15–16
Miner, Bob, 186, 187
minicomputers, 4–7, 66–70, 70–72,
79–80, 213, 376
Mita, Katsushige, 292, 298–300
Mitchell, Duke, 287–288

MITI (Ministry of International
Trade and Industry), 295,
302–303, 329
Miura, Takeo, 301, 327–328
Modcomp (Modular Computer
Systems), 66, 83, 343
Mommony, George, 69
monopolies, 49, 135, 136, 150
Monroe, 89
Montgomery, Gerald, 152
Moore, Gordon, 88, 379
Morell, Mike, 40, 41
Morton, Dean, 354, 356–357
Motorola, 56, 57, 86, 93, 94, 97,
100
multiple virtual storage (MVS), 56,
330
Musser, Bob, 284
Myhrvold, Nathan, 209
The Mythical Man-Month (Brooks),
187

N

Nakayama, Norihiko, 64
NARUC (National Association
of Regulatory Utility
Commissioners), 136, 149
Naruto, Michio, 295–297, 300,
328–329
National Advanced Systems (NAS),
290, 292–293
National Semiconductor, 31, 93,
94–95, 292
NCR (National Cash Register
Company), 3, 4, 13, 14,
27, 28, 58, 157–158, 165,
170
Netscape, 209–211, 371
NeXT, 7, 202
Nippon Electric, 13

X

Y

Z